DEMOGRAPHY

PETER R. COX

C.B., F.I.A., F.S.S.

DEMOGRAPHY

Fifth edition

CAMBRIDGE UNIVERSITY PRESS

CAMBRIDGE

LONDON · NEW YORK · MELBOURNE

312
C877 d5

Published by the Syndics of the Cambridge University Press
The Pitt Building, Trumpington Street, Cambridge CB2 1RP
Bentley House, 200 Euston Road, London NW1 2DB
32 East 57th Street, New York, NY 10022, USA
296 Beaconsfield Parade, Middle Park, Melbourne 3206, Australia

First published 1950
Second edition 1957
Third edition 1959
Fourth edition 1970
Fifth edition 1976
Reprinted 1978

Photoset and printed in Malta by
Interprint (Malta) Ltd

Library of Congress Cataloguing in Publication Data
Cox, Peter R.
    Demography.
    Includes bibliographies and indexes.
    1. Demography. I. Title.
HB881.C783   1976   301.32   75-27262
ISBN 0 521 21003 8 hard covers
ISBN 0 521 29020 1 paperback

(Fourth edition ISBN 0 521 07697 8 hard covers
            ISBN 0 521 09612 X paperback)

Preface to the fifth edition

Although it is only about five years since the Fourth Edition of this book was published, the passage of events and the change of outlook they have wrought have created a need for a material revision of the contents; otherwise, the most recent information could not be presented as an effective comment on the theories expounded or in illustration of the methods described. About one-third of the text has been rewritten with this in mind. There has also been recently some general change of emphasis in demography towards the more political aspects of the subject, as a result of which the refinements of technical analysis assume rather less importance; this change finds its reflexion in a new order of the chapters: they are now grouped within the following main subdivisions:

> Fundamentals
> Population Movements
> General influences on Population
> Technical Analysis

with a concluding section in which the past and future of the subject are surveyed. Material which was formerly spread over twenty-six chapters is now allocated to only twenty; but the coverage of topics is as before and the text as a whole is no shorter in length. The four new subdivisions embrace the contents of the following chapters in the Fourth Edition: 2–6; 7–9; 19–25; 10–17 respectively. The present chapter 1 fulfils the same functions as the previous one, while former chapters 18 and 26 are combined in the new concluding chapter 20.

The gradual diminution of attention paid to the specific demographic problems of Britain, and the broadening of interest to a full international scale, which are features of the development of this book from one edition to the next in the past, have been continued in the transition to the Fifth Edition; there has been a further rebalancing, after which Britain now receives little more emphasis than any other single country and more attention than before is paid to the 'Third World'.

The author's sincere thanks are extended to all those who have helped him so much over the years, notably Bernard Benjamin, Roland Clarke, John Peel and Clifford Thomas, but many others too, and on the present occasion he is deeply indebted in addition to his wife, Faith, for every kind of support.

v

As the prefaces to former editions are omitted, it should be reported here that H.M. Stationery Office gave permission for the reproduction of certain extracts from official papers. These extracts were derived from the Annual Reviews and other publications of the Registrars General for England and Wales and for Scotland; from the Report and Statistics Committee papers of the Royal Commission on Population; and from the Decennial Supplement, England and Wales, 1951, on occupational mortality. Most of these extracts appear again in the Fifth Edition, and H.M. Stationery Office has also given permission for (i) the reproduction of English Life Table No. 11 (Males) which appears in another of the Decennial Supplements of the Registrar General for England and Wales for the year 1951, and (ii) the appearance of figs. 4.1, 4.2 and 4.3, which relate respectively to census, birth and death records and which bring up to date some corresponding illustrations given in previous editions of *Demography*.

March 1975   P.R.C.

Contents

Illustrations

Fundamentals

1 Introduction

1.1 Reasons for population studies

There are many good reasons for studying population statistics. The most general of these is the advancement of science: finding out what happens, formulating theories as to why it occurs and testing these theories against the course of events. Secondly there is practical value in measuring population growth so as to be able to plan ahead for satisfying man's needs throughout life —food, clothing, shelter and other necessities. Thirdly there is the aspect of the subject that is sometimes called 'political arithmetic' —the name that some of the pioneers of demography used to indicate the nature of their interest in population: demographic data may facilitate the making of arrangements for the ascertainment of people's views on important topical questions, the election of representative governing bodies, the collection of taxes, the planning and conduct of industry and commerce, the provision of social services, the maintenance of health and the preservation of law and order. Such data may also help to give some guide to the probable outcome of such activities. The changing balance of young and old people, for instance, affects government expenditure on matters such as education, child welfare, housing and pensions, and the more the demands of the future can be foreseen, the better the planning can be.

Finally, some governments have developed or are developing policies involving legislation or other action designed to have an influence (or to eliminate certain influences) upon the size, trend or distribution of population; and, even where governments have not gone this far, many people believe that they should do so. The study of the appropriate statistics is clearly important, in these circumstances, either in order to monitor progress and check effectiveness or to attempt to establish a case for or against a policy. Some institutions, such as political parties, the Church and scientific societies have set up associated organizations for the analysis or presentation of population material and the development of arguments therefrom.

1.2 Characteristics

Demography is a term derived from the two Greek words, $\delta\hat{\eta}\mu o\varsigma$, the people, and $\gamma\rho\acute{\alpha}\phi\epsilon\iota\nu$, to draw or write. It was first used by Guillard in 1855, and

1

nowadays denotes the study by statistical methods of human populations. This involves primarily the measurement of the size and growth or diminution of the numbers of people. The constituents of change in these numbers are births, deaths and migration, and demographers analyse the related functions of fertility, mortality and population transfer.

They take an interest in the influences —social, political and economic — which operate on these functions, in the interplay between them, and in their effect on the population as a whole.

Populations can be studied also for their characteristics at a single point of time, for example age-distribution or genetic composition. Such characteristics do not often change very rapidly. Moreover, there is a particular association between the numbers of people in an area at different times, namely that those aged x at time t are the survivors of those aged $x - s$ at time $t - s$, subject to the forces of mortality and migration. This association can be a close and ordered one and it imparts a special flavour to the subject because it opens up possibilities for mathematical analysis. Population may also be assessed by means of algebraic disciplines in which conclusions are reached by rigorous logical procedures on the basis of specific fundamental assumptions, Such work leads to theoretical statistical models, and these may be either stochastic or deterministic in character — that is, they may or may not allow for chance variations to individual members of the population. Among the topics which are studied in their relationship to population are natural resources, production and consumption, labour supply, housing, savings and investment, ability and education. Many of these studies are not particularly mathematical in character, but can be pursued with the use of electronic computers able to handle large masses of data with many classifications.

Intense public interest is expressed in the prospects for the future development of the population, and most of the studies mentioned above can lead to some sort of forecast for, or projection into, the years to come, although it is well known that estimates made in the past have not so far been accurately borne out in the event. Our knowledge is at present insufficiently complete for success in forecasting.

1.3 Theory and practice

The study of population may be approached in a number of different ways. For instance, it may be made the subject of very general argument or philosophical speculation without recourse to any statistical analysis. This method of approach belongs mainly to the past, before adequate and reliable data were available, but it may still be of some use in limited fields. A more common discipline today is the collection of statistics as a basis for empirical analysis. The results of individual studies of this kind may be of only local application, but broader generalizations may well be possible upon the basis of a group of such surveys. Besides numerical data, evidence such as newspapers, Acts of Parliament, other public documents, and miscellaneous writings of various kinds may be adduced in demographic research: novels and advertisements have been used as basic material.

In economically well-developed countries today it is customary to register births, deaths and marriages and to hold periodical censuses; the information collected is sufficiently accurate for many demographic purposes. Such information indeed provides most of the raw material of the demographer's work, and some familiarity with the particular characteristics of these data, as well as the statistical returns and reports where they may be found, is essential for their proper use.

1.4   Definitions, and links with other disciplines

It is sometimes argued that certain branches of population analysis should be distinguished from others by a separate title. In this connection the word 'demology' has occasionally been suggested as an indicator of the more learned branches of the subject; but this has not come into general use. Rather more commonly, the expression 'population studies' is used to indicate the simpler and more descriptive demographic work. There is, however, no sharp dividing line between the various parts of demography and these expressions are used, if at all, without much consistency. In this matter, as indeed in all questions of definition, the student who wishes to pursue the question further would do well to refer to the English part of the *Multilingual Demographic Dictionary* published by the United Nations Organization.

The following definition of demography was given by Hauser and Duncan: 'the study of the size, territorial distribution and composition of population, changes therein, and the composition of such changes, which may be identified as natality, mortality, territorial movements and social mobility (change of status)'. This definition introduces several ideas not mentioned above. First, there is territorial distribution — evidently a matter of much importance. This characteristic was not mentioned in § 1.2, because 'population' was used in the sense of 'any group of people' and not a specific group such as the citizens of a town or nation. If any group of people can be chosen for study, then one can select those living in a particular area: hence the idea of territorial distribution is not, strictly speaking, needed as a basic concept. Similarly, other forms of population composition, for instance in respect of occupation, type of dwelling or religion, while very significant in demography, are not perhaps essential for mention in an initial definition. Nevertheless, they enter into a good deal of demographic work. Hauser and Duncan have emphasized that by the word 'composition' they intend the inclusion of

3

'quality', for example, sex, social status, intelligence, and physical characteristics such as height.

Few, if any, people limit their studies to demography alone. Most persons who are interested in population are concerned also with other disciplines, notably actuarial science, agronomy, economics, economic geography, history, human biology, social policy, and sociology. In all of these it is useful to have knowledge of one or more aspects of demography. For instance, in economics, population size and distribution are clearly factors affecting total production and consumption. Social policy is influenced by the relative numbers of infants, children, young adults, people in middle life and the aged. Human biology is concerned *inter alia* with reproduction, birth control, the sex ratio and genetic constitution; population data are useful in connexion with all these subjects.

1.5   The parts of demography and their interrelationship

A diagram has been prepared in order to show how the various aspects of population study are related, and this appears as fig. 1.1. It will be seen that there are nine separate boxed subjects and that some links between them are indicated. Central to the diagram is the analysis of data of population movements, which has connexions with all the other topics. A prerequisite is the

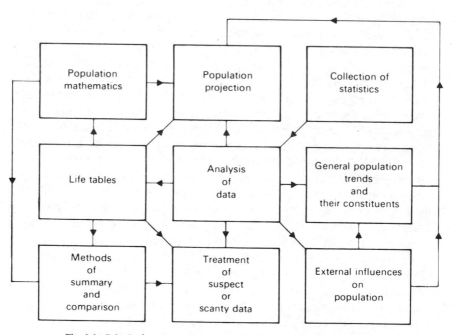

Fig. 1.1. Principal connexions between the main topics of demography.

collection of statistics and this is therefore an inflow, but five other connexions are shown as well, all as outflows, or consequences:

(*a*) analysis throws light on general population trends, mainly through their constituents of fertility, mortality and migration;

(*b*) the effects of external influences acting on population movements, such as social changes and economic progress, should be revealed as part of the analysis;

(*c*) one product is the preparation of life tables;

(*d*) another is projections of population into the future on the basis of assumptions derived from analysis;

(*e*) finally, the demographer's studies may show that the data are suspect or incomplete, but there are means by which he can correct for this (some of which derive from life tables).

Other links in fig. 1.1 relate to population mathematics, which although capable of being pursued entirely in the abstract almost always has a connexion with life tables; mathematics can well provide a basis for population projection, and it also helps with methods of summary and comparison, which derive from data analysis mainly through the medium of life tables. Finally, both general population trends and the influences which act upon them must clearly play an important part in population projection.

1.6 The contents of the chapters to follow

Not all the aspects of demography dealt with in this book find a place in the diagram. The introductory and concluding chapters, in particular, necessarily have links with every one of the nine topics displayed, and therefore figure all through it. Chapter 2 deals with some basic concepts of demographic analysis, which pervade the whole of the science; and chapter 3 explains some of the essential characteristics of the statistics, which must always be borne in mind. Finally, chapter 20 discusses the past, present and future of demography as a whole — a subject which can hardly be properly introduced until all the constituent parts have been elucidated.

When there are so many interconnexions, various orders are possible for the presentation of the topics but the most logical sequence for instruction purposes seems to be as follows. First, there is the collection of statistics in practice (chapter 4). Then it is desirable to list the principal characteristics of fertility, mortality and migration. Each of these principal demographic events has its own individual features, and there is a good deal of variation in nature from one to another — in respect of both the techniques used and the theoretical orientation and interest of the people who specialize in their study. The nature of the available data varies correspondingly, and the way in which the characteristics of these vital events can best be exhibited is peculiar to each one. It is the purpose of chapters 6, 7 and 8 respectively to illustrate these differences and to show how each type of occurrence can best be studied. The subject of marriage is treated first in chapter 5 because its associations with fertility are closer than those with mortality or migration. In the course of these chapters some typical results to be obtained from the analysis of vital events are shown by way of illustration.

1.7 Population trends and the influences upon them

At this stage it is useful to speak of the selection of bases for population projection, which normally derive directly from the analysis of trends in the constituent elements of marriage, fertility, mortality and migration: see chapter 9.

After this, the time has arrived for a look at how populations have actually developed, first in the past — often scantily recorded; secondly, in the present state of affairs, for which there are fuller particulars. Chapters 10 and 11 are given over to these respectively. They lead naturally to an investigation of such general influences upon population development today as resources, in the widest sense of the word, and governmental policies. In order to give the student an elementary introduction to these wider problems, two chapters are devoted to (*a*) population and resources (chapter 12) — the extent to which the world's people are fed, clothed and provided with other necessities of life — and (*b*) the policies of governments towards population, and in particular the issue of family planning (chapter 13). It is then of value to consider some of the demographic projections that have been made in recent years, and the prospects they suggest; this is the subject of chapter 14.

1.8 Formal demography

The ensuing five chapters are concerned with the use of methods of a mathematical nature, mainly in circumstances of deficient or non-existent population data but also when they are plentiful. Demographic data tend to be very voluminous; it is therefore necessary to be aware of the best methods by which their main characteristics can be noted and exhibited simply and concisely. A number of different methods of summarization exist, and any one of them is liable to conceal some important quality of the data. It is therefore necessary to be aware of the limitations of these methods. Chapter 15 deals with life-table techniques. Other systems of summary and comparison are touched on in chapter 16.

Because demographic trends are important in economic and social life, and because of the desire to plan ahead, there is much demand for estimates of future population. This demand persists in spite of the fact that it has not so far proved to predict the future at all accurately. Given a set of assumptions as to the course of mortality, fertility and migration over the coming decades, it is a fairly straightforward matter to work out the consequences for population size and age-distribution, and general methods by which this may be done are discussed in chapter 17. Some basic mathematics is given in chapter 18. Demography does not lend itself very readily to advanced mathematical treatment, and yet one aspect — the stable population theory developed by Lotka — is important historically, and indeed generally today. An elementary introduction to this theory, and to other proposed mathematical systems, is given in this chapter. The practical limitations are also made plain.

Chapter 19 is given over to the problems that arise, mainly in the economically less-well-developed countries, where statistics of one kind or another have been collected but these data may be, and indeed very probably are, unreliable. Methods of appraisal of credibility naturally assume a high importance in these conditions. In this chapter, a different area of uncertainty is also high-lighted: here data are difficult to come by because of the complexity and obscurity of the processes involved; for example in questions relating to the field of the biology of reproduction. Computer techniques, using simulation, have been developed in order that stochastic variability can be provided for in several stages. This is a rapidly developing area of demography, and prospects for future progress are almost as important as the work already done.

1.9 Conclusion

So diverse are the contents of *Demography* that it would seem of little value to try to summarize them concisely in the last few pages of the book. Instead, chapter 20 shows the limitations of what the student has read in the foregoing text; it does so by indicating some of the principal matters to which present-day research is being directed. In other words, attention is paid to the areas of the subject to which thought might usefully be devoted by those who wish to pursue their demographic studies further, after attaining basic proficiency in population analysis. The principal organs of demographic literature are also referred to — the broadening scope of the subject is indicated by the increasing number and length of writings upon it that appear from year to year.

SELECT BIBLIOGRAPHY

(*Note:* As in previous editions, the purpose of the reading lists at the end of each chapter is to indicate the names of a few of the works which contain some reference to the topics mentioned in the chapter and which may be generally useful to the student. The books and papers mentioned are not arranged in order of importance.)

Eldridge, Hope T. *The Materials of Demography: a Selected and Annotated Bibliography* (International Union for the Scientific Study of Population, and Population Association of America, New York, 1959).

Hauser, P. M. and Duncan, O. D. *The Study of Population: an Inventory and Appraisal* (University Press, Chicago, 1959).

Multi-lingual Demographic Dictionary: English Volume (United Nations Organization, New York, 1958).

2 Demographic analysis: some basic concepts

2.1 Observation

The purpose of this chapter is to explain the fundamental nature of population analysis and to give an introduction to some of the necessary statistical methods. The object of study is the demographer's fellow creatures, and he has perforce to respect the rights of individuals and groups. Fully-controlled scientific experiments of the kind that are conducted in laboratories are out of the question. If inquiries become too inquisitorial they may well be rendered ineffective by refusals to respond, by evasions or by untruths. All the demographer can do is to observe the course of events from time to time, open as they are to many conflicting influences acting concurrently. He can be said to have access to 'experimental situations' in the sense that different populations can be studied at the same time, and the same population at different times, so that the effects of the intervention of different variables can be assessed. Nevertheless, interpretation of cause and effect, if this is at all possible, requires considerable skill and judgment, and there may be differences of opinion even between acknowledged experts. Above all, care is required, because it is all too easy to draw the wrong conclusions.

2.2 Objectives

The aim of analysis in demographic work is to identify and measure as precisely as possible the influences that underlie population changes. By so doing it is possible to deepen one's understanding of the variations observed in past experience, and also perhaps to arrive at a basis for the prediction of future trends. There must always, however, be some doubt about the chances that identified influences will continue to have effect in the years to come. Even if a simple extrapolation of an existing trend is accepted as a valid assessment for the future, it should be possible, as the result of prior analysis, to attach some rough measure of confidence to the estimation.

The word 'trend' is often misused. In the world of fashion it frequently implies no more than whatever style happens to be current. More correctly, it refers to a change in time; thus, if the proportion of old people in a population had been 20 per cent fifteen years ago, and 30 per cent at this year's

9

census, then clearly there had been, over this period, an ageing trend. The trap into which many are liable to fall is to assume that this trend *must* continue. In fact, analysis is usually required in order to find out whether or not this is likely to happen. The main tasks of the demographer are, first, to understand the characteristics of his data; secondly, to observe and measure the past experience; thirdly, to study as far as possible the factors influencing the experience and causing the changes; and fourthly, to consider the prospects. In the third and technically most difficult stage, the analysis should be supplemented by an examination of any available information of a social, economic or even psychological kind that could indicate, or illustrate, the background.

2.3 Variations

Great precision is rarely justifiable in demography. Indeed, the observed statistics are subject to considerable variations, both in time and from one group or area to another. Whereas much of mathematical statistics is founded upon some assumption of homogeneity, in the study of population this assumption is rarely justified; frequently, observed variations greatly exceed those to be expected by statistical theory, and the actual fluctuations where large numbers are involved can be as big, relatively, as the random variations observed in small homogeneous groups. Consequently, the refinements of mathematical statistics are only of limited application in practical demography.

2.4 Classification

Population data are normally available on a standard pattern for different groups of people. Some obvious examples are males and females, young and old, working and not working, those in one area and those in another. Further subdivisions are usually possible; thus age can be measured in completed years, or even in months or days. Those not at work can be analysed into those too young for schooling, those at school, the unemployed, the retired, and so on, while people with a job can be classified into employers, managers, the self-employed and the employed. Analysis can be made by more than one characteristic at a time, as in table 2.1. Here, the grouping is two-fold, viz. by status and date. It would not be unusual to see a three-fold analysis, including (say) a breakdown by sex, or even a four-fold analysis (say) including also particulars of age or area. As the table cannot conveniently be presented in more than two dimensions, a wider spread over the page is necessary, and this can be achieved in a variety of ways, e.g. by the printing of two tables in a form similar to that of table 2.1, one for men and one for

Table 2.1. *Active earners classified by employment status, Hungary, 1960, 1970*

Employment status	Number of active earners	
	1960	1970
Employees	2,990,023	3,883,471
Co-operative members	707,511	941,195
Independent workers and family helpers	1,062,082	164,010
Total	4,759,616	4,988,676

women; or by the subdivision of the figures in the 1960 and the 1970 columns between those for men and those for women. A reduction in the amount of detail may be helpful, for example omitting the last three digits and expressing the numbers in thousands. Or it may be that some form of chart or graph may be a more suitable means of communication. Thus, one way of presenting the data in table 2.1 would be as shown in fig. 2.1, which takes the form of a block diagram, or 'histogram'.

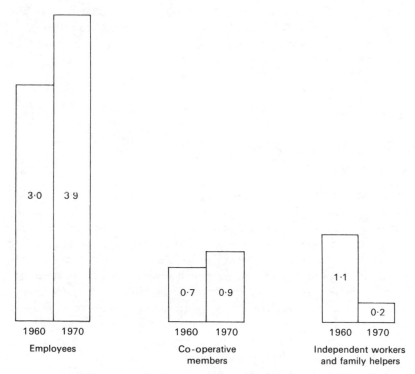

Fig. 2.1. Active earners classified by employment status, Hungary, 1960, 1970.
(Numbers in millions)

2.5 Rates and proportions

Although students of population can often do little more than observe the course of events, they can at least observe them in the most meaningful way. Thus, if they see that the number of births per annum is much larger in the United States of America than in New Zealand, it is evident that little useful can be deduced from the comparison unless the relative sizes of the populations of the two countries are brought into the story. It is customary in exhibiting basic demographic data to show both the number of occurrences and the 'rate', or number per thousand head of the population. Birth rates, death rates and marriage rates in this form serve a useful, if very limited, purpose in the first stage of analysis, although for valid explorations of differences it is usually necessary to go a good deal further.

Rates are functions appropriate to data which record occurrences, for example, death registration statistics; these are sometimes called 'flow' information, to distinguish them from 'stock' data, or in other words statistics of the state of affairs at a given moment, such as are provided by a census. The corresponding demographic function for stock data is the 'proportion', for example the proportion of people in the population who are widowed, or the proportion who live in a given town. The proportions to be derived from table 2.1 are, when expressed as percentages:

	1960	1970
Employees	62.8	77.8
Co-operative members	14.9	18.9
Independent workers and family helpers	22.3	3.3
Total	100.0	100.0

2.6 Risk

The demographer's process of observation is usually directed to some specific purpose, and is organized in relation to ideas, or 'conceptual models', that have been found useful as modes of procedure in analogous problems or in past experience. One of these ideas is that of 'risk'. This is familiar from everyday parlance. There is more risk in backing an outsider than there is in backing the favourite. In a thunderstorm it is more risky to be out under a tree than it is to be indoors. A car is more at risk of an accident if it is on the roads than if it is in its owner's garage. Nevertheless, in common idiom, people often fall into error on matters connected with risk. They say, for instance, that because more road accidents occur at 5 p.m. than at 3 p.m. it is more dangerous to be driving a car at 5 o'clock than at 3 o'clock. They overlook the fact that, with the end of the working day, there is more traffic at 5 than at 3. A further concept is required — that of 'exposure to risk'; only when it is known relatively how many cars are on the road at the two times, that is, how many are 'exposed to risk', can a valid comparison of the driving hazard be made.

2.7   Exposure to risk in demographic analysis

The commonly-used measure, the rate, overlooks the concept of exposure to risk in some respects, because, to take the birth rate as an example, it disregards the fact that children, and women over the age of 50, are infecund. The following figures illustrate the possible extent of error; the data shown have been collected from two populations, A and B:

	A	B
(1) Total female population (all ages)	1,000	3,000
(2) Total women aged 10—49	500	2,000
(3) Number of births in a year	50	180
(4) Frequency of births per thousand females of any age, $[(3) \div (1)] \times 1,000$	50	60
(5) General fertility rate: births per thousand women aged 10—49, $[(3) \div (2)] \times 1,000$	100	90

The results shown in line (4) suggest that the level of fertility is higher in population B than in population A, whereas the more informative ratios in line (5) show the opposite to be the case. The misconception arises because the proportion of women who can be fertile is lower in A than in B.

This is not the end of the story. The risk of pregnancy is less for unmarried women than for married, and it may well be that a still more valid comparison of A and B could be made on the basis of an exposed to risk consisting of the numbers of *married* women aged under 49. If this were done, then strictly speaking the numerator should be, not all births, but only legitimate births.

Risk normally varies according to age, and a further possible development of rates such as those at (4) and (5) — or of any other demographic measure — will be referred to immediately below, namely 'standardization'. Because of its imperfections the type of rate calculated in line (4) is often referred to as a 'crude' rate.

2.8   Standardization

The chances of mortality, fertility, marriage and other demographic events vary considerably from one time of life to another, as many statistical studies have shown. A further refinement of the comparison process is therefore to work out the occurrence rates for each single year of age separately. Thus, in the example given in § 2.7, the rates for ages 10, 11, 12, ..., 49 could be calculated for populations A and B, the numerators being the numbers of births occurring to women of the relevant ages. Such a procedure could be

13

very revealing: it might show, for instance, that the rates for *A* exceeded those for *B* up to age 24 but were lower than for *B* at older ages. The reasons for this could then be investigated (it might be due to later marriage in *B*). Often, however, the picture is more confused, and detailed comparisons can be tedious. To reduce their number to a convenient size, fertility rates might be calculated for short groups of ages, by dividing the number of births by the corresponding exposed to risk.

If rates for groups of ages are used for comparisons, the exposed to risk may not be distributed over the individual ages of the group in precisely the same way in *A* and *B*. In fact, the distributions could be so substantially different that the average ages differed markedly. Such disparities can be corrected by various processes of 'standardization', leading to the production of single-figure index numbers, for instance in place of those shown in lines (4) and (5) of §2.7. The methods by which standardization can be effected will be discussed mainly in chapter 16 below.

2.9 Analyses including both age and time

In the example given in § 2.7, populations *A* and *B* need not be two contemporary populations in different areas. They could be the population of the same area at different times. Let it be supposed that the marriage experience of a country in a large number of successive years is under examination, and that the rates at each age have been calculated. The whole data could then be set out in a square table, with separate columns for each successive year and separate rows for each successive age, in the form illustrated below:

Age	Year				
.	...	1943	1944	1945	...
.	—	—	—	—	—
21	—	x	—	—	—
22	—	—	x	—	—
23	—	—	—	x	—
.	—	—	—	—	—

Now a group of persons aged 21 in 1943 would correspond closely with the group aged 22 in 1944 and that aged 23 in 1945; they would be substantially the same people at different times; the experience of this group would emerge along a diagonal line starting at the top left-hand side and proceeding step by step downwards towards the bottom right.

The following figures are illustrative; they show the numbers of men's first marriages per thousand men (irrespective of marital status) in quinary groups of ages and of years:

Age group	Years				
	1955—59	1960—64	1965—69	1970—74	(Av. 1955—74)
20—24	150	115	95	85	(111)
25—29	560	480	510	580	(532)
30—34	170	120	140	130	(140)
35—39	30	40	60	50	(45)
Total	910	755	805	845	(828)

It will be noted that:

(1) the rate of marriage was higher than average in 1955—59 and 1970—74 and lower than average in 1960—69;

(2) marriage rates at age 20—24 fell as time passed, whereas those at 35—39 tended to rise;

(3) a fall in the rate from one quinary period to the next at one age-group was always followed by a rise in the rate at the next higher group between the next period and the next but one;

(4) a rise in the rate from one quinary period to the next was similarly followed by a fall.

The inference which may possibly be drawn from these observations is that, while the level of marriage activity varies from time to time, a group of men of a given age at a given moment has a propensity to marry which tends towards constancy: if their rate of marriage is high in youth, then it may well be lower at older ages, and *vice versa*.

2.10 Cohorts and generations

A group of people, whose age increases at the same rate as that at which time passes, is often called a 'cohort' or, if the cohort consists of persons all born in the same year, a 'generation'. An example of a cohort is a number of women all married in a particular year. Examination of the experience of cohorts is often fruitful in demography. This is because occurrence rates are often strongly influenced by the length of time elapsed since some event; for example, the event of birth, in relation to infantile mortality, and the event of marriage, in relation to fertility. Many instances of cohort analysis will be discussed in later chapters. If cohorts are not the subject of study, but instead the experiences of particular periods of time are considered, the description 'secular' analysis is sometimes employed. Secular and cohort analyses may on occasion be used to supplement one another, and the two taken together may throw more light on a subject than either used in isolation. Some studies, however, can be usefully carried out only in cohort form, e.g. analyses of survivorship following a diagnosis of cancer.

15

The concept of duration of time is a useful and important one in demography. Louis Henry has suggested that vital events should be related, in general, to those other vital events which necessarily precede them, for instance marriages which must precede legitimate first births, or terminations of marriage which must precede remarriages. If this is done, the important relating factors are the probability of the second event occurring at all and, if it occurs, the distribution of the lengths of time elapsing between the event and its precursor.

2.11 Life tables

If the experience of a cohort is followed, over a period of life, in respect of its passage from one state to another, the result may be exhibited in 'life-table' form. The simplest, and original, version of this form of presentation is a table showing the numbers living and dying at each age, for example:

Age	Living	Dying
0	1,000	41
1	959	20
2	939	11
3	928	.
:	:	:

Here, the numbers living (usually denoted as l_x) are those entering upon a given age x, and the numbers dying (usually denoted as d_x) are those failing to live until their $(x + 1)$th birthday, i.e. the difference between the numbers living at the successive ages x and $x + 1$.

The life-table form of presentation may be adopted in respect of other forms of decrement, for example, bachelors marrying or men retiring from work. There can also be more than one decrement, for example, widows remarrying and dying. (It is even possible to construct life tables with increments in them, though the use of this device is rare.)

The ratio of the dying to the living at any age is the mortality rate, or 'rate of mortality', usually denoted as q_x. Thus $q_x = d_x/l_x$. A life table can be built up from any set of mortality rates, thus forming a hypothetical generation. For instance, the mortality rates experienced at each age in a particular calendar year may be used.

Here are some specimen values of l_x, d_x and q_x for ages 10, 30, 50, 70 and 90, as they might appear in a table representing the recent experience of an economically well-developed country:

Age	l_x	d_x	q_x
10	9601	5	0.00051
30	9377	16	0.00169
50	8753	75	0.00861
70	5316	300	0.05640
90	207	72	0.35015

16

The different trends of the figures in each column are worthy of note (see also figs. 15.1 and 15.2).

2.12 Social and economic groups

In many censuses, questions are asked about occupation and place of work. One aim is to classify the population into active producers and dependants. Another is to measure the occupational distribution of the labour force, which is important for economic analysis. Demographers, too, are interested in occupational differences in marriage, fertility and mortality, for the light they may throw on the factors affecting these elements of population change. In this connexion, a person's status within his occupation is also important: whether he is an employer, a manager, a foreman or a person in no special position of authority − or perhaps he may be self-employed. Retired people can be classified by their former occupation. As there are many occupations, and many statuses within them, the picture presented by occupational analysis is often confusing; efforts have therefore been made to bring out social and economic differences in experience more succinctly by grouping all types of work into a small number of categories. These categories are sometimes called 'social classes', or 'socio-economic groups'. Other similar groupings that may reveal basic differences in experience, by themselves or in conjunction with social classes, are those by sex, race, nationality, tribe, place of birth or place of residence.

2.13 Differentials

If the population can be meaningfully divided into groups, and if the experience of each group, for instance in respect of mortality or fertility, can be measured separately and the results compared, something additional may be learned which will be of assistance in demographic interpretation. In such a case, the study of 'differential mortality' or 'differential fertility' will have been undertaken, to use the normal phraseology (this has no particular connexion with the differential calculus). One example of a set of differentials is an analysis by area or region, and the study of regional differences may indeed be revealing, although because of correlation with race, climate, occupation, industry, etc., interpretation may have to be made with care. Another example is subdivision by occupation; this is a subject of much interest to economists for its effects on demographic rates and proportions; as the multiplicity of occupations is a cause of confusion, their grouping into homogeneous or nearly homogeneous strata is desirable for the sake of clarity.

Among other potential bases for population differentials, it is possible to think of: hours worked; industry in which engaged; wealth; income; housing accommodation; education; and job status. Analysis by the first two of these is probably less meaningful than that by occupation. Wealth is not a subject normally inquired into at a census or a vital registration, and therefore suitable data are unlikely to be available. But the remaining items have all been frequently adopted for the study of differentials. Sociologists are interested in what they call 'social class', a set of groupings into which, historically, people have tended to become divided. Thus, in ancient times, there were the ruler and his court, the large landowners, the church hierarchy, the military men and the peasants. In more modern times, this system has been rendered more complex by industrial development and altered by political acts, which have often been directed against class systems because they are regarded as unfair. In communist countries, class in the old sense has been wholly or mainly abolished, but new determinants of social prestige seem to have arisen between factory workers, agricultural workers, intellectuals, politicians and the like. In other places, some elements of an old class system may remain. Often, social groupings can be found that will conveniently sum up a number of factors, such as job status, income, wealth, domicile, occupation and education. (see § 3.23 below.)

Some specimen figures to illustrate socio-economic differentials are given in table 2.2. It may be noted that the first and third of the categories shown represent specific occupations while the second and fourth represent respectively a position in a hierarchy and a type of work that may be carried on in many different circumstances. It should be borne in mind that people do not necessarily stay in one such category all their working lives, as the figures in the table assume. There may be strong associations between categories by which differentials are measured, as is evidenced by the following selected figures derived from the USA 1970 Census (men aged 25 and over):

	Educational attainment	
Occupation group	Percentage in the occupation group with less than one year at high school	Percentage in the occupation group with one year or more at college
Professional and technical	2	78
Clerical	11	29
Craftsmen	26	10
Operatives	41	11
Labourers	51	5
All	22	27

2.14 Demographic units

The basic unit in demography is the individual person; thus when a population is said to be one of 'about twenty million' the number of living persons (of whatever age or whichever sex) is implied. Frequently males and

18

Table 2.2. *Proportion of people surviving from age*
35 to age 75, (France, 1955—65)

Socio-economic category	Proportion of survivors
Roman Catholic Clergy	0.518
Foremen	0·459
Farmers	0·443
Unskilled labourers	0·331

females are considered separately, for example in regard to mortality, but normally it is best that these should be studied equally as far as possible, no preference being given to one at the expense of the other. For certain limited purposes, other types of units may be employed. Examples of these units are: (*a*) years of potential future lifetime and (*b*) factors representing economic production and consumption. In fertility analysis the married couple, or the 'biological family' of father, mother and children, as it is called, may be referred to, while in housing studies the 'family' may include other relatives as well; the 'household' may incorporate in addition persons other than relatives, for example lodgers. These forms of unit may be regarded as temporary departures, for the sake of convenience in particular studies, from the basic unit of the individual person.

SELECT BIBLIOGRAPHY

Reiss, A. J. *Occupations and Social Status* (The Free Press, Glencoe, 1961).
Chasteland, J. C. 'La Population des Démocraties Populaires d'Europe', *Population* (January-March 1958), p. 79.
Barclay, G. W. *Techniques of Population Analysis* (Wiley, New York, 1958).
Pressat, R. *Demographic Analysis* (Arnold, London, 1972).

3 The nature of demographic data

3.1 How data are collected

Information about population is collected in two main ways: by enumeration at a point of time, and by recording events as they occur over a period. Censuses and social surveys are examples of the first method, and provide 'stock' data (see § 2.5), while birth registrations and migration records ('flow' data) are examples of the second. The information may purport to be complete or it may take the form of a sample. The aim of this chapter is to describe the chief features of the statistics so collected and to indicate the limitations the demographer may need to bear in mind in attempting to interpret the meaning of the published information. In this connexion it is important to consider the relationship the data bear to the biological events in human existence which are the basic objects of study. Although these events are essentially the 'facts of life' with which people generally are familiar, what the student of population needs is a precise knowledge of how they are defined for practical purposes and their consequent place in demographic analysis.

Reliance on 'common sense' may not be enough to prevent serious misinterpretation of the results of statistical studies. While it is obvious what a 'birth' is, the demographer requires to know whether recorded births include or exclude still-births and how still-births are defined. Are the births those which occurred in a given period, or those which were registered during that period? If the latter, what are the rules concerning registration and what delays can occur before registration is effected? Are all births notified to the authorities, or do some escape recording? Such matters can be important when analysing changes in experience, or in measuring differences between populations — more particularly in international comparisons.

3.2 Current and past events

In both censuses and vital registrations, it is usual to ask questions which relate not only to the current status or the happening of the moment but also to events of the past. A census schedule may ask for information about any changes of address within the previous (say) 12 months; the date of marriage may have to be stated when a couple register the birth of their

20

child. Both methods may be combined, as in follow-up surveys, and in systems of continuous registration of the population (under which the records can show both the events that occur and the state of the population at any given moment). Choice of the method to be used is governed by factors such as cost, probable accuracy and political acceptability. The assessment of the accuracy of people's memory clearly must play an important part in the interpretation of such statistics.

3.3 Why data are collected

The keeping of records of births, marriages and deaths originated long before the beginning of the scientific study of population. Its primary purpose was — and still is — the noting down permanently for reference purposes of the most important events in people's lives. The proof of age provided by a birth certificate is useful on many occasions — for instance in order to be able to sit for certain examinations, to receive a bequest which is conditional on the attainment of (say) 21 years, or to claim a pension. The recording of marriages is a feature, *inter alia*, in the enforcement of the law against bigamy. Proof of death is likely to be of importance in the establishment of title to the proceeds of life assurance policies. These are just a few examples of the practical utility of registration.

Although enumeration data normally have no direct administrative uses, censuses help greatly in dealing with the complex problems of social administration in industrialized communities, for instance in the solution of transport difficulties and the determination of manpower available for industry and the defence services.

In neither instance is the process of collecting statistics devised solely or even primarily for the benefit of the demographer. He may, for his own advantage, conduct his own independent population surveys, although considerations of cost normally restrict these to a small-sample basis. Moreover, such surveys usually have to rely upon the voluntary co-operation of the public to a much greater extent than in the regular official enumerations, backed as they are with the force of law; the value of private surveys may therefore be vitiated in some degree by refusals to respond on the part of some people.

3.4 The supplier of population statistics

Demographic information is normally collected by means of inquiries involving a dialogue of some sort between an official and a member of the general public, with the aid of a prepared form. The quality of the results will depend on both persons but, in spite of the help of a trained registrar or enumerator, will vary mainly according to the nature of the respondent.

When a death is registered, for instance, the informant will often be a relative, but the knowledge of this relative about the deceased person's affairs (for example, his occupation) will sometimes be less complete than that of the deceased person when he was alive — who may have completed a census return about himself not long before. At a census, the head of a household, or even of the village, may be required to supply the information; but, in sample surveys conducted from house to house, the housewife will often be the person questioned.

Not only accuracy of knowledge is involved here, but also natural human weakness and bias; relatives may be less inclined than the subject of inquiry to misstate his age or occupation, or they may misstate it in a different way. The type of question asked, and the way in which it is put, will affect the nature of the response; for instance, respondents' memories of events long past will be vaguer than those of recent occurrences. Too protracted a questionnaire may provoke hostility, or boredom, and the recorded results will then suffer accordingly. Response will vary also according to education, social class and area (if there is political or religious bias in some places). There may also be changes in time: people are now more willing, perhaps, than they used to be to disclose information on personal matters associated with fertility.

If the primary supplier is the public, the demographer usually has to rely also on a secondary supplier — a government official — for his data, and here a problem of communication arises mainly because of the very extensive nature of the statistics. This nearly always leads to delay in availability and to ultimate loss of detail arising from a need to condense. The official is often obliged to compromise between the conflicting demands of politicians, administrators, economists and other users of demographic data, and also to keep his costs within bounds, and this necessarily leads to disappointments.

3.5 Vital registration

Although civil registration of births, deaths and marriages is essentially a product of the nineteenth and twentieth centuries, lists of baptisms, burials and weddings were kept by ecclesiastical authorities from much earlier times. The practice originated in France in the year 1308 and in Toledo (Spain) in 1497. While the lists maintained in churches are a useful record, providing material of much value for historical research, they remained local in character and were never brought together centrally; they were normally restricted to those observing the official religion of the State and may not have been fully comprehensive even within this compass.

'Bills of mortality' were an English institution occupying an important place in the history of vital statistics. Such Bills were weekly statements issued by the parish clerks in the time of plague, from perhaps the year

1538 onwards, showing the numbers of deaths and their causes. Their classification of causes was originally crude, and one would not expect medical certificates nowadays to quote such fatal illnesses as 'fever', 'grief', 'headache', 'teeth' or 'suddenly'. Nevertheless, they paved the way for the initiation of the more thorough analyses of today. Civil registration was first introduced in England and Wales in 1836, and in Scotland in 1854, but since the original introduction there have been considerable developments. Thus penalties for failure to register births were introduced in England and Wales in 1874, and compulsory registration of still-births was not enforced there until 1926, although the notification of such occurrences had been required before that date.

Britain cannot be regarded, however, as the birthplace of official vital statistics. This title belongs to Sweden, where a law for the making of tabular records of a population came into force in 1748; this law provided for the regular completion of schedules every year for each parish, showing particulars of births according to sex and legitimacy, of marriages and of deaths by age-group, sex, cause and marital status. From the manner in which they were analysed in conjunction with census data, these schedules may, indeed, be regarded as a beginning of the advanced methods of continuous registration of population that are practised in a few countries today.

In contrast, the development of a national system of vital registration in the USA was slow, mainly because this subject is under the control of the various States, and the Federal Government has no power to enact vital statistics legislation on a national scale. It was only in 1933 that the areas in which birth registration and death registration were at least 90 per cent complete finally expanded to embrace the whole country; and statistics of marriage and divorce are still very limited in scope even today.

3.6 Births

Registration of expectant mothers has been known, but normally nothing is recorded in demographic statistics before a birth occurs. Yet birth is not the earliest point in life to which demographers direct attention; for them, life begins with conception, because today induced abortion is widely used as a method of birth control and needs to be studied. Moreover, spontaneous abortion ('miscarriage' in common parlance) is also a subject of medical interest. Spontaneous abortions that occur in the later part of the gestation period are often included with still-births and with deaths very early in life in the study of what is called 'perinatal' mortality, because these forms of reproductive wastage may have a common cause and doctors are striving to reduce all three kinds of loss. The meaning of the word 'fertility' in demography, for historical reasons, attaches to the production of live-born children. Because of reproductive wastage, and other causes discussed later

23

in this chapter, fertility is quite distinct from 'fecundity', the biological capacity to reproduce.

It is desirable that there should be a clear distinction between live births and still-births; the registration systems of different countries draw, however, a different dividing-line between them. Here is one definition of a live birth: 'the complete expulsion or extraction from its mother of a product of conception, irrespective of the duration of the pregnancy, which, after such separation, breathes or shows any other evidence of life, such as beating of the heart, pulsation of the umbilical cord, or definite movement of voluntary muscles, whether or not the umbilical cord has been cut or the placenta is attached; each product of such a birth is considered live-born.' In order to define still-births it is necessary first to mention foetal deaths: 'Foetal death is death prior to the complete expulsion or extraction from its mother of a product of conception, irrespective of the duration of pregnancy; the death is indicated by the fact that after such extraction the foetus does not breathe or show any other evidence of life.' A still-birth is a foetal death occurring late in the gestation period; 'late' is usually defined as 'after 28 completed weeks of gestation'.

Human births may come singly, and do so in the great majority of cases. There is, however, approximately a 1 per cent chance of twins, and a remoter chance of triplets or even four or more children being born together. The expression 'maternity' is sometimes used for the act of bringing to birth, whether the child is live-born or still-born; where this is done, a multiple birth is reckoned as one act of maternity. Multiple births provide an important source of experimental data for social and psychological research.

The particulars that are recorded when a birth is registered vary from country to country, but ideally the demographer needs to know the marital status of the parents, their ages and occupations, where they live, how long they have been married (or cohabiting), and details of any other children born to them.

3.7 Marriages

All human societies appear to have well-defined rules of one kind or another bearing upon the biological mating process, or 'coitus'. The most common stipulation is that there should be a generally-recognized form of ceremony before mating first begins. Marriage has been defined by the Statistical Commission of the United Nations Organization as: 'The legal union of persons of opposite sex. The legality of the union may be established by civil, religious or other means as recognized by the laws of each country; and irrespective of the type of marriage, each should be reported for vital statistics purposes.' The rate of marriage among the population is sometimes referred to in demography as 'nuptiality'. Marriages are most often solemnized by a religious or a civil ceremony, or both, but in some countries many marriages are merely 'consensual', that is, sanctioned by local custom alone; for example, in the West Indies, consensual marriage is a relic of the days of slavery, when church marriages were not allowed. Such marriages are more difficult for demographers to measure because they are often not registered. In Japan, consensual marriage often precedes legal marriage. In India, however, even today, consummation of marriage may not take place until one or two years after the original ceremony.

Besides being of interest in itself, marriage has significance in demography, for its effect on fertility. Socially, it has important implications in relation to the legitimacy or illegitimacy of the offspring. It is usual to record the ages of the bride and groom together with particulars of residence and parentage, and these data provide material of interest for sociologists and psychologists. Sometimes the occupation is required to be stated but it has been found that the resulting statistics are not very reliable.

3.8 Divorce and separation

Terminations of marriage (otherwise than by death) are not registered in the manner in which marriages are, probably because they are a modern phenomenon and not steeped in history. Some records of legal terminations may, however, be available from other sources. Divorce has been defined as: 'The final legal dissolution of a marriage ... by a judicial decree which confers ... the right to ... remarriage.' In many countries there are various intermediate legal stages before the final decree is issued. There may also be voluntary dissolutions of marriage without the privilege of remarriage; these are often known as 'separations'. It is difficult to collect accurate data of separations, but they are evidently of importance in the study of fertility.

3.9 Deaths

The information collected at registration normally includes particulars of name and address, sex and age, occupation and cause of death. Age is usually reckoned in years, except for infants.

Mortality in the first year of life is of special interest because it is much higher than mortality in childhood, and is strongly correlated with social conditions. On both these counts its study appears to offer prospects for a valuable improvement in survival. The chance of dying decreases rapidly with an infant's advancing age, and this fact governs the choice of time-periods for analysis: the following series is fairly typical:

The first day of life
The remainder of the first week

The following week
Each of the two succeeding weeks
Each of the next two months
Months 4, 5 and 6
Months 7, 8 and 9
Months 10, 11 and 12.

Sometimes the first four weeks are described as the 'neonatal' period, and the rest of the year the 'post-neonatal' period.

3.10   Causes and consequences of death

Unlike fertility, death is a single, final event. Very occasionally, a person may 'die' and be revived after a brief interval, but so far this has not given rise to any difficulty of definition in the study of population: 'Death is the permanent disappearance of all evidence of life at any time after live birth has taken place.' The 'cause of death', that is, the illness or accident to which it is attributable, is of much importance in medicine, and to the demographer for his interest in the probable future course of death rates. Often, the cause is not easy to determine; for instance because people may suffer from more than one impairment in their terminal illness. According to the official definition: 'The causes of death ... are all those diseases, morbid conditions or injuries which either resulted in or contributed to death and the circumstances of the accident or violence which produced any such injuries.'

The death of a spouse causes the 'widowhood' of the surviving spouse and normally terminates the marriage. When the dying partner is the wife, reference may be made to the 'widowerhood' of the husband, but frequently 'widowhood' is used for both sexes. The widowhood of a woman may be followed by a legitimate birth posthumous to her husband's death.

3.11   Typical errors and misstatements

A common fault in national registration systems, from the point of view of their use as demographic records, is incompleteness of observance of the requirements by the public. It is probable that in England and Wales before 1880 the recorded number of births was understated — by about 8 per cent in 1841–5, falling to about 1 per cent in 1871–80. In the USA, even today, there is a certain amount of incompleteness (about 2 per cent for births in 1950). A more striking example is afforded by India, where the fertility data collected amount to perhaps only 50–90 per cent (according to region) of the actual occurrences and so are untrustworthy for measuring long-term trends.

26

Even where the coverage is complete, there are likely to be errors and misstatements of detail in the register; typical examples are incorrect reporting of age and of occupation. Understatement of age by women at marriage is not uncommon. A preference for even numbers and multiples of five has been demonstrated in recorded ages, although this is not quite so prominent as at the census. Different considerations probably apply in respect of births, marriages and deaths according to whether the informant is the person directly affected or someone else. Discrepancies between census and registration data may lead to appreciable errors in mortality rates in respect of certain ages, occupations, and marital statuses.

3.12 Delay in registration

Whereas registration of marriage normally takes place at the same time as the ceremony, a period of grace is usually allowed for the notification of births and deaths. Deaths tend to be notified with little delay when registration is necessary before burial or cremation can take place. The average interval between occurrence and registration of death in many countries is only a few days, and this is not sufficiently important under normal conditions to give rise to any particular need for adjusting the published data of registrations in order to arrive at the number of actual occurrences in any given period of time.

For births, however, a longer interval may elapse after the event before the formal record is made. This can be a cause of misinterpretation or difficulty in close analytical work, especially if the numbers of births are changing. For example, in Britain and other combatant countries the Second World War not only brought about rapid swings in the birth rate but also reduced the delay in registration because of the need to claim a food ration book for the infant. After food rationing ended, the average extent of delay in notification of births increased.

3.13 Re-allocation from place of occurrence to place of residence

Marriages are normally registered at the place where they are celebrated. Births may well be assigned to the district where the parents reside (rather than the area in which the hospital is situated). Deaths occurring away from the place of normal residence may be assigned to the area of normal residence. The practice in matters of this sort varies from country to country, and it is arguable whether a *de jure* or a *de facto* tabulation (see § 3.17 below) is preferable, according to the purposes for which the data are needed. Births, marriages and divorces tend to occur in places that are specially suitable for the purpose, and for demographic measurement it is better that they should

27

be re-allocated to the area of normal residence; for the purpose of studying the extent to which some places are actually favoured by the performance of these events, however, re-allocation is undesirable.

For the calculation of mortality rates by areas, the primary requisite is that the treatment of the deaths should be consistent with that accorded to the living population that is used as an 'exposed to risk'. Where the population can be classified according to either place where enumerated or normal residence, the choice of a *de jure* or *de facto* tabulation of deaths by areas is open, and it is not an easy one to make. For instance, the death from a motor accident in Brighton of a resident of Bradford who happened to be on holiday there might be said to be properly attributable to Brighton; but a death from tuberculosis in a similar case should perhaps be allocated to Bradford, since this disease normally takes some time to complete its course.

3.14 The census

Historians have discovered that enumerations of the people have been carried out from the earliest civilized times. These early counts appear to have been made for limited practical purposes, such as tax-collecting or military conscription, and the results were probably not disclosed publicly. Aims of this kind are fulfilled today normally by special means and not as part of the general population census, which, as indicated in §3.3 above, serves only as the foundation for extensive statistical tabulations designed to satisfy the general needs of economists, social workers, local and other public authorities and government departments.

Early examples of the modern type of census are those conducted in Quebec in the year 1665 and in Iceland in 1703. The practice did not, however, become general until the early nineteenth century: periodical enumerations began in the United States of America in 1790 and in Britain and France in 1801. By about 1860, no fewer than twenty-four countries had adopted the system, and were enumerating populations totalling some 200 millions, or about one-fifth of the world total of the day. Today, over 2,000 millions are enumerated regularly — two-thirds of the world total. The frequency of the census, and its scope as regards the numbers and nature of the questions asked, have also increased: only four topics (housing, families, age and occupation) were included in the British schedule of 1801, whereas by 1911 this had risen to over a dozen.

A modern population census has been defined as 'the total process of collecting, compiling and publishing demographic, economic and social data pertaining, at a specified time or times, to all persons of a defined territory'. For any sizeable territory, a census normally requires:

(1) the choice of a system of local areas, for example, electoral wards, or squares on a map;

(2) the systematic preparation in advance of lists of the dwellings in each area;

(3) the formation and training of a corps of enumerators;

(4) the delivery to each person, household or village of one or more schedules in which information is to be set down;

(5) the giving, by the enumerators, of advice or help in the completion of the schedules — or in some cases the completion of the schedules by the enumerators themselves after questioning the inhabitants; and

(6) the collection, examination and statistical analysis of the schedules.

A recent innovation is the sample census in which not all the persons of a defined territory, but a proportion selected on a strict rotational basis, are enumerated.

3.15 General characteristics of censuses

Censal enumerations vary a good deal in quality in different parts of the world. The best, although highly accurate in many respects, are never wholly free from faults. In the least accurate censuses the data collected may even be so untrustworthy as to be largely valueless: some primitive peoples believe that it is unlucky, or even impious, to hold a census and will consequently do all they can to thwart the most carefully-laid administrative plans; others have no means of accurately measuring the passage of time and so no one can say precisely how old he is. It is the demographer's task to appreciate the character of the statistical material he is using, and to understand the local significance of the items of information tabulated.

There are two general methods by which census schedules may be filled in: either the principal householder — or each member of the household separately — does this or else the official enumerators themselves elicit the information by direct inquiry (they are then called 'canvassers'). In Australia, New Zealand and many European countries the first method is favoured, but in the USA, Canada, Russia and India the second has been adopted. The choice of method is closely linked with the timing of the census, the way in which 'population' is defined, the literacy of the people and the complexity of the questions asked. An advantage of arranging for the householder to complete the schedule is that the census can be taken all at one particular point of time. The use of canvassers usually entails spreading the inquiries over a period of days or weeks; this may cause confusion over births, deaths and removals occurring during this time, and render the results liable to inaccuracy because of lapses of memory.

29

3.16 Timing

The timing of a census presents many problems. The observer has no control over his material; he is unable to provide that the population shall, at the chosen moment, be arranged in such a way as to be representative of its distribution, on average, at all other times. He can only attempt to select a period when disturbances (such as holiday trips) are at a minimum. Within the year, considerable seasonal movements take place between various occupations and areas. The census date should probably be at a time when most people may be expected to be at home and at their usual work; but this necessarily cannot represent the mean situation for the year, which should, strictly speaking, include a due proportion of holiday-makers.

Difficulties may also arise in the choice of the census year. It is clearly desirable to aim at regularity and continuity. Nevertheless, in any time of serious disturbance a census might be unrepresentative, and so of small value. In 1939—45 it was clearly impracticable to have one in many countries because of wartime conditions. In the early 1930s some enumerations were held during a major economic depression, and the interpretation of the occupational data was difficult because of the prevailing unemployment. The choice of census year may nowadays be influenced also by a desire to conform as closely as possible to the recommendations of some international agency for improved comparability of statistics between one country and another.

Considerations of cost seem likely to restrict the holding of full enumerations to decennial or quinquennial intervals. Information that is required between censuses may, however, be obtained somewhat differently — by means of continuous registration systems or by sampling.

3.17 Definition of 'population'

In general, it has to be decided what to do about: (*a*) home citizens overseas, temporarily or permanently; (*b*) persons in transit by land, sea and air, and (*c*) foreign nationals within the area covered by the enumeration on the census date. Thus one might perhaps distinguish between:

(1) *Home population:* comprising all the people actually located within the country,

(2) *Total population:* adding to (1) the national armed forces overseas and also residents who happen to be on holiday abroad, and

(3) *National population:* which would exclude from (2) any visitors from overseas or other non-civilians present in the country.

There are two main ways by which census populations may be classified according to area of residence, namely (*a*) they may be recorded simply wherever they happen to be on the census night (*de facto*) or (*b*) they may be regrouped into their places of usual abode (*de jure*). Thus a London man who was on business in Manchester when the enumeration occurred would be regarded as living (*a*) in Manchester or (*b*) in London. The first is perhaps more suited to householder methods, and the second to canvasser methods, of completing the enumeration schedules. In fact, however, in many countries persons are nowadays asked to give sufficient information to enable a double classification to be made. The 'usual residence' question, introduced into Britain in 1931, permits of this and is of importance in the calculation of local death rates.

In India, in 1951, persons were enumerated as at their usual residence if they had stayed there at any time within a specified period of twenty days. If they had not done so, they were reckoned as 'visitors' wherever they were staying on census night.

3.18 Drafting the census schedule

The schedule consists very largely of instructions, and these need to be very clear, especially in relation to questions about employment and the occupation followed within it, marriages and fertility, birthplace and nationality. Other typical questions relate to sex, age, place of residence, characteristics of residence and extent of education. To some extent, more information about the population of a country can be gained simply by adding to the number of questions asked on the census schedule. If this process is pursued far enough, however, a point will be reached where public indifference, or inability fully to understand what is required, gives rise to such a degree of inaccuracy that doubt is thrown on the validity of the results of the whole enumeration. The limit to the number of questions depends on the degree of literacy and general standard of education of the population, and on public familiarity with and attitude towards official inquiries. If canvassers are used it should be possible to explain the more difficult questions and so help to improve the accuracy of the answers.

Not only the number of questions but also the type of question is important. It is undesirable to ask for any information the giving of which may arouse prejudice or resentment in the minds of ordinary men and women. There may, indeed, be some to whom any kind of official inquiry is abhorrent, but the great majority of people give particulars of residence, family relationships, occupation, age and the like fairly readily — if not always with complete accuracy. It is more likely, however, that inquiries about infirmities, or into financial matters such as wages, salaries, savings or expenses would be resented in too great a degree for success. In the USA, however, information on earnings began to be sought in 1940, with results that are apparently successful. One possible way of removing the objections to questions about

31

income is to ask for no more than the ranges within which they lie, as is done in New Zealand. Considerable skill is called for in framing the questions that are to be put, as the accuracy of the replies will depend to a material extent on their clarity and lack of ambiguity. In many countries small pilot inquiries are held before the census proper in order to investigate the degree and accuracy of response and also other aspects of the work of the enumeration.

3.19 Errors in census data

The first test of accuracy will normally be made by the enumerator when he examines the completed schedule for each household to see if it contains any obvious inconsistencies. A further examination is likely to be made at a regional office or at headquarters before the data are processed. Nevertheless it is likely that, when the census material has been tabulated, a careful study of the results by common-sense methods will still reveal apparent misstatements or even omissions (it is not impossible that fresh errors may have arisen owing to wrong classification or inaccurate tabulation). Typical faults are discussed in ensuing paragraphs; some statistical methods by which errors may be detected are discussed in chapter 19.

Inaccuracy in the total number of persons enumerated has been reduced to a low level in most countries that have held censuses for many years. Even so, errors may not be negligible: the enumerated population in the USA in 1950 was nearly $1\frac{1}{2}$ per cent smaller than it is estimated it should have been, even though the census was conducted by official enumerators. The numbers of young children may be understated. Thus, in 1921 in England and Wales 795,000 children aged 0 and 826,000 children aged 1 year were counted, whereas it was assessed from the numbers of birth registrations, after allowing for infant deaths, that 819,000 and 848,000 respectively should have been returned. The total deficiency for the two ages together was 46,000 or as much as 3 per cent. Subsequently, however, this kind of error has greatly diminished. In other countries under-enumeration may be found at other ages, for instance in early adult life. If the *de jure* method is used there may be over-enumeration, through some people being counted at more than one address.

3.20 Misstatements of age

Generalizing on the basis of international experience, the principal times of life at which discrepancies may be expected to be revealed are as follows:

(1) *in infancy:* sometimes under-enumeration of very young children appears to be associated with overstatement of the ages of such children;

(2) *around the age of legal adulthood:* overstatement of ages under adulthood

32

and understatement of ages immediately succeeding adulthood may bring about heaping of the numbers recorded in this region;

(3) *at pension age:* a tendency to overstate the age, or to correct a previous understatement, is sometimes observed among persons who are about to become entitled to a pension;

(4) *in extreme old age:* very aged persons are prone to exaggerate the length of time for which they have lived.

Sources of difficulty that are not connected with any particular time of life arise, first, from ages that are not stated or are reported to be unknown — ignorance on the subject of one's age still exists in the rural areas of some countries; secondly, from a widespread tendency to quote ages in round numbers, such as to the nearest even number, or five or ten; thirdly, from local variations in methods of reckoning ages in some of the less well-developed countries. The second kind of misstatement leads to heaping of the numbers enumerated at some ages and a corresponding deficiency at less popular ages.

Corrections of errors of the kind mentioned in this and the preceding paragraph are made: (*a*) by assuming some not unreasonable hypothetical age-distribution for persons whose ages are unstated; (*b*) by a process of grouping or graduation in order to eliminate irregular progressions among the numbers enumerated at successive ages; and (*c*) by a variety of procedures, such as the study of sex-ratios, and of the proportions surviving from one census to the next. The extent of misstatements arising at the two extremes of life can sometimes be assessed by reference to details of registration of births and deaths respectively. Adjustments for other suspected forms of bias, such as those occurring under heads (2) and (3) above, are much less easy to make. This is because of the influence of migration, the statistics of which are rarely comparable in quantity and quality with records of vital events; as a result it is often difficult to find any firm framework of reference, from independent sources of data, against which corrections can be made. For similar reasons, a suspected consistency of understatement of ages over a wide range by women is not readily proved or allowed for.

3.21   Bias in the statement of occupation

The variety and complexity of modern employments and industrial processes necessitates the devotion of considerable attention, in censuses in developed countries, to the framing of questions about occupation. One of the commonest errors arises, however, from a very human weakness: a tendency to overstate the status within the occupation. For instance, an unskilled or semi-skilled operative may describe himself as a skilled worker or a foreman. A more genuine kind of difficulty for individuals arose at enumerations taken during the economic depression of the 1930s; men and women who

33

had been out of regular work for a long time had to decide whether to regard themselves as still being engaged in their own industry, in which they hoped to return to work in due course, or to write in details of any other trade which, perhaps, they had followed intermittently while unable to do their main job.

Other principal sources of inaccuracy and lack of comparability between one census and another are retired persons, part-time workers and unpaid family helpers. Such persons may describe themselves wrongly. Some retired men and women return themselves as though still engaged in their former occupation, and deciding whether one is 'unoccupied' or 'retired' apparently causes many difficulties.

A method of testing the accuracy of censal statements of occupation (and of other particulars such as age and marital status) that has recently been investigated is to compare the information given on the schedule with that supplied on subsequent death registration. Such a matching process is naturally restricted to deaths occurring so soon after the census that there has been insufficient time for a change in the occupation or other character-istic, or in the address. For a period of perhaps a month or six weeks after the census, it should be possible in the majority of cases, after a scrutiny of the death record, readily to trace the corresponding census schedule. Tests of this kind were made in England and Wales in connection with the 1951 Census, and showed some discrepancies between the two forms of record. In such work it is, of course, often impossible to be sure which of the dis-crepant statements is the inaccurate one. Reasonable inferences are some-times permissible; for instance, if there has been a general tendency for the position held within the occupation to be described in a more favourable light on death than at the census it may seem probable that it was the registration informant who overstated the position rather than the deceased person himself when making his last census return. It must be remembered, however, that many of those who died very shortly after a census may already have been so ill on the census date that information was then also given by persons other than themselves.

Particulars of occupation, age and marital status given at a census may also be checked against statements made on marriage registration or on birth registration.

3.22 Evidence of marital status and dependency

When information about marital status first began to be collected, a fairly clear-cut subdivision of all persons into the three categories of single, married and widowed was possible in the countries holding their censuses. In more modern times, however, the additional classes of 'divorced' and 'legally separated' have had to be added. Furthermore, many married persons nowa-days are not enumerated on the same schedules as their partners, and some-

34

times this is because of permanent non-legal separation. In other countries, complications are caused by varying customs; child marriage has not yet been wholly eliminated in India; polygamy is not unknown in certain areas; in Central and South America many couples live together as man and wife, without any legal or religious bond, in consensual unions.

It follows that the study of the statistics of marital status, whether for their own sake or as a background to the analysis of fertility, presents a number of problems and requires a knowledge of local customs and attitudes. Misstatements of marital status are likely to occur, especially where events have taken place that may be regarded as a cause for pity or shame. Thus married women who are separated from their husbands may tend to describe themselves as widows, and single women with illegitimate children may record their status as 'married' or 'widowed'; the numbers of divorced persons enumerated may tend to be fewer than would be expected from the particulars of divorces known to have been effected in the law courts and of registrations of re-marriages of divorced men and women.

Where it is desired to tabulate the ages of husbands and wives in combination, this can normally be performed only in respect of schedules on which both spouses are enumerated. It is unlikely that the data will be much reduced in value by this limitation, but a corresponding difficulty of greater magnitude often arises in respect of children, who may be away at school or with relatives. Inquiries into family size or dependency are not, therefore, normally practicable unless special questions are asked regarding members of the family located outside the home on census night.

3.23 Socio-economic grouping

Basically, in capitalist countries a distinction is often drawn between employers and managers on the one hand and employed people on the other. The first of these groups is usually enlarged to include professional workers and it may be divided into a superior and inferior band. The second group is sometimes broken down into three sub-categories, namely:

clerks, foremen and skilled technicians,
semi-skilled workers,
unskilled labourers,

though there is some virtue in analysing the first of these into its three constituent parts. More extensive analyses distinguish also the following as separate groups:

farmers,
shopkeepers,
people providing a personal service
junior ranks in the armed forces,

but these cannot so easily be arranged in any particular order of ascendancy. There is naturally a tendency to move from one class to another as the age increases. This tendency, and other inter-group movements occasioned, for instance, by personal efforts, changes in personal circumstances, or developments from one generation to another, are often referred to as 'social mobility'. In the USA, extensive studies have been made of the approach towards a system of stratification. It has been asked what validity occupation has, as an index of social position; and, given that there is some validity, what widths of occupational grouping are suitable for the purpose. It has been argued that the concept of stratification rests on four postulates, namely:

(1) differences of position occur in many social structures, for example, in the Church, in government service and industry;

(2) these differences are recognized by variations in working conditions, in monetary rewards and in various kinds of honours;

(3) some mixture or other of these various types of recompense may be regarded as constituting 'prestige of position';

(4) social position may be regarded as a combination of prestige of position and the personal esteem which may be conveyed by others in recognition of the efficiency and charm with which the occupational role is fulfilled.

Acceptance of these postulates would indicate a system of classification based on occupation only in part. But, in practice, occupation is the most important single factor that is capable of being investigated in a census schedule. Nevertheless, the Americans place much emphasis on 'popular acclaim' in the judgment of the social worth of occupations, and have conducted sample inquiries to measure this acclaim. In this way, a system of classification of occupations has been evolved; some examples of a suggested scheme of arrangement are given below — the groupings are shown in order of esteem, with the most admired at the foot:

(1) farm labourers, miners, porters,
(2) gardeners, janitors, waiters,
(3) workers in glass and leather,
(4) furnacemen, members of the armed forces,
(5) auto mechanics, painters,
(6) bakers, bricklayers, shipping clerks,
(7) buyers, farm managers, railroad foremen,
(8) auctioneers, dancers, nurses,
(9) athletes, clergymen, musicians, photographers,
(10) accountants, bank managers, engineers, scientists.

The result might not unfairly be regarded as similar to the social class system in Britain, in that it begins with unskilled manual work and proceeds upwards with increasing manual skill towards work involving higher mental

36

ability, creativeness and managerial capacity. Ten groups are, however, preferable to five.

An advantage of the 'public esteem' approach is that it is possible to measure the variations, by age, sex, social position and geographical area, in the opinions of the members of the public who were interviewed. A disadvantage is the limited technical knowledge of the public generally, some of whom may never have heard, for example, of demographers, and a possible tendency of the public to be swayed by ephemeral considerations.

3.24 Continuous registration systems

If at some time immediately following a census, it were decided formally to keep under review not only all vital events but also all migratory movement, including transfer from one locality to another within the country, it should be possible to inaugurate a complete system of 'population accounting' under which the location, sex, age and marital status of each person in the country could be known at all times. Such a system might be termed 'continuous registration'. Its major characteristic, and principal difference from ordinary vital registration, would be that, in order to keep track of all day-to-day movements, some form of personal record — such as an identity card — would be essential. The advantages of continuous registration from the demographic point of view are evident: it would provide full information about the population whenever it was required; if perfected it could even eliminate the need for further censuses (and for other administrative inquiries involving, for instance, registration for national service or establishment of title to old age pension). The disadvantages are perhaps less immediately obvious but are nevertheless important; the system would tend to be laborious to operate, costly, liable to rapidly accumulating errors and, last but by no means least, unpopular with many members of the public.

In spite of the disadvantages, continuous population registers have been successfully set up in small highly-developed nations such as Belgium, Holland, Switzerland and the Scandinavian countries. The Swedish system had its roots in the seventeenth century, as mentioned in §3·5, and the Dutch register has been in force for over a hundred years. A somewhat analogous system was brought into force in Britain during the Second World War but has since been discontinued. It may be noted that none of these countries has found it possible to dispense with censuses, which remain of great value both as checks on the operation of the register and as sources of information on matters additional to those recorded in it.

With the advent of electronic computers, it may be possible, in countries where the system of demographic records is less complete than that provided by continuous registration, to use a process of 'record linkage'. Supposing that enough is known in the census results (say) to identify uniquely each member of the population – the full name coupled with the exact date of birth might well be enough – and that there is another, independent, record system covering all the people which also allows each person to be uniquely identified, for example, the social security records or the data of the national health service. Then, by putting each of these two sets of data on to magnetic tape, or punched cards, it could readily be arranged that the computer should assemble together all the information about each person from both systems. In this way, it might be possible, for instance, to match the particulars of occupation, birth-place and nationality collected at a census with the medical records of the local doctor, the statistics of periods of stay in hospital and the claims for sickness benefit while away from work due to illness. Plans for record linkage systems of this kind are well advanced in many countries, although naturally there are many practical difficulties to be overcome.

3.25   Other sources of demographic data

In the remaining part of this chapter, reference will be made to the uses, for demographic purposes, of a number of sources of statistics. First, records of migratory and passenger movement, essential as they are for a complete tally of national population change. Secondly, social security data, which are often comprehensive enough to be of value in relation to the population generally. Thirdly, miscellaneous systems such as health service records, employment registers, electoral rolls and scholastic files, which might on occasion be helpful, although the chance of their use is smaller. Finally, there is always the possibility of making *ad hoc* inquiries to obtain particulars that would not otherwise be available; such inquiries are often conducted by the use of sampling, and therefore require a knowledge of the appropriate techniques of collection and interpretation of data. The underlying theory of sampling is very well explained in textbooks of statistics, and will be referred to only briefly here, emphasis being placed on practical applications rather than on theory.

3.26   Migratory movements

Total world population is augmented only by births and diminished only by deaths (as inter-planetary transfer may at present be left out of account); but in any more limited area the size of the population is influenced by geographical movements, or 'migration'. Of these, the best recorded are movements across national boundaries, or 'international migrations'. Many of these are quite temporary in character – holiday and business trips for instance – and these are usually distinguished in the statistics from longer-term changes of abode, known as 'permanent' migrations; although in fact they do not all prove to be permanent. Sometimes movements by sea, land and air are not equally well-documented — the more rapid the conveyance, the less time there is for the collection of data.

3.27 Migration records

Where continuous population registers are found to be cumbersome and costly to operate, it is quite likely that records of local migration are not kept either. Movements across the borders of national states are, however, regarded as being politically significant almost everywhere in the world, and many countries have set up machinery for their recording and control, thus providing useful demographic data as a by-product. This machinery is, however, often inadequate from a statistical point of view, and methods of making improvements have frequently been discussed at international conferences. The International Labour Office has also devoted much attention to the subject. Migration statistics are still generally regarded as being incapable of providing a basis for true demographic comparisons between one country and another. The chief problem is to ensure uniformity of definition in distinguishing genuine migrants from passengers going temporarily on travels abroad. To quote the International Conference of Migration Statisticians of 1932, 'In principle, every act of removal from one country to another for a certain length of time should be included in the statistics of migration, with the exception of tourist traffic . . . When the removal is for one year or more the migration should be regarded as permanent migration.'

Defining migrants is not, however, the only problem. Methods of collecting statistics vary, and some movements may pass unrecorded while others are carefully tabulated. Different authorities within the same country may publish apparently conflicting data. The degree of classification by sex, age and occupation varies greatly. In these circumstances, demographers sometimes turn for information on migration to censuses, which can help in two ways.

(1) if successive census counts are differenced, and if allowance is made for intervening births and deaths, the amount of net migration can be deduced;

(2) census tabulations as to birth-place, nationality and mother tongue can give further relevant particulars.

Certain disadvantages are, however, inseparable from this kind of information. The deductive method throws in with the supposed migration any errors in the data at the two censuses and in the intervening vital registrations. The study of birth-places, or other similar census material, does not permit the measurement of movements within a specific period of time — unless, as in the USA and elsewhere, a special question is asked at the census about place of residence a given number of years before the date of the enumeration.

3.28 Records devised from social security systems

As has already been indicated, a number of countries have instituted comprehensive schemes of social insurance covering a large part of the population, and these schemes are a potential source of useful demographic data. Such schemes are usually to be found only in the most advanced societies, and these societies are the most likely to have developed reliable census and registration systems; it seems probable therefore, that social insurance records will not normally constitute a primary source of population statistics but will be of value only in furnishing supplementary information on special matters. A further reason why this should be so is that the exclusion of certain classes, the restrictions on benefits, and the economies in administration that are often features of social insurance systems tend to limit both the scope of the data and the usefulness of the way in which they are presented.

3.29 Employment statistics

The study of the 'labour force', as the body of persons actively engaged in work is sometimes called, is an important instrument of economic policy in most modern industrial communities. Inquiries are therefore addressed by government departments periodically to employers about the number of work-people they employ, and sample surveys are also held, especially in the USA, to obtain additional information. The data thus provided give a picture of changes in the employment situation between censuses, and may be used in order to supplement the occupational tabulations derived from those censuses.

In studying employment statistics and the corresponding census data it is important to understand the distinction between the classification of gainfully occupied persons by industry and their classification by occupation. Some industries employ many kinds of workers; coal mining, for instance, requires the services not only of those hewing at the coal face but also of those who transport the mined material to the surface, of clerks for keeping the books and payrolls, of sales agents and engineers and directing staff. These occupations have counterparts in other industries. The industrial classification may be based on the product made or the service rendered by the employer, whereas for occupations the essential criterion has been the material worked in, with sub-divisions according to the process. Industrial organization and method vary from place to place, and certainly from time to time. Agricultural work, for example, is now far more mechanical than it used to be, except in underdeveloped areas where it may have continued in traditional fashion. As a result, classifications and meanings tend to alter from one census to another and to vary internationally, and great care is needed if comparisons of data collected at different times or in different countries have to be made; some knowledge of industrial processes may be desirable for a proper interpretation of the data.

Social classifications and analyses of fertility, marriage and mortality are usually based on occupation rather than industry.

3.30 'Statistical Accounts'

The comprehensive social surveys of Scottish life which are designated 'Statistical Accounts' may appropriately be mentioned here as a unique source of demographic information. The main purpose of the Accounts has been to collect for permanent record some notes on the principal cultural elements in the life of the British nation north of the Border; particulars of the size and distribution of the population are obtained incidentally. So far the Accounts have been of infrequent occurrence and the inquiries connected with them have been spread over periods of years. The first was held in the last decade of the eighteenth century and the second in 1832—45. The third was started after the Second World War and covered such items as local topography, history, public and social services, housing, agriculture, industries, commerce and way of life — as well as population.

3.31 General value of sampling

Detailed reference has been made in this book so far only to examples of the collection of complete data, mainly by means of censuses and registration. Although it may give a certain sense of finality to have collected the maximum possible material at a given time, even 'total' data are subject to random fluctuations, for instance from one year to another, and can be regarded only as a sample drawn from an indefinitely large 'ideal' population. Further, their bulk may well be such that great delay ensues before they can be tabulated and published. If a truly representative sample can be obtained, several advantages will be secured; not only can the data be collected by a smaller and more skilled staff and the analysis of the results be made more quickly and at less expense, but great flexibility will be achieved —because inquiries can be held more often and the questions asked can be varied. Although there will be a wider margin of statistical error in the information obtained, this margin can be measured and, by suitably varying the size of the sample, satisfactorily controlled.

The problems involved in obtaining demographic data by means of samples deserve attention, and the remaining sections of this chapter will be devoted to a description of what can be (and has been) achieved in this way.

3.32   Advantages of sampling in demography

The uses of sampling in the study of population may be classified into three broad groups, namely:

(1) gaining information independently of any complete count;
(2) bringing up to date the results of a complete count taken some time before; and
(3) supplementing a current complete count.

Although the advantages of group (1) are potentially the greatest, sampling has so far by no means supplanted the taking of complete counts. There are two main reasons for this. First, it may be argued by some people that if a census or registration system is compulsory it should be applied to everyone and not only to a certain selection of the people. Secondly, efficient sampling requires stratification and this can be achieved only if there is a suitable reference framework based on a recent complete count of some sort. Groups (2) and (3), and particularly (3), therefore provide many interesting examples in demography.

Sampling may be employed not only in order to obtain basic statistics but also to check the accuracy of particulars already collected, or to pave the way for a complete count by the acquisition of advance information about the characteristics to be expected or the difficulties likely to be encountered from an administrative point of view. These and other uses are elaborated upon in the next section.

3.33   Sampling in connexion with population censuses

Examples of the successful employment of sampling methods in connexion with censuses can be found in almost every phase of the work of the Registrar General — at the planning stages, in the enumeration itself, in the course of processing and tabulating the data, and as part of subsequent evaluations of the quality of the statistics collected. Before a census is held it is possible, for instance, to test the reactions of members of the public to the number or nature of the questions to be asked or to ascertain in what light people view the proposed enumeration; some may resent what they consider to be an unnecessary State interference in the life of private citizens; some may argue that the details to be sought should differ from those proposed. The general attitude of the population towards the census has a significance that cannot be overlooked.

During the process of enumeration it may be desirable to design the schedule of personal information so that some questions are asked of everyone but others are asked only of a sample. The advantages of this method are that the complete enumeration provides a firm framework for the sample,

42

and a check upon its representativeness, and that the amount of trouble caused to the public generally is minimized. By such means, more questions may be included on the schedule than would otherwise be possible. The labour of tabulation is also considerably reduced. Another use of sampling is connected with tabulation alone. After a complete set of schedules has been collected, tabulation is begun of a sample of them. This method permits the publication of the results of the census much earlier than would otherwise be the case, and also (provided that the sample is large enough) allows of greater complexity in the tabulation for a given cost. If desired, the complete tabulation can be published afterwards at leisure, without holding up the supply of data needed urgently for planning and research.

Finally, after an enumeration, sampling may be used in order to check the accuracy of the data. If the response of householders is suspect, some re-enumeration may be made; or if the local census official is not trusted, new enumerators — or the same men in different districts — may be employed. Checking the census data against other sources of information, such as vital registers, is also adequately effected by means of samples.

3.34 Practical difficulties

While sampling during and after a census is a relatively straightforward matter, surveys conducted independently of a recent enumeration sometimes run into difficulties. These difficulties may arise from limitations to staff and monetary resources, which tend to reduce samples to such a small size that there are hardly enough units to fill all the subsections after the necessary stratification; or sufficient information on which to base an adequate stratification may be lacking — although the missing information may be obtained by holding a pilot survey (that is, a small sample designed to investigate possible problems in advance). In order to concentrate fully on the important problems of securing the co-operation of the public and ensuring that the right sort of question is asked in the right manner, it may be necessary to pay less attention to details in the selection of cases to be interviewed. This may involve some departure from the desired standard of statistical accuracy. If even a small proportion of the public do not co-operate by answering the questions asked, some doubt will be thrown upon the inquiry as a whole.

These problems may lead either to the abandonment of some desirable stratifications or even to the use of a 'quota' system under which it is left to the enumerator, who may be skilled as a collector of information but not as a statistician, to make up his or her own sample, within certain specified limits. Further, an adequate selection of areas may be hampered by loss of time through, and expense of, travelling. In view of these difficulties it is particularly important that the results obtained should be checked whenever

43

possible against any comparable national data to ensure that the sample is, as far as can be seen, properly representative — or, if it is not, that the fact shall not be overlooked.

It is important that the 'field work' should be well organized. It may be best to use the services of university research centres or market research organizations; or interviewers and supervisors may be specially recruited and trained, in which case it will probably be necessary to keep a careful eye on their progress and performance. If the number of field workers is kept small a better quality of data may be collected, but the duration of time required may be lengthened undesirably, so a balance must be struck between these two *desiderata*.

3.35　Selection of samples

The manner in which a sample is chosen is of the greatest importance if bias in the results is to be avoided. If there is any bias present, the data obtained will not be representative of the whole population, and the reason for the inaccuracy will not be random error but will lie in other, avoidable, causes. Such inaccuracy arises when the whole range of actual possibilities is not adequately covered by the sample, and more particularly when, inadvertently, the demographer fails to eliminate all correlation between the degree of inadequacy of coverage and the nature of the characteristics under study.

One example of incompleteness of coverage liable to cause bias arises from the deliberate selection of a 'representative' sample by the choice of individuals who are thought to be typical. This method is fallible because the person making the selection may well fail to envisage all the possible varieties present in the whole population and may therefore choose an unsatisfactory sample. Prejudices — of which the statistician may not even be aware — may also interfere with representative selection. Thus, for instance, he may try so hard to avoid colour prejudice that in the end too many coloured people are chosen.

A very common source of bias is non-response in voluntary inquiries. People who refuse to co-operate are often not a random group but consist of those who do not wish to participate for some reason connected with the purpose of the survey; for example, in a fertility survey the infertile may be unwilling to supply details of their family life. A more subtle form of bias can arise where people are not at home when the interviewer calls: this again could be connected with fertility, as mothers with young children are more likely to be at home than are women without children. The interviewer may well be tempted to approach the person next door for information instead, to save the labour of calling again, and bias could result from this. Census enumerators have been known to avoid physically-handicapped persons, to save such persons any further hardship.

44

Bias has been known to arise even from apparently careful selections, for example, the choice of the middle card in each of a series of drawers, when the number of cards in each drawer was not the same. The results would then be unduly weighted towards the emptier drawers and thus towards the reasons for their emptiness.

Correct sampling procedures involve either the use of processes which are known to be truly random, such as drawing lots or adopting proven systems of random numbers, or the adoption of 'stratification' based on a complete list of possibilities. The simplest form of stratification is the choice, from a complete pack of record cards, of every nth card in strict sequence, for example, the 5th, 15th, 25th, etc. This is called 'quasi-random' sampling. If there were two packs of cards, say one for men and one for women, and a similar selection were made from each and the selected cards combined, this would represent multiple stratification. In such a case, a different sampling fraction could be chosen for men from that used for women, say $1/m$ and $1/w$ respectively, provided that the results were weighted together in the ratio m men to w women subsequently.

In 'quota' sampling, the investigators may be told to interview at random a given number of persons of each kind, for example six housewives for every three students for every four old age pensioners. While such a plan may be very reasonable in its general outline, there is a danger that bias may enter into the selection of the representatives of each class because they may be chosen for their ready availability or geographical proximity. As in all types of survey, much must depend upon the quality of the interviewers.

SELECT BIBLIOGRAPHY

Handbook of Population Census Methods (United Nations Organization, Statistical Office, New York, 1954).

Handbook of Vital Statistics Methods (United Nations Organization, Statistical Office, New York, 1955).

Yates, F. *Sampling Methods for Censuses and Surveys* (Griffin, London, 1953).

Matras, J. *Populations and Societies* (Prentice-Hall, New Jersey, 1973).

4 Demographic statistics in practice

4.1 Quality

The purpose of this chapter is to give some practical illustrations of demographic data, showing how and in what form they are published and how their characteristics vary from time to time and from one country to another. Naturally, reference can be made only to some of the material collected in a few countries, most of it recent. An attempt is made, however, to give some idea of the range of variation, in quality, style and completeness of coverage, that can occur in population statistics between one area and another. As awareness of demographic problems increases, and more data are collected, this range is probably diminishing, and unreliable elements are slowly being rendered more trustworthy. Even where the basic aim is the same, however, the methods used for the collection of information vary because of the need to adapt them to local circumstances − political, legal or educational. Such circumstances may affect the way in which vital events are defined; they may also affect the accuracy of the statistics; if errors of interpretation are to be avoided, close attention must be devoted to both aspects.

4.2 World census coverage

Much valuable work has been carried out by the Population Division of the UN Organization in assembling information from all over the world on population size and characteristics. In this way, estimates for some 250 countries have been brought together. The results are shown in the UN *Demographic Year Book*, grouped into the six continental areas of Africa, America, Asia, Europe, Oceania and the USSR. It is indicated for each statistic in each country whether the assessment is based upon recent census data, on only a sample survey (or some other form of less complete count), or upon no more than general observation. The current record shows that some 95 per cent of the world's population today has been estimated upon the basis of a census held within the last ten years or so. The remaining 5 per cent consists of people living almost exclusively in Africa and Asia; the number of separate countries or dependencies where they reside is about forty − or some 15 per cent of the number of all nations. Those countries where enumerations have not been held are of smaller than average size; study of the areas in question

46

reveals that they are also economically underdeveloped, and probably as they advance into modernity their demographic statistics will also emerge.

The fact that a census has been held in a country does not, of course, ensure the accuracy of the data. In many places, censuses on an adequate modern scale have been held only since 1945, and maturity has not yet been achieved. Experience shows that the first few censuses conducted in a territory rarely achieve such a degree of completeness as those held after a long series of previous enumerations; if completeness is not certain, then correctness in details such as age and marital status is likely to be even more elusive. The question of accuracy will be further discussed later in this chapter.

4.3 General extent of vital registration

The UN Population Division, in supplying estimates of the numbers of births in recent calendar years, was unable to give any figure for about seventy territories for which a population assessment had been made. Thus about 30 per cent of countries do not have any effective registration of births, and much the same will be true of deaths and marriages. It is more expensive and troublesome to maintain a permanent system of registration than it is to hold a census. An occasional effort to recruit enumerators, and to rouse the public to the degree of awareness necessary for an adequate single censal response, is less difficult to achieve than the imposition of a permanent and continuous system of registration upon people who, in poorly-developed countries, may neither see nor desire any advantage from it.

Of the 180 countries for which birth statistics could be given by UNO, the data are regarded as being less than 90 per cent complete in 70; in the remaining 110 countries a 90 per cent standard of accuracy was attained, or exceeded, but in some of these there may still be some shortfall. The total number of recorded births, for all the 180 countries together, adds up to some 30 millions, as against a probable world total (based on the likely levels of the birth rates) of 110 millions. Clearly, therefore, records of births (and deaths and marriages) are, on a world scale, very inadequate. The continents where the biggest gaps occur are Africa, where the numbers of births based on registrations represent only about 5 per cent of expected total births; Asia, where the corresponding ratio is some 10 per cent; and South America, where only perhaps one-half of births are recorded.

4.4 Variations in the scope and organization of censuses

In North America, censuses are far-reaching in scope and are organized efficiently; the characteristics of the demographic data are very well documented. Sampling techniques were used in the USA earlier than elsewhere, and post-enumeration checks were also introduced sooner. A larger number of questions is asked, and more searching inquiries are made, than in most other countries; for instance, particulars of income are sought. Recent methods have included enumeration by interview (1950) and by post (1960); the *de jure* system is employed; thus people are recorded as at their usual addresses rather than where they are present at the time of the census. In 1950 a special count was even made of the numbers and characteristics of certain categories of Americans living abroad. The results of the censuses are published in a very full series of highly informative volumes in which text and tables are intermingled.

In India, censuses have been held since 1881: that of 1961 was most note-worthy for a series of special accompanying surveys, the results of which have been published in a very large number of separate reports.

In Japan there is a long history of successful enumerations. Today, the census is directed by the Office of the Prime Minister and is very thoroughly organized; nearly 400,000 enumerators were employed in 1955. A variety of methods has been used at different times. During the period 1920–40 the schedule usually covered the household, and the head of the household filled in the replies. The questions asked were then comparatively simple. The household schedule was used again in 1958, but, because of growing complexity, canvassers were used to assist in the preparation of the answers relating to employment and housing. In 1947 there had been a schedule for each individual, but possibly this was not a success for in 1950 collective schedules were used; canvassers then themselves filled in the details for the whole of each enumeration district.

Studies of the results of censuses held in Israel before and after political independence suggest that, although in each case there was an effective enumeration, the more recent enumerations have been the more accurate. This may not be just a normal time-trend. It has been suggested that the relative inaccuracy of the censuses in the days of British rule was attributable to political opposition, and in general it seems likely that less satisfactory results will be achieved where there is unrest than in settled periods. The enumeration of Burma in 1953 took place in such disturbed conditions that a complete count was impossible in certain areas; here, sampling had to be employed, and even this was at some personal hazard to the enumerating staff.

Russia has had censuses at irregular intervals, and these seem to have been variable in quality: for some, no data at all have been published. That of 1937 may have been unsuccessful, for another was conducted in 1939, and this seems to have served a useful purpose in plans for the development of the economy and for the conduct of the war which ensued. A further enumeration was held in 1959, and for this the schedule was somewhat simplified, no doubt in an effort to ensure greater accuracy. A household schedule was employed, and information was sought on housing, place of usual residence, age, sex, marital status, nationality, language, educational attainment, occupation and social and family characteristics.

4.5 International differences in registration procedure

The information available from a number of countries in Europe, America and Asia shows that, while most registration systems have a good deal in common, significant differences of procedure do occur, and some of these may have important consequences. First, the administering authority may be one of a number of persons or organizations, for example, the local government unit — such as the mayor or village headman — or a branch of a State organization, or even the Established Church. Secondly, the person charged with the duty of informing the authorities of a vital event may not always be the same. For instance, in respect of a birth, sometimes it may be the parent, and sometimes the hospital or doctor concerned. The extent to which medical evidence, for example on birth weight or prematurity, may be available must depend to some extent on such arrangements. Thirdly, the length of time allowed for notification may vary; this may affect the published data in two ways:

(1) any delay in notification may cause a discrepancy between the numbers of occurrences which actually happen in a year (or other period) and the numbers of occurrences that are registered in that year or period; the longer the delay allowed, the greater may be the discrepancy;

(2) in respect of births, the distinction between still-births and deaths a few days after a live birth may be blurred; the second type of occurrence may tend to be recorded as if it were the first.

In some communities, the classification of a post-natal death as a still-birth may be encouraged, because the parents may thus be spared the expense of a funeral. In others, however, the reverse may occur; parents may prefer to regard a still-birth as a live birth, in order that baptism or other religious rites may be observed. An extreme example of delay in birth registration is recorded in the UN *Demographic Year Book*, in which it is stated that cases have been known in Central and South America where births have been registered as long as 25 years after their occurrence.

Fourthly, the details sought on registration may vary. In some countries, items may be recorded in the registers which in other countries are kept confidential; among other birth particulars that may or may not be sought are the doctor's name, certain medical circumstances, and whether the birth was single or multiple.

Fifthly, the extent to which the registers are organized may be more or less elaborate. Thus, in Japan, family registers are maintained, and these would be expected to show more detail of relationships than are available elsewhere. Births are numbered in sequence, or given codes, in many countries, and this may serve as a check for the purpose of verifying claims for social security benefits, for example, family allowances. In some of the smaller European countries, the locally-maintained registers show who is living in each district, so that records of migratory movements, both internal and external, can be maintained. In all these cases the volume of available statistics may well be greater than is usual in other areas.

4.6 Co-ordination of vital statistics systems

Efforts are being made to reduce unnecessary differences between national registration systems. The Population Commission of the UN has published recommendations for the improvement and standardization of registration data, based on a survey of the practices of many nations and the opinions of numerous experts. The requirements of a uniform international system were considered from the point of view of the day-to-day uses of the registers not only as legal records, but also as (a) the foundation for demographic data, (b) a means of research in matters of public health and medicine, and (c) material for use by professional and business workers. Working definitions were given for various demographic events, and the details to be collected in respect of each event were specified. A tabulation programme was drawn up in considerable detail.

Registration data were considered also at the first international conference of National Committees on Vital and Health Statistics. It was suggested that countries should adopt the international form of death certificate recommended by the World Health Organization and that they might adopt sampling processes to help fill the gaps that exist in registration records in regard to social, economic and occupational characteristics.

4.7 Publications of demographic data

The UN Organization first published a *Demographic Year Book* in 1948, and since then it has become the practice to issue a new volume annually. A table was given in the 1948 volume showing the extent to which replies were received to questionnaires issued to all the countries of the world; the proportion replying varied from 100 per cent for estimated number of inhabitants to the neighbourhood of 50 per cent for details of age, sex, marital status, occupation and mortality, and to as low as 20 per cent or less for particulars such as migration or reproduction rates. Since then, the response has improved.

Although the *Demographic Year Book* is very substantial — recent editions have each contained about 800 pages — it has not been found possible to include all the available material each year, and accordingly it is the practice to devote part of each issue to a different special subject such as fertility, mortality or distribution of population. Among the items regularly published are the numbers of births for a series of years, together with birth rates by age of mother and size of family; the numbers of still-births and of deaths; mortality rates by sex, age and cause; the numbers of marriages and divorces; expectations of life; and the distribution of population by sex, age, literacy, economic activity, household size, and the like. An important commentary on the data is provided by an extensive introduction that draws attention to differences in the definition of vital events between one country and another, and some indication is given of the degree to which various items of information can be relied upon to be accurate.

The UN Organization issues also a *Monthly Bulletin of Statistics*, giving estimates of population, crude birth rates, marriage rates and death rates, and figures of manpower in various industries, as well as a *Statistical Year Book* that includes a few demographic tables. The World Health Organization publishes periodical *Epidemiological and Vital Statistics Reports*, including an annual volume in which deaths and death rates are set out cause by cause; particulars of notifications of infectious diseases are also given.

At the national level, information about registrations of vital events is issued in many countries in series of reports of different frequency of appearance. There may be as many as four types of sources of reference, namely (*a*) weekly statements, (*b*) monthly or quarterly returns, (*c*) annual reports and (*d*) decennial — or irregularly issued — volumes on special investigations. Those documents that are published more often than once a year will normally be relatively brief collections of routine tables of essential information, unaccompanied by any appreciable written commentary. Annual and special reports are likely to be much fuller and will probably include a verbal account of recent experience.

4.8 Accuracy of data

Much attention has been devoted, in many countries, to assessments of the accuracy of census and registration data and, where major deficiencies are revealed, to the consideration of methods by which better statistics could be collected. Checks of this kind made in Japan have established that recent census data have covered the whole population within a margin of error of less than 1 per cent; also that the registration of births is at least 98 per cent complete. This is satisfactory, and the degree of success achieved betokens an efficient organization, backed by a long history of enumerations and a keen national interest in population questions. It would indeed be remarkable if the accuracy of the details, such as age and occupation, collected at censuses and registration, were of equally good quality. The Japanese do not appear to give numerical details, but generally they reckon that errors are relatively few, except perhaps in connection with classification of cause of death, which is an exceptionally difficult item.

An isolated example of an error of detail in a census that in general appears

51

to have been reasonably accurate is provided from Jamaica, where, it is stated, the numbers returning themselves as being 'aged 60' were 80 per cent higher than they should have been, judging by the numbers enumerated at adjacent ages. Post-censal checks on the validity of recent census results in the United States suggests that on balance as much as $1\frac{1}{2}$ per cent of the population escaped enumeration; this represented a net balance between gross under-enumeration and over-enumeration (see §4.9 below). Both types probably occurred because of the *de jure* method of classification which was employed.

Although not negligible, such errors are hardly on a comparable scale with those that may be found in less developed areas, especially where registration is concerned. Thus, surveys have disclosed that birth and death registration in India is only from 30 to 70 per cent complete, varying according to State. In Uganda — one of the few African countries to have any form of permanent registration — only perhaps one-half of vital events are notified. Much effort has been devoted by the Population Commission of the UN Organization to the evaluation of the quality of demographic statistics in the developing countries and to plans for their improvement. These plans have involved especially the training of suitable people from those countries in the necessary skills, and the issue of informative manuals aimed to encourage internationally standardized procedures for the collection and publication of population data.

The remainder of this chapter will be devoted to a consideration one by one of a number of particular areas from the point of view of demographic statistics.

4.9   Censuses in North America

In the USA there are some $\frac{1}{4}$ million enumeration districts, and in Canada about 30,000 districts. The US system is to distribute a form by mail to each household; the members of the household were asked in 1960 to answer the questions and to hold the form for the arrival of the enumerator. When he collected this he transcribed the entries on to another form designed for computer processing. For 1970, however, it was planned that the household should send its return back by post. The questions asked in 1960 included some relating to relationship to head of household, colour or race, place of birth, country of birth of parents, place of residence at an earlier date, school achievement, employment, earnings, service in the armed forces, housing conditions, water supply, value of property occupied and rent paid. Many of these questions were put to only a sample of people. Some completed forms were compared with independent records in order to provide a check on the accuracy of the census as a whole; the independent records related to income tax, social security, vital registration, immigration files and earlier census returns. In 1950 and 1960, it was reckoned that 2–3 per cent of people were never counted; but about 1 per cent of people were erroneously included, with the result that the net under-representation of the population was between 1 and 2 per cent. The degree of error appeared to be rather larger in 1960 than in 1950; but alternative assessments in which an attempt was made to link the results of the two censuses with vital registrations and migration records (themselves subject to error) suggested that the coverage might have been better in the later year than in the earlier one.

The degree of under-enumeration in the USA has varied by sex and race. In 1960, for instance, the shortfall is estimated to have been:

	%
White males	1.1
White females	1.7
Non-white males	10.3
Non-white females	7.1

When analysed by age, these figures show some interesting variations. For non-whites they rise to about 13 per cent in middle life but fall again in old age. For whites they are highest in early adult life. But, for men, under-enumeration turns into quite considerable over-enumeration at ages 65 and over for both whites and non-whites; this over-enumeration did not, however, apply to women. The census in the USA has so far remained decennial, but in Canada it is now held quinquennially, and intermediate counts of limited scope are made also in some States of the USA.

4.10 Vital registration in North America

Each of the States of the USA legislates separately for its system of birth and death registration, though there is a common pattern and conferences of registrars are held regularly so that they may keep in touch. Records of marriages are less uniform and less complete, and statistics of divorces still less so. The US birth certificate gives details of the child's date and place of birth, sex, and any twin, the mother's and father's age, place of residence, race, education, and previous children. As the process of collecting and transmitting the certificates first to the State Office and later to the National Office of Vital Statistics is necessarily slow, special steps are taken to expedite the passage of the assembled data so that the monthly and annual reports for the whole country can be published without too much delay. Coverage is better than it used to be. Before 1933, when birth and death records were first collected on a national basis, the government accepted such records only from States which could show that these were at least 90 per cent complete. The number of such States increased steadily over the years. By 1940, it was found, by comparison with the census enumeration, that for births completeness ranged from 80– 100 per cent. In 1950 and 1960 registrations are assessed to have been respectively 98 and 99 per cent adequate. Similar tests have not been made

53

for deaths, though it is believed that registrations are now about as effective as for births.

The position in Canada is generally similar to that in the United States, with independent responsibility for each Province. In Quebec and Newfoundland the clergy act as local registrars.

4.11 Sampling in North America

Recent demographic work in the USA contains some examples of the use of sampling in which interesting differences from practice elsewhere may be observed. In 1940 it was arranged to secure additional census material by asking certain questions of only 1 person in every 20. At the 1950 Census this procedure was so developed that some data were collected from 1 person in every 5 and others were obtained from only 1 person in every 6 of those chosen in this way, i.e., from a sample consisting of 1 in 30 of the whole population. This enabled very detailed inquiries to be made and represents a more complete application of sampling at a census than that sometimes adopted, in which statistics are amassed in full and are analysed in part only for the sake of speed in producing early results. In fact, the United States authorities also used samples of the schedules in order to obtain preliminary estimates of certain characteristics long before the final tabulations could be produced.

In both the USA and Canada, the accuracy and completeness of the most recent enumerations have been checked by means of a re-survey on a sample basis carried out shortly after the census. The relatively small numbers of persons interviewed on the second occasion no doubt enabled a more thorough investigation to be made of the selected households than was possible during the main inquiry. In order to examine statistically some novel aspects of fertility, an unofficial survey was made in 1941 by asking certain questions of every married couple of a particular type as regards colour, education, religion, and in other respects in one city (Indianapolis) and since then other important fertility surveys have been completed. In both countries, systems of population sampling by regular surveys have been initiated in recent years. In the United States, the whole national area has been divided first into primary sampling units consisting of a single county or a combination of contiguous counties. Some of these have then been selected for analysis by random methods; in these methods, the efficiency of the selection was enhanced by the use of judicious combinations of counties and also by stratification, in order to ensure homogeneity, and further increased by making the chance of selection proportionate to the size of the population within the unit at the previous census. Each of the selected primary sampling units was then divided into smaller areas. By an ingenious arrangement the probability of selection of an area was calculated so that the sample chosen would be representative in certain important respects, not so much of the unit of which it formed a part, but of the greater stratum to which the unit belonged.

A somewhat similar series of surveys has been carried out in Canada. Members of households selected from the smaller areas are interviewed monthly. Part of the sample is changed each month in order to avoid troubling the same persons persistently over a long period. Information of national importance other than demographic data is collected. One example was the Canadian sickness survey of 1950—1.

4.12   Population statistics in Jamaica

Census-taking and civil registration began in the Island in the middle of the nineteenth century as part of a system designed for the West Indies as a whole. Today they provide information sufficient for a survey in considerable detail of the population and of its characteristics and prospects, and the latest census (held in 1970) has been reckoned a sufficiently reliable basis for meaningful population estimates; about 2 million people were enumerated. Other censuses were held in 1943, 1953 (on a 5 per cent sample basis only) and 1960. Tests based on intercensal survival ratios suggest that the census data are adequate, in total and when analysed by age groups, but the numbers recorded at individual ages show a considerable irregularity due to rounding off by respondents. Comparison of birth registration and census records is satisfactory, and it would appear that deaths are also noted with enough accuracy. Migration data are not so good, but even so it is possible to reconcile adjacent census counts with the recorded population changes for the intervening years with a discrepancy of only about 1 per cent.

4.13   Censuses in Britain

Following the holding of the first enumeration in 1801, censuses of gradually increasing complexity have been held at decennial intervals. That of 1911 in England and Wales was noteworthy for the introduction of a full tabulation of age in single years instead of in groups, for questions embracing the industry in which each worker was employed as well as his occupation, and for the holding for the first time of a detailed inquiry into fertility. When the 1921 Census was being planned it was realized that a repetition of the fertility inquiry of 1911 would yield additional data of a little more than historical value because of the special influence of the First World War. It was therefore decided to ask questions instead about the numbers of all live children and stepchildren in the family under age 16, according to age, whether or not those children were enumerated on the same schedule as the parents; this was called 'a dependency' inquiry. A question that had

55

formerly been asked about infirmities, such as blindness and mental illness, was omitted because unreliable answers had been received — no doubt because of a natural reluctance on the part of the public to disclose full information upon such subjects.

In 1931, in the expectation that future enumerations would be held quinquennially, the schedule was simplified by the omission of any questions on fertility or dependency. In Scotland three questions were asked in addition to those put in England, namely:

(1) length of stay in Scotland;
(2) whether insured for medical benefit under the National Health system; and
(3) whether a speaker of Gaelic.

In fact no census was held in 1936 (and the first quinquennial census did not take place until 1966). In 1939, however, immediately after the outbreak of war a modified form of enumeration was conducted in place of the 1941 Census. Each member of the population was identified individually and was thereafter required to hold an identity card. This began a system called National Registration. After the cessation of hostilities in 1945, personal identification continued for some years in conjunction with food rationing, but it came to an end in 1952. The demographic data collected under this system were very limited in scope.

A special inquiry into fertility was undertaken on a sample basis by the Royal Commission on Population in 1946; this is usually known as the 'Family Census'; it was not an official enumeration in the usual sense.

4.14 Recent British enumerations

At the 1951 Census enumeration, the list of questions was longer than in 1931 and included some references to fertility. Details were also sought of the extent of full-time education and there were questions about domestic amenities, such as piped water supply.

In 1961, new questions were put concerning:

(1) scientific and technical qualifications;
(2) changes of address during the year preceding the census; and
(3) persons normally living in the household but absent on census night.

Some major developments took place on matters of procedure. Certain topics were dealt with on a 10 per cent sample basis; as a result 9 households out of 10 received a schedule with fewer questions on it than were received by the remaining 1 in 10. Thus particulars of age, sex, marital status, fertility, nationality and country of birth were among the data collected from everybody; but only 1 person in 10 was asked to provide details of occupation, work-place, recent change of address, standard of education or technical qualifications.

The first year in which the Government took advantage of the provision in the 1920 Act enabling quinquennial censuses to be held was 1966. The census was held on the night of 24 April 1966, and included questions about household ownership and amenities, car ownership and garaging, age, sex, marital status, and occupation — but nothing about fertility. This was the first official enumeration to be held in Britain wholly on a sample basis (10 per cent); although the principle of sampling had been utilized in 1961 (and in a more limited way in 1951), on both these occasions some at least of the data were collected from every household in the country.

The 1966 sample frame was based on dwellings, particulars of which were derived from the 1961 census schedules supplemented by rating valuation records for houses built since the date of that census. In Scotland, the whole range of the sample came from the local valuation rolls. In institutions such as hospitals, prisons, barracks and ships, one-tenth of all people were enumerated; but in hotels, where sampling had proved troublesome in the past, everybody had to take part.

The first checks upon the adequacy of the sampling frame suggest that the number of dwellings actually enumerated was about 1 per cent too low. In one way and another, some 20,000 houses and flats failed to be included in the sample, and on this account the population counted — when rated up to a full national basis — was too low by about $\frac{1}{2}$ million people. When allowance is made for the omission, by respondent heads of households, of some people who should have been included, this deficiency in the population was increased to some $\frac{3}{4}$ million. An independent verification of the dates of birth given in the census schedules in a sample of cases has shown that these dates were completely correct in 94 per cent of cases, and incorrect in 6 per cent; in one-half of the inaccurate statements, the age in years was given correctly.

Another census was held in 1971. At the time of writing, only a few analyses have been published, but the programme provides for reports *inter alia* on housing, migration, economic activity, transport to work, education and fertility. The consultations preceding this census led to the suggestion of some 300 questions of which 32 were finally included on the form used. One of the possibilities eventually rejected was a question on incomes: this was because pre-tests showed that the response was likely to be inadequate. Copies of some of the instructions and notes issued to heads of households are reproduced in fig. 4.1.

A further census is announced for 1976.

These notes are to help you answer some of the questions in Part B (for persons present).

If you have any further difficulty with these, or any other questions, please ask the enumerator about them when he calls to collect your form.

B7 Job last week

A job means any work for payment or profit. In particular it includes:

(a) work on a person's own account

(b) part-time work, even if only for a few hours, such as jobbing gardening or paid domestic work

(c) casual or temporary work of any kind (for example seasonal work, week-end work and vacation work by students)

(d) unpaid work in a family business, for example a shop or farm.

Unpaid work, other than in a family business, does not count as a job.

B8 Students

Do not count as full-time students people who are:

(a) on day release from work to attend school or college

(b) attending night school only

(c) attending an educational establishment provided by employers, such as an apprenticeship school.

B15 Employer's name and business

Describe the business fully and try to avoid abbreviations or initials. General terms such as 'manufacturer', 'merchant', 'agent', 'broker', 'factor', 'dealer', 'engineering', are not enough by themselves and further details should be given about the articles manufactured or dealt in.

For civil servants, local government officers and other public officials give the name of the Government department, local authority or public body and the branch in which they are employed.

For people employed solely in private domestic service write 'PRIVATE' in answer to this question.

For members of Armed Forces see special note overleaf.

B16 Occupation

Full and precise details of occupation are required.

If a person's job is known in the trade or industry by a special name use that name.

Terms such as 'scientist', 'technician', 'engineer', 'machinist', 'fitter', 'foreman', 'checker' should not be used by themselves. Greater detail is required as for example:—

woodworking machinist, civil engineer, toolroom foreman.

For civil servants, local government officers and other public officials give their rank or grade.

B17 Self-employed

'Self-employed, employing others' means having one or more employees other than 'family workers'. A 'family worker' is one who lives in the same household as the employer and is related to him. Although 'family workers' are not counted for the purpose of deciding whether an employer has employees, they should themselves be recorded as employees.

Fig. 4.1. Some of the instructions and notes issued with the English Census Schedule in 1971.

4.15 British census publications

The Registrar General for England and Wales publishes a number of documents following each census, and usually the first of these takes the form of a preliminary report, giving a provisional figure for the total numbers of persons enumerated. Subsequently, county volumes are issued, to provide details of the population of the various administrative areas and of the dwellings, rooms and families, institutions, special premises, and the ages and marital statuses of the people there. Besides the county volume series, the Registrar General publishes volumes on special topics such as those mentioned towards the end of §4.14 above. At the conclusion of these series a General Report may be issued. The Registrar General for Scotland publishes similar data separately, and for some purposes information is now supplied for Britain as a whole.

Another series of volumes closely associated with the census are the decennial supplements to the reviews and reports of the Registrar General. These deal, among other topics, with the national life tables, with occupational mortality and with occupational fertility. Finally, any data that have not been published can be made available for research purposes, on the payment of a suitable fee.

4.16 Registration statistics in Britain

Copies of the local records of births and deaths appear in figs. 4.2 and 4.3. The manner in which they are maintained has not changed greatly since their beginning in 1837, but more recent additions to the system include the compulsory registration of still-births (1926) and provision (1938) for the collection of additional information about fertility on the registration of a birth, still-birth or death; this additional information is confidential and is used for statistical purposes only. It is not entered in any public register.

Members of the public may consult an alphabetical index of births, marriages and deaths maintained by the General Register Office showing the names of the individuals concerned, the registration district in which the event occurred, and also:

(1) for births, the mother's maiden name; and
(2) for deaths, the age of the deceased.

This index is prepared quarterly from certified copies of the local registers.

The Registrars General for England and Wales and for Scotland have for very many years issued weekly and quarterly returns of births and deaths, but their main medium of communication has been in annual reports. For England and Wales, the amount of information is voluminous. Accordingly, the annual reports have been divided into three parts, namely:

59

Regulation 16   Births and Deaths Registration Act 1953, S.1(1)

NHS Number	**BIRTH**	Entry No.
Registration district		Administrative area
Sub-district		
1. Date and place of birth	CHILD	
2. Name and surname		3. Sex
4. Name and surname	FATHER	
5. Place of birth		
6. Occupation		
7. Name and surname	MOTHER	
8. Place of birth		
9. (a) Maiden surname	(b) Surname at marriage if different from maiden surname	
10. Usual address (if different from place of child's birth)		
11. Name and surname (if not the mother or father)	INFORMANT 12. Qualification	
13. Usual address (if different from that in 10 above)		
14. I certify that the particulars entered above are true to the best of my knowledge and belief	Signature of informant	
15. Date of registration	16. Signature of registrar	
17. Name given after registration, and surname		

Fig. 4.2. British local record of a birth (from S.I. 1968, No. 1049).

Part 1. *Tables, Medical*: statements of death rates and disease notifications.

Part 2. *Tables, Population*: the numbers of births, marriages and rates of fertility.

Part 3. *Commentary*: the Registrar's report on the data.

Regulation 48(1) Births and Deaths Registration Act 1953, S. 15.

DEATH	Entry No.
Registration district Administrative area	
Sub-district	
1. Date and place of death	
2. Name and surname	3. Sex
	4. Maiden surname of woman who has married
5. Date and place of birth	
6. Occupation and usual address	
7. (a) Name and surname of informant	(b) Qualification
(c) Usual address	
8. Cause of death	
9. I certify that the particulars given by me above are true to the best of my knowledge and belief....................................	Signature of informant
10. Date of registration	11. Signature of registrar

Fig. 4.3. British local record of a death (from S.I. 1968, No. 1049).

In the *Medical* volume, among many tables there is one showing deaths classified by cause and age. The figures indicate the relative importance of fatal illnesses and accidents at various times of life, and the extent of their contributions to total mortality. In another table the numbers of deaths at various periods in the first year of life are set out. Some pages give particulars of

61

mortality trends over a period of ten years; others even give series for up to a hundred years. Information is supplied about the relative numbers of deaths at different ages and in various marital statuses.

For each separate administrative area, the principal facts about population, births, deaths and infant mortality for the year are provided; typical headings in this table are shown in fig. 4.4. Among other subjects dealt with in the *Medical* volume, the following are worth special mention: the monthly incidence of deaths according to cause; notifications of infectious disease; summaries of temperature, rainfall and sunshine (given in view of their possible importance in connection with the relative numbers of sicknesses and deaths).

The main topics on which information is given in the *Population* volume are marriages, divorces, migration, births and fertility. The numbers of marriages are tabulated according to the sex, age and previous marital status of the persons concerned, and the ages of the partners are also tabulated in combination. Particulars of dissolutions and annulments of marriage (obtained from a card index maintained by the Principal Probate Registry) are supplied in different tables classified according to cause, ages of partners, duration of marriage and numbers of children. Migration statistics are given in a number of different forms according to the method by which they were collected or estimated.

The statistics of fertility are tabulated in considerable detail; for instance, births are classified according to the mother's age and the number of children previously born alive to her. They are classified also by duration of marriage. Details are given of multiple births and maternities. (The maternity record differs from the birth record in that multiple births from a single pregnancy are counted as one maternity, while for the birth record, each child born is reckoned as a separate unit — see § 3.6.) The Registrar General estimates the 'exposed to risk' of fertility and on this basis assesses the rates by age of parent, duration of marriage, and so forth.

Recently, the Registrar General for England and Wales has discontinued the Commentary Volumes and he now plans to issue, for 1974 and subsequent years, smaller volumes each dealing with one topic or a number of closely-related topics. These will replace all parts of the former annual reports. His quarterly returns will be supplanted by a new quarterly journal called *Population Trends*.

4.17 British migration and other records

For many years the only British data available about emigration and immigration were those collected under the Merchant Shipping Act, 1906, which provided that the master of every ship, British or foreign, carrying any passengers to or from the United Kingdom must obtain from them certain

Home population, births, deaths, infant mortality and perinatal mortality, 1966 England
and Wales, regions, Wales, conurbations, hospital regions, counties, Greater London,
City of London, London and county boroughs, urban and rural districts. Note. The perinatal
mortality rate is the number of deaths under one week plus still-births per 1,000 total live
and still births.

	England and Wales	Northern Total	Tyneside conurbation	Remainder of Northern
Estimated home population as at 30 June 1966	48,075,300	3,316,790	848,070	2,468,720
Live births				
Legitimate				
Male	402,876	27,483	6,720	20,763
Female	379,891	25,926	6,396	19,530
Illegitimate				
Male	34,386	1,882	548	1,334
Female	32,670	1,774	504	1,270
Total	849,823	57,065	14,168	42,897
Crude rate per 1,000 home population	17·7	17·2	16·7	17·4
Comparability factor	1·00	0·99	0·98	1·00
Ratio of local adjusted birth rate to national rate	1·00	0·96	0·92	0·98
Deaths				
Male	288,622	20,982	5,300	15,682
Female	275,002	18,719	4,718	14,001
Total	563,624	39,701	10,018	29,683
Crude rate per 1,000 home population	11·7	12·0	11·8	12·0
Comparability factor	1·00	1·10	1·13	1·10
Ratio of local adjusted death rate to national rate	1·00	1·13	1·14	1·13
Deaths under 1 year				
Number	16,147	1,198	309	889
Rate per 1,000 live births	19	21	22	21
Deaths under 4 weeks	10,933	790	194	596
Deaths under 1 week	9,446	660	168	492
Still-births	13,243	963	241	722
Perinatal mortality rate	26	28	28	28

Fig. 4.4. Typical information from vital registration data (figures from the Annual Report
of the Registrar General).

63

information and set this down on returns to be transmitted to the Board of Trade. Provision for the collection of similar information in respect of air travel was made under the Statistics of Trade Act, 1947, but it proved difficult in practice to make acceptable arrangements for the collection of adequate information in this way. At the end of 1963, the methods in force were replaced by a regular system of sampling under which a fixed proportion of those coming and going by long sea or air routes are asked some questions. The sampling fractions are 7 per cent for outward movement and 4 per cent for inward movement. In addition there is a 2 per cent sample investigation of short sea movements.

In order to be able to compare the new sources of information with the old, data were collected simultaneously under both systems for a month before the old returns were discontinued. The Registrar General for England and Wales publishes the numbers of immigrants and emigrants classified according to country of origin or of intended residence, as appropriate; occupation; sex; marital status; citizenship; and route travelled. True migrants form only a fraction of all passengers. Ideally, more data about them would be desirable – for instance in respect of their special qualifications or skills and their actual (as opposed to their intended) changes of country. Various other official records that are maintained in Britain give some information bearing upon migration – for example the health records of immigrants maintained by the Office of Population at its National Health Service Central Register, the particulars maintained by the Department of Health and Social Security concerning new applications and re-applications for National Insurance cards and the records of aliens maintained by the Home Office. All these have their limitations, their principal defect being that they do not provide any details of emigrants. Some of the countries to which the emigrants go, however, publish statistics about them classified by country of origin, and in this way the numbers of those who came from Britain can be traced.

Because the study of the labour force is an important instrument of economic policy, inquiries are made about it in the British Production Censuses that were instituted in 1907 and which the Statistics of Trade Act, 1947, provided should be held annually from 1949 onwards. Information is also collected from time to time, by means of special inquiries, about exits from industry: these may be classified according to cause of exit, for example, change of job, emigration or retirement. Rates of exit are often described as 'turnover' rates, because normally losses of this kind are replaced by special recruitment. Such rates may be combined for different ages, by a life table technique, in order to estimate the average length of working life, and this is a convenient index of variations in the use of manpower from time to time or from place to place.

4.18 Population sampling in Britain

An early use of sampling was made in the Family Census (see § 4.13 above). Questions were addressed to married women asking for the following information:

(1) date of birth (month and year);
(2) date of first marriage;
(3) date of end of first marriage (if applicable);
(4) date of birth of every live-born child;
(5) number of children alive at census and under age 16;
(6) occupation of husband.

The sampling fraction was 1 in 10 over the whole country, the names of the persons concerned being chosen by a quasi-random method from local population records maintained as part of the National Registration system then current. The use of this proportion permitted the collection of extensive data, which could be broken down into many subgroups, while saving greatly in enumerating manpower in comparison with a full-scale census.

A letter was sent to each chosen person with a simple form to be completed. After an interval, enumerators called for the forms and, if necessary, helped to fill them in. In order not to overload the schedule, certain items that otherwise might well have been deemed desirable were omitted. These included the husband's age, the date of any second or subsequent marriage and the ages of surviving children.

As it was expected that some difficulty would be encountered in getting in touch with women who were not at home when the enumerator called, even at the second or third visit, plans were made to send follow-up letters to such persons inviting them to reply in writing. In the event, it happened that a response of 85 per cent was secured; about 9 per cent of women refused to assist in the inquiry and a further 6 per cent could not be reached by means of the normal procedure. The postal follow-up brought responses from about $2\frac{1}{2}$ per cent however, and reduced the total shortfall from 15 to $12\frac{1}{2}$ per cent. It was evident that this incompleteness in the sample could be a source of bias. By comparing their data with the statistics collected under the 1938 Act, the authors of the report deduced that in the original 85 per cent of returns the families of women with children were fairly represented but that there was an understatement of childlessness to the extent of 5 per cent. They considered, however, that the particulars of the missing 15 per cent were probably fairly represented by the postal replies from the $2\frac{1}{2}$ per cent, and they were able to adjust their data on this assumption.

4.19   Further instances of the use of sampling in Britain

Sample data drawn from the schedules were published for the 1951 Census. Various considerations had to be taken into account in deciding upon a method of selection. One of the first was size; as speed in presentation of results was a prime factor, too large a sample was out of the question. Another was that it was desirable to obtain results which could readily be rated up. One-hundredth was used as the sampling fraction, and appears to have been a very satisfactory one. A device of printing the data with a comma before the last digit reminded the user that two noughts had to be added if it were desired to think in terms of the full census statistics.

The time element was also responsible for a plan of requiring the enumerators themselves to select the sample from their schedules according to strict rules of procedure. This saved a large amount of work at headquarters. A slightly better sample might perhaps have resulted from a selection made after the schedules had been collected centrally, but this is of little practical significance. The habitations in each enumeration district were divided by the local registrar into: (*a*) large institutions and analogous establishments for which particular arrangements would be needed ('Special Enumeration Districts') and (*b*) other units ('Ordinary Enumeration Districts'). Over a million persons were found in the first of these two categories, at an average of about 366 persons per Special Enumeration District; local census officers themselves numbered each individual enumerated in these establishments and extracted the sample by selecting in odd-numbered districts everyone whose number ended in 25 and in even-numbered districts everyone whose number ended in 76. Household schedules for the Ordinary Enumeration Districts were selected by the enumerators according to the same rule; on the average each such District consisted of some 270 households in England and Wales and some 150 households in Scotland.

4.20   The accuracy of British census sampling

When the 1951 Census results were processed, it was found that for Britain as a whole the sample reflected the enumerated total within the expected limits of error. There was a difference of only 16 between the sample number, of about half a million, and 1 per cent of the total population of nearly 50 millions. In most smaller areas, too, the comparison was equally satisfactory, but in a few it was not so good. Irregularities due to errors on the part of the enumerators, while not entirely absent, were of negligible effect, but they were not the only difficulty. It had been envisaged that the choice of the number 25 might give rise to some overstatement of numbers and households in the odd-numbered districts, but it was expected that in general this would be counterbalanced by corresponding understatements due to

66

the choice of the number 76 in the even-numbered districts. The reason for such overstatement and understatement is easily seen when it is considered, in regard to the households in excess of the last completed hundred, that if all terminal pairs of digits from 00 to 99 were equally likely in a group of enumeration districts in the sample, schedules with numbers ending in 25 would be chosen in 75 per cent of cases and schedules with numbers ending in 76 would be chosen in only 24 per cent of cases; these balance almost exactly. If all enumeration districts had exactly 360 households, however, then one-half of the enumerators would have four sampled households and one-half would have three sampled households, with an average of $3\frac{1}{2}$ instead of 3·6 — an error of nearly 3 per cent; a balance would not be achieved in such a case. In the event, the errors did balance in many areas but not in all of them. In order that the correct total of households and population should be reproduced precisely in each enumeration district, the Registrars General substituted different schedules for the selected schedules where necessary. Subsequent analysis has shown that the statistical effect of the substitutions was slight and that the 1 per cent sample served its purpose fully as expected.

The method by which the 1961 Census sample was drawn was as follows: the enumeration districts were listed systematically and a random number (between 1 and 10 inclusive) was allocated to each district. If this number was n, the enumerator gave a sample schedule only to the nth, (10 plus n)th, (20 plus n)th, etc., household he contacted. A post-enumeration survey was made in order to verify the accuracy of the data in a proportion of cases; some of the households were asked the same question a second time. This survey revealed that in the fertility inquiry there had been no significant misstatement of either the number of children borne or the duration of marriage.

The 10 per cent sample proved to contain an excess of households occupying a large number of rooms and of households of from 2 to 6 persons, and a corresponding deficit of households occupying a small number of rooms, and of households of 1 person or of 7 persons or over. Sometimes the extent of the error was material; for instance, there were 20 per cent too many households of 2–6 persons occupying 9 rooms or more, and 11 per cent too few households of one person occupying 1 or 2 rooms. In the 1966 Census, as indicated in § 4.14 above, the results of the count differed from the probable true population size by a considerable margin — much greater than on previous occasions. This was largely because of inaccuracies in the sampling frame, and is a common experience when the whole of the census, and not just a part, is conducted on a sample basis.

It was decided for the 1971 Census not to attempt any field sampling; but a 10 per cent sample was selected from the completed returns for use in some analyses.

4.21   Population statistics in India

Census-taking is well established, as is evidenced by the fact that the provisional results of the 1971 enumeration were available within 10 days of the visit of the canvassers. Over a million people were employed on the work of counting a population of 500 million. The results are published in considerable detail and many special studies are made on a sample basis to establish the degree of accuracy of the results and to enrich the information collected.

In such a vast country, where some 80 per cent of the people live in over 500,000 villages, completeness of vital registration has not so far been achieved, in spite of the efforts of the Government. Thus special studies relating to the period 1952—4 suggest that registered births and deaths may have represented only about 60 per cent of the true totals. The extent of the shortfall varies widely from one region to another (see § 4.8 above) and between rural and urban areas. In these circumstances, sample surveys can be of great value, and these began to be made in the early 1950s. With the aid of the UN Organization, a Population Survey was conducted in the former State of Mysore as an experiment in the use of a sampling survey of households to measure the trends and characteristics of the population and to investigate their interrelations with the process of economic and social change in an area undergoing economic development. It was planned as a pilot project, and was designed both to test concepts and methods and to demonstrate what types of results could be obtained.

Even sample surveys can encounter difficulties: in a survey of fertility and mortality in the Poona district (1951—2) the whole of the mortality data were found to be defective. The Indian National Sample Survey has, however, conducted very successful enterprises. About 10,000 representative households all over the country have been interviewed every six months. On some occasions fertility statistics have been collected; for instance, the following questions were asked in the second 'round' of the survey: ages of husband and wife, at marriage and also at the time of the investigation, the duration of marriage at the birth of each child, the sex and age of each child, and the age at death of any of the foregoing who had died. The inclusion of questions relating to events that had happened in the past, perhaps many years before, involved the danger of inaccuracy because of faulty memory on the part of the persons interviewed. As a result the information gained about the trends in time of mortality and fertility was suspect. The investigation revealed the interesting fact that memory could be selective, more important events being remembered and less important events forgotten. Evidence of this is available from the data relating to the sex ratio among children born, which for births shortly before the date of the inquiry was 1·06 boys to each girl but which is recorded as having increased steadily as the time since birth lengthened. For couples married before 1910 it was 1.26. The greater importance attached to male births had apparently caused them to be remembered more completely than female births.

More recently, the Indian surveys have asked for particulars of births, marriages, and deaths during the preceding year and for information about sickness during the preceding month. Other uses of sampling have included checking the accuracy of the census and making special inquiries into opinions concerning family size and other factors governing fertility.

In a study of infant deaths, it was estimated that the proportion omitted in the responses varied from about 5 per cent for recent marriages to over 50 per cent for marriages contracted 50 years before the date of the sample survey, as follows:

Number of years elapsed since marriage	Approximate proportion of infant deaths omitted
0	0
10	10
20	25
30	40
40	50
50	55

As the Indian authorities are making strong attempts to improve the completeness of vital registration processes and data, they apparently feel that sample surveys by themselves are not enough for the demographer's needs. Such surveys need to be varied rather than on a routine plan, and the greater the detail sought the more the need for accuracy and consistency checks and independent confirmation. The most productive methods at the moment are those which correct historical data for lapse of memory at a rate which can be estimated from a variety of investigations.

4.22   East African demographic data

Africa is divided into many independent national States, and those of Kenya, Uganda and Tanzania are chosen here as representative areas. As a whole, East Africa is fairly well provided with demographic data, with some (if incomplete) information deriving from censuses and some particulars of births and deaths for over half the population. In this it is superior to West Africa taken as a whole but it is said to be inferior in coverage to Central Africa. Censuses were conducted in 1948, in 1957–62 and in 1967–9. In the days before many Europeans and Asians left the area registration data were accurate for Europeans, less accurate for Asians but of little value for Africans. Although vital registration is now compulsory in most parts of Uganda and also in Zanzibar, this does not ensure the provision of accurate statistics and it seems likely that the degree of completeness is only in the neighbourhood of 50 per cent.

69

In these circumstances, plans have been made for sample enquiries to be conducted, while some information about fertility is sought by asking questions of adult women when a census is held. The estimation of mortality presents greater problems as census data are not very useful for this purpose. The UN *Demographic Year Book* for 1972 records the numbers of deaths only for Kenya — with a code notice to indicate unreliability; it gives one recent death-rate for Uganda (as estimated by the UN Population Division) and one for Tanzania. The situation respecting birth registration statistics is similar but census data showing female population classified by age and number of children born alive are set out in detail for both Kenya and Tanzania in the 1971 issue of the *Year Book*.

4.23 Some general comments on the quality of demographic statistics in a variety of countries

An even larger and more populous country than India, China clearly presents the greatest problems in the collection of demographic statistics. One census has been held in recent years, but little information is available about population change since then. In contrast, the nearby islands of Japan and Taiwan are very well charted demographically, with a long history of effective censuses and registration. Sample surveys have been used to investigate social conditions and there is a strong interest in family planning which ensures a close attention to population studies.

Much of Latin America is similar to India in that census statistics are generally reliable and informative but vital registration is incomplete and of variable quality in time and place. There is a keen interest in the study of population, however, and many sample surveys have been conducted.

In Eastern Europe there is a strong tradition of good data collection. Though on the whole less information is available from Russia than from the countries to its west a number of censuses have been taken there in recent times (see § 4.4 above). Mortality and fertility are well charted over the whole of the area. In Northern and Western Europe and in Australia and New Zealand, reliable and extensive data have been available for very many years.

Table 3 of the UN *Demographic Year Book* for 1972 sets forth vital statistics rates, national increase rates and expectation of life at birth for about 200 areas; these areas may be classified as follows, in round numbers:

Africa	50
North America	30
South America	15
Asia	30
Europe	40
Oceania	25
Russia	3

Table 4.1. *Specimen vital statistics rates (per thousand)*

Area	Year	Marriage rate	Divorce rate	Birth rate	Death rate
Ivory Coast*	1965–70	—	—	46·0	22·7
Antigua	1965	3·7	0·4	30·4	8·4
Uruguay†	1971	8·1	0·9	22·6	9·8
Sri Lanka‡	1971	6·7	0·2	29·9	7·6
Poland	1972	9·3	1·2	17·4	8·0
New Zealand	1971	9·5	1·2	22·6	8·5
Ukraine	1971	10·7	2·9	15·5	8·9

* Estimated by the UN Population Division: marriage and divorce rates not available.
† Based on incomplete civil registers.
‡ Divorce rate relates to 1967. Marriage statistics incomplete.

Some specimen entries, one from each group, are shown in table 4.1 by way of illustration.

SELECT BIBLIOGRAPHY

World Population Conference, 1965 (United Nations, Organization, New York, 1967), vol. 3. Papers at Meeting B7 — New developments in measurement and analysis of factors of population growth and structure' — for example, those by G. R. Chevry, Forrest E. Linder, P. C. Mahalanobis and G. Vangrevelinghe.

World Population Conference, 1974 (United Nations Organization, New York) Paper — 'The availability of demographic statistics round the world'.

The Mysore Population Study (United Nations Organization, Department of Economic and Social Affairs, New York, 1961). (ST/SOA/Series A/34.)

Vital Statistics in England and Wales 1951. (Issued by the General Register Office, 1967).

Redington, F. M. and Clarke, R. D. 'The Papers of the Royal Commission on Population', *Journal of the Institute of Actuaries*, **77** (1951), 81.

Population movements

5 Marriage

5.1 Relationship to population development

This is the first of four chapters in which some of the principal features of the components of population change will be discussed, against a background of social, economic and political considerations and influences. The aim throughout this part of the book is to show how the features can be analysed and presented in statistical terms and to indicate the likely nature of the results of analysis. Marriage is not, in the most direct sense, a component of population change but it has a profound influence on fertility, which is, and which comes up for consideration in the next chapter. A change of marital status may also have an influence on mortality and migration: how it can do so will be discussed in the ensuring two chapters. Marriage is also, however, a subject of interest in its own right, the main areas of importance being, first, the extent of and the reasons for deferment beyond the time of puberty, and secondly the relationships between the demographic characteristics of the spouses and the way in which these are affected by changes in the relative numbers of men and women becoming available for marriage.

5.2 General characteristics

The definition of marriage has already been discussed — see § 3.7 above. Evidence from the past, and from many types of human society today, suggests that it is a normal state of affairs for adults to marry, usually at an early age. Time is required for courtship, but this need not be protracted, for the manner in which children are educated, by their parents and at school, and the way in which they are brought together in their early years, all serve to prepare them for their adult relationships. Indeed, betrothal of children is a common practice in some parts of the world. Whatever the social system, first marriages — especially of women — take place mainly within a narrow range of ages. There is, however, an important exception to the universality of early marriage. For reasons that are not very well understood, since the Middle Ages late marriage and non-marriage have become much less uncommon in Europe. These features have spread to America and elsewhere as the European population has migrated or exerted an influence. Ireland

72

is well-known as a country in which marriage is much delayed. The practice may have advantages as a method of birth control, and in recent years the Chinese government as an act of policy has laid much emphasis on the need for late marriage.

The effect of this practice is that marriage rates vary according to age or, to look at it in another way, according to the duration of time since puberty (once the minimum legal age for marriage has been reached); remarriage rates vary, similarly, according to age and duration since widowhood or divorce. The incidence of marriage depends on local custom, on occupation and on social class. The numbers of marriages are materially affected by changes in the numbers of men and women in the community from time to time, and in particular by the relative numbers unmarried. Marriages tend to become fewer in bad times, such as an economic depression, when many couples have to postpone their weddings, and to rise above the average level of frequency when more favourable circumstances return. They also exhibit some seasonal variation within the year, as preference is shown for holiday periods and religious festivals; Easter is particularly popular and, in so far as the date when this is celebrated is itself variable from year to year, the seasonal distribution of marriages is not constant. It is also possible for seasonal variations to be occasioned by the taxation laws, because couples will tend to wed at the moment of the year when they can gain most from the system, or pay the least under it.

5.3 Marriages rates

Many works of reference, including the *UN Demographic Year Book*, show 'crude marriage rates' obtained by dividing the total numbers of marriages in given years by the mean total populations in thousands in those years. Crude marriage rates are an unsuitable measure for comparing the experiences of two populations having different distributions by age and sex, for the same general reason as that given in § 2.7. Moreover, the probability of marriage is strongly associated, not only with age, but also with prior marital status. As there is normally no 'exposure to risk' of marriage for children under the age of puberty, or for married couples, these classes should be entirely excluded from the denominator as the first step in calculating any marriage rate. They are not part of the 'supply' of marriageable men and women. The concept of 'supply' is important and will be discussed in the following section.

Some specimen marriage rates are shown in tables 5.1, 5.2 and 5.3. In table 5.1, the figures for Venezuela are incomplete; those for Scotland are based on registrations counted in the year rather than actual occurrences during the year (though the difference is small); all the indexes for the USA and some of those for Belgium, Scotland and the USSR are provisional and so

Table 5.1. *Crude marriage rates in 1968—72*

Country	Year 1968	1969	1970	1971	1972
USA	10·4	10·7	10·7	10·6	10·9
Venezuela	5·8	5·8	6·0	6·1	5·6
Belgium	7·2	7·5	7·6	7·6	7·7
Scotland	8·4	8·3	8·3	8·2	8·1
USSR	8·9	9·4	9·7	10·0	9·4

Table 5.2. *Marriage rates in the year 1950 (per marriageable man or woman)*

Age-group	Japan Men	Women	Puerto Rico Men	Women	Switzerland Men	Women
15—19	—	0·01	0·01	0·07	—	0·01
20—24	0·04	0·09	0·10	0·12	0·06	0·12
25—29	0·14	0·09	0·13	0·09	0·15	0·15
30—34	0·15	0·04	0·09	0·06	0·13	0·09
35—39	0·10	0·01	0·06	0·04	0·09	0·05
40—44	0·06	0·01	0·05	0·03	0·06	0·03
45—49	0·03	—	0·05	0·02	0·04	0·02
50—54	0·02	—	0·04	0·01	0·03	0·01
55—59	0·01	—	0·04	0·01	0·03	—
60—64	—	—	0·02	—	0·02	—
65 and over	—	—	0·01	—	—	—

Table 5.3. *First marriage rates, England and Wales, 1931 and 1962 (per thousand)*

Age-group	Bachelors 1931	1962	Spinsters 1931	1962
15—19	3·3	12·8	17·1	58·4
20—24	72·3	157·5	106·8	267·3
25—29	152·2	187·6	111·9	178·7
30—34	111·5	98·7	57·2	90·4
35—44	49·8	42·8	21·3	33·3

subject to revision in due course. The table gives some idea of the extent to which the crude figures vary from country to country and from year to year.

In table 5.2, first and subsequent marriages are combined and expressed in ratios of the total non-married population in each age-group. Table 5.3 however separates, for one country, first marriages and records them as ratios of unmarried men and women, while table 5.4 shows similar figures for re-marriages and classifies them according to the cause of the termination

74

Table 5.4 *Re-marriage rates. England and Wales,*
         1962 (per thousand)

	Widowed persons		Divorced persons	
Age-group	Men	Women	Men	Women
25—29	207	182	433	450
30—34	162	188	310	219
35—44	133	58	189	115
45—54	83	25	107	51

of the previous marriage. The following features of marriage experience
may be noted:

(1) first marriages occur mainly at ages 20—29;

(2) spinsters marry earlier in life than bachelors;

(3) the rate of second marriage is, in general, greater than that of first
marriage (although the natures of the respective 'exposures to risk' are so
widely different that comparison is rather meaningless) and is higher for men
than for women;

(4) the rates are higher for divorced persons than for widowed persons:
the desire to remarry may, of course, have been the reason for the divorce;

(5) in England and Wales, much higher first marriage rates were experienced in 1962 than in 1931, with the exception of older bachelors.

The fact that marriage rates rise to a peak and then fall, over a relatively
narrow range of ages, indicates that uniform quinary age-grouping may well
be unsatisfactory in analysis and should probably be replaced by calculations
at individual ages. It also indicates that single-figure indexes are to be
avoided if possible. For instance, constancy of the 'average age at marriage',
a statistic that is sometimes used as an indicator, might conceal a reduction
in the age at first marriage, if it were balanced by an increase in the proportion
of remarriages at older ages. Such concealment would be a handicap in the
study of fertility, because of the unequal effects that the two balancing
changes are likely to have upon the number of children born.

5.4 Marriages and the numbers available for marriage

The 'supply' of men and women available for marriage depends not merely
on the total number of unmarried persons but also on the distribution of
ages at which it is customary to marry. A thousand unmarried girls aged
21 in (say) France are likely to experience more marriages in a year than
a thousand unmarried men of that age, than a thousand girls aged 17 in that
country, or than a thousand girls aged 21 in Ireland (where most girls
marry later). If, owing to some economic or political disturbance, the number

of marriages in a population is materially changed, the supply may be disturbed and thus the numbers of marriages in subsequent periods may be affected. For instance, a war scare might cause the numbers of marriages to rise above the usual level for a time; when it died down, there might for a time subsequently be fewer marriages than normal – although no exact compensation would be likely.

Generation and cohort influences (see § 2.10) are important also in the study of marriage rates. Each age-group in tables 5.2 and 5.3 represents a different set of persons, who are unlikely to experience exactly the rates shown for the older ages when they reach these ages; the future marriage rates of each set will probably depend more on the circumstances of the time and on the previous history of the set. Suppose, for instance, that unfavourable conditions caused low marriage rates for ten years but that the rates in the ensuing decade were materially higher. It is clear that, towards the end of the first ten-year period, boys and girls then attaining age 15 would in due course experience higher marriage rates than those concurrently recorded at ages 15–24; this would be because of the change to higher rates. Similarly men and women attaining age 25 towards the end of the first ten-year period would thereafter experience a higher proportion of marriages than those concurrently recorded at 25–34; this would probably be attributable not only to the secular change but also to the experience of the past ten years, as a result of which unusually large numbers of persons would be available for marriage.

5.5 Sex difference in marriage rates

Polygamy is rare, and so equal numbers of men and women are concerned in the marriages in any period; such differences as may exist between the total numbers of the sexes at the appropriate ages will thus be reflected, through the denominators, in their marriage rates. Inequality between the numbers of young adult men and women in the population may arise in various ways. More boys than girls are born each year in most countries; the excess is usually about 5 per cent, but is reduced during infancy and childhood because male mortality is almost invariably heavier than female. As men normally marry at a later age than women, their numbers are still further depleted by deaths before reaching marriageable age. War losses have usually fallen more heavily on men than on women. Migratory movements are liable to affect the structure of the population by sex and age.

Thus, marriage rates such as those shown in tables 5.2, 5.3 and 5.4 may well have been influenced by such events as past wars and migrations. Even changes in the level of births from time to time may appreciably affect the relative supplies of marriageable persons of the sexes, as is illustrated in the following simplified example. Suppose that men aged 25 marry women aged

20, that the chances of surviving unmarried from birth to these ages are respectively 0·85 and 0·90 and that male births are more numerous than female births by 5 per cent each year. If the numbers of births in a community in selected years were as follows:

Year	Boys	Girls
1925	105,000	100,000
1930	84,000	80,000
1935	126,000	120,000

then the numbers of marriageable persons in the next generation (ignoring migration) would be:

Year	Men aged 25	Women aged 20
1950	89,200	72,000
1955	71,400	108,000

In 1950 the supply of marriageable men would exceed that of women, but by 1955 this position would be reversed. The tendency would thus be for men's marriage rates to be low, relative to women's, in 1950 but high in 1955. A higher proportion of women attaining age 20 would marry in 1950 than in 1955.

In practice the severity of the changes illustrated above would be mitigated by the spread of ages over which marriages take place; the effect of a change in the supply of marriage partners at one age or in one year would probably be to alter the numbers of marriages at other ages or in other years.

5.6 Disparities of age between husbands and wives

Statistics are published, for very many countries, showing the numbers of couples classified according to the age of the husband and the age of the wife, in groups, for all combinations of these groups. The point of time at which the data are collected may be a census, or even the occasion of the death of one spouse, but more normally it is the moment of the marriage itself. The picture which these statistics present varies appreciably from country to country and from one time to another. For a number of reasons, the relative numbers of unmarried men and women, and their age-distribution, also change. Time-changes in the population available for marriage account for a material part of the variations observed in the joint age-distribution at marriage; but age-differences between the spouses evolve also through the operation of influences of a social and economic character.

International variations in the relative ages of brides and grooms can also be accounted for, in part, in terms of the relative plentifulness of the unmarried of either sex. To give some idea of the extent to which the figures fluctuate, the following statement shows the excess (in years) in the average age of a wife of a man marrying between the ages of 25 and 29 in three countries over the corresponding average age of a wife in England and Wales in the same year; the figures have been adjusted to allow for the effects of international variations in the numbers available for marriage:

	1951	1966
Austria	+0·5	−0·3
Italy	−0·1	−0·3
Switzerland	+0·8	+0·6

Analysis of such data may be of interest for the light they can throw on the psychological and social processes of mate selection.

5.7 Proportions married

Broadly speaking, the proportion married at any age sums up the experience of a generation of men or women as regards marriage rates at all earlier adult ages. Proportions married – and also proportions single, widowed and divorced – are thus the product of varying marriage (and mortality and divorce) experience in past years. Unless conditions have remained constant for a long time – an unlikely contingency – the marriage rates at each age in a given year will not be consistent with the differences between the proportions married at successive ages in that year. The experience of the year may thus be interpreted in two different ways according to which method of approach is used.

Marriage rates are subject to wider fluctuations than proportions married. (The former may thus provide a better pointer to the immediate future whereas the latter are probably more reliable as an indication of long-term trends). In particular, the proportions married at ages 45–60 tend to be constant in time, and from country to country, because it is usual for about 90 per cent of men and women eventually to marry. At older ages, proportions married are affected chiefly by mortality experience. Sometimes, however, the 'proportion ever-married' is used in analysis; this is the sum of the proportions married, widowed and divorced, and is not appreciably influenced by mortality at the older ages.

Illustrative figures are given in table 5.5. These show in particular the high proportion married in Egypt, the very low proportion married in Eire and the appreciable numbers of the consensually married in Barbados.

5.8 Termination of marriage

Widowhood rates will be obtainable from census and registration data, in countries where the deaths of married men and women are classified and tabulated according to the ages of their surviving spouses. Where such data are not available, widowhood rates can be estimated by using married men's

Table 5.5. *Specimen proportions married in various countries*

Sex	Age-group	Status	Egypt (1947)	Barbados (1946)	Eire (1951)	England and Wales (1951)
Men	20—24	Single	0·69	0·84	0·95	0·76
		Married	0·27	0·08	0·05	0·24
		Consensually married	—	0·08	—	—
		Widowed	—	—	—	—
		Divorced	0·01	—	—	—
		Unknown	0·03	—	—	—
	45—49	Single	0·02	0·15	0·32	0·10
		Married	0·94	0·66	0·66	0·87
		Consensually married	—	0·16	—	—
		Widowed	0·03	0·03	0·02	0·02
		Divorced	0·01	—	—	0·01
		Unknown	—	—	—	—
Women	20—24	Single	0·20	0·68	0·83	0·52
		Married	0·74	0·19	0·17	0·48
		Consensually married	—	0·13	—	—
		Widowed	0·02	—	—	—
		Divorced	0·03	—	—	—
		Unknown	0·01	—	—	—
	45—49	Single	0·01	0·37	0·26	0·15
		Married	0·72	0·45	0·67	0·78
		Consensually married	—	0·09	—	—
		Widowed	0·24	0·09	0·07	0·06
		Divorced	0·02	—	—	0·01
		Unknown	0·01	—	—	—

or women's mortality rates in conjunction with the joint age-distribution of husbands and wives recorded at a census.

In many countries divorces have become material in number in recent years, and may represent an appreciable proportion of marriages. Divorces often occur at the more advanced ages and after many years of married life (indeed, the law generally prevents an early dissolution of a marriage). The numbers of children of divorced couples are often smaller than average, but a high proportion of divorced persons – particularly men – remarry and any shortfall in fertility may be made good in the second marriage. Divorce is now far more important than death as a cause of termination of marriage at ages under fifty in many countries, and accordingly deserves careful consideration in analyses of marriage and fertility. It can be studied, where data are available, in relation to such factors as age at marriage, duration of marriage, and area of residence.

A kind of disturbance in the data that may be encountered when using proportions married and widowed in demographic calculations is the presence in the female population of women who have been widowed by war. If there had been no war, many of them would in the normal course have still been married – the number depending on the length of time elapsed since the war in question – and the excess in the proportions of widows and deficit in the proportions of married women will pass through the age-groups generation-wise as time advances. Thus, in 1941, proportions widowed were high at ages 45–65 in countries combatant in the First World War 20–25 years before; at a census taken in 1951, say, the excess in the proportions would have shifted to the age-group 55–75, and would be less marked because more of the women concerned would in any case have lost their husbands by then through death from normal causes.

5.9 Remarriage rates

Widows' remarriage rates show marked differences according to duration of time widowed in the first few years after the death of the husband. Some illustrative figures drawn from the experience of social insurance schemes in Britain are given in table 5.6. In this table, the 'select' rates give the probability of remarriage, in the year following the duration of widowhood shown, for a woman who had been widowed at the age indicated and was still a widow at that duration; the 'ultimate' rates give the probability of remarriage in the year following attainment of the age shown, after not less than 5 years from the date of widowhood. The figures indicate clearly that aggregate rates for widows such as those in table 5.4 are open to objection as a measure of experience because their values depend so much on the durational distribution of the 'exposure to risk'.

The remarriage rates of widowers and of divorced men and women are probably subject to similar durational influences, but comparable figures

Table 5.6. *Rates of remarriage of widows, Britain, 1937–8*

	Select rates					Ultimate rates	
	Duration since widowhood (years)						Duration since widowhood
	0	1	2	3	4		
Age at widowhood						Age attained	5 years and over
22½	0·076	0·148	0·178	0·173	0·162	27½	0·142
27½	0·062	0·108	0·121	0·113	0·102	32½	0·088
32½	0·048	0·074	0·078	0·072	0·062	37½	0·050
37½	0·034	0·050	0·052	0·044	0·037	42½	0·030
42½	0·024	0·032	0·032	0·026	0·022	47½	0·018
47½	0·014	0·020	0·019	0·015	0·012	52½	0·009
52½	0·008	0·011	0·011	0·008	0·006	57½	0·005
57½	0·004	0·006	0·005	0·003	0·001	62½	—

are not available. No data can be produced here to show the extent of variation in remarriage rates according to other likely factors such as number of children.

5.10 Differential marriage

Just as the extent of non-marriage and of delay in marriage may vary between one country and another, so these features may apply in different strength to different areas within a country or to different economic and social groups. Illustrative statistics are rare but such studies as have been made suggest that the principal variations arise from an economic foundation. In general, this is associated not so much with disparities in the proportion ultimately marrying as with differences in the age at first marriage. Their cause is essentially the length of any training required for an occupation and the associated time needed in order to establish an adequate income. To qualify as a doctor or a lawyer may take five years — more if university education is included — which would bring the qualifier to his or her middle twenties; apprenticeship to a skilled trade would be completed earlier in life than this, while those who become only semi-skilled or who remain unskilled would need little time in which to attain the earnings level at which they are likely to remain for much of their lives. Thus in England in 1931, 54 per cent of semi-skilled and unskilled male workers were married in the age-group 25—29 but the corresponding proportions for social classes I and II were respectively only 38 and 49 per cent. In the same age-group, no more than 15 per cent of the unoccupied were married; a potent reason for this must have been that disablement of some sort prevented the following of an occupation, and this would render marriage much less likely from both a physical and an economic viewpoint.

Marriage accordingly acts as a 'selective' force, in relation to health; similarly it occurs much more frequently among the mentally normal than among those retarded or otherwise handicapped since birth. Mortality, sickness and low intelligence are therefore relatively at a reduced level among married people and at an increased level among the never-married. Widowed people experience higher mortality than those who are married (see § 7.11 below).

5.11 Fertility in relation to marital status

It is possible that marriage selects the more fecund from among the population. This is so at least where a child is conceived out of wedlock and where marriage subsequently takes place in order to make its birth legitimate, for if a child had not resulted from the union of the couple the marriage might

81

not have taken place. The dependence of fertility on marriage is clearly very important. The age at which marriage occurs also has a considerable influence on fertility. This influence may operate in several ways: earlier marriages provide increased opportunities for producing and rearing children; those who want to have a large family may marry early in order to do so; further, those who are the most fecund may also be those who marry early in life.

Changes in the number or age-distribution of marriages arising from economic or other causes may well affect the average fertility of married couples. For instance, a rise in marriage rates occasioned by some such 'external' cause may bring into the nuptial state persons less suited for child-bearing or with different ideas about the family they want to have. In other words, the additional marriages are not to be expected necessarily to have the same fertility as the 'average' marriage.

SELECT BIBLIOGRAPHY

Hajnal, J. European marriage patterns in perspective. In D. V. Glass and D. E. C. Eversley, *Population in History* (Aldine Publishing Co., Chicago, 1955).

Cox, P. R. Sex differences in age at marriage. *Journal of Biosocial Science*, Supplement No. 2, **73** (1970).

Sklar, J. L. The role of marriage behaviour in the demographic transition: the case of Eastern Europe around 1900. *Population Studies*, **28** (1974), 231.

6 The statistical study of fertility

6.1 Introductory

The first part of this chapter will be concerned briefly with the biology of fertility (§§ 6.2, 6.3) and then the sections that follow will discuss the nature of the principal social and other factors which influence fertility from time to time (§§ 6.4—6.8). The remainder of the chapter will outline the various forms of statistical analysis with illustrative examples. Methods for use in analysis where the data available are scanty or untrustworthy will be outlined in chapter 19. It is probably true to say that the demographer never finds ready to hand all the statistics which might be desirable for a full study of the subject; but in the present chapter it is assumed that some reliable information at least is available, with perhaps a subdivision by at least one useful parameter.

Fertility becomes possible when adulthood begins, namely at 'puberty' (for girls the word 'menarche' is also used). Studies of the age of puberty show that it varies from country to country, and between the sexes, while it has also undergone marked changes from one century to another in recent times. It is more meaningful in statistical analysis to measure the number of births against the number of persons over the age of puberty than it is to express births as a proportion of population as a whole.

6.2 Fecundity and fertility

A woman's fecundity varies according to a monthly cycle, and study of this cycle is important in relation to the 'rhythm' method of birth control. Immediately following a birth ('parturition'), or during the 'post-partum' period, as it is called, the cycle is absent ('amenorrhoea') or incomplete ('anovulatory cycle') and it is not possible for her to conceive. The length of this period of infecundity may depend upon the extent of breast feeding, or 'lactation'. Infertility may result also from social or religious rules, or 'taboos', concerning intercourse following a birth. Such questions are of importance in considering the difference that exists, even in primitive peoples, between a woman's actual fertility and the maximum number of children that it is physiologically possible for her to bear. In economically more advanced countries, this difference is often much wider, because of birth control.

Demographers take an interest in the methods of birth control used, because they vary in efficiency and therefore in their practical effect; besides the rhythm method, the main groups are abstinence (within marriage, or more usually by non-marriage), coitus interruptus, appliance methods, coils and oral contraceptives. In some married couples, one partner or the other may prove to be wholly infertile ('sterile') or partly infertile ('sub-fecund'), but the proportion of couples to whom children cannot be born at all is relatively small — perhaps of the order of 10 per cent — and variations in natural sterility do not usually explain the variations in fertility that are observed.

6.3   The fertility cycle

The biological process of reproduction is repeatable until, for women, the 'menopause', or 'change of life' is reached; normally at age 45–50. In recent times, demographers have found it useful to make certain types of calculation in connection with fecundity and fertility on an electronic computer. For this purpose they need a 'flow-chart', or diagram showing the events that can occur, and the connecting-links between them. The diagram on page 85 gives for illustrative purposes a simplified flow-chart for women, initially fecund, during the period from puberty to the menopause. What fig. 6.1 does is to remind the demographic computer-programmer of all the possible sequences of events that can occur, so that he can provide suitably for the probabilities at each stage. Thus, for instance, widowhood or divorce cannot occur before first marriage but may happen before conception, or between conception and the outcome of the conception, or after that outcome. It may be succeeded by remarriage or (if it occurs after conception) by the outcome of the conception; and so on. The flow-chart is simplified because, (*a*) only conception within marriage is considered, and (*b*) the chance of the death of the woman is ignored. Allowance could of course be made for these possibilities, and the chart would then become more complicated (as is normally necessary).

6.4   Some factors affecting fertility

In demography, as well as in most other statistical work, one of the steps in analysis is to examine the experience of recent years and to consider what changes, if any, it shows from that of earlier periods. The second step is to study as far as possible the factors influencing the experience and causing the changes, supplementing the analysis by an examination of any available background information of a social, economic or psychological kind. In drawing valid conclusions from such studies, and particularly in attempting to assess the probable future course of events, it is important to remember that any influential factors are likely to vary, not only in ways that seem probable

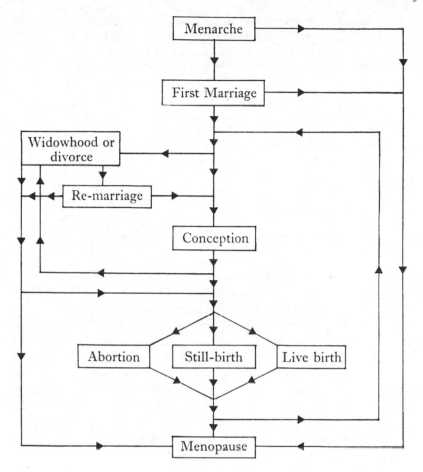

Fig. 6.1. Simplified reproduction flow-chart for women.

in the light of past experience but also perhaps in more unexpected ways. This is particularly true of marriage and fertility, because they are in some degree susceptible to human control, both in regard to deliberate action by individuals and in regard to less conscious effects such as mass changes in fashion and outlook.

Some idea of the influence of human control on fertility may be obtained from table 6.1. The changes from one period to another are quite rapid. In some cases — France and perhaps also England and Wales — they show the effects of the Second World War, which separated young married couples for long periods and so reduced the exposure to risk of fertility during 1940—4 in comparison with the quinary periods before and after this. In Portugal,

85

Table 6.1. *Numbers of births per thousand total population expressed as percentages of the corresponding function in the same country in 1935—9*

Country	Years		
	1935—9	1940—4	1945—9
Australia	100	113	134
Austria	100	130	114
Czechoslovakia	100	122	131
France	100	99	133
Ireland	100	108	116
Norway	100	118	139
Portugal	100	90	93
Sweden	100	122	131
England and Wales	100	104	122
USA	100	116	136

a country very largely unaffected by the war, it also happens that the rate was lowest there in the central period. It will be noted, however, that in Austria fertility was highest in 1940—4, and that in Norway and Czechoslovakia, both of which were occupied and fought over, a steady upward trend is visible. This trend was shared by neutral Sweden and Ireland and by combatant countries as far apart as Australia and the USA. It is difficult to explain all these tendencies convincingly. In part, no doubt, they were the result of economic forces, of social changes and of legislation affecting the family. In part they are probably a reflexion of a change in people's ideas about the number of children they should have, either for reasons of personal happiness and satisfaction or in the national interest.

It may be added that the cause of a sudden fall in fertility in Ireland after the great potato famine there over a hundred years ago is still the object of much interest and speculation today.

A more obvious change was the rise in the birth rate in Rumania after new legislation was introduced, in October 1966, limiting legal abortion and prohibiting contraception. In the four quarters of 1967 the birth rates were respectively 13·7, 15·5, 21·6 and 38·4. (These figures are on an annual basis — each represents four times the number of births in the quarter divided by the population expressed in thousands.)

6.5 Personal attitudes towards the family

Much attention has been paid in recent years to the opinions of ordinary men and women about the number of children they consider it desirable to have; sample surveys on this subject have been conducted in many countries. It has been found that quite often couples do not in the event have, or even intend to have, the kind of family that they have stated to be ideal in theory; much depends upon their knowledge of birth control, on the availability of contraceptives and on their ability to use them effectively — apart from the fact that they may change their minds. Nevertheless, there is sufficient interest in the ideals and sufficient resemblance between favoured and actual family size for the method to be considered to be of some value. Psychological, economic and moral considerations seem to affect people most. From the point of view of psychology, at the present time one child alone is often considered undesirable, two children satisfactory but three or four perhaps better. A large family, however, is usually thought to be too great a burden; this is certainly true from the economic aspect, which appears to have an influence in favour of very small families in some developed countries; here influences are complex, as what people do may be affected by:

(1) their actual prosperity, or lack of it; or
(2) how rich or poor they *feel* they are; or
(3) concern over population pressure on resources.

Moral considerations, apart from (3) above, are concerned mostly with politics and religion. Much of their religious importance relates to the methods by which limitation of the number of children is achieved. Infanticide, an ancient method of population control, is now universally condemned. Induced abortion is considered very undesirable, at least on health grounds, although it is extensively practised in many countries today. Official Roman Catholic Church doctrine is still opposed to contraceptives — although not to methods of limitation that are dependent on abstention from intercourse — and fertility tends to be materially higher in Catholic communities than among adherents of other faiths in the same countries.

6.6 Fertility from the national viewpoint

Normally, men and women are capable of bringing numerous children into the world, and a couple may thus replace themselves several times over. If all married couples did so the population would increase rapidly — unless the mortality experienced was very heavy or relatively few persons married. (At the opposite extreme, a population completely deprived of births and immigrants must disappear entirely within about a century.)

In recent years rates of population increase of up to 2 per cent per annum have been recorded over large areas. The maximum possible rate of natural growth of a human population is probably between 3 and 4 per cent per annum (though it could be higher in exceptional circumstances, for example if the proportion of young adults were unusually large); a continuance of this rate could lead to a doubling of the population size within twenty-five years and thus to a sixteen-fold increase within a century. Even a 2 per cent rate of increase causes a rapid growth in numbers. In order that this shall not lead to famine, and other great hardships, it is essential that food resources, and also the supply of necessities such as clothing, housing and education, should expand correspondingly; this requires the speedy development of all forms of trade and manufacture. The opportunity for such an expansion of resources varies greatly from country to country, and more will be said on this subject in chapters 12 and 14.

The attitudes taken by governments towards population growth also vary. In some countries the need is felt for greater numbers, whether to bring uncultivated areas into use and to allow the beneficial introduction of mass-production methods in the factories, or in order to increase national security and power. Such governments tend to discourage the use of contraceptives and to offer rewards for large families. In other countries the possibilities for expansion of resources are seen to be insufficient to support a rapidly increasing population, and in some of these dissemination of information about birth control is encouraged. The national interest may clash with the personal viewpoints described in § 6.5, and in such circumstances governmental action may or may not be successful in achieving its aims. Official policies may be changed, with corresponding effects upon fertility. Chapter 13 enlarges upon these questions.

6.7 Family size

The secular variability to which reference has been made above is a handicap in the interpretation of the past and in the prediction of the future. Any difficulties may well be diminished by the study of the fertility experience of cohorts or generations, and the use of this form of analysis is desirable wherever possible.

The experience of a cohort in regard to fertility is conveniently summed up in the average number of children per married couple, or 'family size'. This can take two forms: the numbers of children ever born, or the numbers surviving at a given time. For two main reasons, completed family size tends to vary less than annual fertility. In the first place it is a 'stock' function effectively covering a span of some ten to twenty years' experience of 'flow'. Secondly, as family size to some extent reflects the ideas of married couples as to the number of children they should have, if a wanted child is postponed during unfavourable economic or political circumstances there is a good chance that it will be born later when circumstances have improved. Thus, soon after 1945, birth rates rose as couples who had been unable to have children during the Second World War resumed their family building.

It should not, however, be imagined that even completed family size is a wholly constant element in demography. It is subject, *inter alia,* to long-term trends in fashion and to the influence of changes in government policy. Fecundity tends to decline with increasing age, and a postponement of a birth does not signify in every instance that the desired child can be borne later. Family size may also be affected by variations in the average age at marriage; by other changes in marriage rates such as those resulting from an alteration in the balance of the sexes; by trends in divorce; by medical advances, and by other factors.

In order to illustrate variations in completed family size, some recent experience in Britain is shown in table 6.2. As the size has fallen, the proportions of small families have increased and those of large families have decreased. This brings out the point that average family size is a composite function. For many purposes it is desirable to consider the elements of which it is composed, namely: the proportions of married couples with 0, 1, 2, 3, ... children. Another noteworthy feature is that, in order to demonstrate the most recent experience, an element of estimation for the future has had to be introduced. Without this speculative element, the statement would have to be confined to the fertility of earlier decades. This is often a serious disadvantage in generation analysis.

6.8 Further fundamental characteristics of fertility

Although it is often convenient to think of fertility in relation to married couples, illegitimacy cannot safely be ignored. The percentage of illegitimate births to total births, as recorded, varies widely from country to country; thus the UN *Demographic Year Book* gives figures as low as 0·1 per cent for Cyprus

Table 6.2. *Family size in Britain for marriages since 1900*
(All women married at ages under 45.)

Year of first marriage	Number per thousand of married women with specific numbers of live births						Average number of children
	0	1 or 2	3 or 4	5 to 9	10 or more	Total	
1900–9	113	335	277	246	29	1,000	3·4
1910	122	373	282	200	23	1,000	3·04
1915	150	447	254	139	10	1,000	2.51
1920	138	456	258	136	12	1,000	2.54
1925	161	506	221	106	6	1,000	2·21
1930	165	511	220	100	4	1,000	2·10
1935	165	522	215	95	3	1,000	2·05
1940	170	528	210	90	2	1,000	2·00
1945*	145	510	248	95	2	1,000	2·20
1950*	135	510	258	95	2	1,000	2·25
1955*	127	500	275	97	1	1,000	2·40
1960*	124	500	280	95	1	1,000	2·40
1965*	124	520	260	95	1	1,000	2·30

* Estimated by the author on the assumption of a certain level of fertility in the future. The estimate is speculative so far as the distribution by family size is concerned.

and for Macao, but as high as 70 per cent for some parts of the Caribbean. The figures for Europe range from 1 to 25 per cent, at the extremes, though in most countries they come within 5–10 per cent. Clearly the proportion depends very greatly on social conditions. Notable rises have been observed where, for some special reason, marriage has been rendered more difficult, for instance during wartime. While fertility depends in large degree on all the factors that have been shown to affect marriage, owing to marriage selection the degree of dependence will not be exactly the same for fertility as for marriage.

Fertility is, of course, subject also to biological factors affecting fecundity; it commences at puberty and has a tendency to decline with advancing age. For women it ceases at the menopause. One birth is very unlikely to be followed by another within the period of gestation of nine months; thus the exposure of women to risk of childbirth is to some extent dependent on recent fertility experience (and although no special adjustment is normally made for this, an allowance for the point may be desirable in certain forms of analysis, for instance in a close study of fertility rates during the first few years of marriage). It should be noted, however, that births within the first nine months of marriage are by no means impossible; indeed they are very common, particularly for the younger ages at marriage, as the impending birth of a child is often the precipitant of a marriage.

It has been shown that fertility depends to some extent on personal attitudes and aspirations, which in turn depend on intelligence and education; it may be influenced, directly or indirectly, by government policy of one kind or another and by economic circumstances. It is not surprising, therefore, to find that it also varies according to race, religion, occupation, social status, urban or rural domicile and geographical region; the manner of variation in these respects itself varies from country to country. It is high in tropical areas, and there may well be a climatic effect, with a seasonal pattern, rising and falling with the temperature. It may also be affected by altitude.

As a result mainly of biological factors, but also partly of social and other influences, the fertility of men and women, whether they are considered as a whole or whether only married persons are studied, varies according to attained age. For married persons it depends not only on age at marriage, but also on duration of marriage, on the number of children already borne and on the time interval since the birth of the last child. Fertility rates also differ as between men and women, except of course where couples are considered jointly according to length of time married or to the size of their family.

6.9   The possibilities for statistical analysis

The course of analysis must depend, first, on the purposes in mind and, secondly, on the nature of the available data. Interest may be taken in fertility statistics for their own sake, or so as to advance demographic science, although in view of the difficulties that have been described the prospects for theoretical development are not very bright. Knowledge of the subject is more likely to be found necessary in order to assist in the formulation of policy, or in order to determine the true rate of growth of a population, or to undertake a study of different sections or classes of a population so as to show how much each is contributing towards the national trend: the study of 'differential fertility' can be very revealing as to the nature, causes and trend of fertility generally.

The influence on fertility studies of the nature of the available data is indeed profound. If for instance births are classified only by the mother's age, then analysis by marriage duration is unlikely to be possible. Worse still, births may not be classified even by the mother's age (as for example in Britain before 1938). The course of the remainder of this chapter is, therefore, largely determined by the history of the collection of fertility statistics. Attention will first be paid to 'flow', i.e., to rates and indexes that can be developed from annual registration data, because this is the classical mode of analysis. Fertility data derived from censuses will then be described, for the information of the 'stock' type that they present and for the forms of analysis that they permit — for instance the study of family distributions and of differential fertility.

6.10 Simple measures of total fertility

Reference to the crude birth rate was made in § 2.7. As was shown there, it is open to the general objection that the total population is not the proper 'exposed to risk'. A better measure is the general fertility rate, in which the number of potentially fertile adults is substituted for the total population in the denominator. For women, this may be expressed as

$$\frac{\text{number of live births in year}}{\text{number of women aged (say) } 15-49}. \tag{6.1}$$

It has sometimes been the practice in the past to calculate the ratio of births to marriages in a year, but this procedure is unsatisfactory because, in the main, births are the outcome not of contemporaneous marriages but of those of earlier years.

Another measure easily derived from basic census statistics is the child—woman ratio, namely

$$\frac{\text{number of children aged 0 to } x}{\text{number of all women aged } y \text{ to } z}, \tag{6.2}$$

which may be of some use in the comparison of the fertility of different populations. The values commonly used are 4 or 9 for x, 15 or 20 for y and 49

91

or 54 for z. This measure is less valuable, on the whole, than the general fertility rate, because the population that bore the children is not used in the numerator; but it may be a good substitute where birth registration data are absent or unreliable.

If no further data are available, accurate measurement of other aspects of fertility is clearly impossible, but reference will be made in chapter 19 to substitute methods, by which estimates of more elaborate functions may be made with the aid of inferences drawn from a comparison with suitably-chosen populations in respect of which more plentiful data have been collected.

6.11   Legitimate and illegitimate fertility

The general fertility rate may be analysed into components according to legitimacy, first by taking as numerator only legitimate live births and using as denominator married women, and secondly by dividing the numbers of illegitimate births by the numbers of non-married (single, widowed and divorced) women.

The child—woman ratio could be similarly analysed, though as enumerated populations of children are not normally classified by legitimacy the numerator would need to be subdivided in the same proportion as for births. In cases where the child—woman ratio may be of value, however, the numbers and legitimacy of births may not be recorded.

An analysis in which legitimate children are attributed to married women and illegitimate children to non-married women is not perfect: for instance, children born to widows are not all illegitimate — normally they are posthumous to men who have just died. Any censal misstatements by which married women describe themselves as non-married, or *vice versa*, would also affect the subdivision.

6.12   Fertility rates analysed by age of parent

The attained age of the parent is an important variable in relation to fertility, although not necessarily more important than duration of time since marriage or number of existing children. The age at marriage plus the duration of marriage equals the attained age. Thus these three variables are interconnected, and for any specific duration the spread of the parents' ages may be expected to be less than the corresponding spread for all durations taken together. Nevertheless, the averages and spreads will vary from time to time as the ages at marriage change. Similarly with the spread of marriage durations at any given attained age. Whichever variable is used some allowance is made for the other.

The male fertility rate at age x may be defined as follows in respect of legitimate births:

$$\frac{\text{number of legitimate births to fathers aged } x}{\text{number of married men aged } x}, \quad (6.3)$$

with corresponding definitions for illegitimate births and for all births. Similar rates may be calculated for women and also for the sexes combined.

Although both a mother and a father must be concerned in every birth it has been and still is to some extent customary to disregard this for statistical purposes and to treat the mother's share as being the one in relation to which fertility and reproduction should be measured. Paternal factors can, however, be employed as easily and suitably as maternal where adequate data are collected. To develop the subject by the independent use of both men's and women's data should be the best course because if sound processes are used the same results in estimating the future numbers of births should be obtained by each approach, and the check afforded by the necessity for agreement should ensure the elimination of any systematic errors that might otherwise arise. As will be seen later, however, it is not altogether easy to reconcile men's and women's data.

The classification of fertility rates by age alone is of limited value when the numbers or rates of marriages are changing rapidly; but if the rates for all births, irrespective of marital status of parent, are presented in generation form rather than in secular form (i.e. if they are arranged according to year of birth of parent) they can show how population replacement is proceeding, without any analysis of the contribution which is made by marriage. Much useful work has been done along these lines, especially in the USA.

6.13 Illustrations of age-specific fertility rates

Fertility rates of the kind discussed in the preceding section are sometimes known as 'age-specific' rates. Tables 6.3 and 6.4 give certain hypothetical data which may be regarded as relating to some particular community chosen from the population of a European country. It is supposed that in year X there were 3,804 legitimate and 54 illegitimate births, and that in year Y the corresponding numbers were 3,752 and 37 respectively. Table 6.3 shows the relevant sections of the population; women have been chosen for this purpose rather than men because the number of age-groups is smaller, thus simplifying the arithmetical work involved (which has been minimized so that the calculations may readily be verified by any reader who so desires).

Table 6.4 sets out the fertility rates for groups of attained ages which are supposed to have been experienced in years X and Y, and table 6.5 shows results obtained from the data given in tables 6.3 and 6.4.

93

Table 6.3. *Hypothetical population of women at ages 15—44*

Age-group	Year X		Year Y	
	No. of married women	No. of single and widowed women	No. of married women	No. of single and widowed women
15—19	1,000	8,000	1,000	7,500
20—24	5,200	4,000	5,700	3,400
25—29	7,100	1,800	7,200	1,700
30—34	7,900	700	7,600	700
35—39	7,800	600	7,500	600
40—44	8,000	500	7,600	600
Total	37,000	15,600	36 600	14,500
		52,600		51,100
Total population	270,000		250,000	

Table 6.4. *Hypothetical fertility rates by attained age of woman (live births only)*

Age-group	Year X		Year Y	
	Legitimate	Illegitimate	Legitimate	Illegitimate
15—19	0·100	0·005	0·090	0·004
20—24	0·250	0·003	0·240	0·002
25—29	0·150	0·001	0·140	—
30—34	0·090	—	0·090	—
35—39	0·060	—	0·060	—
40—44	0·020	—	0·020	—
45—49	—	—	—	—

Table 6.5. *Crude fertility indexes per thousand (derived from data in tables 6.3 and 6.4)*

Type of index	Value in year X	Value in year Y	Y as a percentage of X
Birth rate	14·3	15·2	106·3
General fertility rate (women)	73·3	74·1	101·1
Legitimate fertility rate (women)	102·8	102·5	99·7

It seems clear from table 6.4 that the intrinsic fertility in year Y was lower than that in the year X to an extent that none of the crude indexes in table 6.5 indicates correctly. To obtain a better result, recourse may be had to standardization. The procedures will be described in chapter 16, using the data from these tables.

6.14   Effects of marriage duration

Some specimen fertility rates classified by the number of years of marriage are set out in table 6.6. In the figures for West Germany, the number of years married means the number arrived at by deducting the year of marriage from the year of the birth; whereas in the data for Switzerland and Scotland the true complete number of years married has been adopted. This difference of definition has had an obvious effect on the rates shown for duration *0*, and it also influences the comparison of the countries at other durations. The chief features of table 6.6 are that the rates are not specific to one sex or the other, but to couples, and that fertility falls steadily with advancing marriage duration.

The calculation of such rates every year requires not only that information about duration of marriage shall be collected at the registration of every legitimate birth but also that data or estimates of the numbers of married couples at each marriage duration shall be available. These requirements are severe, and consequently durational rates are uncommon in world demography. They are not calculated, for instance, in the USA. In England and Wales, although the effects of marriage duration on fertility were demonstrated by actuaries some seventy years ago, national data in durational form could not be regularly published until 1938.

A more generally useful method of incorporating analysis by marriage duration into studies of fertility is to use the original number of marriages, and not the numbers of survivors to each duration, as a denominator. The rates can then be added together for several or all durations for each cohort, showing how the family builds up. Some illustrative figures are given in table 10.3 below.

The distribution in time of the arrival of the first child in a family varies somewhat with age at marriage: it comes more speedily for young couples than for older ones, probably because of a higher proportion of pre-marital

Table 6.6. *Fertility rates classified according to marriage duration*

Number of years married	West Germany 1962	Switzerland 1960	Scotland 1961
0	190	415	365
1	364	296	360
2	253	262	291
3	225	223	269
4	202	189	245
5–9	122	113	149
10–14	52	44	60
15–19	24	15	23
20 and over	10	1	2
All durations	124	76	82

conceptions. For second children and those of higher parities the time-distribution of birth varies little by age at marriage. Naturally, the higher the parity the longer the marriage duration required. As, however, couples who marry young have plenty of time in which to build up a large family, if they wish, whereas older couples at marriage do not have this time, the durational distribution of births of all parities in combination is longer for those who marry young than for those who marry at later ages. This is illustrated by the following round figures for Britain in the years preceding 1950:

	Percentage of total family born by duration			
Age at marriage	2 years	4 years	7 years	10 years
20—22 years	35	55	75	90
33—35 years	40	70	90	95

6.15 Analysis of fertility by birth order

Where suitable data are available, fertility rates can be classsified according to family size; that is, the total number of births in a year to parents who had already had n children may be divided by the total number of parents with n children. Alternatively a double classification involving family size and either attained age or marriage age or marriage duration of parent could be adopted. Many of the comments made in § 6.14 about durational rates would then be applicable to rates arranged according to family size. The birth-occurrence data required for this form of analysis are collected in some countries, but estimates of the corresponding exposures to risk are normally obtained, if at all, only on the occasion of a census. Publication of rates is therefore uncommon. It may be noted, however, that legitimate fertility rates classified according to age or marriage duration may readily be analysed by subdividing the numerator according to birth-order of child (1st, 2nd, . . .) without subdividing the denominator. Thus if the fertility rate after seven years of marriage were 0·102, this might be found to be composed (say) as follows:

First children	0·034
Second children	0·047
Third children	0·019
Fourth children	0·002
Total	0·102

A use for this form of analysis will be mentioned in the next section.

If, at a census, married couples old enough to have completed their families are tabulated according to the number of live-born children they have had, it is possible to calculate ratios of the form:

$$P_n = \frac{\text{number of couples with } n \text{ children or more}}{\text{number of couples with } n - 1 \text{ children or more}}, \quad (6.4)$$

and these can be quite useful for comparative purposes. They are called 'parity progression ratios'. If in P_n the numerator is deducted from the denominator the difference represents the number of couples with $n - 1$ children precisely. The distribution of this function, divided by the total number of couples, is also valuable, as it shows how average family size is composed. Some illustrative figures were given in table 6.2 above.

The degree of time-spacing between births is also significant for demographic analysis, and fertility rates for each parity can be classified by the number of months or years elapsing since the previous birth. This can be valuable for the examination of short-term variations, but experience data are rare. See § 16.25 below.

6.16 Secular, generation and cohort analyses

One reason why a generation approach towards the study of fertility may be more desirable than a secular approach was given in § 6.7. The relative disadvantage of a secular approach may be expressed in another way. There is no particularly strong reason to suppose that women now aged (say) 25 will, when they reach age 35, experience the same fertility rate as do women aged 35 today. Indeed if the women's fertility rate at age 25 ten years ago differed from the corresponding rate at that age today it is quite likely that the rates for the same groups will differ also at age 35. But if statistics relating to women who were born in the same year, or who attained puberty in the same year, are followed through their reproductive lives, the fertility records thus obtained will form a consistent series. Cohort analysis associates births to women aged 25 now with births to women aged 35 ten years hence and shows how their total families build up. For this purpose the rates may, if desired, be subdivided according to order of birth, as indicated in § 6.7. Only all-women's or all-men's fertility rates can simply be followed through in this way. If it is desired to work with legitimate fertility rates, an allowance for the proportion married, derived from a study of the marriage experience of the cohort in question, is necessary. Further, because the size of a cohort steadily diminishes as time and age advance, only the actual numbers of births, or the rates obtained by dividing them by the initial size of the cohort, can properly be added together in order to sum up the long-term experience of the group of persons in question.

Powerful arguments may be found in favour of cohort analysis involving either age or marriage duration as the principal element. Both these elements have their advantages and disadvantages, and neither can be said to be so much superior that it should be used to the entire exclusion of the other. Ryder has shown from the experience of the past that the completed family size for a marriage cohort of duration m at time t (F_1, say) can be related to the completed family size assessed on the basis of the experience of all fertile cohorts in existence at time t (F_2, say). Reduced to its simplest elements, his formula is:

$$F_1 = F_2 \left(1 + \frac{d}{dt}(m),\right) \qquad (6.5)$$

where m is the mean interval between marriage and the average birth to it. What this implies is that if a speed-up in births is occurring, $(d/dt)(m)$ will be negative and F_2 will exceed F_1; if births are slowing down, $(d/dt)(m)$ will be positive and F_1 will exceed F_2. This is reasonable provided that change is not occurring in the ultimate family size but only in the rate at which it is being built up by couples.

6.17 Relative advantages and disadvantages of using various methods of analysing fertility

To sum up the possibilities, it may be said that the principal axes of fertility classification are age of parent, duration of marriage and number of children in the family. Either sex may be considered (or in some circumstances both sexes together) and there is a choice between a secular and a generation approach; so there are many possible modes of analysis.

The relative advantages and disadvantages of the various axes of classification have been much debated in those countries where the available data are of sufficient scope to permit alternative classifications. It has not, however, been possible to reach agreement that some axes can be rejected in favour of others. Thus no single one of these modes can be said to be perfect in itself.

Where fertility is largely under control because of the practice of contraception, a generation analysis (according to year of birth or year of marriage of parent) may be preferable to the study of secular trends, because married couples are likely to have some regard to the existing numbers of their children in deciding to what extent they will attempt to prevent the birth of another child. Unless demographers using the generation approach are prepared to confine their attention to the couples who are past the age of childbearing, however, they are faced with a number of different sets of people, all at different ages of reproductive life, and their data are not easy to present in convenient form. The problem can be tackled by the use of mathematical models and other devices. But the secular approach (according to the year of occurrence) is simpler to handle and will probably continue to be used for this reason, though the use of both approaches side by side may give the fullest explanation possible.

Discrepancies between the results of fertility analysis based on men's and women's data arise mainly from the different ages of the sexes at marriage and from the fact that the proportions of married men to all men and of married women to all women are not equal, owing to inequalities in the numbers of births, deaths and migratory movements of the two sexes. Some attempt has been made to find a solution to the problem by treating the male or the female sex as being 'dominant' in marriage, but no practical solution has been found.

Analysis of fertility solely by number of children in the family is inconvenient because of the absence of a regular measure of time, and for this reason size of family is likely to remain secondary to age or marriage duration.

There has been considerable discussion on the respective merits of age and marriage duration as axes.

The following reasons may be advanced for giving pride of place to marriage duration:

(1) most children are born in marriage, and analysis by age alone mixes proportions married in with fertility;

(2) marriage durations are the same for both husbands and wives, and this helps in the reconciliation of the approaches to fertility by means of the data for the two sexes;

(3) where fertility is partly planned, age at marriage loses some of its significance and marriage duration becomes important.

Those who favour age as the main axis say in regard to (1) that marriage is a selective force and that fertility within marriage cannot be independent of the level and age-distribution of marriage rates, and in regard to (3) that not all fertility is planned and that age at marriage is still influential. It is, of course, possible to compromise by setting out the results of the two alternative approaches side by side or by treating age and duration in a combined analysis.

Yet another issue is between summary functions, such as average family size, and frequency distributions, such as the proportions of couples with 0, 1, 2 ... children. An apparent stability in the average may conceal an important change in distribution — for instance, if the proportion of large families continues to fall but there is an increase in the average size of small families. A similar conflict exists between other forms of 'stock' and 'flow' data — for instance, the number of married men at a given time and the number of men marrying in a given year respectively.

A mathematical treatment of fertility analysis is discussed in chapter 18.

6.18 Fertility censuses

The expression 'fertility census' may relate to special inquiries like that undertaken in Britain in 1946 (see § 4.13) but may also be used in connection with normal censuses at which additional questions relating to fertility are asked. Such additional questions may relate to age at marriage or length of time married, to number of children ever born in marriage or number of children alive on the census date, to children born within a given recent period, or even to the dates of birth of all the children in the family. This extra information need not be obtained from every member of the population, and will normally be limited to appropriate classes, for instance, to married women under the age of 50 (to ask single women about illegitimate children may well be impolitic).

Fertility censuses provide a measure of 'exposures to risk' for the calculation of fertility rates. They are thus a desirable adjunct to birth registration statistics, which supply the numerators for such rates but from which it is often difficult to estimate the denominators. A regular series of fertility censuses, even unsupported by registration data, can reveal much about trends, but a single enumeration, taken entirely itself, requires very careful interpretation and it may even be impracticable to draw many valid conclusions from it.

Where birth registration data are not available, or are inadequate, censal information about children recently born can – if sufficiently reliable – give a good indication of current fertility rates, when related to the numbers of parents, and it may be possible to classify such rates by age, marriage duration or parity depending on how detailed the census schedules are.

The framing of questions for fertility censuses requires great care. It needs to be explained very clearly, for instance, whether the fertility of the present marriage is to be referred to or whether children of any earlier marriages are also to be included; whether or not children away from home on the census night are to be treated as part of the family; whether or not still-births are to be included in the record of past fertility, and whether only currently-married persons or all persons who have at any time been married are to answer the questions. It is important to ensure that persons who have had no children say so directly and do not leave the form blank. Experience has shown, however, that even when the census form is clearly expressed a proportion of incorrect answers is given; obvious mistakes can be put right by suitably amending the answers, but a residue of undetected errors may remain, and some caution in interpreting the census results is therefore desirable.

6.19 Problems of inference from fertility census data

There are several reasons why it is difficult to draw conclusions solely from the results of a single fertility census. Fertility is a function of age or marriage duration and also varies from time to time. If women of given ages or marriage durations are found to have certain family sizes at the census, it is impossible to separate the biological and other effects of age or duration from the secular effects of the calendar years during which the age or duration has grown to its census value. Thus the average marriage partnership that had lasted ten years at a census taken during (say) 1951 might well have produced a family size different from that of the average ten-year-old marriage enumerated at a census taken in 1946, because the influence of economic and political factors during 1936—46 was not the same as during 1941—51. Similarly, marriages that had lasted eight years in 1951 might not have produced the same average number of children by 1953, when they had lasted 10 years. It would thus not be a valid procedure to compare the average family sizes of couples married for 0, 1, 2, 3 . . . years at a census and argue that the differences between successive durations measured the normal rate of family building. The consequence of this is that average completed family size could not be correctly deduced from the statistics of incomplete families. (The problem would, however, be eased if married couples had had to state the dates of birth of each of their children, for then the fertility of (say) the fifth year of marriage could be studied for different cohorts in varying economic and political circumstances.)

The difficulties associated with marriages of incomplete fertility may be avoided by dealing only with the statistics of children in relation to women aged over 45 or 50 — those whose fertility may be said to have been completed. This kind of study brings its own problems, however, as follows:

(1) if living children only are considered, average family size has been affected by mortality in the past, and perhaps also by lack of knowledge where parents have been living apart from their children; if children ever-born are inquired into, errors of memory may influence the data;

(2) data are obtained only in respect of surviving parents; the elimination of those who have died (and perhaps also those who have been divorced) is likely to create a select class by removing a group of couples with a lower than average fertility.

Further analytical troubles arise from the fact that remarriage may have occurred after a first marriage was ended by death or divorce. To pay attention only to unbroken marriages would ignore the probably different experience of the remarried.

Where the census results are used in conjunction with birth registration data, the demographer should be on his guard against differences of classification and definition between the two sets of statistics. For instance, children of previous marriages might be included in the one but not in the other.

6.20   Illustrative fertility census data

Table 6.7 shows the average numbers of children born to British women as disclosed by the 'Family Census' conducted by the Royal Commission on Population in 1946. The principal features of the table are the steady decline in family size as time has passed and the relative constancy of the indexes of

101

Table 6.7. *Average number of children according to age of mother at marriage, Great Britain, 1890—1925*

(Marriages unbroken by death or divorce)

Year of marriage	Age of woman at marriage					
	Under 20	20—24	25—29	30—34	35—39	40—44
	Average number of children per married woman					
1890—9	5·86	4·43	3·24	2·51	1·59	0·89
1900—9	5·20	3·84	2·73	2·07	1·27	0·69
1910	4·89	3·47	2·54	1·95	1·13	0·42
1915	4·02	2·97	2·10	1·70	0·95	0·48
1920	3·94	2·89	2·09	1·63	0·97	0·42
1925	3·44	2·56	1·75	1·39	0·83	0·38
	Indexes of the above based on 100 for age 20—24 at marriage					
1890—9	132	100	73	57	36	20
1900—9	135	100	71	54	33	18
1910	141	100	73	56	33	12
1915	135	100	71	57	32	16
1920	136	100	72	56	34	15
1925	134	100	68	54	32	15

fertility according to age at marriage over the period. When large families were usual, family size was necessarily a function of age at marriage, because only in marriages contracted early in life was there enough time for women to have many children, while late marriages had not the opportunity of producing more than one or two. In later times, when families of only two or three children have on average been born, it would appear to have been possible for women marrying at (say) age 32 to have as many children as those marrying at 22; yet the shape of the curve of fertility according to marriage age has persisted unchanged. Even though a study of the most recent experience perhaps gives some evidence of a loosening of the effect of age at marriage on family size, as the Royal Commisssion expected, it is remarkable how little loosening there has actually been.

It may be noted that the decline in the index numbers with advancing marriage age is rendered much less rapid if attention is restricted to fertile marriages, i.e. to women who have borne at least one child. Further, the indexes in this form have tended to rise somewhat at the older ages with the passage of time.

6.21 The study of socio-economic and similar influences on fertility

Some reference was made in § 6.5 to studies of personal attitudes towards the family. Much work on this subject has been carried out in the USA. The sample drawn in the town of Indianapolis in 1941 (see §4.11) provided data from which variations in family size have been examined in relation to socio-economic status (which was found to be the most important influence), family background, feeling towards the home, personality characteristics, and psychological balance between the spouses. A feature of the inquiry was the subdivision of fertility into four categories, namely: children planned as to number and spacing, children planned in number only, quasi-planned families and excess fertility. The weaknesses of the investigation were its restriction to a narrow class and the smallness of the data, often too scanty to allow definite conclusions to be drawn.

Studies in British sample data made by Dr J. Berent have shown that there is a small positive correlation between the family sizes of successive generations, and that fertility is affected by 'social mobility' (see §3.23).

Perhaps the most prominent of all sociological inquiries into fertility have been concerned with inter-class differences. One of the earliest investigations was that made by Heron in respect of the London boroughs in 1851 and in 1901, in which a marked correlation was discovered between fertility and various indexes of social status such as the proportion of professional men, of domestic servants or of general labourers in a borough. This indirect form of approach was superseded by a direct investigation of social classes when suitable census data became available.

According to the Indianapolis investigation, socio-economic status is strongly correlated with fertility, probably because of the underlying attitudes and psychological characteristics of the various classes.

British official demographic reports have provided illustrations of no less than 4 different methods of collecting and presenting differential fertility data; first, by special inquiries from married women as to their families, past and present; secondly, from the particulars of parents and young children who happen to have been enumerated on the same census schedule – this requires no special questions to be asked and is thus a method that can be used at any time; thirdly, by a comparison of the census data with the registration information collected in the census year; and finally from registration data alone. In the fourth process, as there is no suitable 'exposed to risk', it is possible only to arrange the occupations and classes according to ranking order, and no measure of the numerical extent of differences between classes can be obtained.

The method of analysis must depend very much on the form of the data available for study. Some illustrative statistics are given below.

6.22 Differential fertility in Britain

Comparison of the fertility of social classes and regions may be made in a number of ways. One of these is the outcome of special inquiries from married women as to their families. The available figures (which are approximate for

103

the regions) are shown in table 6.8 for 1911 and 1951. The indexes shown relate to fertility per married woman, standardized for age, the index figure for the whole country being 100. They do not suggest that regional and social class differences have either increased or decreased very markedly, but it must be borne in mind that the social class groupings have greatly changed during the forty-year period.

A second method of assessing differential fertility involves the use of ordinary census schedules without special additional questions. Data are available for 1921 and 1931, and also from the results of the 1 per cent sample inquiry in 1951. The 1921 figures were given for men only, but the 1931 and 1951 data relate to married women and are compared for social classes and regions in table 6.9; the figures are standardized and set out in the same manner as in table 6.8. The 1931 figures relate to mothers and children enumerated on the same schedule, whereas the 1951 particulars relate to all children born during the year preceding the census data.

A third method of comparison (the use of census and registration data together) gives indexes of fertility rates by social classes in 1911, 1921, and 1931. Results are shown in table 6.10. The distribution of the population

Table 6.8. *Indexes of social class and regional differences in fertility within marriage, England and Wales, 1911 and 1951*

Social class	1911 (%)	1951 (%)
I	76	91
II	89	88
III	99	96
IV	102	111
V	113	122
VI–VIII	114	—
Whole country*	100	100
North of England	101	104
Midlands	100	102
South (including London)	95	96
Wales	110	104
London	97	93 (South-East)
County boroughs	100	97 (Conurbations)
Urban districts	99	99
Rural districts	104	107

* The 'whole country' means England and Wales in 1911 and for the regions in 1951, but Great Britain for social classes and density groups in 1951.

Table 6.9. *Further indexes of social class and regional differences in fertility within marriage, England and Wales, 1931 and 1951*

Social class	1931 (%)	1951 (%)
I	79	90
II	84	93
III	94	96
IV	108	110
V	124	123
Whole country	100	100
Urban areas (excluding London)	100	100
Rural districts	107	109
North	102	106
Midlands	102	104
East	104	94
South-West	98	102
Wales	106	106

Table 6.10. *Still further indexes of differential fertility, England and Wales, 1911, 1921 and 1931*

Social class	1911 (%)	1921 (%)	1931 (%)
I	73	70	75
II	81	74	68
III	94	100	99
IV	98*	115	100
V	131	126	127
Whole country	100	100	100

* Excludes miners, agricultural labourers and textile workers.

into classes changed materially between 1911 and 1921 but less between 1921 and 1931.

Summing up the results of the comparisons by the second and third methods, there is little real evidence of a change in differential fertility since 1911, except perhaps for a slight contraction in social class difference since 1931. The lack of marked developments is confirmed by the results of the Family Census of 1946.

6.23   1961 Census fertility data — methodological problems

The socio-economic groups into which the Registrar General for England and Wales subdivided the 1961 Census fertility data were nineteen in number, and they did not correspond exactly with the fourteen categories of 1951. Figures for the five social classes were not published. Some fertility index figures of interest are as follows. They relate to married women aged under 45, and are standardized for age and duration:

Professional workers — self employed	104
Professional workers — employed	89
Employers and managers — large units	88
Employers and managers — small units	90
Workers on own account (non-professional)	94
General average	100

They suggest that there has been at least a continuation, and perhaps an intensification, of the feature found in 1951. In order to investigate the trend more closely, the available data can be examined in two ways:

(1) aggregate the socio-economic classes into groups that are as nearly as possible comparable between the censuses of 1951 and 1961 and then set out the results side by side;

(2) use the 1961 Census data alone, thus removing any uncertainty about occupational classification, and compare the experience of couples married at different times — omitting those whose marriage took place so recently that it is not yet possible to see how their family-building is likely to go.

The second of these methods eliminates one disadvantage but introduces others: couples married in 1936 had been together for 25 years in 1961 but couples married in 1946 had had only 15 years of married life, so the degree of completeness of their family-building will therefore not be quite the same. Moreover, the social class composition of the population varies with attained age, with the result that the extent of segregation into economic groups will not be quite the same for younger couples as for older ones.

There is another problem, which arises under either method. The average age at marriage has become younger over the years, and the pace at which this has happened has varied from one socio-economic group to another. Such variation can be eliminated by processes of standardization; but it may be argued that those groups for which the marriage age has fallen the most are just those groups who wed younger in order to have larger families. If this is so, this propensity would be concealed by the standardization process. Probably, neither the use nor the absence of standardization leads to a perfect answer.

6.24   The fertility picture in 1961

As it happens, the general picture presented by comparisons made by methods (1) and (2) in § 6.23 is reasonably consistent, whether marriage-standardization is used or not. Thus, couples who had been married for only

15—19 years in 1961 had, in the main, a larger average family size than those who had been married for 25—29 years in 1961. This increase was evidently associated with the more recent period in which their family-building took place. The highest rises in number of children were found for self-employed professional workers (about 17 per cent up on both the standardized and unstandardized bases) and employed professional workers (up about 13 per cent on the unstandardized and 7 per cent on the standardized bases) and the lowest applied to manual workers. There was in fact virtually no change for manuals on the standardized basis and a slight fall on the unstandardized basis.

Some of the results of using method (1) are as follows:

	Percentage increase in family size between 1951 and 1961	
	Unstandardized	Standardized
Professional, administrative and managerial workers	+20	+7
Unskilled manual workers	+13	+1

Here, the left-hand column represents an unstandardized approach, and the right-hand column represents a standardized approach, in regard to age at marriage.

The 1961 Census Fertility Tables contain some interesting information concerning the relationship of family size with ages at which education ceased. The picture these data present is one of relatively high fertility for those with a modest degree of education; declining family size as the educational level increases; but then an increase in relative fertility when the most highly-educated groups are reached.

Recent British census data confirm that there is little difference between the classes in the ultimate proportion marrying. As the higher-numbered social classes, such as IV and V, tend to marry earlier than the lower-numbered classes, the length of the generation will be shorter for them. Nevertheless, on the whole, differential marriage probably operates slightly in favour of the élite and so reduces the spread of differential fertility within marriage: but the effect is relatively unimportant, and so differential marriage does little to modify differential fertility.

SELECT BIBLIOGRAPHY

Variables for Comparative Fertility Studies. A Working Paper prepared by a committee of the International Union for the Scientific Study of Population (1967).

Kiser, C. V. and Whelpton, P. K. 'Social and Psychological Factors affecting Fertility', *Population Studies*, **7** (1953), **95**.

Campbell, A. A. 'Concepts and Techniques used in Fertility Surveys', in *Emerging Techniques in Population Research* (Milbank Memorial Fund, 1963).

Blake, J. 'Are Babies Consumer Durables?', *Population Studies*, **22** (1968), 5.

Tanner, J. M. 'The Trend towards Earlier Physical Maturation', in *Biological Aspects of Social Problems* (Eugenics Society, London, 1965).

Matras, J. *Populations and Societies* (Prentice-Hall, New York, 1973).

Pressat, R. *Demographic Analysis* (Arnold, London, 1972).

7 Mortality characteristics

7.1 Introduction

Tabulations of deaths and death rates in demographic publications may be planned for the purpose of providing one or other of the following:

(1) an analysis of mortality by various characteristics of the living — age and sex, for instance — and of its changes from time to time in these respects;

(2) a subdivision of the data by 'cause of death', as certified by a doctor, and a study of the changes from time to time in the distribution of deaths according to cause;

(3) a combination of (1) and (2) — as in occupational mortality investigations.

This chapter will follow a similar tripartite form. The next twelve sections discuss the effects on mortality of such influences as age, year of birth, lapse of time since a significant event, marital status and geographical region. Here, in general, different medical 'causes' of death will not be considered separately. In a further seven sections, however, attention will be directed to the various main causes of death and their incidence. Finally, occupational and social-class differences in death rates will be illustrated. The data on which the observations must be based are necessarily those for countries, and periods, for which reliable information is available.

The demographer's attitude towards the analysis of mortality is somewhat different from his approach to fertility statistics; this is because the characteristics of the two are different. Mortality is almost entirely involuntary and therefore is little influenced by the changes attributable to human volition to which fertility is subject. When wars and pandemics are excluded, mortality experience may follow, in the long term, a reasonably well-defined trend, less sensitive than fertility to short-term variations of a kind that are particularly difficult to predict. This is not to say, however, that mortality is altogether free from temporary fluctuations, or longer-term deviations; oscillations will undoubtedly occur — for instance because of weather or climatic developments, and changes in economic and political circumstances; and the progress of medical science, which could well affect the health picture radically within the space of a few years, may cause a re-orientation of the trend lines.

109

The study of mortality by the demographer is also different from the actuary's treatment of the subject in connection with the administration of financial institutions providing monetary payments dependent on human life and death. The demographer's objectives are to identify and measure all the influences that underlie observed changes. The actuary is interested mainly in the experience of the members or policy-holders of the institution with which he is concerned, or other lives on which the payments depend, and perhaps also in that of similar groups of people (because their data are more plentiful and can be used as an indicator). For both the actuary and the demographer, for many purposes mortality is but one of a number of important factors bearing upon his work, and the degree of importance attaching to mortality will vary widely from one purpose to another.

7.2 Foetal and infant mortality

Although of little interest from an insurance point of view, foetal and infant mortality have a considerable significance in demography. The level of the death rate in early life has been described as a crucial test of the health services and social progress of a country, for whereas at older ages each individual person is to some extent responsible for his own survival, the young child's life is entirely dependent on the care of others.

Because of the difficulties in measuring important segments of reproductive wastage, especially foetal deaths, no fully adequate statistical expression of its magnitude is available in any country, but it would appear that, in the world as a whole, at least one-third of each new generation is lost before or shortly after the time of birth.

The rapidity with which the chance of dying diminishes as the duration of time since birth increases is attributable, at least in part, to the fact that some infants are born with genetic defects that give them little chance of survival. It is important from the point of view of medical progress to analyse infant deaths into those due to external factors, such as accidents and infectious diseases, and those caused by inborn defects. The normal method of separation is either to go through the list of certified causes of death and from general knowledge allocate them to one group or the other or, more simply, to subdivide deaths into those occurring before and after the completion of four weeks of life. Mathematical methods have also been proposed, but the efforts now being made to improve the quality of infant death certification are perhaps more likely to lead to a fuller understanding of mortality very early in life.

Although the infant mortality rate is often calculated by dividing the number of deaths at ages under one year in a given period by the number of births in the same period, this is only a rough-and-ready method which may become appreciably inaccurate at times when the numbers of births are fluctuating rapidly. The inaccuracy arises from the fact that the true 'ex-
110

posed to risk' of mortality in a given year includes some of the births in the previous year and only part of the births in the given year. Reference to more accurate methods of calculating q_0 is made in chapter 15 below.

The demarcation line between still-births and infant deaths varies from country to country; thus the numerator as well as the denominator of the death rate in the first year of life needs careful consideration. Both should, of course, relate to occurrences in the same area; as many births take place in hospital at some distance from the mother's home, the adjustments required in order to satisfy this criterion may be quite material when the experience of local areas is under consideration. The infant mortality rate could become inaccurate also if the completeness of vital registration in a given country differed as between births and deaths early in life.

Infant mortality varies according to most of the environmental and other influences that will be mentioned in this chapter. Indeed it is to some extent correlated with general population mortality in childhood and at older ages (see the index figures in table 7.1 below). It is also associated with a number of additional factors such as the size of the family, the intelligence of the mother and the legitimacy of the child. Some demographers draw a distinction between 'endogenous' infant mortality — arising from the baby's constitution, from congenital malformations and from the circumstances of its delivery — and 'exogenous' infant mortality, attributed to outside surroundings after birth.

Studies in the USA show that infant mortality varies greatly by weight at birth and by the number of days elapsed since birth, and to a lesser extent by sex, plurality and colour and by the education, occupation and area of residence of the parents. Here are some specimen figures for the chance of death, they relate to the year 1960:

	First week	Rest of first month	Rest of first year
Birth weight			
1000 grams or less	0·621	0·176	0·074
2001–2500 grams	0·019	0·005	0·018
4000 grams or over	0·002	0·001	0·004
Plurality			
Single	0·006	0·002	0·007
Multiple	0·034	0·007	0·017
Colour			
White	0·006	0·002	0·005
Non-white	0·009	0·004	0·015

7.3 Permanent and temporary influences on mortality

Among the characteristics of the living that may influence mortality, three broad groups may be distinguished as an aid to thought, namely those characteristics that represent (*a*) innate differences which are present

111

throughout life; (*b*) the effects of particular events in life, which may vary in importance according to the duration of time elapsed since the event; and (*c*) temporary or semi-permanent differences of environment and conditions of life.

It is difficult in practice, however, to disentangle the effects on mortality of these various groups of characteristics. Where two populations have experienced differing death rates it is nearly always possible to catalogue long lists of factors all of which may have contributed in some degree to the differences, and attempts to distinguish the effects of each separate factor involve dangers of misinterpretation.

7.4 Innate characteristics affecting mortality

The most sharply defined innate qualities are sex and race. Some typical variations according to these qualities may be seen from the following statement of mortality rates at certain ages in the whole of the USA in 1950:

Age-group	White males	White females	Non-white males	Non-white females
Under 1	0·0340	0·0257	0·0599	0·0475
15—24	0·0015	0·0007	0·0029	0·0022
65—74	0·0486	0·0324	0·0525	0·0398

Over a wide range of ages, the rates for women are consistently below those for men and the rates for non-whites are consistently above those for whites. It must be recognized, however, that the influence on mortality of the two elements, race and sex, as shown in the statement, is not unmixed with other influences that are not innate. The conditions of life of women differ from those of men; non-whites have a lower average standard of living than whites and the geographical distributions of the races are not the same. Thus the rates are to some extent affected by environmental factors such as occupation, housing conditions and climate. Further, the degree to which deaths are not registered and the propensity towards misstatement of age in the official returns probably vary from group to group.

A study of the mortality of religious brothers and sisters whose lives and surroundings are very similar has suggested, however, that intrinsically male mortality is heavier than female.

Among the innate characteristics that affect mortality may be reckoned physique and other genetic endowments. The most important of these are congenital defects and abnormalities, some of which result in early death. The evidence of a more general inheritance of longevity is uncertain. Actuarial and other studies of the effects of health impairments on death rates are primarily concerned with the consequences of a recent history of specified illness, and are thus by no means directed to the study of innate characteristics as such.

7.5   The influence of age

Age is probably the most important single characteristic affecting death rates. It is a special category and can only rarely be ignored in mortality investigations. As age is the length of time elapsed since birth, it could perhaps be regarded in the same light as the durational factors to which reference is made in the next section, but mortality variations by age cannot be due entirely to the passage of time, and to the development and decay of the body, because people pursue their lives in different surroundings, and the environment undoubtedly plays a part. Some specimen mortality rates for the female sex in different parts of the world are shown in table 7.1. The index figures are included in order to illustrate variations in the age-pattern; at ages under 45 their variations are less marked than those in the death rates themselves; at higher ages the rates vary less than the indexes, showing that mortality differs from country to country less in old age than it does earlier in life.

7.6   Selective events having a durational effect on mortality

The events that have an influence on mortality —apart from crimes, accidents and wars which directly cause death — are those that tend to be associated with the state of health or environment of the affected individuals. When the mortality of a group of such persons in the years following the event differs from the mortality of an otherwise similar group drawn from the whole population, the event is said to have acted in a 'selective' way. The difference due to selection may largely disappear after a short period or it may persist to a varying extent throughout life. In the world of life assurance, persons accepted for ordinary policies at normal rates of premium are usually selected, because those whose health is impaired are not admitted on those terms; the mortality of assured lives will thus be below the general average, at least to start with, but the difference may well tend to become small after a few years. In a similar sense, the mortality of annuitants has tended to be light because in general only those persons who have realized themselves to be healthy have taken out contracts. They selected themselves for this purpose, and because such annuitants also generally belonged to particular social classes the effect of selection has tended to be more permanent. In the opposite direction, disabled persons or ill-health pensioners form a select group with above-average mortality rates.

Selective events in demography include entry into an occupation, retirement, migration, enrolment for military service and marriage. All these, except the second, are more likely to occur to healthy persons than unhealthy

113

Table 7.1. Mortality rates of females in various countries in specimen years

(Note: the figures in italics show the rates expressed as percentages of the rate for the first year of life.)

Age group	Barbados (1965)		Mauritius (1965)		Mexico (1965)		Thailand (1960)		Belgium (1964)		Bulgaria (1965)		England and Wales (1965)		Scotland (1965)	
Under 1	0·0402	*100*	0·0591	*100*	0·0608	*100*	0·0626	*100*	0·0225	*100*	0·0280	*100*	0·0166	*100*	0·0208	*100*
1–4	0·0024	*6*	0·0072	*12*	0·0098	*16*	0·0100	*16*	0·0008	*4*	0·0014	*5*	0·0008	*5*	0·0008	*4*
10–14	0·0001	*—*	0·0007	*1*	0·0011	*2*	0·0017	*3*	0·0002	*1*	0·0003	*1*	0·0003	*2*	0·0003	*1*
20–24	0·0006	*1*	0·0025	*4*	0·0025	*4*	0·0029	*5*	0·0006	*3*	0·0005	*2*	0·0005	*3*	0·0005	*2*
30–34	0·0013	*3*	0·0031	*5*	0·0035	*6*	0·0040	*6*	0·0009	*4*	0·0010	*4*	0·0008	*5*	0·0010	*5*
40–44	0·0042	*10*	0·0039	*7*	0·0050	*8*	0·0063	*10*	0·0021	*9*	0·0019	*7*	0·0022	*13*	0·0027	*13*
50–54	0·0049	*12*	0·0089	*15*	0·0087	*14*	0·0085	*13*	0·0052	*23*	0·0049	*18*	0·0052	*31*	0·0062	*30*
60–64	0·0191	*47*	0·0217	*37*	0·0213	*35*	0·0160	*26*	0·0125	*56*	0·0130	*46*	0·0129	*78*	0·0159	*77*
70–74	0·0381	*95*	0·0426	*72*	0·0434	*71*	0·0352	*56*	0·0386	*172*	0·0425	*152*	0·0368	*222*	0·0442	*213*
80–84	*		0·1277	*216*	*		0·0778	*124*	0·1130	*502*	0·1201	*429*	0·1071	*645*	0·1157	*556*

* Not available.

ones; in the case of retirement the reverse is true. All of them may also involve a change of environment, so that selective and environmental effects will probably be acting in conjunction. Illustrations of mortality variations according to some of these characteristics will be found later in this chapter.

7.7 Environmental influences

Among the characteristics with which differences in mortality are generally considered to be associated and which may be termed 'environmental' are: climate; weather; standard of living (implying social status, income, nutrition-level and the like); housing conditions; population density; industrial development; sanitation; medical facilities; occupation; habits of life, including smoking, drug-taking and consumption of alcohol, the frequency of travel by air and other means of transport and the pursuit of hazardous sports such as motor racing; and political conditions, especially war. Marital status may also be considered an environmental influence, at least for women.

Environmental influences do not continue unchanged throughout life, and it should always be considered how long they have operated. If, for instance, a man spent most of his working life as a coal-miner but, after being disabled, became a clerk and then died, it would probably be inadvisable to attempt to associate his death only with the occupation he was pursuing at the time of his death.

The only characteristics whose influence on mortality is worth measuring demographically are those that affect substantial proportions of the population and for which trustworthy data are available. Much of the remainder of this chapter will be occupied with illustrations of the analysis of the influence of such environmental characteristics on mortality, especially with occupational effects. Before these illustrations are given, however, it is desirable to consider the following subjects, which are of general importance throughout:

(1) long-term developments in death rates in the course of time, i.e., 'secular' changes;

(2) the effects associated with being born, or with attaining an important stage in life, in a given period, i.e., generation influences;

(3) the medical certification of deaths according to cause;

(4) the attempted separation of the influences of individual factors affecting mortality where several factors have operated together concurrently.

Another important question is the choice of indexes in order conveniently to sum up the mortality rates that have been analysed by age and other characteristics. In this chapter little reference will be made to indexes. Their special features are discussed in chapter 16.

115

7.8 Secular changes in mortality

In almost every country, the experience since death rates first became measurable has been that mortality has fallen, perhaps after an early period during which death rates were fairly constant, apart from fluctuations. Some figures are given in table 7.2. Attention has to be paid to variations as the years go by, both in the total number of deaths and in the deaths from specific causes. The study of trends is of interest in itself and is also a necessary preliminary to the assessment of future mortality in a manner suitable for the purpose of population projections. (Comparison of one country with another in the same year is less useful in this table, because of the severe limitations of crude death rates where age-distributions differ widely.)

Whilst many changes in environment — such as improvements in sanitation and advances in medical technique — are gradual in their effect, the application of scientific discoveries can sometimes cause a sudden change. An example of this is the very rapid decline in mortality after the Second World War in malarial countries, largely attributable to the use of new and highly successful measures against mosquitoes. This fall, from this cause, cannot be repeated. Either the lower mortality will continue unchanged, or death rates could even rise as a result of the evolution of a new strain of mosquito resistant to chemical agents. A further fall might then ensue if a new anti-malarial agent were discovered.

It is also possible that, in areas where natural resources are poorly developed, rapid increases in population resulting from reductions in death rates coupled with undiminished high fertility could lead to lower standards of nutrition and thus to an environment unfavourable to low mortality. The

Table 7.2. *Crude death rates in various countries, 1920—70*

(Total number of deaths at all ages divided by total population numbers in thousands.)

Period of calendar years	Chile	Egypt	Japan	Malaya	Italy	Norway	Yugo-slavia	England and Wales	Scotland
1920—4	30·2	25·7	23·0	*	17·5	11·8	17·1	12·2	14·0
1925—9	25·5	26·5	19·8	*	16·6	11·1	20·0	12·2	13·7
1930—4	23·9	27·1	18·1	21·6	14·1	10·4	18·4	12·0	13·2
1946	16·6	25·0	17·6	20·0	12·1	9·4	*	12·0	13·0
1947	16·1	21·3	14·6	19·4	11·5	9·5	12·8	12·3	13·2
1948	16·7	20·4	12·0	16·3	10·7	8·9	13·5	10·8	11·8
1949	17·3	20·6	11·6	14·2	10·5	9·0	13·5	11·6	12·3
1961	11·6	15·8	7·4	9·2	9·4	9·2	9·0	11·9	12·3
1962	11·8	17·9	7·5	9·4	10·1	9·4	9·9	11·9	12·2
1963	12·0	15·4	7·0	9·0	10·2	10·1	8·9	12·2	12·6
1964	11·2	*	6·9	8·1	9·6	9·5	9·4	11·3	11·7
1970	9·4	15·0	6·9	10·8†	9·7	10·0	8·9	11·7	12·2

* Not available.

† Estimated by the UN Population Division; it suggests that the figures for some earlier years may be too low.

demographer should be fully aware of possibilities such as this when studying improving trends and the likelihood of their continuation in future.

7.9 Generation influences

Although to study mortality by generations involves the insuperable difficulty that the conditions of life of each generation have steadily changed as it has grown older, there remains the possibility that generation influences on mortality are significant, and theories of mortality along these lines have been propounded. The importance of the early, formative years of life has been stressed as having effects which, if not as profound as innate differences, may at least be more potent than those of influences felt later in life. Such theories have not been fully established; it appears that there may be some 'wearing off' of generation effects with advancing age, and the most appropriate attitude towards them is a lively interest coupled with suspended judgment. There are, however, occasions when a generation analysis can be very revealing, as in the following example.

Table 7.3 shows the male death rates from tuberculosis at certain ages in Massachusetts in various years; in the left-hand part of the table they are arranged according to year of occurrence, and in the right-hand part they are arranged according to year of birth. If the secular trend is examined from the left-hand set of figures, it is evident that the rate of diminution in tuberculosis mortality has been more rapid at ages 15 and 25 than at later ages, with the result that the shape of the curve of death rates measured against age has changed from one with a peak at age 25 followed by a plateau to one with steadily increasing rates. The figures on the right-hand side show, however, that three generations have all experienced the same general shape of tuberculosis mortality curve — one with a peak at age 25 followed by a steady decline.

Table 7.3. *Tuberculosis mortality rates (per thousand) of men in Massachusetts, USA, arranged according to year of occurrence and year of birth*

(Approximate figures.)

Central age	Mortality in year			Mortality of generation born in year		
	1880	1910	1940	1870	1890	1910
15	1·3	0·6	0·1	1·3	0·9	0·5
25	4·4	2·2	0·3	3·7	2·1	0·8
35	3·8	2·6	0·6	3·0	1·6	0·5
45	3·7	2·6	0·9	2·6	1·2	*
55	3·7	2·6	0·9	1·8	0·9	*
65	4·9	2·5	1·0	0·9	*	*

* Not available at the time of compilation.

117

The missing values in the right-hand columns of table 7.3 (and in other similar presentations of mortality rates) relate to years yet to come when the table was drawn up; they could then be estimated in a variety of ways from the known experience of the past and present. The study of secular trends involves the assessment of future mortality rates at age x on the basis of only one kind of factor — the mortality rates at age x in the past. Generation approaches involve two factors, relating respectively to age and period of time.

7.10 Theories of general mortality involving mathematical formulae

Formulae which connect the mortality rate at age x with the rate at age y at the same moment of time will be discussed in § 15.12. Those which are of immediate concern in this section relate to the course of mortality over a period of years and involve secular and generation trends at all ages.

Kermack, McKendrick and McKinlay suggested that the rate of mortality at age x in year N might be regarded as the product of a function of x and a function $N - x$.

Greenwood applied a formula of this type to English death rates from all causes in combination and tested the graduated result against the original data by the χ^2 method. He found, however, that it was not probable that the divergencies between observation and expectation were mere chance fluctuations. Somewhat similar conclusions were reached by Cramér and Wold, who used exponential functions for the progression of mortality rates with both advancing age and advancing time.

Derrick, in a paper to the Institute of Actuaries, drew on logarithmic graph-paper a series of generation mortality curves arranged in the same way as the figures in the rows in the right-hand part of table 7.3; there was one curve for each group, with year of birth as abscissa and rate of mortality for any particular year of birth as ordinate. The available data suggested to him that over a period there had been a broad kind of parallelism between these curves; he considered, therefore, that in the long run the curves for the mortality rates at the older ages would continue to run parallel to those for the younger ages. This provided him with a basis for forecasting mortality.

Derrick's paper was written in 1926. His approach was re-examined 20 years later in the course of the investigations made in connection with the work of the British Royal Commission on Population. By that time it appeared as though parallelism between the mortality curves at the older ages and those at the younger ages was not being fully maintained. The improvement in vitality between one generation and the next tended to diminish towards zero as the age advanced (compare the international differences in table 7.1). New methods of approach to the problem of forecasting mortality were therefore developed, in which an allowance was made for some 'wearing away' of generation effects in old age. It might be supposed that the influence of secular factors on the mortality of the stock increases as the period lengthens during which individuals have been exposed to them. Alternatively, it might be argued that survival in early and middle life, which is largely associated with resistance to accidents and infections, is more amenable to generation influences than longevity in old age, which is more a matter of rate of decay and may to some extent depend on biological inheritance.

More recently, Professor W. Brass has proposed the use of the formula

$$_1Y_x = A + B \cdot {_2}Y_x \tag{7.1}$$

where A and B are constants, subscripts 1 and 2 refer to different generations and

$$Y_x = \tfrac{1}{2}\log_e\left\{\frac{1-l_x}{l_x}\right\}. \tag{7.2}$$

Derrick's 'parallelism' formula may be expressed as

$$_1Z_x = B \cdot {_2}Z_x, \tag{7.3}$$

where

$$Z_x = \log_e(l_x), \tag{7.4}$$

and thus relates time changes in the probability of dying at any age to the proportion still alive at that age (l_x) (see §2.11 above). The equation proposed by Brass is expressed instead in terms of the proportion no longer alive: $(1 - l_x)/l_x$. The new function Y_x has been found useful in bio-assay studies of the responses of animals to drugs, and it is possible to interpret Brass's formula in terms of the concept that death is a response to a 'dosage' of time on a particular scale.

Attempts to represent mortality in mathematical form should be based on theories that do not appear implausible in the light of modern scientific knowledge. The idea of death in small doses is certainly tenable. Professor R. E. Beard has tested a number of alternative mortality models satisfying a similar criterion of reasonableness. For instance, in a demonstration delivered to the Royal Society, he analysed the course of lung cancer death rates in Britain by age and sex over the last fifty years and showed that they could be reasonably represented by the product of three components, one associated with age, one varying with the year of observation and one depending on the year of birth. He suggested that the generation element could well represent the proportion of persons who smoke cigarettes and the secular element the amount smoked per head; on this basis he was able to correlate his factors successfully with measures of the volume of smoking.

119

While these notable contributions do much to develop theories of mortality, there remains scope for further research and experiment in the future.

7.11   Mortality in relation to marital status

Ordinary healthy persons are more likely to be selected as partners in marriage than ailing or abnormal people. At the ages at which marriages take place, therefore, one would expect to find that the population of either sex had become subdivided into two categories with different mortality experiences — the married with lighter rates and the unmarried with heavier rates. That this is so may be seen from table 7.4, which shows that in Scotland bachelors' mortality materially exceeded that of married men at all ages. A similar effect was not observed for women in Scotland in 1930—2, but the figures for England and Wales given in table 7.5 show not only that marriage selection did have a material influence in that country in 1930—2 but also that the extent of the selection had become much more marked by 1950—1. The reason for the increase in selectivity is that marriage rates had risen, as is evidenced by the fall in the proportions of spinsters shown in the table; the additional marriages doubtless occurred among the medically fitter women and left a higher proportion of the unfit among the unmarried.

As married couples grow older, the difference between their mortality and that of men and women of all marital statuses probably becomes smaller.

Table 7.4. *Mortality rates according to marital status, Scotland, 1930—2*

Age	Rate of mortality			
	Unmarried	Married	Widowed	Whole sex
Men				
20	0·00332	0·00250	*	0·00326
30	0·00481	0·00312	0·00725	0·00383
40	0·00955	0·00599	0·01141	0·00676
50	0·01549	0·01036	0·01608	0·01151
60	0·03227	0·02294	0·02976	0·02518
70	0·07574	0·05723	0·06989	0·06295
80	0·15469	0·13834	0·16003	0·15098
Women				
20	0·00271	0·00440	*	0·00293
30	0·00350	0·00414	0·00520	0·00392
40	0·00533	0·00552	0·00594	0·00551
50	0·00932	0·00924	0·01085	0·00945
60	0·01969	0·01995	0·02136	0·02021
70	0·04562	0·04541	0·05261	0·04866
80	0·12156	0·11691	0·12857	0·12582

* Data insufficient to provide a valid result.

Table 7.5. *Ratios of spinsters' mortality to all women's mortality, and corresponding proportions of women unmarried (England and Wales)*

Age-group	Ratio of spinsters' mortality to all women's mortality		Proportion of women unmarried	
	1930—2	1950—1	1931	1951
20—24	0·98	1·17	0·74	0·52
25—29	1·04	1·48	0·41	0·22
30—34	1·09	1·53	0·25	0·14
35—39	1·05	1·51	0·21	0·13
40—44	1·13	1·38	0·18	0·14
45—49	1·12	1·21	0·17	0·15

The end of marriage by the death of one of the partners affects the mode of living of the survivor, whose vitality is temporarily influenced and may even be permanently impaired. The mortality rates of widowed persons shown in table 7.4 are above the average for men and women as a whole.

The married state itself may have various direct effects on mortality, both physical and psychological. This is particularly so for women, who may undergo a change of occupation and are liable to extra risks to health arising from childbearing. Bereaved women, and more particularly bereaved men, suffer poorer health than those still married, and their mortality is higher too, more particularly in the years immediately following the loss of the partner.

7.12   The effects of war

An increase in death rates in wartime may be caused not only directly through enemy attacks, both on persons in the fighting Services and on civilians, but also indirectly by a growth in diseases resulting from worsened conditions of living at home and on the battle field. Needless to say, the extent of additional mortality depends entirely on the nature of the war and on the military and scientific equipment of the countries engaged, and it is wholly impracticable for a demographer to forecast future wars and their effects.

If the population statistics are subdivided between Service men and women on the one hand and civilians on the other, and if in any age-group a material proportion of persons have been called up, there is likely to be an appreciable selective effect in the mortality rates. This is because only the healthiest will have been chosen for the military forces; the civilian section will therefore contain all those of relatively poor physical quality, those who have been invalided out of the Armed Forces, and only relatively few healthy persons. Thus in England and Wales in the war years 1941—5, male mortality

121

among civilians aged 20—24 was 5·0 per thousand, whereas in 1931—5 it had been 3·2 per thousand.

7.13 Regional variations in mortality and the effects of urbanization

If the death rates for the various regions of a country are compared, any differences between them that are found may well have resulted from the influences of a number of factors acting concurrently. There will probably have been environmental forces such as climate and soil; these in turn may have determined the principal local occupations, with their attendant risks, and the geography of the area may also have had a bearing upon the degree of urbanization and consequently upon population density. Innate differences such as those attributable to sex and race may have made their contribution — although it should normally be possible to separate the main classes in this respect with the aid of the available statistics. Selective influences will probably have been at work, such as the migration of retired persons, and of the more well-to-do, from the towns to the country-side.

If regional variations and density differences in mortality have to be studied, it will be desirable to analyse the data as far as possible in every way in order to separate the effects of each of the complex forces at work. It may be that no clear-cut picture will emerge. Thus when Spiegelman compared the experience of the north, south, east and west of the USA in 1939—41, he found that the mortality rates of white persons were the lowest in the country in the north at ages under 45, in the south at ages 45 to 74 and in the west at older ages; the death rates of white persons in cities with a population of 100,000 or more were lighter than those in rural areas at ages under 35 but heavier at ages 45 and over. The data for 1959—61 exhibited similar features.

Estimates based on census data for India show variations in the crude death rate from 16 to 27 per thousand according to State; these variations probably reflect in part differences in the pace of the spread of the health services. Regional disparities of similar size have been observed in many developing countries, Brazil and Ceylon for instance, and also in developed areas. Data for Scotland have shown relatively high mortality in Glasgow — a feature probably associated with high population density, the occupations followed and the social class of the majority of the residents, as well as with the climate. The mortality variations are of different importance at different ages. There is a higher rate than average for young men in the outlying areas of Scotland, attributable perhaps to the selective migration of the fitter people to other areas.

Generally, death rates are higher in the industrial belt than in the more rural regions. A similar feature is revealed by the index figures in table 7.6

122

Table 7.6. *Ratios of actual deaths in density aggregates to expected deaths based on the national experience, England and Wales, 1950–2.*

Density aggregate	Men	Women
Conurbations	1·065	1·026
Urban areas with over 100,000 population	1·065	1·037
Urban areas with 50,000 to 100,000 population	0·989	0·966
Urban areas with less than 50,000 population	0·981	0·998
Rural areas	0·876	0·941

for the ratio of actual to expected deaths at all ages for density aggregates for the whole of England and Wales in the years 1950–2.

7.14 Medical certification of death and classification by cause

Two general requisites for a successful tabulation of deaths according to cause are:

(1) a scientific and consistently-used system of classification; and
(2) a clear distinction between main and subsidiary causes where there has been more than one ailment.

The first attempt to prepare a scientific classification of diseases would appear to have been made towards the end of the seventeenth century, since when other systems have been published from time to time. Acceptance of a standard nomenclature throughout the world was not, however, achieved until the 1890s – many years after the commencement of registration in some countries. At the 1893 meeting of the International Statistical Institute, Bertillon presented, on behalf of a special committee, a draft 'International List of Causes of Death', which was found generally acceptable and was subsequently adopted by the various member countries. This list followed a principle advocated by Farr in arranging diseases as far as possible by their anatomical sites. It is periodically amended in the light of advances in medical science, and conferences have been held at roughly decennial intervals for purposes of revision. The 1948 revision was important in that it provided for the first time a single list for the classification of both morbidity and mortality terms.

It is not easy to determine a really good method of selection of a single cause of death for tabulation in cases of multiple illnesses. A system was, however, internationally recommended in 1948 whereby the main line of causation is separated from merely contributory features, and the time-sequence is given of the series of causes that directly led to the immediate cause. It followed that in use in England and Wales since 1935, illustrated in fig. 7.1. It is, of course, desirable to go further than to select a single main

123

cause; one should also know which causes act together and how frequently they do so.

The medical certificate in the USA has now been brought into line with the pattern recommended by the World Health Organization and thus resembles that in Britain; judging by recent tabulations, however, there are still some differences in certification practice between the two countries.

7.15 Accuracy of reporting of cause of death

Although less liable to inaccuracy over details than other items of registration, medical certificates of death are not always perfect. The physician may

Name of deceased...................................

Date of death as stated to me .... day of .... 19..

Age as stated to me ....

Place of death...................................

Last seen alive by me .... day of .... 19..

* {
1. The certified cause of death takes account of information obtained from post-mortem.
2. Information from post-mortem may be available later.
3. Post-mortem not being held.
}

* {
a. Seen after death by me.
b. Seen after death by another medical practitioner but not by me.
c. Not seen after death by a medical practioner.
}

		These particulars not to be entered in death register.
CAUSE OF DEATH I	I	Approximate interval between onset and death.
Disease or condition directly leading to death†	(a)	....
	due to (or as a consequence of)	
Antecedent causes.	(b)	....
	due to (or as a consequence of)	
Morbid conditions, if any, giving rise to the above cause stating the underlying condition last. }	(c)	....
II	II	
Other significant conditions, contributing to the death, but not related to the disease or condition causing it. }	....	....
	....	....

* Please ring appropriate digit and letter.
† This does not mean the mode of dying, such as heart failure, asphyxia, asthenia, etc.; it means the disease, injury, or complication which caused death.

Fig. 7.1. Extract from medical certificate of cause of death (England and Wales).

occasionally wish to spare the feelings of relatives, where the patient has suffered from a disease of a kind likely to arouse popular superstitions, and where in his lifetime it has been generally supposed that the trouble was of some other kind. It has been argued that the remedy for this kind of mis-statement would lie in making the medical certificate confidential to the registrar; but a recent special study in New York, where confidential certificates are employed, provided little evidence that they improved the accuracy of statistics of cause of death.

The proportion of death certificates reporting causes in vague terms such as 'senility' has tended to decline over the years, and the proportion reporting complex causes has tended to rise. These trends suggest an improvement in accuracy, no doubt attributable largely to favourable developments in methods of diagnosis. But, recently, comparisons of the opinions of doctors on causes of death in selected cases have revealed some big differences between the statements of the hospital doctors who treated the patient and of the pathologists who carried out the post-mortem.

The study of time-trends and of international differences in mortality from separate causes is fraught with many difficulties of interpretation.

7.16 Analysis of mortality by medical cause

Although sufficient material is often provided for extensive investigations of the ways in which different illnesses combine to bring about death, and although such investigations are made from time to time, for ordinary purposes each death is classified according to one cause alone. This fact needs to be remembered as an important limitation in most demographic analyses of cause of death. Furthermore, the doctor is not required to state in what circumstances the deceased person was living, or whether in his view there was an increased risk of death arising from environmental factors such as occupation or housing conditions.

General medical opinion on causes of death is prone to change from time to time, under the influence of fresh discoveries and, of course, there may also be variations between the views of individual doctors on the cases coming to their notice. Despite these several kinds of difficulty, many of the certified causes can be combined for practical purposes into more or less realistically independent aggregates. For instance, industrial accidents, road accidents, infectious diseases, heart impairments and cancer represent largely unrelated cause-groups. The contributions of such cause-groups to the total mortality of either sex at different ages, and their secular changes, are of considerable interest both medically and demographically; they may assist in the consideration of possible future changes in total mortality — see § 9.12 below.

Most deaths can be considered as belonging to one or other of two broad categories, namely:

(1) those that are largely the result of the impact of the environment, such as infectious diseases and accidents; and

(2) those that appear to be mainly the result of the wearing out of the body, such as senility and some diseases of the circulatory system.

These groups cannot be sharply separated or defined, because accidents and diseases help to wear out the body and a worn-out body is more liable to accidents and diseases. Moreover, there is a third, although limited, group of causes arising from inherited defects. Nevertheless, the contrast between (1) and (2) is important because for some years efforts at reducing mortality have been far more effective with the former than with the latter.

7.17   Prevalent causes of death

A few specimen figures of male death rates from certain causes are given in table 7.7. The validity of causal comparisons between different countries must be suspect, especially in regard to such evidence as the low mortality in Ceylon from malignant neoplasms (cancer), which may perhaps be attributable to lack of diagnostic facilities.

It is not easy to give comparable figures for a later year, as the WHO publication from which the statistics are taken now shows the data in a different set of classifications.

Generally speaking, in the developing countries the leading causes of death are gastro-enteritis, influenza and pneumonia, accidents, heart disease and cancer. In the best-developed countries the balance is different — the two causes last-named above taking precedence because of the older average age of the population and because of better control over infectious diseases.

7.18   Time-trends in mortality from specific causes

In 1964 Sir John Charles asked the question, 'who in 1900 would have imagined that the death-rate from typhoid fever in England and Wales which was then 216 per million population would be 16 in 1920 and 4 in 1940?' Another kind of question can equally well be put however: 'Who in the year 1910, when salvarsan had just been discovered by Ehrlich, would have expected that deaths from syphilis, then running at around 2,000 a year in this country, would still be as numerous as 500 a year 40 years later?' Even in 1970 some 200 deaths were recorded in England and Wales (see fig. 7.2). True, some delay in the eradication of the disease should have been thought likely in respect of the time required:

126

Table 7.7. *Male death rates per thousand persons from specified causes in different countries, 1953*

(*Note*: the internationally-agreed classification code is shown in brackets)

Age	Australia	Ceylon	Japan	Portugal	England and Wales
Respiratory tuber-culosis (B 1)					
1—4	0·005	0·032	0·079	0·290	0·007
20—24	0·015	0·155	0·569	0·584	0·071
40—44	0·117	0·527	1·061	1·058	0·229
60—64	0·592	1·195	1·907	1·755	0·805
Malignant neoplasms (B 18)					
1—4	0·116	0·032	0·062	0·035	0·114
20—24	0·124	0·025	0·062	0·062	0·105
40—44	0·491	0·189	0·620	0·435	0·731
60—64	4·669	0·805	5·474	3·304	6·789
Arteriosclerotic and degenerative heart disease (B 26)					
1—4	0·005	0·002	0·036	0·032	0·001
20—24	0·028	0·035	0·083	0·031	0·009
40—44	0·728	0·234	0·302	0·284	0·453
60—64	9·918	1·977	1·975	2·825	7·116
Motor vehicle accidents (BE 47)					
1—4	0·122	0·007	0·106	*	0·112
20—24	0·780	0·048	0·095	*	0·307
40—44	0·310	0·059	0·101	*	0·109
60—64	0·324	0·069	0·133	*	0·186

* Not available.

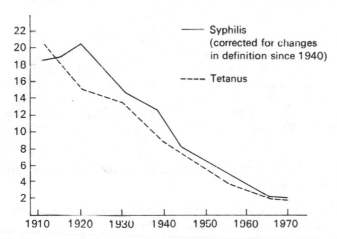

Fig. 7.2. Numbers of deaths per annum from syphilis (in hundreds) and from tetanus (in tens), England and Wales.

(1) for the drug salvarsan to be manufactured in sufficient quantity;

(2) for knowledge of its value to spread to all doctors; and

(3) for cases of consequent circulatory and other impairments to clear themselves by death;

but these could hardly require sixty years to take effect.

It does not appear that analytical studies of the history of the decline in mortality from specific causes such as this are capable of tracing all the reasons for the course of the figures but, in general terms, the literature indicates that salvarsan is not, in fact, always curative (though it prevents the spread of infection); it is indeed now replaced by other chemotherapeutic agents as the treatment of choice. Just as important, many affected persons do not consult their doctors soon enough to obtain the full benefit of the discovery.

Similarly, tetanus mortality is still with us although it is over fifty years since effective anti-toxin became generally available. Indeed, as fig. 7.2 shows, the rate of progress is similar for both diseases.

Social inequalities can cause an appreciable wagging in the tail-end of a process of improvement in the death-rate from a disease. Thus Brewer listed a number of infectious diseases the incidence of which lingers on in the USA from causes which might be thought highly unlikely to operate in such a generally prosperous country: insufficient nutrition accounts for some tuberculosis; poor housing and overcrowding allow rheumatic fever to continue; racial discrimination in the health services is alleged to be responsible for the prevalence of trachoma in some areas.

In general, the development in time of mortality rates from specific causes cannot be traced to specific scientific discoveries or to changes in medical practice. To quote McKeown:

Biologists ... have been interested particularly in the behaviour of individual infectious diseases and a considerable literature has been devoted to discussions of possible reasons for the decline of mortality from tuberculosis, smallpox ... and other infections. The biologist has not had the incentive of the economic historian to explain the behaviour of mortality as a whole ... Medical achievement has not been a theme of medical history in the way that population growth has been a theme of economic history.

7.19 Difficulties in the interpretation of trends in mortality from specific causes

Table 7.8 shows a series of mortality rates over a period of time; the data refer to selected cause-groups in England and Wales over the years 1861–1940. It will be seen from the following observations how important it is to understand the background to the figures before attempting to interpret them.

Table 7.3. Standardized mortality rates from certain causes (using the 1901 Census age-distribution in conjunction with the death rates in each age-group for each cause and period), England and Wales, 1861–1940

(Per million persons.)

1921 International list no.	Cause	1861–70	1871–80	1881–90	1891–1900	1901–10	1911–20	1921–30	1931–40
6	Smallpox	149	228	45	14	13	0	1	0
7	Measles	377	322	392	399	318	308	142	74
8	Scarlet fever	857	625	300	152	109	51	28	13
10	Diphtheria	166	108	148	254	183	152	105	99
11	Influenza	—	—	20	363	208	566	308	191
31–37	Tuberculosis (all forms)	3,263	2,882	2,444	2,021	1,646	1,375	992	695
43–49	Cancer (all forms)	396	484	610	767	867	928	985	974
99	Bronchitis	1,680	2,167	2,059	1,792	1,146	1,029	682	558
100–101	Pneumonia (all forms)	990	937	1,034	1,214	1,254	1,147	936	704
{165–136, 201–203}	Violence (all forms—except war casualties among armed forces)	742	707	626	632	567	555	450	536
	Total of above	8,620	8,460	7,678	7,608	6,311	6,111	4,629	3,844
{90 ((1)–(4))} {88 ((1)–(2))}	Valvular disease, endocarditis	Not available	Not available	255	341	438	582	550	378
143–150	All puerperal causes (per million females)	341	350	318	301	206	157	Not available	Not available

Smallpox　Mortality has declined to zero, thus providing an example of the elimination of a disease in this country. This has occurred during a period when there was compulsory vaccination; also personal cleanliness and general standards of hygiene have improved, and a careful watch for cases of the disease has been maintained at the ports.

Scarlet fever　A large decline in the death rate since 1911, when notifications of the disease were first tabulated, is known to have been accompanied by a marked fall in the degree of fatality. Doubtless standards of medical care and treatment have improved, but there is a suggestion that the reduction in the number of deaths may be partly accounted for by the evolution of a milder strain of the causative organism.

Measles and diphtheria　Mortality for a long time fluctuated, without showing any marked general change, but later there was a sharp fall, especially in the case of measles. This was principally due to a very great reduction in the risk of secondary respiratory infection − partly through improvement in the general health of children and partly on account of the introduction, mainly since 1940, of the sulphonamide drugs. The voluntary immunization of young children was no doubt responsible for the reduction in the diphtheria death rate in the years following 1940 to a much lower level than that shown in the table.

Influenza　The sudden 'appearance' of this disease in 1881−90 and its subsequent 'growth' are almost certainly due not to the importation of the virus but to the late recognition of the ailment as a separate infection. The very high death rate in 1911−20 is accounted for by the prevalence of a particularly virulent variety after the First World War. Other fluctuations may have been influenced by changes in medical fashion in attributing deaths from uncertain or mixed causes to the various respiratory diseases.

Tuberculosis　The disease has declined steadily through such causes as improved standards of living, more effective sanitation in the towns, better nutrition, more ample sanatorium facilities and chemotherapy. Earlier discovery of the presence of the infection consequent upon the introduction in recent years of mass radiography should ensure future improvements in pulmonary cases.

Bronchitis and pneumonia　These ailments have continued to cause large numbers of deaths, although the incidence of bronchitis is recorded as having declined. Since 1940, drugs such as penicillin and the sulphonamides have saved many lives that would otherwise have been lost. Further reference to bronchitis appears in the comments on heart disease below.

Puerperal causes　The fall in the death rate here has followed the decline in the birth rate. Maternal mortality remained for several decades in the region of five deaths due to or associated with child-bearing per thousand confinements, although it has fallen more recently to well below this figure

130

as the use of antibiotics has reduced the risk of sepsis and standards of antenatal and postnatal care have improved.

Violence   There has been an almost continuous decrease in the numbers of violent deaths in spite of the expansion of road and air transport, and increases in mechanization generally. This is due in part to the greater use of safety precautions. There has also been a great saving in life attributable to improved medical care. The 'case fatality rate' (i.e. the number of deaths per accident) cannot, however, be measured, in the absence of proper records of non-fatal accidents.

Cancer   The growing death rate shown in the table cannot be taken as a conclusive indication that the incidence of cancer has increased, because methods of diagnosing the complaint have become more efficient, and cases which would formerly have been attributed to other causes are now properly classified. Nevertheless, there is evidence that malignant growths have become commoner on some sites. In any event, with the ageing of the population, cancer is a complaint of increasing incidence and the need to combat it is steadily growing.

Heart disease   Records of the many varieties of cardiac impairment have been much influenced by changes in medical custom in attributing deaths from several causes, especially amongst old people, to the principal disease, and by alterations in the system of classification. The cause of death most frequently associated with heart disease is bronchitis, which has declined, while heart disease has apparently increased. In 1940 a new international list of causes was put into operation simultaneously with the abandonment of the rules of selection which had hitherto operated in joint causes. This caused a sharp discontinuity in the rates of mortality from heart disease, bronchitis and several other major causes of death.

Crude death rates from specific causes in the USA for the period 1940–62, quoted by Spiegelman, show further substantial reductions in mortality from communicable diseases of childhood, from influenza, pneumonia and tuberculosis, in infant and maternal mortality and in accident mortality. Death rates from cancer and heart disease have continued to rise.

7.20   The use of 'potentials' in the analysis of mortality by cause

While the fundamental unit in the study of population is the human person, and this unit is the basis of most demographic measurements, one exception has arisen in the study of loss of life attributable to certain diseases. It was suggested by Hersch that, as the relative deprivation to the community was not the same for a child death and a septuagenarian death, some recognition should be given to the fact by counting each life lost not as a uniform item but as a unit varying according to the normal expectation of life at the age of death. This expectation was to be considered as an expression of the 'potential' lifetime if death had not supervened.

One disadvantage of this approach is that expectations of life are not independent of the mortality rates which are the object of study; another is that they are liable to considerable change in the course of time. These difficulties may be mitigated by using as a measure of value not the expectation of life but the difference between the age at death and a given higher age.

7.21 Attempts to separate the effects of multiple influences

In the classical methods of the more exact sciences the aim has been to study the effects of variations in a single factor in conditions under which all other factors are unchanged. This process is often possible under laboratory conditions, but in mortality investigations, as in other social analyses, laboratory conditions are usually unattainable, and to isolate any characteristic is nearly always impracticable. It is true that in some cases the pattern of the other characteristics may not differ greatly, and relative isolation of one factor combined with random variation of the other factors may be possible. For example, this is so in respect of changes in the weather. In many important instances, however, several characteristics affecting mortality are closely interlinked, and proper interpretation of statistical differences becomes very difficult.

Messrs Buck and Wicken have used discriminant analysis to study mortality from lung cancer and bronchitis in Northern Ireland. Measurements were made of the characteristics of people who had died from these diseases, and of a control group of people of similar age who had died from non-respiratory causes. A linear function of the measurements on each individual was calculated, and individuals were then assigned to one of two populations (e.g. (I) lung cancer and (II) not lung cancer) according to whether or not their corresponding value of the function was below or above the average value. The function was calculated so as to minimize the number of wrong classifications that occurred. In this way they showed, *inter alia*, that the male lung cancer mortality rates experienced fit closely to a model consisting of a basic rate multiplied by factors representing: (*a*) amount smoked, (*b*) presence or absence of morning cough, and (*c*) whether resident in town or country.

By the use of regression analysis, an attempt was made to find out how much of the large fall in the death rate in Ceylon between 1925 and 1960 was attributable to malaria control (which was found to be responsible in appreciable part), to improvements in health services (which contributed little) and to general economic development (which had an important effect).

7.22 Epidemics and seasonal variations

By the term 'secular' changes in mortality, long-term developments are implied rather than variations from month to month or from year to year. Shorter-term variations often have a cyclical character rather than a steady movement in one direction. In many countries the number of deaths rises or falls from season to season; some ailments are more prevalent in cold weather, and others in hot weather. Epidemics of infectious diseases of all kinds show marked seasonal differences. They also exhibit some tendency to occur at intervals of several years, and the strength of the seasonal effect in a given year may depend on the severity of the epidemic as well as the character of the weather.

Table 7.9 sets out the numbers of deaths in a series of years, in two different countries, from four separate causes of death. The principal features of the table are:

(1) the irregularities in the annual incidence of influenza and measles; it will be noted that the good and bad years are not the same in the two countries;

(2) the upward trend in motor accidents, especially in Belgium, attributable probably to increasing use of the roads;

Table 7.9. *The numbers of deaths, 1954—61, from certain causes in Belgium and Hungary*

(*Note*: the internationally-agreed classification code is shown in brackets.)

	Number of deaths attributed to			
Year	Influenza (B 30)	Measles (B 14)	Motor accidents (BE 47)	Bronchitis (B 32)
Belgium				
1954	409	84	977	1,870
1955	1,208	35	1,007	1,920
1956	432	50	1,160	1,826
1957	1,508	30	1,305	1,767
1958	707	23	1,477	1,572
1959	584	42	1,478	1,339
1960	2,660	16	1,748	1,661
1961	158	36	1,691	1,275
Hungary				
1954	1,662	97	557	227
1955	919	213	494	242
1956	858	198	761	363
1957	2,129	147	720	540
1958	988	258	521	448
1959	2,371	113	690	462
1960	2,025	174	642	537
1961	806	48	693	386

(3) the comparative steadiness of the bronchitis figures, although there are variations — which do not necessarily reflect the ups and downs for influenza;

(4) the different relative numerical importance of the causes; in Belgium, motor accidents and bronchitis are prominent, whereas in Hungary influenza and measles account for a larger proportion of deaths.

The seasonal incidence of deaths in England and Wales in 1945 is shown in table 7.10 for four causes. The figures show a marked seasonal effect in all the columns except that relating to acute endocarditis.

7.23 Mortality and social class

Many of the environmental influences on mortality that were mentioned in § 7.5 are correlated with one another. Persons with higher incomes tend to live in better houses, to reside in healthier and less-crowded areas, to eat choicer foods and to have better medical facilities — although they may also smoke more cigarettes, drink more spirits and do more motoring. Demographers find it convenient to group together the related factors that have an influence on mortality. Attempts have been made to assess the influence of 'housing density', or mean number of persons per room, on mortality by correlating the average level of each over a series of different areas (somewhat similar work has been carried out in connection with fertility). These methods are of limited value, however, and suitable data are not available

Table 7.10. *The numbers of deaths in England and Wales in 1945 by cause and month, for certain selected causes and for all causes in combination*

(*Note*: the internationally-agreed classification code is shown in brackets.)

Month	Number of deaths attributed to				
	Influenza (480–483)	Measles (085)	Accidental drowning (E 929)	Acute endocarditis (430)	All causes
January	666	103	63	71	61,642
February	503	134	82	64	46,851
March	284	200	96	61	44,000
April	123	114	131	62	37,030
May	90	71	124	52	37,786
June	80	41	128	46	33,739
July	49	27	209	49	33,033
August	41	10	160	61	31,978
September	50	4	95	45	31,944
October	124	4	68	40	35,252
November	156	10	50	47	37,312
December	515	4	53	49	48,546

for the estimation of the demographic effects of most of the factors associated with social status.

Table 7.11 shows some indexes of mortality for different socio-economic groups in the United States of America; the data relate to gainfully occupied men aged 20—64. The differences between white and non-white men in these figures do not accurately measure racial disparities in mortality, for within each class the non-whites tend to fill lower-grade positions than do whites.

Some figures relating to England and Wales in 1949—53 are shown in table 7.12. It will be observed that differences in total mortality have been well-defined for both men and their wives and that they have been sharper for children than for their parents. Somewhat similar disparities were ob- served for still-births and for maternal mortality, but it should not be thought that the same is found for every individual cause of death. Table 7.13 shows how steep the social class gradients can be for certain causes — sometimes running in the direction opposite to that for all causes in combina- tion. Social-class differences in mortality arise partly from disparities

Table 7.11. *Indexes of mortality for the USA, 1950*

	Mortality index (All men = 100)	
Socio-economic groups	Whites	Non-whites
Professional people	84	101
Proprietors, managers and technicians	87	151
Clerks, skilled workers	96	120
Agricultural workers	88	167
Semi-skilled workers	100	123
Unskilled workers	165	263

Table 7.12. *Percentage ratios of actual mortality in each social class to the expected mortality by the national standard, England and Wales, 1949—53*

Social class	Men aged 20—65	Married women aged 20—65 (by husband's class)	Legitimate children (by class of father)	All still-births (by class of father)	Maternal mortality (by husband's class)
I	98	96	63	67	90
II	86	88	73	92	90
III	101	101	97	98	93
IV	94	104	115	104	106
V	118	110	138	110	137
All groups	100	100	100	100	100

135

Table 7.13. *Standardized mortality ratios* for certain diseases by social groups in England and Wales, 1950, at ages 20—64 years*
(*Note*: the internationally-agreed classification code is shown in parentheses.)

Cause of death	Social class group				
	I	II	III	IV	V
Men					
Cancer of stomach (151)	57	67	100	114	132
Coronary heart disease (420)	150	110	104	79	89
Diabetes (260)	167	97	97	91	108
Bronchitis (500—02)	33	53	97	103	172
Married women					
Cancer of breast (170)	144	100	106	76	97
Cancer of uterus (cervix) (171)	61	69	98	109	150

* See § 16.7.

in exposure to hazards and partly from a social structure of access to medical treatment and cure. Other associated factors are income, area of residence and standard of education. These seem to have an effect even in countries with a free national health service.

7.24 Analysis of social class differentials in mortality

In order to understand the full significance of data such as those exhibited in §7.23, analysis will often be necessary. A number of different methods have been tried for this purpose, in varying circumstances and with varying success. Thus, in Hungary, a thorough subdivision by causes of death was made, and this was developed into a classification of the social groups according to the number of causes, and extent, for which each of them exhibited the lightest mortality. No very clear conclusion emerged from the result, however. In the USA, class-differences have been measured in association with factors such as education, income and place of birth; this work was carried out actually in respect of illness and disability, but in principle could be applied in relation to mortality. A somewhat similar type of analysis has been made, on an international scale, of the differences between the mortality experiences of richer and poorer nations, in which the correlates included urbanization, literacy, energy consumption; again the outcome was rather inconclusive, but a parallel approach would be possible in relation to social groupings within a country.

Subdivision of the social classes, or study of their circumstances, can be very helpful. Thus, in a survey of mortality in Amsterdam by professions, it was found that the highest rates were experienced by clerks; this was explained on the ground that many men have to fall back on clerical work

136

where they become unfit for heavy manual work or, because of impaired health, cannot obtain admission to the professions.

Unless the social classes have already been broken down into smaller socio-economic groupings, they may well contain too great a miscellany of disparate occupations to have a coherent definition. Analysis into smaller groups should be of value — provided that the groups are not too numerous — but the search for the most meaningful assemblages of occupations is still in progress. Discussions have been going on at an international level in an effort to standardize socio-economic groupings between one country and another, but wide differences in the structure of industry and society are likely to make this very difficult to achieve.

A general study of a large number of social class mortality investigations made at different times has suggested that:

(1) class differences are small when mortality is very high and also when mortality is very low; they thus emerge mainly during the transition from high to low rates; the upper classes are in the lead during this period;

(2) in developed countries, differentials are tending to decline in strength, no doubt because of the general progress towards a low mortality experience.

7.25 Occupational mortality

In the nineteenth century, it seems, the chief recognized purpose of the study of occupational mortality was the assessment of the actual risks involved in particular types of employment. A certain amount of success was achieved in showing up the worst factory and other employment conditions, and their improvement followed in due course. The industrial environment today is far different in the more developed countries from what it was fifty or a hundred years ago, and it is now difficult to attribute most deaths at work to any specific hazard. Where there are risks from materials or processes these are quickly identified and corrected. Consequently, occupational mortality investigations are less necessary than before, although they still play their part in drawing attention to possible fruitful fields for more searching study; they are unlikely to produce data of direct use for the assessment of extra risks in life assurance. Nevertheless, there still exist material differences between the mortality indexes of various fields of employment; for instance, in the USA in 1950 the standardized mortality ratio (see § 16.7) for miners was 180 whereas that for mail carriers was only 69. Part of such differences must be due to the nature of the particular types of work. Another part may be attributable to the surroundings in which jobs are carried on; for instance, most commerce is urban in nature, whilst agriculture is rural; cotton spinning requires a humid atmosphere such as is found in south-west Lancashire. Yet a further reason for occupational disparities in death rates

137

is the social and economic status that is associated with work, as has been demonstrated in the two sections immediately preceding.

Some occupations are traditionally recruited from special classes or races. Others require particular physical features — for instance the slight build of jockeys and the strong muscular powers of general labourers. They therefore exercise selective effects, some of a permanent nature. Much as for the Amsterdam clerks (§ 7.24), the mortality of relatively sedentary employments in the mining industry in Britain is heavier than that of men working at the coal face; investigation reveals that the disparity arises chiefly at ages over 50 and is undoubtedly associated very largely with the fact that many men whose health has deteriorated are found lighter work within the industry. The difficulties in analysis which are created by this state of affairs might be avoided by investigating mortality according to such factors as age at entry to and length of time spent within the occupation, and previous employment history, but the extensive subdivisions of the data that such an approach requires usually prevent the effective carrying out of such an elaborate programme of research.

In spite of these difficulties, occupational mortality investigations have a longer history and a fuller treatment in Britain than in other countries. In 1851 the deaths of males aged over 20 in 300 types of employment were tabulated for each geographical division. Not until 1921, however, were occupations studied quite independently of industries, so providing a more direct assessment of their special risks. The classic instance of the effects of the change is that of cutlery grinders, who in 1911 had been grouped with other workers under the heading 'cutlers and scissors makers'; the group had exhibited a mortality exceeding the general average by 63 per cent. The separation of the occupation of 'cutlery grinder' in 1921 revealed an employment with mortality no less than 240 per cent in excess of the national. The excess was shown to have arisen from diseases such as tuberculosis, bronchitis and pneumonia, which were associated with the inhalation of siliceous dust from the abrasive materials used in grinding, and the need for some effective form of personal protection, or the substitution of a less harmful industrial process, then became evident.

7.26 Special features of occupational mortality data

Inaccuracies in the statistics often limit the value of the results likely to be obtained. In the USA occupational data, although collected in 1910 and 1920, were not published because of suspected errors, and in 1930 tabulations relating to only ten States were released. Fuller statistics have been issued in connection with the 1950 Census, but even these were restricted to ages 20—65 and to carefully-selected occupational groups. It will be appreciated that, if the numerator and denominator of a mortality rate are based on discrepant information, then material errors are possible.

138

Special problems arise in connection with the estimation of occupational exposures to risk of mortality; the use of the census method, which is normally obligatory because the means of tracing personal case-histories are wanting, assumes that the enumerated population is a good approximation to the exposures to risk. It does not matter if individual circumstances change, in regard to the occupation followed, during the period of the investigation so long as all the variations balance one another. Such a balance cannot, however, always be relied upon, especially in times of economic disturbance such as the depression in Britain in 1930–2.

7.27 Illustrative examples in the analysis of occupational mortality

A few specimen index figures for selected occupation groups in Britain, north and south of the Border, are given in table 7.14 which relates to the period 1930–2.

The standard national mortality to which reference is made in the heading of the table, and on which the expected deaths have been calculated, is that of England and Wales in the first column of figures, and that of Scotland in the second. Most of the occupations exhibit the same features in both countries, but entertainment and sport and clerical employments seem to differ appreciably; it is of interest to note that the corresponding figures for single women aged 20–64 in England and Wales were well below 100 in both instances in 1930–2.

A few interesting examples of some more detailed analyses of occupational mortality in England and Wales are given by a comparison for men and married women of the ratios of actual deaths at ages 35–64 in certain

Table 7.14. *Percentage ratios of the actual deaths in selected occupation groups to the expected deaths based on standard national mortality, England and Wales and Scotland, males, 1930–2*

	Ratio of actual to expected deaths (%)	
Occupation group	England and Wales (men aged 20–64)	Scotland (men aged 25–64)
Agricultural workers	73	69
Miners and quarrymen	106	106
Metal workers	101	105
Textile workers	105	95
Building workers	88	96
Workers in commerce	96	98
Workers in entertainment and sport	115	85
Clerks and draughtsmen	90	101
Workers in other and undefined employments	119	118

occupations to the expected deaths based on the national experience, according to cause of death. In some occupations the wife in many cases is involved, as a worker, in the direct effects of the husband's occupation, and in other jobs she is not. In the case of farmers, the suicide rate is high and may be attributed perhaps to financial worries which appear to affect the man more than the wife. Otherwise the man's mortality is the lighter of the two. Innkeepers, on the other hand, experience higher death rates from many causes than do their wives, whose mortality is, however, above that of other married women. Cirrhosis of the liver, which arises from heavy drinking, is most noticeable.

In some of the occupations, data for married women are unfortunately scanty, but the high silicosis risk of masons and stone-cutters, dressers and carvers is evident; this is not, of course, shared by their wives.

SELECT BIBLIOGRAPHY

Kusukawa, A., 'Social and Economic Factors in Mortality in Developing Countries', *Second World Population Conference* (United Nations Organization, New York 1965).

Antonowsky, A. 'Social Class, Life Expectancy and Overall Mortality', *Milbank Memorial Fund Quarterly*, **45** (1967), 31.

Freedman, R., Coombs, L. C. and Friedman, J. 'Social Correlates of Foetal Mortality', *Milbank Memorial Fund Quarterly*, **44** (1966), 327.

Rees, W. D. and Lutkins S. G., 'Mortality of Bereavement', *British Medical Journal*, **4** (1967), 13.

Beard, R. E. 'Some Observations on Stochastic Processes with Particular Reference to Mortality Studies', *Transactions of the Seventeenth International Congress of Actuaries* (London, 1964).

Buck, S. F. and Wicken, A. J. 'Models for Use in Investigating the Risk of Mortality from Lung Cancer and Bronchitis', *Applied Statistics*, **16** (1967), 185.

Spiegelman, M. *Significant Mortality and Morbidity Trends in the United States since 1900* (The American College of Life Underwriters, Pennsylvania, 1964).

Madigan, F. C. 'Are Sex Mortality Differences Biologically Caused?', *Milbank Memorial Fund Quarterly*, **35** (1957), 202.

Brass, W. 'A Generation Method for Projecting Mortality'. Proceedings of the International Seminar on Demography, Edinburgh, May, 1967.

Gray, R. H. 'The Decline of Mortality in Ceylon and the Demographic Effects of Malaria Control', *Population Studies*, **28** (1974), 205.

McKeown, T. 'Medicine and World Population'. In *Public Health and Population Change* (University of Pittsburgh Press, 1965).

Brewer, T. H. 'Disease and Social Class'. In *The Social Responsibility of the Scientist* (Collier — Macmillan, London, 1971).

8 Migration and other socio-economic data

8.1 Introduction

This chapter is mainly concerned with migration; at the end, however, (§8.10) it also makes reference to certain data which are not strictly demographic but which have an important bearing upon population situations and developments.

Brief mention has been made in §3.26 above of migration as a residual factor in demographic movement. This is a complex subject but one which may not assume much importance in practice unless the net migratory streams have a significant influence on population size and distribution. It is complex because both an origin and a destination are involved, because of the difference between permanent and impermanent movements and because changes of geographic location can not only happen much oftener in life than for the biological elements of fertility and mortality but are also much more subject to social, political and economic influences than those elements are. Migration also has a personal aspect as well as an impersonal one. A consequence of these complexities is that many definitions of migration are possible, and the results of analysis depend very much on the definition adopted. An outcome of the volatility of migration is that it is difficult to record; the definition often has to be chosen according to what one can accurately measure. In all the circumstances, the types of occurrence rates and indexes used for measurement are best kept as simple as possible.

As with births, marriages and deaths, migratory movement varies in intensity from year to year and from season to season, and is associated with such factors as race, sex, age, occupation and geographical region. It may also vary in direction because of these factors. In order fully to understand the nature of migration, it is necessary to explore first the reasons why people may have to change their domicile; such reasons will be considered in §8.2. Some of these movements do not lead to any net change in population distribution; others, however, have a permanent effect on a large scale, and the broader social and economic influences are examined in §§8.3 and 8.4 below together with such generalizations that can be made as a result of researches, and the theories to which such generalizations can give rise.

To illustrate the theory, some important migratory streams in demographic history will be discussed in §8.5, and to give examples of statistics in practice

141

some data from various countries will be exhibited in §8.6. Methods of measurement will be the subject of §8.7. Two further sections will then deal with differential migration and with the principal interrelationships between migratory flows and mortality and fertility experience; the second of these is relevant because mortality and fertility may both be changed as a result of population transfers, and also may themselves be an influence on the direction and intensity of migration. Finally, in §8.10, brief reference is made to questions of employment, social security, savings and investment, housing and education.

8.2 Personal reasons for migration

The happening of certain events may oblige or influence people to move to a new place, and movers may have various aims in mind when they go. For instance, when a couple marry they may move to live in a district that is new to at least one of the partners; and on retirement from employment, some people, free from the need to be near their work, may decide to change the area in which they reside. Among the possible personal reasons for moving are:

(1) to help, or be near, relatives;
(2) to find a climate more suitable for health;
(3) to find more congenial neighbours;
(4) to render voluntary military service.

Such motives may lead to a short or a long journey within the native country, according to circumstances, or even to permanent emigration to a new country. Taking the population as a whole, however, the net effect of all such changes would be expected to be small; most of them are related to a person's age, and as this advances so a supply of younger people comes forward to fill the gap. Similarly, the availability of housing must influence the distribution of the population: thus, when a person moves away on retirement, his house may be occupied by a married couple who had previously lived in another district.

A more significant group of reasons for migration, from a demographic point of view, are those connected with work and economic opportunities. Young men may be obliged to travel, in order to find suitable employment; or technological change may enforce transfers, for instance when coal mines are closed and new jobs have to be found; some types of work normally involve frequent changes of location without any change taking place in the industrial classification; for example, bricklayers frequently move from one building site to another; people may seek career advancement, or better wages, by a move to a richer area — such as emigration to the USA from Europe.

142

A third group of motives is political: religious or racial intolerance may bring about large population transfers, often very hastily; or people may be attracted by political conditions elsewhere – for example, by a better social security system, or opportunities for greater freedom of expression.

8.3 General causes of migration

Most significant migratory movements have their origin in economic developments, though the influence of these developments may be exerted through the medium of political, social or even demographic pressure of some kind or another. There are also important factors which operate to suppress migrations. The principal causes and obstacles will be discussed in this and the next section respectively; but by way of introduction it must be stressed that it is possible neither to account precisely for past movements in terms of specific causes nor to make accurate predictions of the future on the basis of past trends.

In primitive societies in the past, and even today in remote or inhospitable areas, man lives in small groups which are permanently nomadic, because of the need to search for food. When man's ingenuity has enabled him to organize a more assured food supply, his numbers have increased and have encouraged a more permanent spread of population to new areas – much of the land area of the world has been occupied in this way, for instance the colonizations of America, Australia and Siberia, often without any need to come into serious conflict with existing inhabitants. The expansion may result in either an enlarged social or political unit or in the formation of independent groups.

In more modern times few untenanted areas are available, and normally migrants must assimilate themselves to the customs of the country to which they go. They may nevertheless be attracted by economic considerations. The main principles that have been found to have some application to population transfers in recent years are listed below:

(1) when the population growth in a region exceeds the economic growth there, it tends to create 'pressure', and emigration to an area of lower pressure may then occur, unless barriers of some sort are erected; correspondingly, a region of low population pressure will tend to attract immigration;

(2) such population movements are probably economically desirable, and on the international scale should benefit world production;

(3) trade fluctuations are associated with unevenness in migratory flows – this is a natural consequence of (1) above;

(4) immigration and emigration may be associated with one another, in the sense that areas with a relatively large intake may also be those with a relatively large outflow;

143

(5) the intensity of migration varies inversely as the distance travelled; this is probably more true of internal migration than of external, and is a correlate of the cost of travel;

(6) migration may be selective as regards sex, age, occupation and skill — the 'brain drain' is a well-known phenomenon in many parts of the world;

(7) immigration of unskilled labour is unfavourable to local unskilled labour but may benefit skilled labour.

The value of these principles for the purpose of prognostication must be regarded as being limited. For one thing, governments often take steps to encourage, or discourage, migration and thus influence the prevailing flow. Secondly, the principles taken as a whole do not account for all the variations in the experience that have been recorded. Many of the changes in speed and direction that have taken place are still unexplained. Finally, the principles are not altogether coherent as a set of rules; there are gaps and overlaps between them. Economic development is to some extent allied with demographic growth, and can lead to significant and permanent net migratory changes. The high state of development of Britain, as compared with that of the West Indies and some other Commonwealth areas, has attracted immigration into Britain. Similarly, workers have gone from Italy into Switzerland, to the economic gain of both these countries: the prosperity of the Swiss economy was thereby supported, while unemployment and under-employment in Italy were reduced, and the Italian balance of payments was helped by the remittances sent home by the workers abroad.

Much of what has been said above can be applied to internal migration within a country. Indeed, there has been a great deal of movement of this kind in recent years in many countries, notably migration into the towns in developing areas (see §12.14 below).

8.4. Obstacles to migration

When man first developed agriculture, he naturally became settled on the land, and ever since then agrarian societies have formed a barrier to migratory movements. At times in European history, men on the move were regarded as vagrants, as such socially undesirable and liable to prosecution. Traditions became established in which a number of factors combined to operate against migration, for instance hostility to strangers, strong community loyalty and social systems in which status and rewards were earned for long residence or service.

The extent and the distance of movement must alike be limited by the availability of communications networks and of transport. They also depend on the willingness of people to go away permanently, or for long periods, and on their capacity to adapt to new places and situations. In the nineteenth century, and the early part of the twentieth, the British were, on the whole, willing migrants and the Scots were particularly notable for this; but the French and the Japanese, in spite of having territories overseas to which they could go, appear to have been much less active in colonization.

Where people do have the incentive, and the opportunity, to migrate, and some do so while others do not, the migrants and the non migrants may sort themselves into groups with different characteristics — see §8.9 below.

8.5 Some important migratory streams

During the period 1820—1960, the numbers of immigrants into the USA amounted in all to some 40 millions; the pace of intake varied considerably from time to time. In the years before 1880 it rose steadily from under 1 million per decade to 3 million per decade. During the four decades 1880—1920 the numbers admitted were successively 5, 4, 8 and 7 millions. Since then the numbers have been considerably smaller, because restrictions were imposed.

The composition by nationality of the immigrants to the USA in the years up to 1935 was broadly (numbers in millions):

British and Irish	9
German	6
Central European	5
Mediterranean	5
Russian	3
Scandinavian	2
French, Belgian	1
Other European	2
Non-European	5
Total	38

The contrast between Britain and France is striking. The French population was larger, yet it provided less than one-tenth as many migrants. This accords with what was said in §8.4 above. France is, indeed, more a recipient than a donor country where migration is concerned, and its population was augmented by some 4 millions in this way over the period 1801—1935.

There have been similar migratory flows to South America, Australia and New Zealand. In all cases, the natural increase of the local population outweighed the net intake from immigration, which represented, for Australia, not more than 50 per cent of the natural increase in any single quinquennium over the period 1861—1935. There were, in fact, two five-year periods when a small net emigration from Australia occurred, namely, in 1901—5 and 1931—5. Another area that largely became populated through immigration in the nineteenth and twentieth centuries was the Asiatic part of Russia — namely Siberia. More recently in the USSR, there has been an immense movement into urban areas. In 30 years, some 40 million people made this kind of

145

transfer, while many more continued to live in villages which grew into towns.

The country from which perhaps the highest proportion of population has emigrated is Ireland; since the middle of the nineteenth century not less than 4 million Irish have gone overseas, and the resident population has fallen from 8 to 4 millions.

The precipitants of these general movements consisted mainly of the economic opportunities provided by the opening up of promising new lands, and population pressure in Europe. Political oppression may have played some part. In Ireland, famine was an important cause at one time; its economic lessons provided the stimulus at other times. The variations in the strength of the flow from one period to another have been the object of studies in which economic booms and slumps in the supplying and receiving countries have been shown to have an important influence.

A migratory movement of a different character was the sudden transference of population between India and Pakistan after political independence was granted by Britain in 1947. No less than 8 million people moved in each direction. The causes were political and religious, and the movement was accompanied by much violence. It is of interest to note that the occupations and social classes of the migrants were not the same: the Muslims who left India for Pakistan were mainly rural dwellers — such as farmers and semi-skilled craftsmen. The Hindus who came in replacement were mainly urban clerks and small tradesmen.

8.6   Data which analyse migration

The extent to which migration can be analysed into its component parts, or between types of migrant, varies a good deal from country to country, and there is no standard pattern. A few examples are given below for illustrative purposes. Table 8.1 shows some statistics, taken from the UN *Demographic Year Book*, which indicate the composition of the annual movements in and out of a country. The countries chosen subdivide their data more than most other countries do.

This table shows a high proportion of total movement with little or no demographic significance, which is nevertheless recorded for administrative purposes. It also indicates an inconsistency of subdivision between inward and outward movement and, as regards more permanent migration, shows both that this may be relatively small and that valuable information may be lost through merger with less significant movements.

Some data relating to internal migration in Sri Lanka (then Ceylon) are given in table 8.2. They show some typical features of the information at the disposal of demographers in many countries, for example, the differences between districts, the degree of discrepancy between two different methods

146

Table 8.1. *Entrances to and exits from Hungary and Kenya in the year 1961*

Type of migrant	Numbers (thousands)			
	Hungary		Kenya	
	In	Out	In	Out
Long-term migrants			6	9
Short-term migrants		254		
Holiday-makers	337		15	14
Persons on business trips		12	7	7
Other visitors		73	2	1
Persons in transit	329	320	18	17
Movements of residents	381	374	30	46
Total	1,047	1,033	78	94

Table 8.2. *Net migration within Sri Lanka (then Ceylon) during the 7 years 1946—53*

(Expressed as % of population)

District	Net migration as assessed by		Natural increase
	One method	Another method	
Colombo	+ 3·2	+ 2·7	+15·8
Kandy	− 4·0	− 3·1	+19·2
Trincomalee	− 7·0	− 5·8	+15·8
Anuradhapore	+22·9	+ 27·2	+21·4

of assessment and (with the exception of one district) the relative unimportance of the migration in comparison with the natural increase of population.

Variations in time are illustrated in table 8.3, and differences according to age are indicated in table 8.4. Both sets of data relate to net movements within the USA. The influence of economic conditions is clearly visible in table 8.3: when the economy was depressed, as in the 1930s, movement diminished. The growth in Negro migration over the years is no doubt the outcome of an increasing degree of freedom to travel, as well as a search for more congenial districts; a rise in the number of Negroes relative to whites must also have played a part by increasing the 'exposed to risk' of movement. The decline in the movement of foreign-born whites since 1930 is perhaps associated with a general reduction of immigration into the country.

The fall in the extent of movement as age advances (after early adulthood), as illustrated in table 8.4, is normally more pronounced for external migration than it is for internal migration. Of 50,000 emigrants from Britain in the period 1921—32, only some 300 were aged 65 or over.

Marginal in character as they are, and open to changing economic influences, migration data are variable, and therefore comparatively un-

147

Table 8.3. *Displacement of population attributable to migration between States of the USA, 1870–1960*

Period	Rate of displacement per thousand *total* population per decade		
	Native whites	Foreign-born whites	Non-whites
1870–9	30	17	4
1880–9	27	26	4
1890–9	18	16	4
1900–9	27	23	4
1910–19	19	11	6
1920–9	26	12	9
1930–9	16	2	4
1940–9	30	3	11
1950–9	31	4	9

Table 8.4. *Indexes of rates of migration to cities, USA, 1935–40*

(All ages = 100.)

Age-group	White men	White women
14–17	70	75
18–19	88	118
20–24	131	159
25–29	159	157
30–34	146	133
35–44	110	93
45–54	73	65
55–64	54	58
65 and over	50	55

reliable as pointers to future prospects. The few isolated examples given in this section are intended to provide a general idea of the nature of the statistics. They may well not be reliably indicative of migration experience at other times, or in other places. They are thus less representative of inherent characteristics of experience than are the mortality and fertility illustrations in the two preceding chapters.

8.7 Measures of migration

As the available data are not in standard form, even from time to time within many countries, there is no standard practice for their analysis or comparison. The fragmentary nature of the statistics and the impermanence of trends both militate against technical elaboration on the part of the demographer. The chief points to note are perhaps as follows:

(1) data will often be in 'stock' form, relating to people enumerated at a census classified according to current residence in conjunction with place of residence *n* years ago; thus proportions may be more useful than rates as a measure;

(2) net movement may well be much smaller than gross movement, so both forms may be worth showing; but if a choice between them is essential, the net form is the more significant for many demographic purposes;

(3) the net flow may be divided by the total population to derive a crude rate of migration; but in analysis by areas of a country this may be expressed in terms either of the ceding population or of the receiving population;

(4) net immigration may be expressed also as a ratio of total inward *plus* outward flow;

(5) the relevance, to studies of internal migration, of expressing the net flow from A to B as a function of the distance between A and B, of the populations of A and B and possibly also the composition of A and B by age and class;

(6) the particular importance that attaches to movements from rural to urban areas (see §12.14).

Subject to these general points, there is no reason why migration rates should not be calculated for different ages, if the data are available, or why these rates should not be standardized, or reduced to index form, in a manner similar to those outlined in chapter 16. This would, however, be worth doing only in special circumstances.

8.8 Interrelations between migratory flows and mortality and fertility experience

In dealing with population problems in countries experiencing a material amount of migration, the demographer will have to contend with special factors. Thus, in interpreting the trend of (say) marriage experience in Australia, he will have to consider the effect of immigration on sex – and age – distribution, and also the degree to which the immigrants are 'assimilated', i.e. the extent to which they mix freely with the native population and to which both groups intermarry. In relation to mortality experience, immigrants (and emigrants) may change the balance of the population by sex, age, area and occupation, and so influence general death rates. They may also select themselves for health, although this is nowadays largely offset, as regards international movements, by the effect of the medical checks imposed by the authorities. Health could, however, be affected by a move to a new climate, and measures of health could be changed as a result of (say) better diagnostic facilities.

The selective effects of migration on fertility may be more complex than those for mortality. First, people may leave or join a country for the economic opportunities it offers, in order ultimately to be able to have a larger family. They may even move to improve their chances of marriage. Or those who transfer may be the more ambitious people, whose desired progress is likely to inhibit family-building. Besides the selective effects there can be direct influences. 'Urbanization', or departure from the country towards the town — a general feature of population movement today — is liable to bring people from one cultural atmosphere into another, and especially from one in which high fertility is an accepted fact of life to one in which there are aspirations towards a small family size. Much will depend on the degree of assimilation, which in turn may depend on the housing available: where the trend to the town is very rapid, those who move may end in shanty areas in the environs of towns and assimilate but little of the urban cultural atmosphere. The contrary effects — those of mortality and fertility experience on migratory flows — may be more evident, especially in the light of what was said in § 8.3 above. The impact of high fertility may be to cause an outflow of population, because of 'pressure', into an area of lower fertility. Somewhat similarly, an area of low mortality rates may repel population, because of pressure — but it could also attract because of favourable occupational or climatic conditions.

8.9 Differential migration

The most notable feature of migrants generally — whether internally to a country or internationally — is their age. People aged between 15 and 35 are the most mobile, and the rate of movement declines in middle life and old age. Differences by sex, occupation and colour may also exist. Within the USA, for instance, it has been found that men are more migratory than women, whites than blacks, professional people than less-skilled workers. The unemployed are more likely to move than are the employed, because of their need to seek work.

In international migration, there is usually selection for health, because of the conditions imposed by the receiving countries and also because the unfit are unlikely to be able to make such a major change in their lives. Some countries will take in only those with certain skills or qualifications which are needed. Others have turned out people of alien race; or such people may have felt impelled to flee because of hostilities or for political reasons.

This is an area of study, however, where generalizations are of small value and could even be misleading.

8.10 Other socio-economic data having a bearing on population

The principal socio-economic data which have a bearing on, or are affected by, population trends are:

(1) education;
(2) housing and households;
(3) labour supply and employment;
(4) savings and investment.

The interrelations between demographic elements and these socio-economic features are complex and will be referred to more fully in chapter 12.

As has been mentioned above, prospective population increases affect the likely number of future scholars and so the requirements for schools and teachers. Reference has also been made to the influence of education, directly or via social status, on mortality and fertility. It remains to list a few other ways in which education has a bearing upon demographic trends:

(1) men and women tend to choose a marriage partner of approximately the same educational level as themselves, and their children's scholastic progress will be influenced by this level;
(2) education is often positively associated with migration, especially towards cities;
(3) rates of divorce may vary with educational level.

As has been indicated, a household is a unit which may serve a useful purpose in demographic analysis, and convenient data are collected at most censuses. The total need for housing is clearly influenced by population growth, and the quality of the buildings needed must depend upon the age-distribution and the distribution of biological families by size. Housing standards are also an indicator of social status and have an association with mortality and fertility — as well as marriage; they vary from area to area and influence the distribution of population, for example, by race.

Estimates of labour supply are often made by multiplying population data by 'activity rates', i.e. the proportions employable or employed. Such rates vary by age, sex and marital status, and therefore the distribution of population in these three respects clearly has an important bearing upon the size of the 'work force'; so also has fertility, in its effect on that distribution in the long term. The local demand for, and supply of, labour will be an influence upon migration, as has already been indicated. The type of labour demanded is significant, for instance whether it is family employment (and often, in the less-developed countries, under-employment) on farms or skilled labour in the cities. Quality of labour is, of course, closely akin to socio-economic status, and has a corresponding link with the principal elements of demographic movement.

Questions of savings and investment are important in relation to economic development and will be referred to more fully in chapter 12. These economic elements do not, perhaps, have much direct association with fertility and mortality, although naturally a man with a small family is more likely to be able to save than one with a large family. In a loose way, however, population growth demands more investment in 'social overheads', such as housing, and leaves less room for investment in industry. Investment promotes economic growth and may thereby affect mortality and, more especially, fertility.

SELECT BIBLIOGRAPHY

Selected Studies of Migration since World War II (Milbank Memorial Fund, 1958).

Thomas, Brinley. *Migration and Economic Growth: a Study of Great Britain and the Atlantic Economy* (Cambridge University Press, 1st ed. 1954; 2nd ed. 1973).

Matras, J. *Populations and Societies* (Prentice-Hall, New York, 1973).

Methods of Measuring Internal Migration (United Nations, New York, 1970).

9 Population projection: general considerations

9.1 Introduction

In recent years a big demand has developed for estimates of future populations. The main reason for this demand is probably economic: plans for the production of food, the supply of power and the manufacture of goods all need to be based on advance knowledge of likely changes in the numbers of people for whom the production is designed. For instance, demand in the perambulator and baby-carriage trade depends on the number of future births and also on whether they are first births in the family or later children (who may 'inherit' such appliances from their elder brothers and sisters). National and local government administration also calls for an appreciation of the outcome of population trends. Demographic changes may affect the relative military strengths of neighbouring countries, the demand for housing and other amenities, and the need for public transport. There is an obvious connection between the size of the future population at the appropriate ages and plans for the construction of schools, the training of teachers, the recruitment of labour and the provision of health services. Calculations of future population for periods varying from one to thirty years, or sometimes even further ahead, are a feature of social security planning: short-term assessments are required for budgetary purposes, and projections of longer range are wanted in order to illustrate the broader financial trends.

An example of a requirement of more limited scope is the assessment of the size and distribution of the population at various points of time between censuses; this is needed as a base for the calculation of birth rates and death rates in the local administrative areas each year and for the country as a whole.

9.2 Population estimation in the short term

A general rule for forecasts of all kinds is that the further ahead one tries to look the more obscure the prospect. This chapter begins with the type of assessment for which the problems are least awkward — estimates for the short term. In this area of work, the methods of calculation of past and current population, and the accuracy of the results obtained, must depend to a large extent on the nature of the available data. Thus, if there was a census five years ago and if births, deaths and migratory movements have been recorded by sex and age during those five years, the only errors likely to arise from the use of the component method of estimation are those occasioned by inaccuracies in and incompatibilities between the census and movement statistics. These would be revealed by a comparison of the estimate with the results of a further census.

Such a comparison of expected and actual population is shown for England and Wales in table 9.1, where the actual relates to the 1931 Census and the expected is based on the previous enumeration. The expected population in April 1931 numbered 39,950,000 and the population actually enumerated was 39,947,931. In table 9.1 the enumerated numbers have been projected to 30 June 1931, and have been suitably adjusted to allow for probable understatement in the numbers of young children; the expected numbers based on the 1921 Census and subsequent registrations have been rated up so as to agree in total with the 1931 enumeration. The table thus shows the inaccuracies in age-groups but not in the total population.

The main reasons for the discrepancies in table 9.1 are probably inadequacy of migration statistics and misstatements of age. In the absence of records of internal migration the Registrar General's estimates for local areas were more inaccurate, the total population in each area being incorrect on the average by $4\frac{1}{2}$ per cent. Comparisons of a similar nature for relatively less well-developed countries are shown in table 9.2, which indicates some much more substantial discrepancies. This table is due to Dr J. G. C. Blacker. Evidently, in at least some of the countries in question, serious errors occurred in census enumerations, or in vital registration, or

Table 9.1. *Expected numbers of persons on the basis of the Registrar General's annual estimates compared with the numbers actually enumerated, England and Wales, 1931 (adjusted to mid-1931)*

(Numbers in thousands.)

Age-group	Estimated	Enumerated	Difference
0–14	9,537	9,530	− 7
15–29	10,362	10,272	−90
30–44	8,480	8,533	+53
45–59	7,067	7,010	−57
60–74	3,741	3,813	+72
75 and over	801	830	+29
Total	39,988	39,988	—

Table 9.2. *Estimated population and census total (millions) revealed in the 1960 round of censuses*

Country		Estimated population	Census total	Deficiency in estimate (%)
Philippines	(1960)	25·1	27·1	8
Thailand	(1960)	22·6	26·3	16
South Korea	(1960)	23·4	25·0	7
India	(1960)	411·7	439·1	7
Pakistan	(1961)	89·6	93·8	5
Brazil	(1960)	66·0	71·0	7
Ghana	(1960)	5·0	6·7	34
Kenya	(1962)	7·5	8·6	15
Zambia	(1963)	2·5	3·5	40
Nigeria	(1963)	37·0	55·0	49

both. Whatever the cause, the actual population always proved higher than the estimated.

In the absence of trustworthy movement data, mathematical formulae may be used for estimating population, for instance in interpolating between or extrapolating from the results of consecutive censuses. These formulae are appropriate only when trends are known to have been uniform and steady.

9.3 Estimates of population according to marital status

Except in countries where continuous registration systems are maintained, the subdivision of a population according to marital status is normally possible only when a census is taken. As censuses are relatively infrequent in relation to changes in the intensity of marriage, accurate denominators for the calculation of marriage rates based on true exposures to risk will not always be available. This limits the possibilities for the close study of the subject.

Estimates of the numbers of single, married, widowed and divorced persons in years other than those in which a census is taken may be prepared in two ways. One is to extrapolate proportions married on the basis of the latest known figures; the trend of marriage is, however, rarely uniform enough to justify this method. A second approach is to adjust the latest recorded numbers of persons in each status, for the period between the census and the year in question, by allowing for actual (or estimated) deaths and widowhoods and for the marriages of the unmarried and the re-marriages of the widowed and divorced. This type of calculation can be very laborious and is liable to inaccuracies. Nevertheless it has proved useful, and the

155

estimates of the Registrar General for England and Wales are especially valuable in the study of the course of marriage rates from year to year.

9.4 Nomenclature

Population forecasts of longer term are often referred to as 'projections'. When the results of projections made in the past are compared with the population changes that have actually taken place, it is frequently found that the projections have not, in fact, succeeded in portraying accurately what subsequently occurred. The prospects of success are somewhat similar to those of weather forecasting (if one allows for a big difference in time-scale: one day where depressions and anticyclones are concerned is equivalent to (say) twenty-five years for populations). Like meteorologists, population experts are very well aware that they cannot at present precisely 'forecast', 'foretell', or 'predict' the future. Demographers therefore avoid the use of these words, in order to make it plain that they do not claim that they can prognosticate. Instead, they tend to use less ambitious verbs, such as 'estimate' or 'project'. An 'estimate' should, according to generally-accepted interpretation, be based on surer ground than a 'projection' and should be more precise; it commonly consists of an assessment of current numbers, or numbers in the immediate past or future, taking into account the results of the latest available census and any figures that are available of subsequent births, deaths and migratory movements. A 'projection' ranges into the further future: it depicts what would happen if certain assumptions as to mortality, fertility and migration were borne out; but little or no claim is made that these assumptions will in fact be borne out in practice. Indeed, alternative sets of calculations are often prepared and displayed together, without any preference for one at the expense of another.

The difference in time-scale noted above is worth remembering, for population projections range further ahead than almost any other form of prediction, e.g. economic forecasts. This means that, in general, population projections cannot usefully be derived, by linkage, from other types of forecast.

In recent years, some scientists have constructed elaborate global models, with the aid of electronic computers, in which parameters of population have been introduced in conjunction with hypotheses concerning economic development, natural resources, scientific advance and pollution of the environment. The predictive value of these models appears very slight, however, as too little is known of the nature of the interconnexions between the parameters; the outcome of the exercise is highly sensitive to the combination of assumptions introduced. Alarming predictions can be produced by those who wish to startle, but others have found it possible to view the future with hope (see § 14.10 below).

9.5   Speculative nature of projections

Population projections for Britain that had been published respectively in 1937, 1942 and 1944 had shown expected totals for 1951 of 45·0, 47·5 and 46·1 millions respectively. The actual population recorded at the 1951 Census was 48·8 millions. Thus, in about ten years, discrepancies between actual and expected total population of from 3 to 8 per cent arose. Much of the difference was concentrated at ages under 15; here the numbers expected were respectively 7·8, 9·1 and 8·7 millions, but those actually enumerated were 11·0 millions. As the period ahead in respect of which projections are made is often thirty years or more, such discrepancies after a much shorter lapse of time must render projections insufficiently reliable for many purposes. This example, and similar comparisons that have been made for other countries with much the same results (table 14.7 below gives some figures), give some idea of the indifferent prospects of success in this kind of exercise.

It might be thought that, cautioned by past errors, demographers should now do better; but there is in fact little real foundation for hopes of material improvement. Our knowledge of the social forces underlying changes in mortality, marriage, fertility, and migration is very incomplete, and the precise effects of suspected causes cannot at present be ascertained. Even if our understanding of the past were more thorough, the future would inevitably be uncertain, because many political and economic events cannot be foreseen, and these influence demographic trends. There is only one respect in which demographers can be sure of improving on the projections of ten or twenty years ago; they know what has actually happened in the interim. The first of the three British projections mentioned above gave 38 millions as the probable population in 1971 — a total lower than in 1931. A projection published in 1955 gave a revised figure of 51 millions for 1971 — one-third higher, and a larger population than ever before in Britain. About one-half of the difference of 13 millions arose from the fact that in 1955 it was known that the population was already about 6 millions higher than originally expected; the remainder is attributable mainly to an expectation of larger numbers of future births, based on the fact that fertility had proved in the intervening 18 years to be higher than had seemed possible in 1937. (The actual population in 1971 proved to be 54 millions.)

The demographer has, indeed, been likened to a car driver who with his instruments and his field of vision before him, is attempting to steer his vehicle clear of all obstacles. His outlook at any time depends on his current speed and bearing and upon such other traffic as he can see; but the situation is constantly changing, and he must adjust his actions accordingly. Similarly, a population projection can be based only on current information about speed of growth, direction of flow, and so on, and will require to be

157

amended from time to time. The car driver can see the next few yards ahead more clearly than the road further on; similarly with a projection. The number of persons under age t in the population t years hence depends on future births, less an allowance for deaths and for migration, whereas the numbers aged t and over are determined, after an adjustment for deaths and removals, by the present living population. Because the level of future fertility, in so many countries, is much more uncertain than the effect of future mortality and migration, there is more doubt about the numbers under age t than about those over age t.

Estimates of population at the older ages (mainly over 65) are likely to be less accurate than in middle life because mortality at the older ages is heavier and more open to changes in the future than during working life.

9.6 Methods for making projections

Many methods have been developed for assessing future population size. They differ from one another mainly in the different circumstances in which they are applied — depending principally on the extent and accuracy of the available data. In Graunt's day there were no statistics at all except the records derived from the Bills of Mortality, and he drew what conclusions he could from these and from such 'sample' information as he could obtain. By the time of Malthus, data were just beginning to emerge, and he used such as were available to justify his theories. A somewhat similar situation exists today in much of Africa and Asia, but the prospects for estimation are more favourable there, because (a) the technique of representative sampling is now known, (b) resources are being made available for the purposes of estimation, and (c) it is possible to make inferences by reference to the situation in countries for which suitable data already exist. The methods that are used in such areas vary greatly according to particular circumstances.

Systems of population projection and estimation by 'mathematical' and 'component' methods are of more general application and will be referred to in succeeding sections of the present chapter.

9.7 Mathematical methods

Where successive censuses have been taken but there is no registration system, mathematical formulae are sometimes used for estimating and projecting population. These have the merit of simplicity, although they have proved to be uninformative analytically — for instance if total population size is the subject of estimation no details are likely to be provided of age-distribution. Success in forecasting by this method has been elusive, and interest has resided more in studying the behaviour of the numbers in the past. If the method is adopted, however, the type of curve chosen should be in harmony with correct general notions of what a population may have been and may become. (Thus a curve should not be chosen which shows a negative population size at some date.) In a population increasing at a constant rate, the curve for the population ^tP at time t is the logarithmic:

$$^tP = Ce^{\rho t} \tag{9.1}$$

where C and e are constants and ρ is the momently rate of increase. This is of limited value for projection, because it is clear that there must be some ultimate limit to the numbers that can inhabit a given space. The rate of growth cannot, therefore, remain constant indefinitely but must diminish. Instead of the differential equation

$$\frac{1}{^tP} \cdot \frac{d^tP}{dt} = \rho \tag{9.2}$$

that underlies the logarithmic curve one may expect some modification as

$$\frac{1}{^tP} \cdot \frac{d^tP}{dt} = \rho - f(^tP). \tag{9.3}$$

The simplest form for $f(^tP)$ is k^tP (where k is constant) and if this is used the 'logistic' curve is obtained, namely

$$^tP = (Ce^{-\rho t} + k/\rho)^{-1} \tag{9.4}$$

that was originally developed by Verhulst and later studied by Pearl and Reed. It is an S-shaped curve, and the upper limit for ^tP is ρ/k.

An interesting series of experiments was made by Pearl and Reed in which the rapidly breeding fruit-fly *Drosophila* was used. The numbers of these flies existing, with an adequate food supply, in a confined space were measured at regular intervals, and it was found that they reached an upper level beyond which they did not pass. Some evidence was thus found in favour of a logistic or related form of population growth (many different formulae produce rather similar S-shaped curves).

9.8 Limitations of mathematical methods

The conditions of human life are complex, and it is questionable whether one logistic would adequately express the trend of the numbers of men and women in any country over a long period if the actual data were available for such a test. Although success has been achieved in fitting the logistic to the populations of England and Wales, France and the USA, for much of the period since censuses began, the sections of the curve that have been used are only partial. Yule drew a logistic through points on a chart representing the data for England and Wales for the years 1801 to 1911 and obtained a not

159

unreasonable fit; the upper limit to this trend was assessed by him as being 90–100 millions according to the precise method adopted. There is nothing inherently impossible about such an ultimate size, but since 1911 the enumerated populations have been considerably less than those on the curve, and projections that take the various aspects of the current population situation into account show that there is little chance of the recorded numbers rejoining the curve within the next few decades.

If it is supposed that the total population size changes in accordance with some mathematical function it must be admitted that there is a definite relationship between the courses of the constituent items of movement, namely births, deaths and migration. These and the corresponding rates per thousand population cannot then be considered as independent but must be regarded as subject to a constraint. Given, for instance, a certain expected development in the death rate and certain assumptions about migration, the trend of the birth rate is already determined and cannot be considered as a separate entity. Various methods of analysis of mortality, fertility, and migration have not suggested, however, that there is any such master connection between them — although looser associations are possible.

Three features of mathematical methods as applied to population projection seem worthy of separate mention:

(1) the use of formulae involves assumptions of continuity in population progression which may not always be justified by the irregular course of some developments, e.g. scientific advance; but wave-curves can be used to fit cyclical elements;

(2) formulae may be applied in the projection of components of population change, for example mortality, instead of to total numbers;

(3) the application of a given projection formula to the population of each constituent area of a country may not produce the same result as the application of the same formula to the total population of the country.

9.9 Component methods

Shortly before the time when Yule published the results of his researches with the logistic curve, Bowley had made some calculations bearing on the future size of the population of Britain. In these he employed as bases the mortality rates of England and Wales in the years 1910–12 and the average annual number of births in Britain during 1921–3. On the assumption that these would continue unchanged, he examined what the course of the total population size would be for some decades to come. Although each author disclaimed that his work was a prophecy for the future, there was a natural tendency to compare and contrast the two methods as forecasts. Yule explained the shortfall in the population of 1921, as compared with the logistic curve, as being due to the war of 1914—18; apart from this, the logistic still appeared plausible at that time as a curve representing population growth. He regarded Bowley's estimate for 1971 of 49 millions in Britain as being too low — as indeed it is now seen to be, although by no means an unreasonable figure for a projection over so long a period.

Since 1925 it has become clear that suitable formulae in connection with changes in the total size of the population have not been developed and that those tried thirty years ago have not proved successful. No doubt today it would not be impossible to obtain plausible results by joining two or more logistics together or by using more tortuous curves, but there could be little confidence in their predictive power unless special regard was paid to the present age-structure of the population and the current tendencies of birth rates and death rates.

Attention to age-distribution and vital rates is fundamental to the methods of population projection that have found favour in recent years. If some assumption is made about the rates of mortality that will be experienced during the period to be covered, for each age of the population, it is readily possible to calculate survival factors and so ascertain the numbers of people among the present population who will still be living at any time or at any age in the future. In order to complete the picture it is necessary to add in an estimate of the number of births in each future year and then to assess the proportions of them likely to survive to various ages. The details of the method are illustrated in chapter 17.

9.10 Sets of projections

The success of a population projection by the component method depends on stability in mortality rates, fertility rates and migratory movements, or uniformity in their trends. In most countries where enough data are available for the use of this method such stability and uniformity cannot be relied upon. Demographers have therefore tried to give some idea of possible future variability, and the improbability of any single projection proving accurate, by making at any one time several different calculations. Thus the British Royal Commission on Population used various combinations of two alternative mortality bases, five sets of marriage rates, five fertility bases and a range of possible types of migratory movement. Sixteen projections in all were completed, and they may if desired be regarded as consisting of one 'master' projection on a particular set of assumptions, with other projections successively examining the effects of variations from the master set in each separate component: although the master set is not necessarily the most probable projection.

This use of a range has the merit of caution. It must be remembered, however, that no precise statistical significance can be attached to the upper and lower limits of the range, nor indeed would these necessarily be chosen to represent extreme assumptions. (A broad idea could perhaps be given of the relative likelihoods of the various bases.) Perhaps more important, however, is the fact that a range of figures may not be best suited to the politician, the economist or the administrator at whose request projections are made. He may want only to have a 'most probable' answer, and may make his own selection of one projection from the range if the demographer has not already indicated his favourite choice. He may indeed choose the one that best suits his policy, without regard to the probabilities. It is for such reasons that official projections tend to be single ones. They are, however, often revised — sometimes annually, or even more frequently.

9.11 Choice of bases for projections by the component method

There are few established methods of approach to the selection of bases for population projections. Each demographer relates such matters to the general concepts he has formed and is employing as a background to his work; these concepts may be economic or sociological or medical but are unlikely to be purely mathematical, because although continuity is desirable it is not enough to extrapolate blindly from past trends. A range of assumptions necessarily has an upper and lower limit, and in order that the effects of diverging experiences may be illustrated it is desirable that the limits should be sufficiently widely separated. It may be convenient to have a central assumption as well, perhaps representing a compromise between the extremes. It is not essential that all the bases should be entirely 'reasonable'. One or more of them could be chosen as representing a target to be aimed at or a 'calamity' to be avoided at all costs.

The projections should be so arranged that the approximate effects of a change of basis in respect of each separate element can readily be seen. It would not be sufficient to make two calculations — one, (a) with high fertility and low mortality and the other, (b), with low fertility and high mortality — without also preparing at least a third. Thus a projection, (c), based on the high fertility and the high mortality, would serve to illustrate, by difference, the effects of changed fertility, mortality being constant ((c)−(b)) and also of changed mortality, fertility being constant ((c)−(a)). An investigation of the consequences of assuming different directions and speeds of migratory flows may if desired be made by treating those who migrate as a distinct class, projecting them separately from the rest of the population and then combining them with the non-migrants as necessary at the final stage.

9.12   Mortality bases

Although projections are sometimes made upon the assumption of un-changing mortality, it is generally recognized as being desirable to make provision for future reductions in death rates. There are two main avenues of approach to the task of deciding by how much they may fall. One is to draw curves representing the experience of the recent past and then to extend them to show that of the years to come; the other is to consider how far mortality may be expected to fall 'ultimately', and then inter-polate values for the death rates during the period between the present and the assumed date of attaining the final level. The difference between these two methods is largely one of emphasis; whichever one is used principally, it is desirable to test the results obtained in the light of an approximate application of the alternative approach. Within each broad method there are several possible variants. One way of using the 'ulti-mate' approach was demonstrated by Whelpton in the United States. He examined the death rates of native white males during recent years and compared the figures for the whole of that country with those for the separate States and for foreign countries, by age and by cause of death. The aim of this analysis was to look for the effects of two sources of im-provement in vitality, namely:

(1) the spread of medical knowledge and of advances in social welfare — it is said that the death rates of the United States as a whole have tended in the past towards those of the States with the lowest figures — and
(2) advances in medical diagnosis and treatment.

The estimation of the effects on mortality of both these developments is necessarily speculative. Regional differences in death rates do not arise simply from degrees of social betterment but are due also to climatic and occupational variations. The movements among deaths from separate causes are influenced by changes in practice in diagnosing illnesses and in selecting the prime impairment for certification where several exist together; in such matters the past may not condition the future. Thus it is not surprising that Whelpton chose three alternative levels of mortality and sought to justify these only in broad terms.

The alternative general approach to the projection of death rates, whereby trend curves are drawn through points on a chart representing the rates ex-perienced in the recent past and then extended, is often used. In doing so it is not necessarily supposed that the curves represent any 'law' of mortality; it may well be appreciated that they are empirical and that the mortality rates of the future are probably not going to be conditioned to any overriding extent by the events of the past. Nevertheless, in extending the curves thus obtained into the coming decades, use is made of the only firm information available as the starting point, and having considered the obvious hazards in all projections the demographer may find that the simplicity and convenience of the method commend themselves.

Various ways in which mortality trends may be determined have been indicated in chapter 7, and many of these can be adopted as a basis for estimating future changes. As mortality decreases generally, the death rates for a country as a whole will necessarily move in the direction of the current rates for the best areas and social classes. Such a tendency is sometimes studied as a basis for projection, as was done by Whelpton. Mortality differences in time are not, however, of the same character as those by class or area. Although the best areas and classes may point the way to improvements that will follow owing to the spread of advanced methods of health administration and better medical care, part of their superiority arises from constant factors such as climate. Further, in so far as medical discoveries yet to be made will lead to greater longevity, present differentials can afford no clue to future developments.

A few details of some recent mortality projections — only some of which have been used for population projections — are given in table 9.3.

9.13 Marriage bases

It is not essential to consider marriage as a separate element when making population projections. Estimates of future births may be arrived at by

Table 9.3. *Comparison of the results of some mortality projections made by a variety of methods*

				Mortality rate	
				Men aged 40—44	Men aged 70—74
Demographer	Country	Year	Method of projection		
P. K. Whelpton	USA (native whites)	1939—41	(Actual rates)	0·0062	0·067
		1975	'Ultimate level approach' High	0·0045	0·066
		1975	Medium	0·0034	0·066
		1975	Low	0·0025	0·054
A. H. Pollard	Australia	1931	(Actual rates)	0·0043*	0·048*
		1968	Secular trend (main causes of death considered separately)	0·0038*	0·064*
		1968	Secular trend (all causes of death together)	0·0028*	0·038*
		1968	Generation method (graphic)	0·0027*	0·033*
		1968	Generation method (formula)	0·0025*	0·021*
Government Actuary's Department	Britain	1942—4	(Actual rates)	0·0042	0·042
		1978	Exponential trend curve	0·0022	0·036
		1978	Adjusted generation method	0·0013	0·034
		1978	Unadjusted generation method	0·0018	0·029

* Central ages 40, 70 respectively; figures are approximate.

means of 'fertility rates per woman' — or per man, for that matter. Such rates, analysed according to age, were customarily adopted for projections made during the 1920s and 1930s. The British Royal Commission on Population, however, found its task considerably complicated by the fact that there had been a sharp rise in the number of marriages at the beginning of the Second World War, and a further peak after the end of the war, and that the number of births had fluctuated in response to these movements. In these circumstances it was felt that it would be more appropriate to relate fertility to duration of marriage irrespective of age at marriage than to associate it with age attained — even though changes in the age-distribution of marriages had occurred and were a disturbing factor. This approach required a projection of the numbers of marriages as a separate element in the calculations.

Either marriage rates or proportions married may be adopted as a basis for calculating the numbers of marriages in future. It has, of course, to be remembered in fixing a basis that the marriage rates of any particular year would not produce the same results as the use of the proportions married in that year would because the proportions in effect sum up the experiences of all the years in the recent past. Proportions are simpler to use, but in view of the effects of population structure (particularly the balance of the sexes) on marriage rates the employment of rates is worth some consideration. Three questions that should be asked when deciding on bases are as follows:

(1) are the marriage factors appropriate to the existing unmarried population, having regard to the marriage experience of their generation?

(2) are the fertility factors appropriate to the existing married couples with uncompleted families?

(3) are the fertility and survival factors for couples reasonable having regard to changes in the average age at marriage? Analysis by age at marriage as well as duration would probably be illuminating although rather laborious.

The choice of basis lies not only between higher and lower marriage rates but also between younger and older ages at marriage. In this connexion it should not be forgotten that, as indicated in § 5.11, changes in the incidence of marriage may affect the rate of fertility. Similarly, although this is of less importance in population projections, marriage and mortality are not wholly independent of one another, and the bases used should be as little inconsistent as possible, one with the other.

9.14 Fertility bases

In view of the appreciable difference between male and female reproduction rates, consideration should be given to the question of projecting by the use of male or female fertility functions, or both. If the bases are properly chosen the two approaches should yield broadly the same result. The use of women's fertility in the calculations is simpler in operation — because of the smaller number of age-groups involved — and is also customary because more data are likely to be available. In some circumstances it may be desirable to provide a check on the results by using the men's rates, but the purely illustrative nature of many projections renders this unnecessary. As remarked in chapter 6, the level of fertility in many communities today depends largely on the individual decisions of parents who practise family limitation and who space out the births of their children. In making these decisions, they may well be influenced by social conditions, such as the economic and political situation, the cost of rearing babies and of maintaining them as they grow up, the amount of leisure needed to be given up in caring for them, and so forth. There are also, it seems, psychological considerations. Each class and each generation has its 'outlook' depending to some extent on custom and fashion, often rebelling against the ideas of the previous generation, and possibly influenced in some degree by leading thinkers and writers. This outlook includes views upon family size.

In these circumstances there can be little possibility of adequately 'forecasting' fertility. To assume that past trends will continue into the future has no particular justification. Indeed, even the choice of a set of working assumptions upon which to project can be warranted only in very general terms. A lower limit for fertility might be defended on the ground that it was not unreasonable, having regard to the tendencies observed from differential fertility investigations, for in the last few decades the families of the lower social classes in some Western countries may have decreased in size so as to approach more nearly the conditions pertaining to the upper classes. Such a tendency might well, however, be submerged by movements of another kind. It is not inconceivable that an improving economic outlook, coupled with a change in the attitude of many parents towards children, might cause some increase in fertility. Similarly, a fall in births might result from unsettled conditions, or even from talk of overpopulation.

In view of the provision of material for compiling fertility rates according to marriage duration and birth order as well as by age, opportunities are now available for improving the technique of projection. So far, however, little has been published concerning methods to supersede the use, which has prevailed in the past, of fertility rates analysed according to the age of parent only. Estimating populations of married women according to age and duration of marriage involves a considerable amount of trouble, even with an electronic computer, and it may well be asked whether, in view of the arbitrary nature of the assumptions upon which a projection is based, the use of such refinement in the calculations is justified. One possible simplification would be to employ a set of fertility rates classified according to age that have been

166

specially chosen, after tests of their suitability in the light of the latest available information, as an approximation to the use of more detailed processes. Another would be to use fertility rates by marriage duration, without distinction by age. If it is desired to make projections implying a change in the future distribution of families according to size, fertility rates by birth order may be used, i.e., proportions having a first child, second child and so on.

9.15 Migration

The effects of migration on the population have been of the greatest importance in countries such as Eire or New Zealand, but in others its influence has been relatively small. The treatment of this subject must depend on individual circumstances. It will only rarely be found that migratory movements have been so regular that the future can be predicted with confidence and, further, as shown in chapter 8, the available data are often rather unsatisfactory. Close attention to detail is unlikely to be required. If all consideration of migration is omitted in the main projection, and then, in a separate series of tables or charts, the general effect of some arbitrary assumption is given, the position will be shown with sufficient clarity. Migrants tend to have a particular kind of age-distribution and their fertility and mortality experience may be different from that of the remainder of the population. These are further reasons for treating them quite separately from non-migrants.

Generally, separate population projections are desirable in respect of any clearly defined sections of the population whose experience is markedly different from that of the remainder. Thus, in New Zealand, the Maoris, and in the United States the non-whites, have been treated separately from the white races. On the other hand, while conditions in Britain are different between the three constituent countries, and between races, groups of occupations and social classes, such distinctions are not in general sufficiently marked or sufficiently important to warrant separation in projection calculations unless specially required for some particular purpose.

9.16 Value of recent population projection work

It does not seem very clear to what extent the projections that have been made, in all parts of the world, in recent years have been of real value, in the sense of offering a reasonable foundation for the making of population and other governmental policies. Certainly the projections have not, on the whole, been very successful as predictions of what actually happened in the event (as chapter 14 will show). No country can be singled out as more successful than another in this respect. Part of the trouble has stemmed from inadequate or inaccurate data or from inappropriate models; but the major

167

difficulty is that social and economic changes, and their effects on mortality, fertility and migration, are so hard to foresee.

As a consequence, rates of decline in mortality have often been under-estimated, and unrepresentative projections of fertility have been made (these constitute the biggest single cause of error in many different countries). Nonetheless, as a result of the continued growth of public interest in population questions, and the need of forward planning of all kinds, there is an increasing demand for projection work; in spite of repeated failures to predict accurately, demographers are being asked to try again; doing so can be justified on the ground that where there is a strong need it is sure to be met from one source or another, and if those best able refuse to act then others less experienced will take on the work with poorer results.

SELECT BIBLIOGRAPHY

Glass, D. V. 'Demographic Predictions', *Proceedings of the Royal Society*, B, **168** (1967), 119.

'Mortality Trends and Projections 1967', *Transactions of the Society of Actuaries*, **19** (1967), D428.

Blacker, J. G. C. 'Population Dynamics', *Intermedica* (1967), **14**.

Brass, W. 'Perspectives in Population Prediction: Illustrated by the Statistics of England and Wales', *Journal of the Royal Statistical Society* (1975).

Pressat, R. 'Mortality Projections and Actual Trends'. In *World Health Statistics Report*, **27**, 8 (WHO, 1974).

General influences on population

10 Population in history

10.1 Introduction

Demographers are often concerned with real populations seen as a whole, and for this purpose neither the analytical methods used in relation to particular characteristics described in chapters 5 –9, nor the indexes and models to be described in chapters 15 –19, tell the whole story. It is therefore desirable that some attention should be paid to the way in which, in all their complexity, real populations have evolved, especially in relation to the historical, political and economic circumstances that have prevailed from time to time. The purpose of the present chapter is therefore to outline the past development of particular populations – and in so doing to give to some extent a practical illustration of the methods of analysis and summary that have been outlined in this book.

The tale can begin in fact before recorded history. Although for obvious reasons not much is known of prehistoric days, and so little can be said about primitive man, nevertheless certain generalizations are possible from the work of palaeontologists, and also of anthropologists, who can even today make observations on tribes living in very remote regions. As time unfolds, and history begins, the record gradually becomes clear and it can be seen in more detail. For Europe and the United States, analysis in considerable depth becomes possible from the early part of the nineteenth century onwards; for many other areas, there is much less scope for study until the middle of the twentieth. The present chapter takes the story up to that point and is thus mainly European in character. Current demographic situations and particulars on a world scale are exhibited in chapter 11. A further chapter (14) will discuss *inter alia* the prospects for the future, as far as they can be assessed at the present time.

10.2 The earliest times

Man is said to have emerged about half a million years ago, during the greatest of the Ice Ages. He lived in tiny family groups, without any permanent settlement, gathering food and hunting much as wild animals do today. His numbers were necessarily limited by the natural resources he could use, and lifetimes were brief. Probably only about 20 million square miles of the

169

earth's surface could have been used by hunters, and it has been estimated that about 2 square miles would on average have been necessary to maintain one person. On this basis, the world population could not have exceeded 10 millions, or less than one three-hundredth of its present-day total. It has been tentatively estimated — presumably on the basis of studies of present-day aboriginals — that the average expectation of life at birth might have been no more than ten years.

In due course man discovered how to make and use stone tools; this gave him an enhanced food supply and enabled not only a longer life to be enjoyed but also quicker and more selective multiplication leading to the development of the species. The result was population growth. Mastery of the use of fire led to the burning of clearings in the forests, and later to metallurgy, to bigger settlements and again larger tribes.

10.3   General tendency of population to increase

The growth in man's numbers recorded above began a process which, apart from temporary fluctuations, has continued ever since and at an increasing rate. The basic reason is that his technology has, in broad terms, been continually advancing and that each advance has enabled larger numbers to be sustained. When man relied solely on hunting for his food, his numbers were determined by the supply of edible animals and of natural roots and fruits. But then came an important technological revolution — the development of agriculture: growing crops and cultivating live-stock was associated with a large increase in population size and also with a more settled way of life. This development did not, of course, happen all at once, but emerged gradually, and indeed is still taking place today, as improvements in methods of farming are introduced. Some of these improvements are known to have had dramatic effects. For instance, the population of the Danube basin rapidly doubled after the introduction of maize as a crop there, and the population of Ireland increased as a result of the importation of the potato. (Both these new foods arrived as a result of the discovery of America.) Population growth has itself determined to some extent the methods used, by creating a demand and so both encouraging the development of new techniques and enforcing their use.

A second great economic change in man's affairs was the industrial revolution which began in the eighteenth century. Its first main effect was a reduction in mortality, by the improvement of personal cleanliness and the introduction of an enhanced level of nutrition. Supplementary effects of this 'revolution' have caused the process to continue: the betterment of living conditions — especially in sanitary matters — and the development of pest-destroying chemicals have had obvious effects. The consequent saving in

170

lives, especially of infants, children and young people, enabled a very massive population increase to occur.

Although man's destructive power has increased, and new ways of limiting population growth have been devised, so far these have not prevailed over the factors that lead to a steady accumulation of numbers. (In the future, the continuance of world population growth is less certain, and indeed it will be shown later in this book that at some stage it must necessarily cease.)

10.4   Classical times

These may perhaps be regarded as having begun with the neolithic age some 10,000 years ago. Studies of ancient settlements suggest that population had increased and become more stratified than it could have been before. The largest cities may have contained 20,000 or more inhabitants. There is some evidence to suggest that over a considerable period such cities did not increase in number or size; this may have been because population had reached the maximum density possible in the circumstances of the day. The arrival of the Iron Age was required to trigger off a further growth.

Near the beginning of the Christian era, censuses began to be held, and ancient manuscripts and other records are still extant which provide some sort of detail of imports, taxes and military strength. From such sources it has been estimated that the total population of the Roman Empire, at its height, amounted to 50 million people. By that date there were also in existence considerable populations in India and China — probably each at least as large as that of the Mediterranean area — and in other Asian regions which are known to have been well-developed at that time. The world total might have been some 250–350 millions. This represents an enormous increase over the 10 millions before the Stone Ages; yet the rate of advance was nevertheless slow by modern standards, because thousands of years elapsed while it was taking place.

The place in the Roman Empire for which the best records are available is naturally the city of Rome itself. Figures quoted by Livy suggest that the population of the city increased from $\frac{1}{4}$ million in 250 BC to about a million by 50 BC. Different authorities, however, offer varying assessments for the maximum numbers in Rome, varying from $\frac{1}{2}$ to $1\frac{1}{4}$ millions. Attempts to deduce such items as age-structure, average length of life or family size are not generally accepted as truly representative, because tests suggest that the lapidary inscriptions on which the estimates are based are incomplete because they omit certain classes and groups. On general grounds, however, it seems likely that the expectation of life at birth was of the order of twenty years; fertility was high (in spite of its reputed decline in the heyday of Rome). Nevertheless, there is evidence that contraception was practised to

171

some extent. The population had a young age-distribution, by modern standards.

10.5 Post-classical history

Some reduction in population size may well have accompanied the collapse of the Roman Empire and the passage of the Dark Ages. For Britain, archaeological evidence suggests a population of perhaps a million during the Roman occupation, and the same order of size appears to be implied by Domesday (AD 1086). Little or no increase can therefore have occurred, on balance, over a thousand years. Information from China, as interpreted by scholars, indicates that there were 70 million people there in the year AD 2 and 120 million people in the twelfth century AD, but only 100 millions in the fourteenth century AD. Very probably, wars or pestilence caused heavy losses to offset, or more than offset, any general upward tendency.

Evidence from other areas supports the idea of population fluctuations. Large areas of Ceylon, at present under jungle, betray signs of an elaborate system of irrigation dating from an earlier time. The associated civilization reached its highest point in the twelfth century AD, when the population probably exceeded that in the nineteenth century. Similarly, Egypt had at least 5 million people at the beginning of the Christian era but only 3 millions for a long period thereafter – up to the nineteenth century at least. The causes of these fluctuations are almost certainly military and political, on the one hand, and medical, on the other – plagues being recurrent. Probably the two often acted together. The European discovery of America led to a catastrophic fall in the indigenous population of countries such as Mexico and Peru, as well as the decline of the Red Indian. In some regions, crop failures may have brought starvation and so reduced numbers. Recently, the attention which has been devoted to old parish records in various countries of Europe has provided clear evidence of very lean years, when deaths multiplied and marriages and births sharply diminished in number, even as late as the seventeenth century.

Hollingsworth has produced a provisional list of places which, in the period 1348–1630 AD, lost more than 25 per cent of their population in one year for any reason. It contains nearly 100 names and includes the effects of plagues and earthquakes. The Black Death is reckoned to have wiped out about one-third of the people over a large part of Europe. In spite of such setbacks, the population of the world as a whole was nearly twice as high by the end of the seventeenth century as it had been in the time of Christ: the total numbers had reached 500–600 millions. Of these, about one-half lived in Asia and the rest were more or less equally divided between Europe and Africa. America (North and South) and Oceania are estimated to have contained no more than about a million each at this time.

An estimated life table for rural England in or about the year 1700, prepared by Renn, is given in table 10.1. It shows a rate of mortality very high (by modern standards in developed countries) in infancy and childhood, and also, to a lesser extent, in middle life.

Table 10.1. *Estimated abridged life table for England, rural areas, A.D. 1700*

Age x	l_x	$_5q_x$
0	100	0·30
5	70	0·04
10	67	0·04
15	64	0·07
20	60	0·10
25	54	0·12
30	48	0·13
35	42	0·13
40	37	0·14
45	32	0·14
50	28	0·17
55	23	0·17
60	19	0·21
65	15	0·21
70	11	0·27
75	7	0·36

10.6 The eighteenth century

Much of our information about this period is derived from historical research among Church registers, and it relates mainly to Europe and North America. The defects of this material are incompleteness — the data for some years are missing, and there have been failures to register; 'non-conformists' in religious observance were not included, and there is also a lack of an appropriate 'exposed to risk'. Such an exposed to risk could be built up if it were not for migration. On the other hand, data bearing upon illegitimacy, and on epidemics and other natural disasters may be available from the registers. The features shown by such investigations naturally vary from place to place, and from time to time, but in general the following statements are reasonably representative of experience during the period:

(1) birth rates were steady;

(2) death rates, and especially the incidence of child burials, began to decline at some time within the century;

(3) at times, marriages and births were lower in number than the average, and deaths were more numerous than usual; it would appear that epidemics or poor harvests were responsible;

(4) population began to grow steadily, mainly as a consequence of (2), although in some places also because of increasingly early marriage.

It appears from other research, for example, that into the demography of the aristocracy and of the ruling families (for whom reliable records are available for longer into the past than for the population generally), that late marriage, and more particularly non-marriage, had been popular as a method of limiting births, but that this form of control broke down in the eighteenth century. Birth control within marriage appears to have become prevalent among the upper classes in France from about the year 1780 onwards. The scale of its employment was not sufficiently widespread, however, to have any noticeable effect in retarding population growth generally.

The causes of the decline in mortality in the eighteenth century are not definitely known, but it is possible to point to such changes as the improvement in nutrition and clothing resulting from changes in agricultural and industrial technique, and improved production of fabrics. Agricultural production had previously been at only a moderate level, and little was known about the relative values of different foods in the promotion of health and strength. The first reductions in mortality almost certainly came about as by-products of other developments. One of the earliest of these developments was the commencement of large-scale farming and the introduction of new agricultural methods; these increased the food supply and hence the general standard of nourishment. Discoveries leading to the manufacture by machine of an abundant supply of textile goods enabled clothes to be purchased more cheaply and to be changed more frequently and, by improving personal cleanliness, brought about a reduction in insect-borne diseases. Better sanitation, a cleaner water supply and an expansion and improvement of medical services may also have contributed, but the main benefits from these sources were probably not experienced until the nineteenth century. On the other hand, industry was still rural in character in the eighteenth century, and had not caused a big migration into crowded conditions in the towns.

How greatly the growth of population was speeded up can be seen from the following estimates (numbers in millions):

	Europe	USA	Latin America	Asia	Other areas	World
1650	100	—	10	400	40	550
1750	—	—	15	500	70	725
1850	275	25	35	900	90	1,325

10.7   The ninetenth century: France

From this point onwards, attention can be directed to the experience of individual countries, and much interest resides in the different ways in which their populations have developed. Details of France, Britain, the USA and Ireland are perhaps sufficient to show the main range of experience in countries which at this time were rapidly achieving an economic sense. The developments in these four countries during the first half of the twentieth century will also be discussed.

France today has a population only twice as large as that estimated for the year 1700. From 1770 onwards there was a spread of knowledge of birth control, followed by a fairly general trend towards family limitation, and it is considered that by 1850 some form of control was probably practised by the majority of French families. No other European country can show such a marked development so early in its history.

According to one school of thought, the first tendency towards family limitation was economic in character and originated in the costly efforts of members of the bourgeoisie to rise into the aristocracy. Others emphasize the importance of political and religious effects such as the French Revolution and the accompanying decline in the influence of the Church. Certainly, good practical reasons for having fewer children were provided by a change in the law whereby the testamentary powers of the individual were limited. It became impossible to leave country estates wholly to eldest sons, and instead they had to be shared between the children. People therefore sought, by restricting the number of children, to avoid the repeated division of holdings into smaller portions. They thus avoided also any intense rural population pressure, and this may explain, at least in part, the relatively small 'drift to the towns' which has occurred in France.

The consequence of prolonged low fertility was that births only narrowly exceeded deaths in number, as may be seen from the vital statistics rates set out in table 10.2, and net reproduction rates were little above unity. The total population size, probably 28 millions in the year 1800, had not reached 40 millions by 1900, and this in spite of the fact that — uncharacteristically of the rest of Europe — there had been, not a net emigration, but a net immigration of $1\frac{1}{2}$ millions during the century.

Although the birth rate was relatively low in 1800, it did decline throughout the following 100 years, as table 10.2 shows, though recent researches have shown considerable variation from one part of the country to another, and something less than a steady downward trend in some areas. Mortality also fell, and so did the rate of natural increase. The history of the country can be seen in the figures for individual years, in several of which deaths exceeded births, for reasons of war (as in 1870), cholera or influenza. The age-distribution gradually became older, the proportion of people aged 60

Table 10.2. *Birth and death rates in France in the
nineteenth century (per thousand)*

Period	Birth rate	Death rate	Rate of natural increase
1801–10	32·0	27·8	4·2
1811–20	31·9	26·1	5·8
1821–30	31·0	25·1	5·9
1831–40	29·0	24·8	4·2
1841–50	27·4	23·3	4·1
1851–60	26·3	24·0	2·3
1861–70	26·4	23·2	3·2
1871–80	25·4	24·1	1·3
1881–90	23·9	22·1	1·8
1891–1900	22·1	21·4	0·7

and over rising from some 8 per cent at the beginning to $12\frac{1}{2}$ per cent at the
end of the century. Such developments, coupled with France's defeat at the
hands of Prussia in 1870, suggested to many people that lack of population
growth was making France too weak.

10.8 France in the first half of the twentieth century

The total population size remained virtually static from the beginning of the
present century until after the Second World War. Natural increase remained slight and of equally important influence upon numbers are such
factors as:

(1) immigration, which continued to augment the population;
(2) territorial changes: Alsace and Lorraine were regained after the First
World War;
(3) wartime losses attributable to enemy action; and
(4) reductions in the birth rate occasioned by the separation of married
couples in wartime, often rendered permanent by the death of the father.
The proportion of people over the age of 60 rose to 16 per cent.

Since 1945, population growth has become more notable; successive
French governments have offered inducements to married couples to increase the size of their families and these policies have achieved some success.
The sale of contraceptives has been prohibited since 1920, except where they
are prescribed on medical grounds, and from 1940 until very recently a severe
penal code was directed against abortion. Family allowances on a voluntary
basis began to appear in industry in 1916, and by 1930 almost half the working population was covered. Government intervention began in 1931 to
remedy complaints of uneven operation of the system of allowances, and

an extension to agricultural workers was effected after 1939. By 1945 the practice of granting allowances had developed into a large, integrated and costly social security system and the allowance represented a substantial proportion of the standard wage. In consequence, despite the illicit contraception and abortion which a repressive law tended to encourage, the birth rate in France recovered from 15·1 per thousand in 1935—9, when it was actually below the death rate of 15·7 per thousand, to a level of 18·7 per thousand in 1953, when the death rate was 12·9 per thousand. Although the birth rate has fallen since then, it has not declined far and France has been fairly successful in its aim of maintaining population growth.

Table 10·3 shows the development of family-building for couples married in certain recent years. The family sizes illustrated are larger by 10 per cent or more than those which would be needed for mere replacement, and it is estimated that as many as one-third of couples have more than 2 children. Families of 6 or more children are still not negligible, especially among farmers and other agricultural workers. First marriages are taking place earlier in life than they used to be, though rather more than before are severed by divorce.

Agriculture still retains an important place in the French economy. Rural population, which at the beginning of the present century accounted for about 60 per cent of the whole, still accounted for some 35 per cent in the 1960s.

10.9 British population in the nineteenth century

The first census held (in 1801) revealed a total population of over 10 millions, with a young age-distribution and a mainly rural domicile, agriculture being the principal source of livelihood: of the whole number 35 per cent were children, and more occupied persons were engaged in some aspect of farming than in any other pursuit. Registration of births, deaths and marriages had

Table 10.3. *Average size of family in France according to year of marriage 1943—63 and duration of marriage*

Completed duration of marriage in years	Year of marriage				
	1943	1948	1953	1958	1963
1	0·40	0·40	0·40	0·41	0·43
6	1·48	1·51	1·57	1·62	1·62
11	2·00	2·01	2·11	2·14	2·13
16	2·25	2·24	2·35	2·37	
21	2·35	2·32	2·45		
26	2·38	2·35			

not begun, and so details of mortality or fertility are not available, but it is known from the succeeding enumerations that population increased by nearly 1½ per cent per annum during the first half of the nineteenth century. The rate of growth was rather less at the beginning and the end of this half century than it was in the middle decades, possibly because of the Napoleonic Wars in the first instance and the 'Hungry Forties' in the second, as compared with the more prosperous and peaceful central period.

When registration began, the crude death rate was found to be about 22 per thousand; the recorded crude birth rate was about 33 per thousand, but this is known to be an understatement, and probably 35 per thousand is a more correct figure. It is believed, from general evidence, that a hundred years before this time the fertility rate had been much the same, but the death rate had been considerably higher than in 1840. Because of this reduction in mortality, the population had begun to grow rapidly in number. The mortality rate declined little immediately after 1840, however, and probably the improvements in longevity achieved during the eighteenth century had reached their limit, or were being offset by the bad effects of the industrial revolution in the mid-nineteenth century. The transfer from an agricultural way of life to urban slum conditions for the mass of the people was well under way. Large numbers were crowded into insanitary settlements. Hours were long in the factories and there was little or no protection from industrial accidents and diseases. Children suffered especially until the Factory Acts gradually placed restrictions upon their employment.

The second half of the nineteenth century was a period of rapid technological development and of relatively peaceful foreign relations. The population, which had already doubled since 1800 to reach about 20 millions by mid-century, nearly doubled again by 1900. Mortality rates fell substantially, as the result mainly of improved sanitation and public health measures, but also because of medical advances, such as antisepsis. The USA provided good opportunities for emigration, as the lands of the Far West were opened up, and many people availed themselves of these opportunities: perhaps a million persons left in this way, in a stream the irregularity of whose flow reflected the variations in economic circumstances from time to time on both sides of the Atlantic.

The period is most remarkable, however, for the first emergence of a significant decline in fertility; beginning about 1870, the fall developed steadily and by the end of the century it had amounted to as much as 20 per cent. Judging by the experience of some countries, the decline in the level of fertility in Britain is remarkable not for its emergence but for the lateness of its occurrence. In France, the practice of family limitation had started to grow during the eighteenth century (see §10.6). In Britain, the subjugation of women to men, the influence of religion and the impact of popular prejudice for a long time prevented public discussion of any form of

178

birth control except Malthus's 'moral restraint' (see §20.4). There is no doubt, however, that many women found it a great strain to bear and rear a large family: Queen Victoria herself recorded this in her diary. They would naturally desire to reduce the strain if suitable and acceptable means of doing so were provided. Eventually Bradlaugh and Mrs Besant defied the current conventions by publishing a book about birth control, and were brought to trial amid great publicity. Enormous interest was aroused; many people realized for the first time that convenient and effective methods of contraception were available, and the fall in fertility started almost immediately afterwards. It seems likely that economic conditions were propitious for the change at the moment of time. According to Banks, twenty-five years of prosperity had increased the appetite of the upper classes for the appurtenances of wealth, but an economic recession was beginning to demand personal economies, thus reinforcing the desire of many people to reduce family size. Other writers have stressed that, for the lower classes, children had ceased to be the financial asset that they had become before the passage of the Factory Acts, and by reason of the Education Acts were instead becoming an increasing burden. This burden has since been greatly accentuated (per child born) by falls in infant and child mortality and by increases in the school-leaving age.

Fig. 10.4 shows how the numbers of large families have been drastically reduced over the years. The long continuation of the fall in fertility was not associated with a general decline in economic standards, for on the whole these rose steadily. The fact is that once fashions and views started to change, for a variety of reasons the new way of life came in due time to be adopted by almost everyone. Education and the emancipation of women proceeded apace, and there was little or no chance of a reversion to the older order of things. This change was naturally reflected in a decline in the annual rate of population growth, and in a change in age-distribution. The proportion of children aged under 15 to persons of all ages fell to 32 per cent by 1900, and the proportion of the middle-aged rose correspondingly, the relative numbers of the aged changed little — only from $4\frac{1}{2}$ per cent in 1850 to 5 per cent in 1900. The changes in age-distribution and size may be seen from figs. 10.1 and 10.2 below, which show the numbers in the various age-groups and, in the smooth curves, the life-table populations based on the then-current births and mortality (see § 10.11). Judging by the experience of other countries, the decline in fertility is not exceptional; it was the normal consequence of a complex of social factors associated with the industrial revolution. As elsewhere, the fall began in the upper classes, but by 1900 had hardly begun to affect the working population.

Some particulars of birth and death rates are given in table 10.4 by way of illustration of the foregoing. The contrasts with the French data in table 10.2 are illuminating: a much higher birth rate coupled with a lower death rate

Table 10.4. *Specimen birth and death rates for Britain
in the nineteenth century (per thousand)*

Period	Birth rate	Death rate	Rate of natural increase
1856—60	34·3	21·7	12·6
1876—80	35·2	20·8	14·4
1896—1900	29·4	17·8	11·6

gave rise to a relatively rapid population increase in Britain and an age-distribution which was still comparatively young at the end of the century.

Although international comparisons of crude vital rates can be misleading, and too much reliance should therefore not be placed on these contrasts as a precise measure, the general picture cannot be in doubt. Indeed, the British woman's net reproduction rate was probably of the order of 1·40 in the second half of the nineteenth century, or about one-third above the French level. It may be noted that the decline in the birth rate had not gone very far in Britain by the end of the century: a drop of only perhaps 15 per cent from its peak value had taken place.

10.10 General developments in Britain 1900–50

The first part of the twentieth century was dominated demographically by the First World War, 1914—18, not only for the losses sustained, which distorted the age-distribution and balance of the sexes and consequently influenced the marriage rates, but also for its economic and social effects. Foremost among these was a speeding-up in the emancipation of women, naturally accompanied by an increase in the rate of fall in family size. The war not only brought casualties caused by the actual fighting but also changes in mortality and fertility that occurred under its influence; for instance, there were more civilian deaths because of lowered resistance to disease, and fewer births owing to the enforced separation of married couples.

The war losses may be set out approximately as follows for England and Wales:

Military losses	550,000
Excess civilian deaths	150,000*
Loss of births	600,000
Total	1,3000,000

* Excluding some 200,000 influenza deaths in the pandemic of 1918—19, for which the war may or may not have been directly accountable.

It has been estimated that the total 'loss' of population in England and Wales between 1911 and 1945, i.e. the difference between the numbers enumerated in the later year and those which would have been counted if there had been a continuation of the mortality and fertility of 1911, was no less than 7 millions. The losses shown above, together with the relatively small 1939–45 war deaths, constitute therefore a low proportion of the whole change in this period. The foregoing figures are, of course, speculative and they are given as an indication of the order of magnitude of the effects discussed and not as precise estimates.

Another powerful force, consequent to some extent on the war, was the economic depression of the early 1930s, during which up to 20 per cent of the working population experienced unemployment. Owing to the stringency of the times, many marriages had to be postponed, and fertility fell temporarily to replacement level, or even below, opening up the apparent prospect of a declining population. One result of the depression was to speed up the fall in fertility of the working classes, who had already begun to have fewer children than before. As a result, the differentials in family size that had appeared before the beginning of the century were considerably narrowed.

Longevity improved during the whole period, mortality falling principally at the younger ages. The main cause was the further medical progress achieved in the elimination of infectious diseases and their more important consequences. The inevitable result of a long period of falling fertility was a marked ageing of the population; the proportion over retirement age (65 for men, 60 for women) had increased to over 15 per cent by the middle of the century. The proportion of children aged under 15 was then only 22 per cent.

Emigration, which had continued at a high level in the early part of the period, diminished — mainly because of restrictions on entry into the USA. A net inward balance was recorded in the 1930s, resulting from the arrival in Britain of the victims of persecution in Europe. Subsequently, emigration to the Old Commonwealth of Australia, Canada and New Zealand has been more or less balanced by an influx from the New Commonwealth (The West Indies, Africa, India and Pakistan).

In the Second World War, fatal casualties among members of the British Armed Forces amounted to 252,000, and in addition there were 60,000 deaths of British civilians due to enemy action. It is doubtful whether any loss of births or excess civilian deaths from other causes resulted from the conflict, although some births were probably postponed for a while. The Second World War thus did not cause such a big extinction of life as did the First, and the casualties fell less exclusively among the younger men.

10.11 British population growth and distribution

As a result of these developments, the total population of Britain increased from 37 millions in 1900 to 50 millions by mid-century, an average annual rate of increase of about $\frac{1}{2}$ per cent. The proportions of males and females have remained in the neighbourhood of 48 : 52 for all ages together, but at the marriageable ages there has been a significant development: the proportion at ages 15—35 was below that for all ages up to 1921 but higher than that for all ages in 1941 and 1961. In the nineteenth century and the early part of the twentieth century, when emigration was substantial, the balance of the sexes was affected, particularly at the young ages, because more men than women went abroad. Moreover, male mortality exceeded that of females, and this difference reinforced the selective effect of emigration. In recent years, however, the cessation of emigration and the fall of mortality at young ages to a low level have removed the selective effect. In these circumstances, the fact that some 5 per cent more boys than girls are born each year is now the predominant factor, and this will, other things being equal, raise the male/female ratio at older ages in the course of time. Changes in the age-distribution are illustrated in figs. 10.1, 10.2, and 10.3 which give 'population pyramids' for England and Wales in 1901, 1931 and 1956 respectively. Curves have been added to show the corresponding outlines of the stationary populations that would be supported by a constant inflow of young children in the same numbers as in the year in question if the mortality then current continued to be experienced.

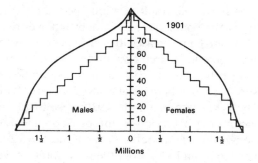

Fig. 10.1. Population pyramid, 1901 (England and Wales).

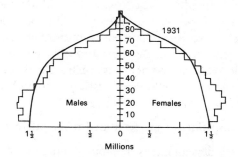

Fig. 10.2. Population pyramid, 1931 (England and Wales).

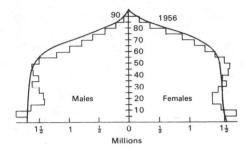

Fig. 10.3. Population pyramid, 1956 (England and Wales).

In 1901 the stationary population was greater than the actual at all ages except the first. The excess is proportionately about the same as in 1841 it is the consequence of a net fertility of more than replacement level (see also fig. 18.1 below and accompanying text).

In 1931 the theoretical curve followed the outline of the pyramid more closely at the older ages, although the actual population of the aged was still smaller than the numbers to be expected on the basis of current births and current mortality. The actual numbers at the reproductive ages, however, considerably exceeded those in the stationary population. If, therefore, children continued to be born in the same numbers each year, if migration was negligible and mortality remained constant, the 'bulge' which had been located at ages 5—40 in 1931 would move as people grew older; it would be present at ages 30—65 in 1956, and at ages 50—85 in 1976, and so on, slowly diminishing in size all the time. The pyramid for 1956 confirms the expected upward movement for the 'bulge' and shows, at the base, the relatively large numbers of children resulting from a recent increase in fertility. Because of this increase the 'bulge' does not protrude so much outside the theoretical curve as it might otherwise have done.

The effect of two world wars may be seen in the pyramids. That of the first is the more evident, and shows up as a flattening of the side for males, as compared with females, at ages around 50—45 in 1931 and around 65—75 in 1956.

The most notable features of the recent changes in the distribution of the population by area of residence are a decline in the numbers living in Inner London and in the rural Eastern and South-Western regions in favour of an increase in the South-Eastern region as a whole.

10.12   The fall in British fertility 1900—50

During the 1930s, fears began to be expressed that the population of Britain would set itself on a downward track, and as a consequence of the general disquiet at this prospect a Royal Commission was set up to investigate the matter. Its Report was published in 1949 and this showed that the fears were unlikely to be realized. The detailed study of fertility trends made by the Commission enable a fuller picture to be given of the changes in the half century than would be presented by a series of crude birth rates, and the problem which was the cause of this study renders it desirable to set forth a few further particulars here. Analysis of fertility was made as between (i) marriage and (ii) family size on a generation and a cohort basis respectively.

The marriage experience up to the middle of the century is shown in table 10.5, which gives the relative numbers remaining unmarried at various ages among the men and women who attained age 16 in various groups of years, in the form of 'gross nuptiality', mortality and migration having been eliminated. The table indicates a trend towards earlier marriage (even though, as is often the case with analysis in generation form, it cannot be finished off because the experience of the later generations has not yet been completed). It also suggests that the proportion ultimately marrying was on the increase, so in itself it contained no suggestion of a potential decline in fertility.

Fig. 10.4 gives more information mostly derived from the Family Census of 1946. The percentages in the various categories of completed family size (no children, 1 child or 2 children, 3 or 4 children, 5—9 children, 10 or more children) are shown by the thickness of the bands between the dividing lines. The chart has been brought up to date and the dotted lines give not un-

Table 10.5. *Numbers remaining unmarried out of 1,000 at age 16 according to the experience of generations, England and Wales*

Age	1917—20	1921—4	1925—8	1929—32	1933—6
	Men who attained age 16 in the years				
16	1,000	1,000	1,000	1,000	1,000
20	987	987	985	983	982
25	661	676	668	611	553
28	414	424	393	332	337
30	304	304	266	250	—
32	237	225	197	193	—
35	171	153	146	—	—
	Women who attained age 16 in the years				
16	1,000	1,000	1,000	1,000	1,000
20	937	937	926	912	888
25	544	549	522	432	364
28	368	370	324	250	234
30	302	296	245	203	—
32	260	249	204	172	—
35	222	208	175	—	—

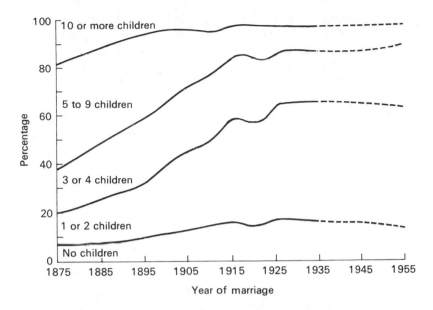

Fig. 10.4. Percentages of families of various sizes, 1875–1945 (Britain).

reasonable forecasts for families that will be completed in the near future. The year of marriage of the parents is shown along the bottom of the chart. The tendency towards a small and uniform family size is clearly seen in a widening of the band representing 1 or 2 children and in the narrowing of the bands for 5 children or over. In comparison with the big alterations of the past half-century the change expected in the next two decades was small.

A tabulation of the Census data that had a considerable influence upon the deliberations of the Commission is reproduced in table 10.6, which compares the average numbers of births per married couple reaching durations 1, 2, ..., 21 years of marriage by the end of 1938, i.e. those married respectively in 1937, 1936, ..., 1917, with the corresponding post-census data for 1948. At the high durations each 1938 figure exceeded the corresponding 1948 figure by a considerable margin; thus the couples married in 1917–25 had had by the end of 1938 more children than the couples married in 1927–35 by the end of 1948. At shorter durations, however, the 1938 and 1948 figures were much closer together, and it was deduced that no material fall in family size had taken place. The conclusion was reached from this and other analyses that average family sizes had tended to be stable for about twenty years.

A number of criticisms have subsequently been made of the Commission's assumption of stability in the size of the family. One of the points made has been that the Commission concentrated too much on the average of the

185

Table 10.6. *Estimated average number of births to cohorts of married women reaching similar durations of marriage at the end of (a) 1938 and (b) 1948, Britain*

(Women whose first marriages terminated before they reached age 45 are excluded.)

No. of years since end of calendar year in which the group of couples were married (1)	1938 Year of marriage (2)	Av. no. of births per married couple (3)	1948 Year of marriage (4)	Av. no. of births per married couple (5)	No. of births to end of 1948 as % of corresponding duration group in 1939 (6)
1	1937	0·40	1947	*	*
2	1936	0·64	1946	*	*
3	1935	0·84	1945	*	*
4	1934	1·02	1944	1·01	99
5	1933	1·16	1943	1·20	104
6	1932	1·31	1942	1·26	96
7	1931	1·43	1941	1·42	100
8	1930	1·56	1940	1·46	93
9	1929	1·61	1939	1·56	97
10	1928	1·71	1938	1·70	100
11	1927	1·80	1937	1·75	97
12	1926	1·89	1936	1·82	96
13	1925	1·99	1935	1·89	95
14	1924	2·09	1934	1·92	92
15	1923	2·15	1933	1·96	91
16	1922	2·23	1932	2·02	91
17	1921	2·34	1931	2·04	87
18	1920	2·47	1930	2·12	86
19	1919	2·60	1929	2·11	81
20	1918	2·51	1928	2·12	84
21	1917	2·50	1927	2·16	86

* Not available.

family distribution and did not pay enough attention to its dispersion. As may be seen from fig. 10.4 the relative numbers of large and small families have not remained stable. Large families have continued to decline in number in accordance with a long-established trend; but the rise in the size of the smaller families which balanced it was a new and unprecedented development, the future course of which is much more speculative.

One effect of the large changes in fertility, mortality and age at marriage in recent decades is that the vital pattern of people's lives has altered considerably. Thus the average woman born in 1870 married at age 26, had her last child at age 35 and lost her husband (if he died first) when she was 58; the average woman born in 1930, however, married at age 24, had her last child at 28 and is not expected to become a widow until she is 65. The later couple should thus normally enjoy a considerable period of life together after the children had grown up, whereas the earlier couple could hardly expect to do so.

10.13 The population of the USA in the nineteenth century

Although today there are some 200 million people in the USA, in 1820 the population was only 10 millions and was lower than that in England. Historical research has shown that the birth rate had begun to fall even before the beginning of the nineteenth century, but even so the population grew rapidly in the first decades of the century — perhaps by 35 per cent every ten years; indeed the attention of Malthus was attracted to this outstanding example of increase. It might be natural to suppose that migration played a substantial part in the rapidity of the demographic upsurge, but in fact this was by no means the most important factor. The big inflow had hardly begun at that time, and even when it was at its height it never rivalled the increments from natural increase.

The fall in fertility, which led to differences in birth rates between States even by the time of the first census in 1800, could be due in part to purely 'demographic' factors such as an increase in age-distribution or an imbalance of the numbers of the sexes. In the absence of full data for the period, there can be no certainty about the precise extent of the contribution of these factors, but it is believed that more esoteric influences also played a part. The industrial revolution can hardly be blamed, for it had not effectively begun in the USA by Napoleonic times; but a tendency towards the formation of towns, and the beginning of urban life, has been detected, and this may have played a significant part in the early fall of fertility. It would seem that the large families prevalent in the eighteenth century were a concomitant of ample land availability, and that the tendency to live in towns, in more restricted space, had an effect in reducing the number of children (this occurred before the opening up of the West). At some stage, also, the dominance of men in domestic matters began to give way to a greater equality of the sexes, or even to the female dominance which is regarded by many as a feature of American life today. This change also may have had an effect on fertility. It will be noted that these causes of the fall are quite different from those for Britain. It is known for instance, that contraceptives were freely available as early as 1820, whereas an attempt in Britain to distribute information about birth control at that time was abortive. The Bradlaugh—Besant trial was, indeed, concerned with a pamphlet that had been freely circulated in the USA since the early 1840s.

It has been estimated that the total number of immigrants during the nineteenth century was about 18 millions. In that century there was an excess of births over deaths of 53 millions.

187

10.14 The first half of the twentieth century in the USA

During the late 1920s and early 1930s, the USA experienced a period of acute economic depression. Marriage rates fell to a low level, and births were relatively few. Net reproduction rates fell to just below unity. In due course, however, prosperity returned and the birth rate rose again. So also did marriages, as may be seen from table 10.7.

Divorce rates followed a generally increasing course over the half-century, but at a much lower level. After the Second World War large families became common. After the immediate post-war peak, which was largely the result of the uniting or reuniting of many married couples after long separation, births remained at a relatively high level instead of falling as predicted. People married young and in high proportions, and in the very favourable economic circumstances of the country it is not surprising that they have also been raising large families — going beyond the one or two children that were customary before the Second World War, to have three or four children or even more.

Table 10.8 shows the average annual numbers of births of various orders in 1940–1 and 1954–5, respectively, and the percentage increases in the numbers. The population of married women aged 15–45 rose by about one-fifth between the first period and the second; the right-hand column therefore shows the percentage increase in fertility rates after allowing for this growth in the exposed to risk. By 1950, children under 15 formed a very material part of the population — not far short of 30 per cent — as against only 8 per cent aged 65 and over.

10.15 Ireland

The course of population growth in Ireland since 1841 is shown in table 10.9. The 'six counties' referred to are the north-eastern region now known as

Table 10.7. *Marriage rates for unmarried men and women aged 15 and over USA, 1900–50 (per thousand)*

Year	Men	Women
1900	61	68
1910	67	77
1920	85	92
1930	64	68
1940	83	83
1950	100	90

Table 10.8. *Number of children born by birth-order, USA, 1940—1 and*
1854—5

Order of birth	No. of births per annum (thousands)		Increase in numbers (%)	Increase in rate per married woman aged 15—45 (%)
	1940—1	1954—5		
1st	933	1,060	+ 14	−11
2nd	638	1,073	+ 68	+34
3rd	348	766	+ 120	+72
4th	202	436	+116	+70
5th	128	232	+ 81	+50
6th and higher	281	333	+ 19	− 7
Total	2,530	3,900	+ 54	+22

Table 10.9. *The population of Ireland, 1841—1951*

Census Year	Total population (thousands)		
	6 counties	26 counties	Whole
1841	1,646	6,529	8,175
1851	1,440	5,112	6,552
1861	1,397	4,402	5,799
1871	1,359	4,053	5,412
1901	1,237	3,222	4,459
1951	1,371	2,961	4,332

Ulster, and the remaining 26 counties are the part of the country known in recent years as Eire. There are estimated to have been some 3 million persons in the whole of Ireland in 1750. During the ensuing ninety years their numbers grew as fast as, or perhaps even faster than, those of persons in England; but in 1950 the population had fallen to less than $4\frac{1}{2}$ millions, and thus it had decreased by nearly one-half during a period when the British population more than doubled. As the numbers of people in Northern Ireland declined relatively little, the fall in Eire was all the more striking.

Except among primitive peoples, a declining population is unique in the recent annals of the world. The origin of this trend was one special event — the great famine of 1846—7 during which the potato crop failed. It was the development of this crop that had supported the growth of the Irish population, and its failure provided convincing evidence that the country was overpopulated. Emigration, mainly to the USA, which had started in the eighteenth century, then developed on a large scale. This, however, was not the only factor at work. To quote Professor D. V. Glass, 'emigration was not the sole cause of the continuous and unique fall in the population of Eire after 1841. The responsibility for that fall is shared by the spread of moral restraint, by the steady rise in the proportions of men and women who

189

did not marry.' Further, those who marry now do so at a relatively late age. The pattern of bachelorhood and emigration, once formed, persisted so long as to become a tradition. Originally very effective in preventing a disastrous increase in population in the nineteenth century, it continued to operate perhaps too potently in the twentieth.

Apart from Dublin, towns have not grown, and the dispersion of the people throughout the area has changed but little. Investment is on a small scale, and although industry has grown in recent years it might well have done so more rapidly. Imports exceed exports in value and external trade has declined; in 1952 the volume of exports was only 76 per cent of that of 1928. A change certainly appears to be necessary in order to revitalize the economic life of the country.

As fertility within marriage has remained relatively high in Eire — a Roman Catholic country — a reduction in average age at marriage should have the effect of increasing the rate of population growth. Various steps have therefore been recommended for encouraging early marriage — such as the removal of the bar to married women in some spheres of employment, the promotion of housing schemes and the framing of a suitable education policy for the schools.

10.16 Some notes on the population history of certain other countries

Russia

The Union of Soviet Socialist Republics is more than eight million square miles in extent — a space into which Great Britain and France together could be fitted no less than twenty-eight times — and it is approximately equal in size to the combined area of Central and North America. Up to 1950 there had been only three complete modern censuses, in 1897, 1926 and 1939, registration of births and deaths has been incomplete and the publication of statistics intermittent; the demographic history and present situation of the Union are thus less clear than for some other countries. It is believed, however, that in the earlier part of the eighteenth century there were about 20 million people in Russia, mainly in the European part, and that by the middle of the nineteenth century the number of persons had increased to 60 millions. In 1939, 171 millions were enumerated, and within the enlarged boundaries of today the population is probably now in excess of 200 millions. This tenfold increase in 200 years is similar to the rate of growth of the British population in the same period, but the circumstances of the two increases are different. The number of persons per square mile is far lower in Russia, and much of the development there has taken the form of opening up new territories. It is estimated that there was a net movement of $3\frac{1}{2}$ million people from the western to the Asiatic part of the country in the nineteenth century, and of another $3\frac{1}{2}$ millions in the years 1900—14. In more recent times internal migration is said to have been on a massive scale.

The rate of population growth in the Soviet Union has remained appreciable. In 1926, the reported birth rate of 44 per thousand for the European part exceeded the reported death rate by 25 per thousand and, although the birth rate for the whole territory has now fallen to under 20 per thousand, mortality has fallen also and the rate of natural increase is still about 10 per thousand. The fall in fertility may have been associated with a movement towards the towns, in which nearly 60 per cent of Russians now live, compared with 15 per cent in 1926, and with social and economic changes under the communist regime. But some while ago the Soviet government called upon parents for an increase in the numbers of their children, and proclaimed a three-child, rather than a two-child, family to be the national ideal. The doctrine of Malthus is regarded as heretical, and it is the official view that the added productivity arising from any likely increase in population in future will provide all the resources required.

India

On the strength of very limited information, it is believed that the population of India increased, probably in a somewhat irregular fashion, during the seventeenth to nineteenth centuries. In more recent times, the rate of growth has been rapid, and from rather more than 250 millions in 1921 the number of people rose by 1951 to over 360 millions. Incompleteness of registration of births and deaths has made it difficult to give an accurate picture of mortality or fertility, but from indirect assessments it appears that, except in the years of famine, the rate of natural increase remained positive and averaged over 10 per thousand. Although some Indians have moved overseas, emigration has necessarily been insignificant in relation to so large a population. The problem has been accentuated by a number of special social, economic and demographic factors. First, early marriage is highly prevalent: so much so that in spite of laws to the contrary, many children are wedded before the attainment of puberty. The 1951 Census disclosed that between the ages of 5 and 14 there were 3 million married boys and 6 million married girls — not to mention 200 thousand widowed persons. With such early marriages are associated high fertility and high maternal and infant mortality. Marriage is not only early but also universal; the social system offers no emotional obstacle and the prevailing economic set-up offers little financial deterrent.

Another, more unusual, factor is a deficiency of women in the population — around 5 per cent of all ages together. This appears to be the result of the

191

greater value that parents have put upon boys than upon girls, with the result that the girls are relatively neglected in childhood. Female mortality is high relative to male mortality. Possibly — although this is not certain — the shortage of women has acted as an encouragement to large family size. Another encouragement has been the social ban on the remarriage of widows, which prevents child-bearing among an appreciable proportion of the potentially fertile women.

Japan

In stable national conditions, 1725—1850, the Japanese population, which was partially enumerated every six years, is known to have remained nearly constant at about 30 millions. The advent of the modern era, after the opening of the country to foreign trade and influence, was accompanied by an increase in numbers, as in other countries, and by 1920 the population had grown to 56 millions. The recorded birth rates and death rates both rose during this period. This change may have been due in part to an improvement in the proportion of events registered, but there was also a real upward movement in fertility that precipitated the increase in population, and this was attributable, at least in part, to measures designed to suppress abortion and infanticide. The population continued to increase after 1920, despite a fall in fertility due to urbanization and other effects of industrialization such as a rise in the age at marriage.

Emigration has never supplied an adequate outlet to Japanese population pressure and, even when prospects were favourable because of national expansion of territory, only about $3\frac{1}{2}$ million Japanese lived in Korea, Manchuria and elsewhere overseas. Since 1945 many of the pre-war opportunities for outward movement have been lost.

China

Great interest attaches to China's population, not only for its enormous size, and consequent importance in world demography today, but also for the characteristics of a distinctive and inventive people. For many centuries China's culture was well ahead of that of other peoples, and so it is not surprising to learn that many censuses have been held through the ages. Unfortunately, the past century has been a period of great economic and political disturbance, inimical both to population and to records of population. Wars and political upheavals have been accompanied by famine and pestilence as well as flooding of the big rivers near which so many people live. After the inception of the communist regime in 1949, however, a census was held in 1953, when no less than 600 million people were recorded — although this includes a relatively small number of Chinese living in Formosa and elsewhere overseas from the Mainland. The birth rate was then assessed at 37 per thousand and the death rate at 17 per thousand.

Australia

As in the United States, immigration has made a substantial but not a dominating contribution to population growth in Australia. During the period 1861—1900, 71 per cent of the increase in numbers (from about 1·1 millions to 3·7 millions) was attributable to an excess of births over deaths, and in 1901 the proportion of people who had been born in Australia was 77 per cent. A similar contribution has been made by natural increase to the further growth of the population to its present size of between 9 and 10 millions. During the six years 1948—53 the detailed movement was as follows (numbers in thousands):

Year	Births	Deaths	Net natural increase	Immi-grants	Emi-grants	Net gain from migration	Total increase
1948	178	77	101	66	17	49	150
1949	181	75	106	167	18	149	255
1950	191	78	113	175	21	154	267
1951	193	82	111	133	22	111	222
1952	202	82	120	128	30	98	218
1953	202	80	122	75	32	43	165

From these figures the important but variable contribution of migration to total growth may be seen. The period shown was a favourable one economically, and both fertility and immigration were relatively high at that time.

Out of the 175,000 immigrants in 1950, 156,000 were drawn from Europe: 52,000 came from the United Kingdom; 57,000 from Germany and 17,000 from Italy. 102,000 were men and 73,000 women, and the proportions of various ages were:

Age group	0—9	10—19	20—29	30—39	40—49	>49
Percentage	18	11	33	21	10	7

10.17   European experience generally — transition theory

European countries, and also the countries peopled by persons of European origin, have all exhibited a major decline in mortality and a major decline in fertility during the last two centuries, although the timing has varied widely. Demographers have naturally sought to generalize on the whole compass of this experience, in order to form theories of change that should be applicable over as wide an area as possible. Such attempts are naturally of much interest, and they could also have a prognostic value in the process if the deductions made as a result could be applied to countries which today have not yet begun to show comparable developments. A number of theories of 'demographic transition' have been advanced by various writers; they tend to suggest that the concomitants of the industrial revolution are:

(1) first, a decline in mortality, from the level experienced in wholly agricultural economies to a much lower level;

(2) then, a fall in fertility of a similar character, ending when the birth rate
reaches a new level;

(3) finally, a state of stability in mortality and fertility, both having attained
a value appropriate to an industrial nation.

These statements by themselves consist of a series of empirical observations and little more. The theory seeks, however, to attribute specific causes
to the changes. In the case of mortality, it is argued, both the increased
scientific knowledge and the enhanced economic wealth acquired during
development necessarily lead to a saving of life in infancy, childhood and
early adulthood and, generally, a prolongation of existence at all stages of
life; this is, indeed, fairly evident. For fertility, the effect of modernization is
less obvious; it is not physical but psychological. Traditional values decline;
the need for children is lessened; people may perhaps prefer to have modern
household appliances rather than additional babies; the wish to advance
socially may inhibit family building; certainly if people desire to have fewer
children than are physiologically possible they have the means to ensure
that they have no more than they want. Modernization may well proceed
quite far before these ideas ripen into action, owing to human conservatism;
the fall in fertility will then be delayed well beyond the start of the decline
in mortality.

The possible applicability of this theory to countries not yet industrialized
will be touched upon in chapter 12. In relation to Europe, the theory may be
questioned, *inter alia*, on the following grounds:

(1) it does not fully explain why in some countries the fall started later than
in others, but then proceeded all the more rapidly; although this could be
regarded as the outcome of local delays holding up the change for a time
and causing a greater sense of urgency, it is not really catered for in the
general thesis;

(2) the relationship between the timing and speed of the mortality decline
and those of the fall in fertility have been so variable that the theory does not
appear to account satisfactorily for all the events which have happened;

(3) the social-class pattern of the fertility decline is not completely accounted for; if the theory explains the change for the rich, it seems hardly sufficient in the case of the poor, and vice versa;

(4) once the transition period has ended, fertility has not proved steady, as
provided for in the model, but has tended to rise again — see the next chapter;
although such an occurrence could be said to be outside the range of application of the theory, the fact that an unexplained contrary movement happened
subsequently must detract from the force of the supposition.

Table 10.10 shows the course of the crude birth rate in the first half of the

194

Table 10.10. *Crude birth rates in certain European countries in the first half of the twentieth century*

(Per thousand.)

Period	Belgium	Germany	Holland	Hungary	Sweden	England and Wales	France
1901–10	26	33	30	36	26	27	21
1920–4	21	23	27	30	20	21	20
1935–9	16	19	20	20	14	15	15
1950–4	17	16	22	22	15	16	20

twentieth century in five European countries, with figures for England and Wales and for France for purposes of comparison. The fall in fertility started later in Germany, Holland and Hungary and in the latter two of these countries it remained relatively high even at the mid-century. The table brings out the recovery in France's birth-rate since the Second World War.

10.18 World population growth 1800–1950

The growth — nearly a trebling — of population over the 150 years is illustrated in table 10.11, which shows how the newly-colonized areas of America and Oceania increased the fastest — about 14 times. Europe's trebling seems modest by comparison. Africa and Asia started their growth late but the vast numbers in Asia (more than half the world total throughout) renders it of the greatest importance.

Table 10.11. *Estimated world population, by regions, in 1800, 1850, 1900 and 1950 (to nearest five million)*

Region	1800	1850	1900	1950
Africa	100	100	140	220
Latin America	20	35	65	160
North America	5	25	80	165
Asia	600	750	900	1,350
Europe	130	195	300	390
Russia	65	85	130	180
Oceania	—	—	5	15
Total	920	1,190	1,620	2,480

SELECT BIBLIOGRAPHY

Ohlin, G. 'Historical Outline of World Population Growth', *World Population Conference, 1965*, (United Nations Organization, New York, 1967).

Blacker, J. G. C. 'Social Ambitions of the Bourgeoisie in 18th Century France, and their Relation to Family Limitation', *Population Studies*, **11** (1957), 46.

Hopkins, K. 'Contraception in the Roman Empire', *Comparative Studies in Society and History,* **8** (1965), 124.

Renn, D. F. 'The Past Population of Britain — an Archaeological Approach', *Journal of the Institute of Actuaries Students' Society,* **15** (1960), 445.

Hollingsworth, T. H. 'Population Crisis in the Past.' In *Resources and Population* (Academic Press, London, 1973).

Conceptión, M. B. *Wanted. A Theory of the Demographic Transition.* IUSSP Australian Conference Papers, 1967.

van de Walle, E. and Knodel, J. *Demographic Transition and Fertility Decline: the European Case.* IUSSP Australian Conference Papers, 1967.

Lee, R. 'Estimating Series of Vital Rates and Age Structures from Baptisms and Burials.' *Population Studies,* **28** (1974), 495.

11 Populations today

11.1 Introduction

The purpose of this chapter is to complete the historical picture set forth in chapter 10 by discussing the principal characteristics of populations as they are today, all over the world. These characteristics represent, too, the starting point for the projected prospects for the future with which chapter 14 will deal. An analysis of the world population situation at the present time is also a useful precursor to the matters to be referred to in chapters 12 and 13, namely the economic implications of and political influences upon population trends.

The present chapter starts by showing some data relating to the world as a whole; thereafter it enters more into the detail of the principal component populations. Subsequently it gives some idea of the pictures presented, in a demographic sense, by some of the most recent censuses, indicating how populations are distributed with regard to such elements as age, area of residence, and family structure, and how far the distributions vary. The data will be drawn in the main from the statistics shown in the UN *Demographic Year Book*, which are a very comprehensive collection, and useful in spite of their imperfections.

11.2 World population today

Table 11.1 gives some information about recent world population growth, and illustrates the well-known features that:

(1) the numbers of people are large and increasing;
(2) the rate of growth has increased but is tending to level off;
(3) the growth rate is higher in some areas than in others.

Prominent among the features of the table are the decline in growth rate in North America, Russia and East Asia in recent years, and a continued increase in growth in Africa and the rest of Asia. About one-half of the world's population is growing at nearly 3 per cent per annum; one-quarter at around 2 per cent per annum; and the remainder at roughly 1 per cent per annum.

197

Table 11.1. *The recent growth of world population*

Region	Estimated total populations (millions)		Estimated annual rate of increase (%)		
	1960	1970	1950—60	1960—62	1965—72
North America	199	228	1·8	1·6	1·2
Europe	425	462	0·8	0·9	0·8
Oceania	16	19	2·5	2·2	2·1
USSR	214	243	1·6	1·7	1·0
All richer areas	854	952	1·3	1·3	1·0
Africa	270	344	2·2	2·4	2·6
Latin America	213	283	2·8	2·8	2·9
S.W. and S. Asia	646	839	1·8	2·4	2·8
S.E. Asia	219	287	2·4	2·7	2·9
E. Asia	780	930	2·0	2·3	1·8
All poorer areas	2,128	2,683	2·1	2·4	2·5
World total	2,982	3,635	1·8	2·1	2·1

11.3   World fertility, mortality and migration

On the scale of any area containing hundreds of millions of people, migratory movements into or out of the area cannot contribute appreciably to population changes of the size of 1—3 per cent per annum, because it is physically impossible, given man's transport facilities, for people to be moved on this scale. Even 0·1 per cent of 500 million represents $\frac{1}{2}$ million, and in general transfers of above this magnitude do not occur in a year except in extreme circumstances such as a major war. For any meaningful explanation or analysis of table 11.1 it is necessary, therefore, to consider essentially mortality and fertility.

While there are still notable differences between countries in mortality experience, it has proved relatively easy in the past three decades for the more advanced countries to convey to the less-favoured countries some helpful advice on improving health and longevity and to back this up with the necessary medicines, services and training so that practical effect can be given to the advice. Thus the crude death rates in the developed countries — Europe, North America, Russia and Oceania — which have a range of roughly $\frac{3}{4}$—$1\frac{1}{4}$ per cent per annum (depending largely on age-distribution) are much less disparate than they used to be from those in the less well-developed areas, where the ranges are now of the order of:

Africa	$1\frac{1}{2}$—$2\frac{1}{2}$ per cent
Latin America ⎱ Asia ⎰	$\frac{3}{4}$—2 per cent

Clearly, therefore, differences in mortality are not largely responsible for the varied growth features indicated in table 11.1. They must be attributable to fertility, and this is borne out by the following round figures for crude birth rates in specimen countries in recent years:

Developed countries		Less-developed countries	
USSR	$1\frac{3}{4}$%	Dahomey	5%
USA	$1\frac{3}{4}$%	Tunisia	4%
Australia	2%	Brazil	4%
Britain	$1\frac{1}{2}$%	Saudi Arabia	5%
East Germany	$1\frac{1}{4}$%	Burma	4%
Spain	2%	Sri Lanka	3%
Japan	2%		

These rates give a reasonable idea of the range of fertility levels for the two categories of area and for the three main constituents of the second category, namely Africa, Latin America and Asia.

In spite of the predominance of fertility as a cause of difference between areas, it is of interest to note that the principal net migration transfers in recent years are assessed to have been (for the decade 1960–70; numbers in millions):

Africa	−1·6
Asia	−1·2
Europe	−0·3
Latin America	−1·9
North America	+4·1
Oceania	+0·9

Much of the movement out of Africa, and some of that out of Asia, was into Europe, where it was largely balanced by outward movement to North America and Oceania. The net transfers out of Asia and nearly all movement out of Latin America went into North America too. While these outcomes of migrations are small in relation to general population growth, they are still substantial enough to be important economically and politically.

11.4 The biggest populations

The country with the largest number of people – China – accounts for no less than one-fifth of the whole world population. The next two largest – India and the USSR – together have broadly as many people again. The USA is not far behind the USSR. For these four countries the numbers, areas, population densities and rates of change are set out in table 11.2, as well as they can be estimated today. (The more vast the population unit, in general the smaller the quantity and the poorer the quality of available statistics, because of difficulties of collection.)

The figures for population density are somewhat misleading, as they do not allow for international diversity in the proportion of land which is uninhabit-

199

Table 11.2. *The populations of the four largest countries*

Country	Population 1970 (millions)	Area (thousand km²)	Density of population (persons per km²)	Rate per thousand (1970) of Birth	Death	Natural growth
China	775	9,600	81	33	15	18
India	545	3,300	165	40	17	23
USSR	240	22,400	11	19	8	11
USA	205	9,400	22	16	9	7

able or can be occupied by only a few people. Certainly, population density varies very widely within each country and all of the four shown in table 11.2 have areas of heavy population pressure and areas which are thinly occupied. Even so, the disparity between the USA and Russia, on the one hand, and China and India on the other is very notable. So also are the crude birth rates, death rates and rates of natural growth. Reference will be made later in this chapter to the age-distributions, but correction for variations in this respect will not greatly lessen the difference between the two pairs of nations. How the governments of China and India react to their population situations, and what success their policies are achieving, will be discussed in chapter 13.

11.5   The developing countries

Developing countries are numerous and vary greatly in size. After China and India the next largest is Indonesia (120 millions) and there are four others with a combined population of over 200 millions. Some are very small, however, for example some African territories and Caribbean islands. The UN *Demographic Year Book* lists as separate units roughly the following numbers of populations:

Africa	60
North America	40
South America	15
Asia	60
Oceania	25

and most of them may be classed as 'developing' rather than developed.

As will have been seen from table 11.1, rates of population growth in the economically poorer areas are mostly in the range 2–3 per cent per annum. Analysis of fertility and mortality rates (see table 11.3) discloses a wider range of variation, but in general the birth rates are in the range 30–50 per thousand for many of the countries concerned, and the death rates are generally between 10–30 per thousand. The mortality now being experienced

Table 11.3. *Recent birth rates and death rates in certain territories and countries*

Country or territory	1945—9	1955—9	1960—4	1968—72
	Death rate per thousand			
Réunion	24	14	11	8
Zanzibar and Pemba	17	8	5	21
Costa Rica	14	10	8	6
Martinique	19	10	8	7
Mexico	18	12	10	9
Jamaica	14	10	8	7
Bolivia	16	9	8	19
Venezuela	14	10	7	7
Brunei	20	13	7	6
Ceylon (Sri Lanka)	16	10	9	8
Singapore	12	7	6	5
Fiji	12	8	6	16
Puerto Rico	11	9	7	7
	Birth rate per thousand			
Réunion	42	47	44	33
Zanzibar and Pemba	22	19	23	47
Costa Rica	45	48	45	33
Martinique	35	40	35	27
Mexico	44	46	46	43
Jamaica	31	39	40	35
Bolivia	40	27	25	44
Venezuela	39	47	44	39
Brunei	45	54	45	38
Ceylon (Sri Lanka)	38	37	35	30
Singapore	46	43	36	23
Fiji	40	40	40	30
Puerto Rico	41	34	31	25

is in most instances well below the level of even a short while ago, and often the decline that has occurred is not wholly the result of rapid economic development within the countries in question: it may be more the outcome of medical aid received from more developed countries. Such aid can be given quite readily, often without great cost, and is universally acceptable. Its effect on birth rates has not been to reduce them: if anything it has tended to raise them, because of the improved health of the mothers.

The implications of these developments, and especially the problems they bring and the issues of policy that they raise, will be discussed in the following two chapters. While the general drift of the data shown in table 11.3 is clear enough, some of the figures shown are not reliable. This applies particularly to the birth rates in Bolivia, which almost certainly have not fallen to the extent indicated, and perhaps even have not fallen at all. In the same country, the decline in the death rate also has probably not been as dramatic as the data suggest. Nevertheless, in some places there has been a startling decline in mortality — in Mauritius, for instance, where the expectation of life at birth increased from 33 years in 1942—6 to 51 years in 1951—3, after the eradication of malaria.

It should not be supposed that the level of fertility is always the same in countries that are underdeveloped by modern standards. Indeed, the existence of differences, attributable perhaps to climate, race, tradition or even differing prosperity, is clear from table 11.3. Study of gross reproduction rates for a number of areas shows as wide a variation as that table might suggest, for instance:

Cocos Island	4·2
Ceylon	3·7
Costa Rica	3·4
United Arab Republic	3·1
Guyana	2·9
India	2·6
Trinidad	2·5

11.6 Europe

Figures similar to those in table 11.2 are set out in table 11.4 for some European countries. Eight of the forty or so countries for which the UN *Demographic Year Book* gives particulars are included, and they account for nearly one-half of the whole population for which details are given in the bottom line. With the exception of Albania — with its high figure for births — rates of birth, death and natural increase are fairly uniform. Population densities also fall mostly within a narrow range, the notable exceptions being

Table 11.4. *The populations of some European countries and of all Europe*

Country	Population 1970 (millions)	Area (thousand km^2)	Density of population (persons per km^2)	Rate per thousand (1970) of Birth	Rate per thousand (1970) of Death	Rate per thousand (1970) of Natural increase
Albania	2	29	70	35	8	27
Denmark	5	43	116	15	10	5
France	50	547	90	17	11	6
Britain	54	230	235	16	12	4
Poland	33	313	105	16	8	8
Spain	34	505	66	20	9	11
Sweden	8	450	18	14	10	4
Yugoslavia	21	256	82	18	9	9
All Europe	462	4,936	94	17	10	7

Sweden, which is sparsely populated, and Britain, with its much higher-than-average density. But the size of the population varies widely, mostly because of the extent of the area the country occupies. If tables 11.2 and 11.4 are compared, the similarity of the European experience with that of the USSR and USA becomes apparent.

As crude birth rates and death rates are relatively unreliable measures of experience if precision in analysis is required, the next two sections of this chapter give rather fuller details of the incidence of fertility and mortality in recent years in four developed countries — namely Britain, France, Sweden and the USA — and in selected countries that are less well developed. One other general feature of the recent European experience is worthy of mention at this point, namely migration between countries. The nine Common Market countries have between them counted, at recent censuses, something like 7 million people who originated in other countries. Much of this immigration has come from the Mediterranean area, notably from Italy, Turkey and Yugoslavia. While the rate of population movement entailed is small, relative to natural increase in either the donating or the receiving countries, this migration is of interest because of the economic forces producing it — for example surplus labour in the donating countries and relatively higher wealth in the accepting countries — and because the political and other problems involved (such as overcrowding, and lack of complete social assimilation) sometimes act in a manner which is inimical to the economic attractions.

11.7 Some current trends in fertility and mortality

A full discussion of the subject of current trends in the two principal forces affecting population is hardly possible within a short space. This is because it is often not easy to establish what the trend is, over a few years, in the face of fluctuations; moreover, if it does appear likely that there is a trend, analysis in detail is desirable. In the end, however, its causes may be obscure and its continuation doubtful. Nevertheless, one or two factors may be mentioned which are well known to have an influence on population changes today, and to illustrate these a few figures for crude birth rates and crude death rates are set out below for eleven selected countries for each of the years 1964, 1968 and 1972:

	Birth rate (per thousand)			Death rate (per thousand)		
	1964	1968	1972	1964	1968	1972
Mauritius Island	38	31	25	9	9	8
Guadeloupe	34	33	29	8	8	7
USA	21	18	16	9	10	9
Sri Lanka	33	32	30	9	8	8
Czechoslovakia	17	15	16	10	10	10
France	18	17	17	11	11	11

203

	1964	1968	1972	1964	1968	1972
Italy	20	18	16	10	10	10
Roumania	15	26	20	8	10	9
Scotland	20	18	15	12	12	12
Australia	21	20	20	9	9	8
USSR	20	17	18	7	8	8

It would appear that, in general, the movement of the birth rate has been downward over the eight-year period. This movement was slight or negligible in some countries in the statement (France, Australia) but very marked in one (Mauritius Island) and rather less prominent in four (Guadeloupe, USA, Italy and Scotland). In Rumania the movement was first sharply up and then down again, but in the remaining countries shown it was gently downwards.

The insertion of the figures for the intervening years would enrich the picture but not change its general outline; but the addition of data for some previous post-war years would make a greater difference for the more developed countries such as the USA and Scotland, where the current fall negatives a previous rise and could well be part of a long-term fluctuation rather than a trend. In contrast, the declines in countries such as Sri Lanka are recent developments resulting from private and governmental plans to lessen rapid population growth, and here it is certainly the intention to establish a trend if possible. The rise in the birth rate in Roumania between 1964 and 1968 was the outcome of a sudden official ban on abortion and on contraceptives, imposed because of the official view that population growth had become too low. In these circumstances, some fall from the first peak might be expected — the figures for intervening years are:

1965	15	1969	23
1966	14	1970	21
1967	27	1971	20

In contrast, the figures for the crude death rates are generally unvarying, and do not exhibit any notable trend over the period, as would be expected.

11.8 Analysis of marriage on an international scale

Rates of marriage, per marriageable person, are shown for each sex for certain recent years in table 11.5. The impression given by the table over all is one of uniformity, and this is as might be expected on general considerations, as most people marry ultimately. Even so, the figures do vary, both between countries, within a ratio scale of 2:1, and from time to time. Marriage rates were high in the immediate post-war period, as couples who had been separated now had a delayed opportunity of marrying. As between countries, the age-distribution of the population may affect the rate, while disparities between the experience of the sexes arise from variations in the general balance of the numbers of men and women.

Table 11.5. *Marriage rates per marriageable person*

Country	Years	Rate per thousand Men	Women
England and Wales	1950—2	70	52
	1960—2	68	51
France	1945—7	82	59
	1961—3	56	43
Sweden	1949—51	53	50
	1964—6	50	48
USA	1949—51	97	87
	1959—61	88	74
Chile	1951—3	54	50
Taiwan	1955—7	74	83

11.9 Analysis of fertility on an international scale

Some fertility rates classified by age of mother are set out in table 11.6, for the same developed countries as in table 11.5 but for two different developing countries. Two kinds of rates are shown: one with a denominator of women irrespective of marital status; the other with a denominator of married women, in which case the numerator is restricted to legitimate births. Rates of the first kind are not available for the USA and rates of the second kind are not available for Honduras or Indonesia. The married women's rates bear a general similarity between the four countries; but those for France are smaller at the younger ages than for the other three developed countries and

Table 11.6. *Fertility rates classified by age of mother* (per thousand).

Country	Under 20	20—24	25—29	30—34	35—39	40—44	40—49
I. All-women's rates
England and Wales (1967)	25	165	165	92	43	11	1
France (1967)	13	160	168	103	50	15	1
Sweden (1967)	25	136	146	82	35	9	1
Indonesia (1964)	46	217	178	143	159	40	14
Honduras (1966)	63	273	265	250	197	93	24
II. Married women's rates
England and Wales (1967)	463	239	181	94	42	11	1
France (1967)	303	298	196	112	35	17	2
Sweden (1967)	453	255	180	92	39	10	1
USA (1960)	479	354	222	123	62	10	1

relatively large at older ages. This feature is noticeable also in the all-women's rates. An idea of the reproduction rate can be obtained by adding the figures in the rows and multiplying the result by $2\frac{1}{2}$. If this is done it will be seen that the rate for France is about 1·3, slightly higher than for England and Wales (1·25) or Sweden (1·1), and the accompanying larger family size accounts for the greater prolongation of child-bearing in France. Such a feature is much more prominent still in the two developing countries, which have reproduction rates of around 2 and 3 respectively.

An idea of the proportions married may also be obtained from the table, by dividing the figures under heading II into those for heading I. This is possible for only the three European countries, in which marriages occurred earliest in England and Wales.

Disparities in family size between countries are further illustrated in the following figures: the average numbers of children born alive to women enumerated at ages 45—49 were, at a recent census:

Kenya	4·1
Canada	3·1
Puerto Rico	5·6
Cyprus	4·2
Belgium	2·2
Hungary	2·4
Fiji	6·3

The following are specimen child—woman ratios, the age-groups being respectively all ages under 5 and ages 15—49:

Algeria	0·940
Jamaica	0·693
USA	0·488
Finland	0·382
Turkey	0·700
Portugal	0·398

The child—woman ratios, though crude, do indicate the outcome of more recent fertility than do the average numbers of children borne.

The following figures show the varied proportions (in round figures) of recent births which are first, second, third and fourth or higher-order children in the family:

	First children (%)	Second children (%)	Third children (%)	Further children (%)
Japan (1967)	50	35	10	5
Mexico (1968)	20	20	10	50
Egypt (1966)	20	25	10	45
USA (1969)	40	25	10	25

Fertility trends are not static at the figures given for particular years, and there are further points of difference between countries. In the next few sections some notes will be given on features of special interest in the experience of particular countries.

11.10 Current fertility trends in Britain

After remaining fairly static in the first half of the 1950s, the birth rate began to rise and continued to increase for about ten years. By 1965 it was roughly 20 per cent higher than it had been ten years before. A fall then set in, and this has approximately restored the position in the mid-1970s to that which applied twenty years before. Analysis by age of mother, duration of marriage and family size does little to throw light on this rise and fall, because much the same feature is observed in all the various subdivisions. What would be of special interest would be to discover whether the changes that have occurred represent a fundamental development of outlook on the part of married couples or whether they reflect merely the influence of a difference in timing in the arrival of a family of children of the same ultimate size. Many demographers believe that couples' objectives are unaltered but that currently they are aiming to reach them less quickly.

11.11 Marriage and fertility in the Caribbean

The following racial groups have been enumerated in the area: African (2 million), East Indian (half a million), Mixed (half a million), European and Other (100,000). Fertility varies between the races, and is particularly high for East Indians, whose relative numbers are increasing. In table 5.5 a special status — 'consensually married' — was shown for Barbados. This and other forms of non legal union account for the high proportion of illegitimate births; in the Caribbean territories as a whole these constitute 60 per cent of all births. To quote Roberts, 'the slaves uprooted from various environments and thrust into oppressive slave regimes where the maintenance of stable family unions had no social or economic advantage to slave owners and where in fact formal marriage was often not allowed, inevitably experienced a dissolution of their traditional family pattern. The subsequent introduction of marriage ordinances based on English law brought no basic change; the formation of unions by means other than formal marriage continued . . . Marriage in the West Indies does not always signify the establishment of a union. Many, if not the great majority of marriages represent no more than the cementing of unions long in existence . . . demographically it (marriage) does not necessarily connote commencement of exposure to the risk of child-bearing.'

11.12   Abortion in Japan

The Japanese Government is conscious of an acute population problem in an area that is less than 150 thousand square miles in extent and of which only one-fifth is suitable for food production. In 1948 abortion was to all intents and purposes legalized, and the desire of people for family limitation expressed itself in a remarkable decline in the live birth rate — from 34 to 18 per thousand in eight years. It is estimated that in 1952 there were about one and a half million abortions (reported and secret) while the number of live births was 2 millions. It seems likely that more effective and less drastic methods of limitation will become widespread in future. As a result of advances in medical treatment, the death rate has fallen from 18 to 7 per thousand since the beginning of the war, and thus even today there is a net rate of natural increase of 11 per thousand.

Japan has a special interest of its own in being one of the few nations composed of people of non-European origin to have become fully developed industrially. The fact that fertility has declined in broad accordance with the Western pattern is often cited as a particularly hopeful sign for under-developed countries in the East and elsewhere. Yet doubters have been able to point to a number of factors which are peculiarly Japanese and may thus not help others — for instance their exceptional ability and industry as a people, their climate and natural resources, and their religion. Moreover, since the occupation of the country in 1945, American influence has been paramount.

It is of course highly significant that the method of achieving birth control has been socially undesirable and medically dangerous. Perhaps, however, abortion was the only practicable initial solution for the achievement of a big fall in fertility in a short time. Surveys have shown that even in rural areas the Japanese are aware of safer and more modern methods, and are motivated towards small families. In time, therefore, the same end may well be achieved by more satisfactory means.

At present, the Japanese Government is attempting to substitute an effective family planning service for the policy of legal abortion, as a means of fertility control. It would appear as though the people can be persuaded into less drastic — if more troublesome — means of achieving the material benefits that can accrue from family limitation. In spite of the marked level of control over fertility in Japan today, it is still appreciably higher in agricultural occupations than in non-agricultural and for people of education only up to the primary level than for those of higher attainment.

11.13   Differential fertility in Taiwan

Taiwan (Formosa) is another country in which fertility has been greatly reduced in recent years. By 1966, the birth rate had fallen from 45 per thousand (in 1955) to 32 per thousand and since then it has fallen much further. An analysis relating to the year 1966 revealed the differentials shown in table 11.7. The rural figures are consistently higher than the urban, and both show a marked influence of better education in favour of lower fertility, which was also associated with local migration, with non-agricultural work and with women's work away from the home (except on the land).

11.14 Fertility trends in the USA

After the Second World War the birth rate rose to a higher level in North America than in Western Europe and for a long while it remained higher. Thus in comparison with France:

Birth rate per thousand

Years	USA	France
1944—9	23	20
1950—4	25	19
1955—9	25	18
1960—4	23	18

As in Britain, however, fertility in the USA fell over a period of ten years and by 1975 the birth rate stood at only about 16 per thousand.

This fall does appear to have been associated with a change in outlook — from one in which a large family seemed both economically possible and psychologically desirable to one in which such a family represented too

Table 11.7. *Number of children ever born to women aged 15—49 for cities and townships of Taiwan, 1966*

	Cities	Rural townships
Husband's education		
Primary	3·6	3·9
Junior	3·2	3·8
Senior	2·8	3·4
Wife's education		
Primary	3·3	3·7
Junior	2·6	3·0
Husband's occupation		
Agriculture	3·8	4·0
Commerce	3·4	3·7
Government service	3·0	3·6
Wife's occupation		
Agriculture	3·4	4·1
Housekeeping	3·4	3·8
Non-agriculture	2·7	3·2
Migration (viz. recent change of address)		
None	3·5	3·9
Rural or urban	3·4	3·6

great a drain on both personal and national resources. Thus while the fertility rates of 1948 were consistent with a completed family size of perhaps 3·1, and those of 1957 pointed to a family size of about 3·8, the corresponding figures for 1969 and 1973 are respectively of the order of 2·5 and 1·9.

11.15 Mortality in further detail

Some figures illustrating variations in death rates from one age-group to another in selected countries were given in table 7.1 above. These rates related to girls and women. The further examples set out in table 11.8 show the disparities between the sexes and (for the sexes combined) between urban and rural areas.

In addition to a wide disparity between countries, particularly in infancy, the table shows that rates for males are generally greater than those for females. The only exception is in the Central African Republic at ages 15—19 and 35—39, where health risks associated with childbearing may well have accounted for the excess of women's over men's mortality. This exception is paralleled in the data for other under-developed countries and for European countries in past centuries.

Rural mortality was higher than urban mortality in the Central African Republic, probably because of better general conditions in the towns than in the country. This is, however, an unusual feature and the picture presented by the data for Holland, in which rural mortality is generally lower than

Table 11.8. *Death rates (per thousand) at selected age-groups for specimen countries, showing differences by sex and type of area*
(U = urban, R = Rural)

Country		Age-group				
		Under 1	15—19	35—39	55—59	75—79
Central African Republic (1959—60)	M	201	12	15	41	*
	F	178	15	17	32	*
	U	173	12	13	26	*
	R	194	14	17	43	*
Guyana (1960)	M	71	2	4	26	96
	F	61	2	4	17	76
Israel (1971)	M	25	1	2	12	86
	F	18	1	1	9	68
Holland (1971)	M	14	1	2	13	82
	F	10	†	2	10	56
	U	3·1‡	0·6	1·3	9·9	67
	R	3·1‡	0·9	1·2	8·5	64

* Figures not available.
† Less than ½.
‡ Ages 0—4 inclusive.

urban, is more representative; it will be noted, however, that in infancy there was no difference in that country and that at ages 15—19 (where accidents are a prominent cause of death in developed countries) the rural rate was the higher of the two.

It will be noted that the rates for the Central African Republic are omitted for ages 75—79; this is because the figures quoted in the UN *Demographic Year Book* are obviously unrepresentative.

Recently, a dispute arose between an American actuary and a Russian professor as to which of their countries had the higher true mortality and fertility rates. So far as mortality was concerned, this argument appears to have arisen because death rates are the lower in the USA at ages under 50, whereas recorded death rates in the USSR are the lower at higher ages. Any result in the form of a single-figure index must therefore depend upon the system of weights used in arriving at the index figure. If the Russian popula-tion is used as the weighting system, then Russian mortality appears to be 3 per cent higher, overall, than American. If, however, the US population is adopted for this purpose, then American mortality appears to be the higher overall — by the same margin of 3 per cent. Neither of these average disparities is particularly meaningful. It would be more useful if valid and comparable analyses by cause of death could be made, as these might throw some light on the real medical and social differences between the two countries.

11.16 Population distributions by age and sex

Figures are set out for seven specimen countries in table 11.9. These show the age-distributions for sexes combined. The three countries to the right of the table have lower proportions of children than the others, and more old people, and this feature reflects their recent fertility history of birth rates

Table 11.9. *Population age-distributions for selected countries*

Age-group	Ghana 1970	Barbados 1969	Peru 1970	Iraq 1965	France 1968	Norway 1970	USSR 1970
0—4	18	11	18	20	7	8	9
5—14	29	25	28	28	17	16	22
15—24	17	20	18	15	16	15	14
25—34	14	11	13	12	12	14	14
35—44	9	8	9	10	13	11	15
45—54	6	9	7	6	10	13	9
55—64	4	8	4	4	12	11	9
65—74	2	5	2	3	8	8	5
75 and over	1	3	1	2	5	4	3
Total	100	100	100	100	100	100	100

falling from a high level to a low one. Barbados is in an intermediate position in this respect.

The balance of the sexes is fairly even in all these countries, notably in Ghana, Peru and Norway. Males slightly exceeded females in number in Iraq but there was a deficit of men in Barbados, France and the USSR. For Barbados, emigration is probably responsible, and for Russia war losses. The recorded age-distribution of the sexes for Barbados and for Russia are as follows:

	Barbados		USSR	
	Males	Females	Males	Females
0—4	12	10	9	8
5—14	28	23	25	21
15—24	22	19	16	13
25—34	10	12	16	14
35—44	7	10	15	14
45—54	8	9	7	10
55—64	8	8	6	10
65—74	4	5	4	6
75 and over	1	4	2	4
Total	100	100	100	100

An excess of males over females in the first years of life affects the sex-ratio at birth, and this is common to the two countries, as for most others. The corresponding deficit comes earlier in Barbados (mainly at 25—44) than in Russia (45—74) reflecting the different causes of disparity mentioned above.

11.17 Miscellaneous other characteristics of population

Among the further particulars which may be collected from people at censuses are education or literacy; occupation and industry; social or industrial status; place of work; place and type of residence; place of previous residence; size of household; state of health; race or country of origin; religion. Most of these topics are suitable for discussion in the chapter which follows, and reference to them will be found there. In the present chapter it remains only to mention briefly two matters — the proportion of aliens and the relative numbers of various religious affiliations. People of a nationality different from that of the country in which the census is held are normally few in relation to the size of the population. Typical percentages are:

Tunisia	1 %
Kenya	2 %
Nigeria	2 %
Costa Rica	2 %

Higher ratios are found in countries which import foreign labour, to which there is a considerable immigration or which lie close to other countries in which people of closely similar race are found, e.g.:

France	4 %
Australia	4 %
Sweden	5 %
Ceylon	10 %

The highest proportion is shown by Monaco (85 %), for reasons which must be obvious.

The UN *Demographic Year Book* does not give many details of religion. Here are some specimen figures from recent censuses (percentages):

	Christian	Moslem	Buddhist	Hindu
Ceylon	8	7	66	19
Egypt	7	93	—	—

SELECT BIBLIOGRAPHY

Demographic Year Book (United Nations Organization, New York, 1967).

Recent Population Trends and Future Prospects. World Population Conference (United Nations, New York, 1974).

Report of the Population Panel (Cmnd 5258), (HMSO, 1973).

Spiegelman, M. *Introduction to Demography* (Harvard University Press, Cambridge, Mass., revised edition, 1968).

Manual of Demographic Statistics in Japan (Japanese National Commission for UNESCO, Tokyo, 1958).

Chandrasekhar, S. *China's Population* (University Press, Hong Kong, 1959).

Roberts, G. W. *The Population of Jamaica* (Cambridge University Press, London, 1957).

12 Resources and Population

12.1 Introduction

By 'resources' is generally meant those things which are necessary for human life, for instance water, land — for the production of food — and some sort of housing shelter. Energy is also required: in primitive societies this is provided by the muscle-power of men and animals; in more advanced countries it may be derived from combustion, steam, wind-power, waterfalls, electricity, atomic furnaces or even tides. For the transition to these complex and more efficient forms of energy, scientific and technical knowledge is essential, and 'know-how' can be reckoned as a significant resource. In order to deploy his resources, man must carry on various kinds of economic activity, such as employment in industry or in agriculture, with their different occupations, trade, capital investment (requiring saving) and economic aid. The effectiveness of these activities depends on numerous subsidiary characteristics of population, such as people's physical fitness for work, their social structure, the urban or rural nature of their domicile, their migratory movements in pursuit of work, their literacy and education, and so on.

This chapter begins with an account in fuller detail of the principal types of resource, and of the associated characteristics of society, and then goes on to deal with the information about them which can be obtained from censuses and other demographic statistics. In the final sections, attention is paid to the effects on population growth and development which may be produced by an abundance or a shortage of various resources; and also to the stimulus or retardation which population increase may bring about in the production and use of resources. Past and present interactions between population and resources are considered, but the prospects for the future are deferred to chapter 14.

12.2 Land

It is an enormous asset for a country to possess within its borders the land on which its economic development can be based, and this may indeed be essential for progress, although there may be exceptions where aid and trade from outside can produce sufficient growth. Trade and aid, while valuable, tend to be of secondary importance; for instance, only 7 per cent of all the

214

food produced enters international trade. An assessment of land resources per head of population is therefore significant as an indicator both of the level of living and of the prospects of progress. A world-wide quantification of resource endowments is impracticable owing to the lack of data for certain areas and materials, but it is possible to make observations on selected resources and trends.

The land is a resource of limited quantity. As part of its surface is needed for factories, dwellings and forests, not all of it can be cultivated, and indeed much of it is unsuitable for food production. Only one-third of the world's land area is agricultural land, and only one-third of this is under cultivation (as opposed to permanent pastures). Nevertheless, agriculture of various kinds is undoubtedly the principal produce of the land. Fertile land varies greatly in quality, and agricultural output is dependent on soil fertility, the method of cultivation involved, the amount of fertilizer used and other factors. Table 12.1 shows the great variation in agricultural productivity that exists. The disparities are probably accounted for mainly by differing techniques and by variations in the use of fertilizers. The figures seem at once to emphasize the present difficulties and to point to glowing possibilities for the future.

Yields can no doubt be increased by the adoption of improved techniques and by better management, including perhaps the amalgamation of small holdings, and by the use of fertilizers; there is thus much scope for raising production from existing land. There is also scope for bringing into production some of the land that is at present unused. Clark has estimated that the world's land area of 131 million square kilometres (excluding Greenland and Antarctica) could be made to yield as much produce as 77 million square kilometres of temperate European farmland if the right methods were used. On the basis of Dutch agriculture, which is the most intensive in the world, capable of producing 730 tons of grain equivalent per square kilometre, and on the basis of a consumption of 2 tons of grain equivalent per head per

Table 12.1. *Variations in agricultural production from one country to another in recent years*

(Centners* per hectare, over a large group of countries)

	Highest	Mean	Lowest
Wheat	43	11	3
Rye	29	11	3
Barley	41	13	2
Maize	48	19	4
Oats	33	12	4
Rice	57	18	6

* A centner is roughly 50 kilograms.

annum (a very high rate) he estimated that the world could provide food, fibre and all the other agricultural requirements for almost ten times its present population. This is, however, only one among many speculative calculations of this kind, and too much importance should not be attached to the results of such an exercise when present-day yields are so poor by comparison. Irrigation projects are invariably long in gestation, and are immensely costly in terms of capital equipment; the purchase of fertilizers can also be discouragingly expensive. While, therefore, the earth's physical resources are sufficient, in the light of man's present knowledge, for a substantial increase of food production, such an increase will be possible only if there is adequate investment in agriculture, to which should be allied changes in the system of tenure, and other social and economic institutions, and an expansion of internal and international trade. Further reference to agriculture will be made in § 12.5 below.

12.3 Water

The water in all the earth's seas is vastly more than mankind needs, but the cost of making it drinkable is prohibitive. Although there are many desalination plants in service in various parts of the world today their total output would supply only about 10 million people. The water man uses is derived from the natural cycle, in which water drawn up from the seas in the form of vapour by the warmth of the sun is precipitated as rain. Such precipitation of fresh water can be increased by scientific means, but this too is costly. On the whole, natural rainfall is more than adequate for the world population, and it is indefinitely renewable, but there is a shortfall in some areas. This is remedied in some degree by storage in reservoirs and by spreading through irrigation. But at present, much water is wasted through running taps and by pollution resulting from the discharge of industrial waste from factories. As population grows, storage and irrigation can be further developed and waste cut down, but this will call for considerable capital expenditure and so will constitute an important demand upon man's other resources and on his labour force.

12.4 Food needs

The energy man requires from food is usually measured in calories. The number of calories required by the average person has been assessed at 2,100 a day, but there are appreciable variations by age — an infant needs only perhaps one-tenth of what an adult wants — by region, body size, occupation and hours of work — and indeed between individuals. The extreme range of variation is probably from 400 to 4,000. It is not easy to assess the requirements with any precision. Studies of calorie supply suggest that in the world as a whole there is an approximate balance with requirements, but in some areas there is an excess, and in others a deficiency. The worst shortfall is in the Far East, where the calorie supply may amount to some 10 per cent less than the minimum. Further variations are found within regions. On the basis of sample surveys it has been estimated that 10–15 per cent of the world's population is underfed, i.e. does not have enough food to live on. While this figure is tentative, it appears to have been accepted by many experts. The quality of the diet is, moreover, often ill-balanced. The proportion obtained from grains, starchy roots and sugar is too high, and not enough protein is consumed. Some years ago, this proportion was put at 64 per cent in Latin America, 74 per cent in Africa, 72 per cent in the Near East and no less than 80 per cent in the Far East. Perhaps one-third to one-half of the world's population is experiencing malnutrition, i.e. suffering from the effects of an insufficiency of certain types of food, although the total quantity consumed is adequate.

Recent studies in India suggest that perhaps one-sixth of the population receives neither enough calories nor enough proteins, while another one-sixth lacks one or the other but not both these essentials.

12.5 Agricultural production

In a paper submitted by the UN Food and Agriculture Organization to the Third World Population Conference, figures were given for each country showing the dietary energy per head and the percentage of requirements which this represents. For Europe and other developed countries the index of calories per person varied from about 2,400 a day to about 3,400 a day, and this was always in excess of standard requirements, with the exception of Albania where there was a 2 per cent deficiency. The range of calories per person a day for the less developed countries, however, was from 1,700 (Algeria, Haiti, Tanzania), representing some 70 per cent of needs, to about 2,500 (with Argentina and Uruguay as exceptions with higher figures); more countries in this group showed a deficit than showed a surplus of food.

Some data for particular foods are shown in table 12.2, and they illustrate the wide imbalance that exists between different types of nutriments. The first problem for agricultural producers is to try to keep pace with the growth of population. This is hard enough in itself, and clearly it must be much more difficult still to eliminate calorie and protein deficiencies and thus to equalize food sufficiency round the world. True, 'know-how' can be exported from countries with high levels of production from the land to the less successful countries, but it is an expensive and time-consuming process to (i) reduce deficiencies in soil quality by the use of fertilizers, (ii) educate farmers in order that they may be ready to use the most efficient methods and (iii) provide the necessary machinery and equipment. Moreover, so far as item (ii) in this list

217

Table 12.2. *World food production and needs, 1961—2*
(Million metric tons.)

Type of food	Production	Needs	Ratio of production to needs
Meat	60	150	0·40
Milk	350	1,050	0·33
Grain	500	300	1·67
Vegetables	500	800	0·63
Other	200	650	0·31
Total	1,610	2,950	0·55

is concerned, not only education but centuries of tradition, even religion, may be involved and a whole way of life may have to be changed.

Recent developments in production and in productivity per head are illustrated in table 12.3. While all areas show a big increase in production, in Africa, Latin America and the Far East this has only just matched the growth of the population, whereas with their more modest demographic developments North America, Europe, Russia and Oceania have been able to raise production per head substantially.

Another way in which food inequalities may be reduced is by trade. Table 12.4 shows how net food imports (+) or exports (−) relate to local production. It will be seen that the effect of trade is relatively small in its value to the developing countries, and adverse in Latin America and Africa.

Poor health on the part of agricultural workers in some countries is a further obstacle to improving conditions there (see § 12.16 below).

Table 12.3. *Indexes of food production and food production per head*
(1934—8 = 100.)

Area	Food production		Food production per head	
	1965	1971	1965	1971
North America	184	217	121	133
Western Europe	164	198 ⎫	146	168
Eastern Europe and USSR	191	232 ⎬		
Oceania	168	213	100	113
Africa	187	225	99	102
Far East	164	202	99	105
Near East	202	239	121	121
Latin America	206	239	102	100

Table 12.4. *Net trade in food as a*
proportion of food
production, 1963—5

Area	Percentage of trade
North America	− 13
Western Europe	+ 16
Oceania	−102
Africa	− 10
Far East	+ 6
Near East	+ 7
Latin America	− 9

12.6 Energy

It is not easy to measure the world's energy reserves. For coal, oil and natural gas this is a matter of geological survey, and new sources are still being discovered in quantity. For atomic energy, and the use of tidal forces, the answer must depend on how much capital investment can be managed. What is clear, however, is that the consumption of energy and of the resources which provide it is high and increasing. This may be seen from table 12.5. From 1937 to 1960, it shows, consumption in the poorer countries increased by over 300 per cent, and consumption in the richer countries (where the level was of course much greater) by nearly 100 per cent. These improvements have emerged much more rapidly than the rate of population increase. Moreover, energy is becoming more equitably shared, one reason being the mobility of supplies.

Table 12.5. *World energy consumption, 1937 and 1960*
(Thousand million kilograms of coal equivalent.)

Region	1937		1960	
North America	800		1,560	
Western Europe	580		800	
Eastern Europe and Russia	320		900	
Oceania	20	1,720	50	3,310
Africa	25		70	
Latin America	30		140	
China	35		420	
Rest of Asia	120	210	240	870
Total		1,930		4,180

12.7 Types of energy

Some further details are given in table 12.6, which illustrates the recent growth of use by type of energy, and in table 12.7, which contains some assessments of the numbers of years of supply of certain minerals which are left if current rates of consumption remain unchanged.

If a way could be found of controlling thermonuclear fission, the energy picture would be completely transformed, as then unlimited supplies could be derived from the sea. For the moment, at least, this is not available and the world still depends largely on coal and oil, the geographical distribution of the reserves of which is very uneven. About 75 per cent of the world's coal lies in the northern hemisphere, and the concentration of oil wells in the Middle East is well known. As total energy consumption has risen there have been increases in the demand for some sources and decreases for some others. For the USA, in 1900, coal accounted for 90 per cent of the energy, oil less than 5 per cent and natural gas 3 per cent, whereas in 1955 coal represented less than 30 per cent, oil 40 per cent and natural gas 25 per cent. This illustrates man's adaptability, and given this there is hope for the future — see below.

Table 12.6. *World consumption of energy, 1950 and 1969*

(Million metric tons of coal equivalent.)

Type	1950	1969
Solid fuels	1,569	2,357
Liquid fuels	636	2,608
Natural gas	273	1,303
Other	41	148
Total	2,519	6,416

Table 12.7. *Estimated ratios of world reserves to current annual consumption*

Commodity	Ratio
Iron ore	600
Manganese ore	250
Tungsten	125
Copper	50
Lead	30
Zinc and tin	40
Petroleum	100
Coal	2,000

12.8   Technical knowledge

The ability to develop modern, efficient, methods of production must depend largely on the general standard of education in a country, a subject to which reference is made in § 12.15 below. It must also depend on the social structure (see § 12.12) and on the quality of the education. Too often, technical and vocational training is neglected. The proportion of students in higher education who are receiving such training appears to be lower in Africa (25 per cent), Latin America (25 per cent) and Asia (15 per cent) than in Western Europe (35 per cent) —though some doubt may be expressed about the true comparability of these figures. It is, however, possible for countries to aid one another in this particular respect, and to do so without great diversion of resources. This is perhaps the most effective form of international assistance and in recent years large numbers of experts have visited the developing countries in order to advise, educate or train.

12.9   Investment

In order to develop resources, investment is necessary and this in turn depends in the main on savings, though international aid can also be of considerable help. Investment takes two main forms: direct investment in enterprises, and social overhead capital: the second of these consisting of an 'infrastructure' — for example roads, railways, harbours and power installations —which, although not directly productive, is essential for the functioning of productive activities. As saving —and aid too —tends to represent the residual element in an economy, i.e., the extent to which more can be earned than is required for immediate use, it is closely interrelated with such other economic characteristics as employment, migration, urbanization with which the next few sections deal.

12.10   Labour forces

The percentage distribution of the male actively working population into broad groups of industries is given in table 12.8 for the most recent census in half a dozen countries in varying stages of economic development. The proportion of the workforce engaged in mining is small throughout —and clearly dependent on the resources of the country. For transport the figures do not vary widely; this is a common need, but even so it operates more intensely in the developed countries than elsewhere. The greatest international differences are in agriculture; the majority of the population are engaged in this in Guatemala and in Algeria, as opposed to one-third in Bulgaria and only about 5 per cent in the USA and Britain. These disparities are reflected in an opposite differential in manufacturing and construction,

221

Table 12.8. *Percentage distribution of male labour force according to type of industry*

Country	Year	Percentage engaged in					
		Agri-culture	Mining	Manufac-ture and Construc-tion	Trade	Trans-port	Other
Algeria	1966	51	1	12	6	4	26
Bulgaria	1965	36	3	38	4	7	12
England and Wales	1971	4	2	51	12	8	23
Guatemala	1964	74	—	13	5	2	6
Japan	1970	15	1	40	17	9	18
USA	1970	5	1	35	19	6	34

and in trade which is often (though not always — see Bulgaria) associated with it. 'Other' occupations include finance, insurance, personal services and social work of various kinds. On the whole, the more developed the country the higher the proportion of men at work in these spheres, but Algeria provides an exception, possibly because of a difference in definition.

12.11 Dependency ratios

The efficiency of a labour force must depend to some extent on its size in relation to that of the population as a whole. Some figures to illustrate variations in this respect are given in table 12.9. They exhibit results generally concordant with the fuller details (over a more limited selection of areas) of table 11.9.

Table 12.9. *Ratios of dependants to workers, 1970 and 2,000 (estimated)*

Area	1970	2000
Europe	1·28	1·30
Russia	0·97	1·02
North America	1·54	1·36
Japan	0·98	1·08
Temperate South America	1·86	1·82
Australia and New Zealand	1·47	1·30
South Asia	1·63	1·66
East Asia	1·20	1·15
Africa	1·60	1·95
Latin America	2·28	2·42
Oceania	1·25	1·45
World	1·42	1·52

12.12 Social stratification

Information on social stratification is in terms of status at work, which is not very revealing as it displays only one rather limited aspect of a complex of associated variables. A selection of such data as are available internationally is set out in table 12.10, which shows such wide differences between countries in the proportions of employers, employees, people working on their own account and unpaid family workers as to suggest that the manner in which these categories are defined must itself vary widely from one place to another. The 'own account' group probably does not delineate accurately a type of worker of which it would be valuable to know, namely the truly entre-preneurial class — a group of people able both to see the need for develop-ment and to ensure that it is achieved. Any benefits, material and intellectual, accruing to this class should provide the motives for the development of standards of efficiency essential for rapid economic progress.

12.13 Households

International data on household sizes are selectively illustrated in table 12.11. They show how large numbers of people living as a group are characteristic of developing countries and uncharacteristic of developed ones. One-person households are, in contrast, little known except in the more developed areas. Even households of 2, 3 and 4 persons are much more usual in Australia, Bulgaria and Germany than in Africa, Asia and Latin America. Much of this difference reflects disparities in family size but it is doubtful whether such disparities are the whole cause. Where fertility is high, very often also behaviour patterns are traditional; and 'extended family system' usually prevails — married couples live with their parents and other relatives —and there is little scope for the individual to exercise initiative.

Table 12.10. *Proportions of workers of various kinds*

Country	Year	Employers (%)	People working on own account (%)	Employees (%)	Unpaid family workers (%)	Other (%)
Australia	1966	7	9	83	—	1
Ecuador	1962	2	42	47	7	2
Libya	1964	1	31	51	6	1
Poland	1970	—	20	70	7	3
Tanganyika	1967	1	66	16	17	—
Turkey	1965	2	44	33	20	1

Table 12.11. *Households classified by numbers of members*

Country	Year	\multicolumn{5}{c}{Percentage of people in households of}	Average household size

Country	Year	1	2—4	5	6	7 and over	Average household size
Australia	1966	3	53	19	12	13	3·5
Bulgaria	1965	5	59	17	11	8	3·2
Germany	1964	11	69	10	5	5	2·5
Kenya*	1962	4	24	11	10	51	4·9
Mexico	1970	2	26	13	14	45	4·9
Tunisia	1966	1	23	14	15	47	5·1
Turkey	1965	—	20	16	16	48	5·1

* Towns only.

12.14 Urbanization

A town may not be a 'resource' but urban life is often associated with economic advance. The proportion of urban to total population recorded at the most recent censuses, when compared with the corresponding proportion recorded twenty years ago, shows a substantial increase in all parts of the world. This increase has occurred in rich and poor countries alike. Table 12.12 gives some data for the years 1950 and 1960. Although the definition of an urban area has sometimes changed during this period, it seems improbable that this has made any appreciable mark on the general picture of a drift to the town, a movement which has indeed been amply confirmed by general observation and has been described as one of the most significant demographic features of the present time.

A survey of representative countries, made on the basis of the published statistics, shows that the range of proportions of urban to total population has risen from 15—70 per cent just after the Second World War to 20—80

Table 12.12. *Proportions of urban to total population, 1950 and 1960*

Region	1950	1960
North America	43	46
Europe	37	40
Russia	31	36
Oceania	46	53
Africa	10	13
Latin America	25	32
Asia (excluding China)	17	19
China	10	15
Total	21	25

per cent, and the average from about 40 to about 50 per cent. Annual growth rates in this proportion varied up to 1 per cent of the population, or up to 5 per cent of the proportion urban, in the 1940s. The increase in urban population during the last twenty years indeed accounts for a high proportion of the total growth of population, especially in the economically-developed countries. Even in the poorer areas, it often represents two-thirds of the total increase.

In part, this abandonment of the countryside is enforced by under-employment, or even unemployment, on the land, resulting from population pressure; in part, it reflects the lure of city lights. It often leads to high concentrations of population in unsightly and unhygienic shanty towns on the outskirts of major cities.

Some current figures for the proportion of urban to total population for individual countries show a variation from as high as 80 per cent for Denmark, and 76 per cent for Canada, to 15 per cent for Afghanistan and Laos, and 10 per cent for Ethiopia. The pace of development in the USSR is indicated by a growth in the urban proportion from 55 to 58 per cent in only 4 years —from 1968 to 1972.

12.15   Education

Education has a special value of its own; but it is also a resource which clearly influences both agricultural and industrial productivity. The improvement of crop yields, for example, depends on overcoming farmers' traditionalism by spreading the knowledge of new techniques, including the use of dressings. Literate people are more likely to adopt such methods than illiterate ones. Likewise, industrial production is more efficient when management and labour have both acquired the relevant knowledge. At the managerial level, as industry becomes more sophisticated, highly specialized educational attainments become particularly necessary.

To establish and operate educational facilities creates a considerable drain on the resources of a poor country. Yet inadequacy in secondary schooling is a serious deterrent to economic growth, for the educated people to provide initiative and undertake creative work will then be absent. Another feature of education in the poorer countries is the neglect of technical and vocational training in the schools. Table 12.13 gives some information about scientific and technical education in various regions. There must be considerable doubt about the true comparability of the figures from region to region. The figures for Asia are swollen by the very large numbers in 'higher education' in India, Pakistan and the Philippines who are in fact doing work only of secondary school level. In any event, the data shown in the first two columns are clearly affected by the age-distribution of the population.

It is hardly possible to make any assessment of the quality of the 'culture'

Table 12.13. *Students in higher education*

| Region | Proportion of students to total population | | Science and technology students as a proportion of students of all faculties (%) |
	All faculties (per million)	Science and technology alone (per million)	
Western Europe	3,500	1,170	33
Africa	720	180	25
Latin America	1,990	550	27
Asia	2,740	445	16

in a population; this is too nebulous a concept for satisfactory statistical measurement, but it is obviously associated with the general level of educational attainment of the inhabitants and, indeed, the whole concept of life including fertility.

Census data have been summarized in the UN *Demographic Year Book* on the basis of grades completed, but the meaning of this expression must vary considerably from one country to another, as the following figures suggest:

| Country | Percentage of men reaching | | |
	Grade 1 only	Grade 2	Grade 3
USA	6	51	43
France	79	20	1
USSR	0	88	12
Japan	37	52	11

But the fact that in Zambia, Sierra Leone and Nicaragua less than 20 per cent of people went beyond grade 1 is indicative.

Statistics of educational attainment are not plentiful, but some figures relating to lack of literacy are given in table 12.14. The standard is low, particularly as the test of literacy usually adopted is a modest one; but if the data are reasonably consistent from one census to another —as appears to be the case — considerable improvements have been achieved. There are, however, indications that recently population growth may have outpaced the extension of schooling. According to the UN, the numbers of the illiterate grew by some 200 millions during the period 1960–5. It is also estimated that, in a group of poorer countries, only 115 millions out of a total of 373 million children of school age go to school; 750 million adults — half the population — cannot read or write.

12.16   Health

Interactions between population growth, the health of the people and their economic development are complex and difficult to measure, but improved

Table 12.14. *Proportion illiterate among the population of certain countries*

(Ages 10 and over)

Country	Percentage illiterate	
	Latest pre-war census	Latest census (mostly 1960)
Bulgaria	31	13
Chile	28	15
Egypt	85	77
India	91	76
Mexico	52	33
Portugal	49	34
Turkey	79	60

health is generally reckoned an asset not only for itself but also as something which facilitates development. Reductions in the incidence of disease may promote new wealth through increased labour productivity, through a reduction in absence from work, and through the ability it may give to open up previously uninhabitable areas. It may also improve morale, leadership, inventiveness and generally a favourable change in behavioural patterns. If, however, the result is to promote increased population growth this may reduce the availability of necessities, worsen the environment and increase demands upon the health services.

While these and similar conclusions are drawn from surveys of various kinds, data are scanty. Many demographers concentrate their attention on infant mortality as an indicator because it is easy to measure, and gives a general idea of health standards (see §7.2 above). Moreover, it may react on programmes for fertility control, on the thesis that the higher the mortality rate the greater must be the desire for more children and the greater the opposition to family planning. It is believed that the direction of efforts towards the reduction of child loss should shorten the lag between the decline in mortality and fertility rates. At the same time, a health system developed with the aim of improving child care can logically and readily be combined with family planning services.

12.17 Interactions of population and resources

There is evidence that increased resources enable population growth to occur, and it is evident that a larger number of people need more resources than do a smaller number. But to determine which is the more important of these interactions, or to ascertain more clearly how the relationships work, are very difficult tasks and only rather vague generalizations are possible. Resources are many and varied and in the mass are not easy to define. People are adaptable and their demands on resources can be varied. Thus it has been found that where more than one method of resource production is known, the one involving the least effort or cost will be used unless the need is urgent in which case a more elaborate system will be developed. Moreover, people's cultural attitudes and expectations influence their perception and use of resources. Again, a different distribution of population by age or degree of urbanization may involve an increased demand for some resources and at the same time a reduced demand for others. These variables are all linked in a complex system the nature of which is but dimly understood at present. Such efforts as have been made to programme a computer to handle them statistically have been easier to criticize than to believe because too many untested assumptions have had to be introduced (see § 14.10). Thus not only the number of people is involved in demand, but also the nature of the social and political structure and the general standard of living; not only the amount of resources but also their quality and permanence, the cost of processing them, the efficiency applied to their use and the extent to which pollution is created (which in the long run will either have an adverse effect on the quality of life or will need the use of further resources to eliminate this danger).

Because in a number of countries a major economic advance has been associated with a considerable fall in the rate of population increase, it has been plausibly argued that industrialization and urbanization lead to new standards in which smaller families are needed (in association with better chances of infant survival and with new methods of caring for the old) or desired (preference being given to labour-saving household equipment and to the entertainments of the town rather than of the home). This is the thesis of the 'demographic transition' (§ 10.17 above) but it is essentially an empirical observation and in recent years much doubt has been cast upon its validity as a means of forecasting the future. It has been observed both that family size has not fallen in some types of economic development and that family size has increased again after its initial developmental fall.

Although the interaction of population and resources is a complex subject, it does not follow that all further discussion is of little value. Indeed, it is all the more fascinating and important. The next sections will therefore go into rather more detail.

12.18 The effect of population pressure upon the demand for resources

The demand for natural resources is in the last resort governed by the demand for final products, in the manufacture of which the resources are used; it is thus influenced by the rate of population increase and by the rate of growth of real income. Occasionally, as industrialization proceeds, there may be a decrease in demand for particular raw materials or products because of the

228

introduction of substitutes, and so innovations can have an adverse effect on the trade of the poorer countries. In general, however, the pressure is to develop natural resources, although as average income rises there is a less than proportionate increase in the consumption of natural resources. (There are exceptions to this rule: thus, as income rises, meat replaces cereals in the diet, which means an increased demand for land.) The pattern of income elasticity of demand is markedly different in the developed and in the under-developed countries. In Europe and North America a 1 per cent increase in real income per head could well manifest itself in a mere 0·2 per cent increase in expenditure on food. The rest would consist of minerals and energy. In less-developed countries, however, a much higher proportion of any increase in real income could well go into food. Because of this difference, it is necessary to distinguish between various phases of development, as follows:

(1) *Undeveloped countries* In purely agricultural economies, population exerts an influence on the amount of economic activity but is hardly affected at all by any changes in the activity. Increase in population creates a high proportion of children, and by this adverse effect on the dependency ratio, calls for a larger increase in the production of food, and of the more essential non-food items. Actual growth of food production is frequently associated with a reduction in food production and consumption per head, because of reduced marginal productivity on the land. Death rates, although perhaps lower than they were, are still high, especially in infancy, and deficiency diseases exert a heavy toll. As population grows, the incidence of such diseases may increase. As there are few educational facilities, and com-munication is difficult, the people remain largely ignorant of birth control.

(2) *Partially-developed countries* These have some industry, and there are towns. With urbanization, the development of educational facilities and the emergence of a market economy, such developments as the cinema may have been introduced, which encourages the awakening of social and economic aspirations. More women may have entered the labour force. In this situation the advantages of family limitation can begin to be appreciated, as less family rearing gives more time for paid employment. A positive association between income per head and population can develop. As income rises the people are able to start saving and, with a suitable fiscal policy and an appropriate institutional framework, there can be capital accumulation on a growing scale, which will in turn promote further industrialization and growth of income.

(3) *Developed countries* Here fertility is mostly under control. In the past, industrial development in many of these countries was first of all accom-panied by rapid population growth, as death rates fell before family limitation began. Birth control then came to be more and more widely practised, and the rate of growth of population fell for a considerable time, although latterly

229

there appears to have been an increase again. Continuation of this increase would result in rapid population growth. Income is coming to be positively associated with family size. This new relationship between population and income, and *via* this with resources, is a complex one. Children satisfy a basic human need, and so part of the demand for children is independent of income, but beyond this the demand for children is in competition with the demand for consumer goods. As income grows still further, a large family and economic prosperity can both be had.

12.19 Population and food supplies

Historical research has found many examples of famines in the past, some so severe as to have led to cannibalism. The death rate rose sharply, usually in association with a concurrent reduction in the marriage and birth rates. Such crises seem to have been mainly rural, and to have been caused by bad weather involving more than one successive poor harvest. It appears that the famine did not persist for long, either through a recovery in food production or a reduction in population, or both of these together. Certainly, population growth in the longer run was not held up, probably because increased areas came under cultivation and possibly also because population pressure provided an incentive for the development of more intensive production methods. Malthus's pessimism about population outrunning supplies was not justified in developing countries in the nineteenth century, but more recently there has appeared to be some evidence, from the developing countries of today, that supplies might not be able to keep up with population growth. The figures given in table 12.2 earlier in this chapter certainly suggest that the balance is a delicate one, and the bad world harvests of 1973 and 1974 have undone much of the gains made in the preceeding years. Prospects for the future are discussed in chapter 14 below.

Broadly, indexes of population and food production for recent years have progressed in close parallel. The relationships between these two economic elements are, however, many and varied. In spite of pressure of numbers on the land in many areas, there are still countries with tracts largely untouched by man. One of these is Ghana, of which Omaboe has written that 'vast areas have been brought under cultivation during the last half-century ... during this same period the population ... increased considerably ... we do not know the extent to which the development of these new areas has been brought about by the population increases. It is undoubtedly true that the ... growth has had some effect.' This statement is probably representative of much past history the world over. Estimates have been made of the positive effect of population growth on production by increases in the agricultural labour force and other more indirect consequences; but the outcome represented only 0·3—0·7 per cent for each 1 per cent rise in population, varying according to location. This lack of 'efficiency' might be explained generally on the basis that the areas newly opened up are likely to be both remoter and less productive than those already in use.

12.20   Adaptability in agriculture

There is ample evidence from both archaeology and history that the size of human populations has responded dramatically to the introduction of new agricultural methods or crops. For instance, rural population in the Danube basin is known to have speedily doubled after the introduction of maize; the population of Ireland grew with the potato and fell after its failure. It is less easy to establish that population pressure influences methods of cultivation, but some interesting evidence comes from Central Africa, where it has been shown that non-intensive and intensive methods of agriculture are both well known; the less effective form is preferred because it is not so laborious, but where population is sufficiently dense the more productive system is employed. It has been suggested that the general transition from a nomadic life to village settlement was similarly enforced on man against his will. Similarly, Martin argues that in Africa 'the growth of population has reduced the extensive method of farming and brought about continuous cropping of the land'. It appears that food-raising methods in Europe have been remarkably susceptible to the price mechanism, which itself reflected the falls in human numbers arising from wars or epidemics and the rises that occurred in undisturbed periods.

Clearly, much depends on such factors as a country's climate and geography, its state of development, its type of political and social organization, the policy of its government, and the amount and nature of any aid it receives. In some cases, a 'feedback' relationship of one kind or another may be in operation (see § 14.10 below). For instance, increasing yields from the soil may encourage population growth and thus prevent the average living standard from rising; or population pressure may lead, through reduced consumption per head, to poorer nutrition and so a weaker general state of health and hence lower agricultural output. Such effects are sometimes described as 'population traps' and they help to explain why the indexes of population and food output keep close together.

There may also be favourable 'feedback' effects. For instance, a country's development is usually accompanied by urbanization, because population growth leads to unemployment on the land and hence drives people to cities, which is widely thought to have a favourable effect on agricultural output because farmers are encouraged to grow exportable food surpluses rather than just aim to feed themselves. But in order thus to escape from the population trap, it is necessary to develop capital and probably to improve education, and both are difficult to achieve without aid from outside.

231

12.21   Population growth and industrial development

It is widely believed, though not universally held, that at present the rapid growth of population in some areas is slowing down investment and so preventing production from rising as fast as it should. Production per head thus tends to remain stationary, or even to fall. The mechanism by which population increase tends to defeat economic growth is that it calls for the concentration of too much human and material resources in 'social over-heads' —such as housing —in order to maintain basic standards and services for the increased numbers. These overheads are not productive and the effort would have been better directed to investment in economically advantageous projects. The trend towards urbanization accentuates these difficulties.

While mitigating factors may be found in the plentiful supply of labour and in the creation of a 'mass market', these cannot be relied on in practice to redress the balance. Although lower death rates tend to give rise to a longer active life and to a reduction in absence from work through sickness, the age-distributions of growing populations are economically disadvantageous. Some economists hold that growing populations lead to unemployment, or at least under-employment, but this is disputed and it may be that such features arise more from geographical, political, or social causes. Whatever the cause, considerable unemployment exists —figures of 5 per cent in India, 9 per cent in the Philippines and 11 per cent in Puerto Rico have been recorded in recent years, to give but a few isolated examples.

Opponents of the idea that population growth impedes economic advance can point to many potentially useful ways in which the growth can be productively employed. Undoubtedly such ways exist. But they often involve radical political and social policies which seem to be beyond the grasp of many countries, for example, the totalitarian restriction of consumption or forced direction of labour.

The relationship between demographic upsurge and economic develop-ment is clouded over, in the data, by complicating factors such as the nature of economic and social institutions, the state of technology, the level of education. For instance, in young and relatively empty countries, high demographic and economic growth are found together, while in some European countries high economic growth is associated with a low rate of population increase. In Holland, population growth is regarded as a handi-cap, whereas in Ireland and France the lack of population growth has been thought to be a defect that should be remedied so as to improve the economic well-being of the nation. But the European experience may prove to be an inappropriate guide to newer countries unless analysis can reveal more precisely than at present the underlying causes at work. Moreover, economic development may itself influence demographic characteristics, especially by altering the balance of urban and rural population and by changing people's traditions and outlook.

12.22   Economic development and family size

Fertility at the maximum physiological level is found in few human societies. Even in under-developed countries the number of children per couple is well below its upper limit, and the reasons for the shortfall are known: fertility is influenced by religious, social or economic considerations. Changes in these considerations are potentially capable of affecting the size of the family. Optimists hold that reduced fertility will accompany the development of wealth, as it has already done in many countries (see § 10.17 above). They can give specific reasons for the likelihood of this development: when more women earn their living, they will have less time and desire for children; children will be valued more as individuals; a family will cost more to raise; there will be less need to replace wastage through early death; competing interests and desires in a modern society will militate against large families.

These arguments are plausible, and it is reasonable to expect that the number of children will indeed fall from its present high level — even though this cannot prevent a big rise in population in the immediate future. Nevertheless it is by no means certain that a big fall will occur. For one thing, development has already occurred in some places without being accompanied by much decline in fertility. Again, even where family-planning advice is available, and the people generally are conscious of the need for taking it, it is not used. Thirdly, some religious and political groups are using the quasi-scientific argument as a basis for suggesting that, as family size will fall in the normal course, there is no need for the adoption of national policies of family planning. (It is only a short time since some of these groups were arguing that a low rate of population growth represented 'decadence', and this motivation could be political rather than scientific.)

It would be helpful if the experience of the developed countries over the last hundred years could be analysed so as to identify the precise causes of the decline in fertility. It seems likely from the work already done in this direction, however, that particular stages or factors in economic progress could be assigned any given share in the demographic trend. Changes in the economy and in fertility did not correspond in time in many instances; in North America fertility began to fall before the industrial revolution took hold, whereas in Europe, with the exception of France, fertility did not begin to fall until long after economic development had begun.

Discrepancies over timing do not necessarily throw doubts on the validity of the connexion between economic development and fertility decline. It is well known that social conditions, and the religious background, can cause delay, as they did in England in the nineteenth century; ideas can spread from one country to another ahead of economic development, and this may explain the American experience. A further element of social delay can be seen in the gradual spread of family limitation down the classes, which

233

found its statistical expression in the rise and subsequent fall of fertility differentials in Britain.

Nevertheless, the discrepancies make it harder to state by what social processes technical and economic change have induced new personal motives for family limitation, or how different social and cultural conditions affected these processes. In spite of the high correlation between low fertility and development, which has been shown for broad aggregates of countries, it is more difficult to interpret the data both for individual countries and for groups, over periods of time. It seems likely that their varying size, history, geography and religion are complicating issues. It has been stated that 'no published version of the theory of demographic transition states precisely what conditions are essential for a fertility decline'. Under the extended family system, the full economic cost of each new child is not borne by its parents, who may thus not realize the burden it imposes. Not only is the level of education too low for a full knowledge of birth control but the average person's wealth is insufficient for the purchase of the necessary devices. Any rises in production merely encourage a greater growth in the population where the people do not yet appreciate the need for family limitation.

12.23   Some illustrative data

By way of illustration of the problems associated with population and resources, this chapter concludes with a few illustrative tables of a general character, which bring out the sharpness of international contrasts.

Table 12.15 gives some figures for the year 1958, and shows that 30 per cent of the world's population lived in the economically more developed areas and produced 90 per cent of the world's output of industrial goods. (Although some of the products of the richer countries are exchanged by means of

Table 12.15 *Population and industrial production as proportion of world total, 1958*

	Industrially developed countries	Other countries
	(%)	(%)
Population	30	70
Industrial production		
Mining	75	25
Light manufacturing	87	13
Heavy manufacturing	93	7
Electricity and gas	91	9
All industrial production	90	10

international trade for the produce of the poorer countries, the bulk of the trade in manufactures is between the industrial countries themselves).

More detail of a similar kind is given in table 12.16, relating to the year 1961. Gross national product 'in real terms' here indicates the purchasing power of the national product in terms of US prices. It is a rough estimate obtained by increasing the purchasing power of various countries by a factor (varying from 20 per cent to 100 per cent) to allow for the underestimation that, according to many authors, results when ordinary exchange rates are used.

Inequalities of national wealth are again illustrated in table 12.17. It has been estimated that an immediate trebling of world industrial output would be necessary, as well as a considerable expansion of agriculture, for the people of the poorer countries to benefit from modern technology on the same scale as the inhabitants of the richer areas. If it were not for population growth, this might be gradually achieved over not too long a period; but as world population is growing it will be necessary for the same purpose to

Table 12.16. *World population and gross national product, 1961*

Area	Population Proportion of world total (%)	Gross national product in real terms Amount ($ thousand millions)	Proportion of world total (%)	Amount per head ($)
USA	6·2	513	29·4	2,790
Canada	0·6	38	2·2	2,048
Oceania	0·5	34	1·4	1,513
Western Europe	8·7	385	22·0	1,472
USSR	7·2	212	12·1	986
Eastern Europe	3·3	82	4·7	825
Japan	3·2	58	3·3	613
South Africa	0·5	9	0·5	598
All richer areas	30·2	1,333	75·6	1,460
North and South Europe	2·2	34	1·9	501
Latin America	7·0	89	5·1	425
Middle East	3·5	29	1·7	257
North Korea	0·3	2	0·1	211
North Vietnam	0·6	3	0·2	199
China	23·2	116	6·6	167
Africa	6·9	34	1·9	164
Remainder of Asia	26·1	120	6·8	154
All poorer areas	69·8	427	24·4	204
World total	100·0	1,760	100·0	584

Table 12.17. *World income distribution, 1961*

Gross national product in real terms per head ($)	Proportion of world population (%)	Proportion of product (%)
Under 100	0·4	0·1
100—299	50·9	16·6
300—599	8·7	6·4
600—1,200	15·1	21·9
Over 1,200	15·9	55·0
Total	100·0	100·0

achieve an expansion of world industry to more than three times its present size. Expressed as a rate of growth of gross national product, a rise of perhaps 6 per cent per annum may be required. At present, very few countries are able to achieve such a rate of increase in total product, let alone product per head. The rates of advance actually achieved by the economically advanced countries in the course of their development history are indicated in table 12.18; none of them nearly approaches 6 per cent. Perhaps the only redeeming feature is that while these countries had to develop their industrial techniques as they progressed, today the other countries can acquire the knowledge much more readily.

Table 12.18. *Rates of annual growth in national product (in real terms) for selected countries over long periods*

Country	Period	Rate of growth	
		Gross national product (% per annum)	Gross national product per head (% per annum)
United Kingdom	1841—1959	2·1	1·2
France	1840—1960	1·8	1·5
Germany	1841—1960	2·4	1·4
Sweden	1861—1960	2·4	1·4
Russia	1913—1928	0·5	—
	1928—1958	4·4	3·7
Japan	1878—1922	4·1	3·0
	1918—1960	3·9	2·6

SELECT BIBLIOGRAPHY

The Determinants and Consequences of Population Trends (United Nations, New York 1973).

Population, Food Supply and Agricultural Development, World Population Conference (United Nations, 1974).

Population, Resources and the Environment, World Population Conference (United Nations, 1974).

Cox, P. R. and Thomas, C. J. 'Population and Resources', *Journal of the Institute of Actuaries*, **94**, (1967), 1.

Mudd, S. (ed.), *The Population Crisis and the Use of World Resources*' (Junk, The Hague, 1964).

Sukhatme, P. V. *Feeding India's Growing Millions* (Asia Publishing House, London, 1965).

Malin, K. M. 'Food Resources of the Earth', *World Population Conference*, 1965 (United Nations Organization, New York, 1967), **3**, 385.

Zhavoronkov, N. M. 'Chemistry and the Vital Resources of Mankind', *World Population Conference, 1965* (United Nations Organization, New York, 1967), **3**, 346.

Jones, G. W. 'Effect of Population Change on the Attainment of Educational Goals in the Developing Countries.' In *Rapid Population Growth* (Johns Hopkins, 1971).

Conceptión, M. B. *Wanted. A Theory of the Demographic Transition*, IUSSP Australian Conference Papers, 1967.

van de Walle, E. and Knodel, J. *Demographic Transition and Fertility Decline: the European Case*, IUSSP Australian Conference Papers, 1967.

Cox, R. and Peel, J. (editors). *Population and Pollution* (Academic Press, 1972).

Benjamin, B., Cox, P. R. and Peel, J. (editors). *Resources and Population* (Academic Press, 1973).

Heer, D. M. 'Economic Development and Fertility', *Demography*, **3**, (1966), 423.

Omaboe, E. N. 'The Population Pressure and the Development of New Areas', *World Population Conference, 1965* (United Nations Organization, New York, 1967), **3**, 400.

Bantegui, B. G. 'Demographic Factors affecting Food Supplies and Agricultural Development', *World Population Conference, 1965* (United Nations Organization, New York, 1967).

De Vries, E. 'Historical Evidence concerning the Effect of Population Pressure and Growth of Technical Progress in Agriculture', *World Population Conference, 1965* United Nations Organization, New York, 1967), **3**, 425.

13 Population policies

13.1 Introduction

The economic issues affecting population are, as chapter 12 has shown, unclear in many respects. There is probably as much room for difference of opinion on these issues as there is on other economic questions of present-day significance. In addition, many further types of consideration are important in relation to population – social and moral questions, for instance, and matters affecting health. Before the prospects for the future can be viewed, in chapter 14 which follows, it is clearly necessary to pay some attention to the ways in which people are currently regarding such issues and questions, for it is in these ways that they will be conscious of demographic problems and their actions in regard to marriage, fertility and migration may well spring out of their consciousness.

13.2 Attitudes of governments

In an attempt to get some information on various aspects of population policy, the UN Organization conducted an inquiry among member nations in 1963 in order to ascertain the views of governments as to whether there was a relationship between economic development and population change. The inquiry document was rather vaguely worded, and left much latitude for the replies. Perhaps for this reason, there was a good response. Answers were received from over fifty countries, with a wide geographical distribution and very varied states of economic development. From the replies it is possible to make a broad classification of countries according to whether they regard population growth as:

(1) a brake on the economy;
(2) a spur to progress;
(3) a factor having little effect, on balance, on general development.

The majority of the African, Latin American and Asian countries that responded regarded population growth as a brake. Answers of a different character came mainly from developed and communist economies; while these economies have their difficulties they are hardly of the same character and it seems clear that the 'population problem' is confined to the countries

238

in poverty. Where subsistence agriculture obtains, where there is very little industrial development, where education is rudimentary and communication, whether of ideas or goods, difficult, procreation seems to be unaffected by current economic considerations. There is usually a fertility cult that has prevailed for centuries. People do not see any rational motives for limiting procreation; on the contrary, they may think of a large family as a form of social insurance in old age. It is only at a more advanced stage of economic development that rational motives for limiting the number of children seem likely to emerge.

Sometimes a Government's reply might reflect a general lack of concern about population increase. Thus the Cameroon Government stated that its growth rate of 2 per cent per annum 'appears to be a factor favouring the country's development. A higher rate would have made it difficult to increase income per head, while if the rate had been lower there would not have been sufficient population pressure to encourage urbanization, which is an essential factor in the economic development of the country.' Not all countries are in this happy situation, however. Tunisia felt that, 'In addition to the special burdens which it imposes on the country, the continuation of the rate of population growth at the current level necessitates a considerable increase in production, not only in the agricultural sector but in all the sectors producing the goods required for a modern, even if modest, way of living. It is useless to increase agricultural output if manufactured goods are lacking and have to be imported in their entirety. Such a situation would imperil monetary stability, necessitate the imposition of price controls and, in general, make it difficult even to maintain the level of living.'

More recently, the UN conducted a second inquiry among Governments, with questions put differently from those in the first one. It was noted from the replies that, in summary:

(1) the most populous countries on the whole had the slowest rate of economic advance;

(2) agricultural output has increased but population growth has prevented much rise in output per head;

(3) there have been severe unemployment problems the root of which lies in part in population expansion;

(4) housing difficulties also exist and can be attributed at least in some degree to the same root cause;

(5) while national plans and forecasts often assume an improvement in the future, past experience suggests that actual performance tends to fall short of hopes.

Nevertheless the responses varied a good deal between individual governments and were not usually capable of proper comparison with those given in 1963. Evidence from other sources suggests, however, that in some

239

countries the family planning movement has, for one reason or other, developed more widely than before, with more official support than it had previously received.

13.3 Government action: the possibilities

Human behaviour in matters associated with reproduction is very largely a question of 'culture', in the widest sense. Fundamentally, therefore, the aim of any government which wishes to effect a change should be to influence the culture. In some countries, there is little or no official population policy; there, the importance of pressure groups such as Roman Catholics or Marxists is relatively high in relation to the importance of demographic problems, and the political disturbance likely to be created by a step in any definite direction is a sufficient deterrent to action.

Where it is desired to raise the birth rate, official action can take the form of legislation banning abortion or even prohibiting the import or dissemination of contraceptive materials, and this can be enforced with penalties. Where it has been tried success has been achieved, mainly in authoritarian regimes, though even there it has tended to be short-lived. There can also be encouragement, in the form of family allowances, and propaganda in favour of larger families, notably towards the ideal of three children per couple rather than two.

Where it is desired to reduce the birth rate, the possibilities for governmental action are also limited. Human behaviour cannot in the nature of things be directly controlled, and no one can lay down that families above a certain size are not permissible, without resorting to measures of greater extremity than of any past time in respect of fertility. Abstinence from sexual intercourse can hardly be enforced. Nor can the use of contraceptives be made compulsory. Artificial termination of pregnancy could not be insisted upon, because it is often dangerous to the mother's health.

In these circumstances, the options open to a government are:

(1) the provision of facilities and advice; or
(2) exhortation and encouragement; or
(3) fiscal action, involving special taxation arrangements or grants.

The possibility of control by dictatorial or repressive legislation is excluded because even in the most authoritarian of regimes this has been little attempted and, where tried, unsuccessful. Obstacles arise from political and religious opposition, from public apathy and from financial problems: apart from the question of cost, there is the moral difficulty that the larger a family of children is, the more State aid it may need; on humanitarian principles this leads to the payment of family allowances in cash, whereas
240

in order to discourage the formation of large families a financial deterrent would require additional taxation for each extra child in the family.

As demographic prospects in many countries must depend very considerably on the relative strength and effectiveness of government action, and of the opposition to it, it is desirable to consider the forces on both sides in more detail.

13.4 Support for, and opposition to, family limitation

The principal components of opposition to population policies of various kinds are in character either political, or religious, or humanitarian or traditional, though mixtures of these principles may well be experienced.

Political The best known theory which rejects the idea of a limit on procreation is that which derives from the teachings of Marx. These teachings imply that whatever the population size it should be possible for suitable provision to be made for it if the political system is right. Communists advance this view not only because they believe in it but also because, in respect of under-developed countries:

(1) it discredits the type of help provided by non-communist countries, which is based on birth control; and

(2) the absence of limitation of birth tends to increase economic difficulties, and hence dissatisfaction with the existing regime and so (it is hoped) opens the way to communism.

Most communist countries have, however, permitted, and even encouraged, birth control practices within their own borders on the ground that it was used for the benefit of the mother's health. Such substantial falls in birth rates have occurred in many communist countries, however, that this State concern with the mother's welfare has had much the same practical effect as voluntary family limitation in certain European countries.

Religious It has been argued that effective birth prevention opens the way to the indulgence of sex without the natural consequences, and that as a result the institutions of marriage and the family are weakened, and, more generally, a hedonistic (pleasure-seeking) outlook upon life is encouraged. Such views probably still influence a large number of people, although others may argue that such traditional values are becoming outmoded in a changing world.

Religious views on the family have varied a good deal from time to time and according to the particular religion. One general feature that all religions have in common to some extent is a pronatalist view, based on a desire to spread the influence of the faith and to avoid being outnumbered by the adherents of some other faith. Roman Catholics take the view that man is provided with various vital organs to perform certain functions, and that

241

these functions should not be prevented. Birth control by artificial means is 'unnatural' and therefore not allowed. Not all Catholics accept this teaching today. The Jewish and Protestant religions have changed their outlook on questions relating to the size of the family, and are now prepared to support the practice of limitation. Mohammedanism, while strongly in favour of marriage, has never presented a strong bar to birth control, but Buddhism, with its belief in reincarnation, regards contraception as the blotting out of an already existing 'life' and as such insupportable.

Humanitarian   There are groups which oppose pro-natalist and *laissez faire* population policies on the ground that mankind is using up resources too fast and therefore leaving too little for the benefit of future generations. This is the conservationist viewpoint.

Tradition   This represents, in general, the unthinking adherence to moral and religious views and practices that may have lost their relevance. At its lowest it consists of nothing more than the will to do just the same as one's forebears. It is associated with other traditional values, such as those connected with rural life, agriculture and in particular with the 'extended family' system, in which all generations and branches of a kinship group live together and support one another. It is also associated with the dominance of men over women (whose wishes in family matters may thus be overridden), with taboos on the discussion of matters of sex, and with 'machado' or 'machismo'. This is a primitive masculine pride in the power to copulate, which can be proved to one's fellows at any time only by the birth of a new child.

13.5   Technical problems of family limitation

The main difficulties over the successful implementation of family-planning programmes, other than those mentioned in the preceding section, arise from technical sources. These may be divided into two groups:

(1) persuading people of the necessity for the limitation; unless they see good reason in it, action will not follow in practice; and

(2) inducing widespread action which requires steady and unrelenting perseverance, where activities are concerned which are of an emotional and impulsive nature.

In some places, the availability of birth control advice and appliances has made little difference to public behaviour in family matters. Where this is the case, attempts have sometimes been made to teach people the need for birth control and the correct manner in which to practise it. Even then, however, knowledge has not led to action on the part of the public. In part this has been attributable to difficulties of technique: simple people have been unable to use the devices available. Much more, however, it has been found that motivation is lacking; in other words, the need for birth control is not appreciated. National prosperity, and overcrowding, seem less significant than the personal satisfaction that children can bring, and the support they may provide in one's old age. However, family limitation came about in Britain, in other European countries and in Japan without the need for any teaching, and sometimes in defiance of accepted conventions. It is against this varied background that governmental action in various countries today must be considered.

Tests and surveys made in many developing countries recently show that there is a desire among the people to limit the size of their families. This springs not so much from a consciousness of national economic need but from motives of better health and an easier life for mothers and children, and of personal economic benefit, coupled with a realization that a large family is no longer necessary for support in old age. This desire is often ill matched by sufficient knowledge or perseverance to learn or apply most of the birth control techniques at present readily available. Neither oral contraceptives nor uterine devices have proved successful in India, for instance. Methods which are easy to produce are either unpopular (for instance total abstinence from intercourse), too complex (such as effective intermittent abstinence — the 'rhythm' method acceptable to Roman Catholics on grounds of ethical and religious rectitude) or too unreliable (withdrawal). Some of the newest and most convenient and reliable methods are too expensive for the developing countries (e.g. the pill and even condoms and sheaths).

Governments which are convinced of the need to implement a family-planning programme, in spite of all the difficulties, use a number of devices of which the following are examples:

(1) free availability of the use of contraceptives at public expense;

(2) education and training programmes in schools and clinics;

(3) incentives in cash or goods — a campaign sponsored by the Indian Government, under which free transistor radios are given to men undergoing vasectomy (sterilization) has been successful;

(4) strong moral pressure, generally used in countries with highly authoritarian governments, in which people are or have to become accustomed to a close regulation of all aspects of their lives.

In many countries, the people have resorted to induced abortion where contraception has failed — notably in Japan (see § 11.12) and in Eastern Europe. Abortion is a subject on which strong views are held by most people. No nation appears to have decided to legalize abortion solely as a means of family limitation, but many have done so as a welfare measure in order to make it as safe as possible for those people who would otherwise resort to the operation clandestinely and at considerable risk. Historically, abortion has been the solution for women who do not wish to bear the child they have conceived, and all experience indicates that they will continue to attempt to

243

achieve this solution whatever the laws of their country may say. For obvious reasons, there are no very good statistics of the incidence of illegal abortions, but recent surveys in connection with family-planning programmes in Chile and South Korea, for example, suggested that there is probably one illegal abortion for every two live births and there can be little doubt that the practice of abortion is widespread in many countries.

Many countries have taken the view that the welfare of the people demands the legalization of abortion in certain cases, and have passed laws to this end. In the Soviet Union abortion was made legal in 1920, then illegal in 1936, then legal again in 1955. Soviet medical and social opinion is aware of the peril of dangerous illegal abortions and of the peril of too numerous legal ones, but has attached different degrees of importance to the two at different times. One trouble is said to have been the poor quality of contraceptives. Hungary and Czechoslovakia now allow legal abortion on a large scale; so too did Rumania from 1957 until recently, when it was decided to limit it to certain special circumstances, such as rape or where there were dangers to the mother or child.

Britain liberalized its abortion law in 1968 and France and other countries are preparing to follow suit.

13.6 The progress of Government plans: India and Pakistan

India was the first country to adopt a national programme of limiting population growth by means of family planning. During the first five-year plan (1951–6) a number of studies were made to provide information for the preparation of the programme, and experimental projects were established based on the rhythm method. In the second five-year plan, an organization and a few training centres were set up; interest in family planning was promoted through mass education media and services were provided through clinics and hospitals. In the third five-year plan, the programme was reorganized and intensified. By a change from a policy of availability of clinics to one of more direct encouragement, some progress was made towards creating a favourable climate for overcoming apathy towards the acceptance of family planning. It has become clear that an extensive community-aimed effort has to be organized to take the programme to the people. Medical family-planning officers with supporting staff are now being appointed to districts containing between 1 and 2 million people, and educational and field staff covering the population in smaller groups of perhaps 100,000. A Family Planning Committee has been set up at Cabinet level and the Ministry of Health has been renamed the Ministry of Health and Family Planning. A demographer has been elevated to Ministerial rank. In the five-year plan for the years 1966–71 some 200 million US dollars was allocated to family-planning, but although this is a large sum it represented only about 8 cents a year per person — too little with which to hope to cut fertility by one-third, the target necessary if effective inroads are to be made on the rate of population growth.

In Pakistan a family-planning programme was devised in 1960. This soon passed through the preliminaries and reached the stage of implementation. The State budgeted about 12 cents a head during each year of the five-year plan, which began in 1965, and family planning has been accepted as a government responsibility of high importance. Field staff have been appointed in the villages. Coil (IUD) insertions now exceed 50,000 a month, and it was planned to reduce the birth rate from 50 to 40 per annum by 1970. During the years 1970–5, oral contraceptives were introduced and a corps of specially-trained men and women have replaced the village midwives who have in the past played the major role in the plans. The separation of Bangladesh from Pakistan has altered the direction of the programme in Bangladesh to one of sterilization.

13.7   Family planning in the Far East

According to Chou En Lai in 1964: 'We do believe in planned parenthood, but it is not easy to introduce all at once in China and it is more difficult to achieve in rural areas, where most of our people live, than in the cities. The first thing is to encourage late marriages ....' Although the degree of official interest in family planning has varied from time to time the government continues to advocate late marriage and small families, and to provide an active programme of contraceptive services of various kinds. The minimum legal age for marriage is 20 for men and 18 for women but marriage earlier than 28 and 25 respectively is discouraged. The will of the government appears to be accepted by the people.

In Hong Kong and Singapore, two territories with a population concentrated into a small area, official family-planning programmes have shown quick success, and the birth rate has been halved. By contrast, in widely-scattered Indonesia, where a Government policy of information and services was first announced only in 1968, progress has been as yet slow. Another Asian country to have organized a national family-planning programme is South Korea. In 1963 there was an energetic 'mass enlightenment' campaign which resulted in the registration by more than a million couples of their interest in family planning and their acceptance of a trial supply of traditional contraceptive devices. Tests were also started on IUD. There are signs that fertility has begun to fall here, and also in Taiwan.

Thailand approved a family-planning programme in 1970 under which IUDs and oral contraceptives are available in hospitals and health centres. The Philippines also began a programme in that year with the aim of enrolling one-half of young couples as acceptors of contraceptives by 1976. In both

245

countries, 'KAP' surveys have been conducted: these are programmes of dissemination of correct Knowledge of, Attitude towards, and Practice of, contraception.

13.8   The Middle East and Africa

A policy to reduce the rate of population increase was officially adopted in Egypt in 1965. It was hoped to bring it down from 4 to 3 per cent per annum in ten years, and in the first five years over a million people accepted oral contraceptives or IUDs. In Turkey, too, 1965 was a significant year; government policy then changed from anti-contraceptive to pro-family-planning, and this appears to be in line with popular feeling. In both Egypt and Turkey the current rate of population growth is still over 2 per cent a year. These countries were preceded by Tunisia, which in 1964 became the first North African country to adopt a national family-planning programme. Pilot studies were made and an initial experiment conducted. The aim was one IUD insertion a year for every twelve women of child-bearing age, in the hope of reducing the birth rate by one-quarter in five years. Abortion is permitted for women who have already borne more than four children.

Nigeria's national population policy dates from 1973, and its aim appears to be to encourage the citizens to develop a balanced view of the opportunities for individual family planning on a voluntary basis, with the aim of raising the quality of life for their offspring. No targets for specific reductions in the birth rate have been set.

13.9   America south of the USA

The UN Fund for Population Activities is now supporting family-planning projects in 22 countries. Not all the governments of these countries have adopted national population policies (Roman Catholic influence is strong) but the UN incentive may provide the necessary groundwork, as may also the work of private organizations such as family-planning associations, women's societies and charitable foundations.

SELECT BIBLIOGRAPHY

Glass, D. V. 'Family planning programmes and action in Western Europe', *World views of Population Problems* (Budapest, 1965), p. 105.
Report of the Secretary-General on an Inquiry among Governments on Problems resulting from the Interactions of Economic Development and Population Changes (United Nations Organization, New York, 1964).
The Determinants and Consequences of Population Trends (United Nations, New York, 1973).
Macura, M. 'Population Policies in Socialist Countries of Europe', *Population Studies*, **28** (1974), 369.

14 General prospects for the future

14.1 Introduction

This chapter refers to three separate aspects of likely future population trends. First, it discusses the prospects for the world as a whole, as they appear today, both treating population as a variable which is independent of specific economic influences and considering it in relation to the prospective supply of the various kinds of resources needed by mankind. Secondly, it shows what expectations have been entertained by demographers in the past — these have varied appreciably from time to time in various countries — and what subsequently happened. This part of the analysis also looks at those parts of the projection which were most successful and which were least successful. Finally, the chapter discusses the details of the latest available assessments, at the time of writing, which have been made for selected countries and areas.

14.2 Future world population

The latest published projections made by the Population Division of the UN Organization show that a steady growth in numbers is expected in all parts of the world. Some figures are set out in table 14.1; these relate to the 'medium variant' and show that a doubling in the grand total is envisaged between the years 1960 and 2000. The pace of advance differs little between the first and second halves of this period. As between the 8 regions, the pace is lowest in Europe (34 per cent rise in the forty years) and is below the world average also in Russia (54 per cent), North America (67 per cent) and East Asia (81 per cent). In other less-developed regions considerably more than a doubling in population size is envisaged.

Besides the medium variant, the UN usually issue figures for a low and a high variant, and they may also give results on the assumption of constant fertility. In the 1966 projections, the medium variant world population for the end of the century was 6,130 millions; on the other three bases the corresponding figures were respectively 5,449, 6,994 and 7,522. In no region is a fall in numbers expected on any of these bases, and even on a subdivision of the world into twenty-four sub-regions there is growth to be expected

Table 14.1. *Population projections for the world and its major regions, published by the UN Organization in 1971 (medium variant)*

(Millions.)

Region	Year		
	1960*	1980	2000
North America	199	261	333
Europe	425	497	568
Russia	214	271	330
Oceania	16	24	35
East Asia	785	1,095	1,424
South Asia	865	1,486	2,354
Africa	270	457	818
Latin America	213	377	652
Total	2,986	4,468	6,514

* Actual.

everywhere. Northern Europe is the sub-region with the slowest growth (5 per cent in forty years according to the low variant).

Some indication of the recent past growth and estimated future increase in population is given in fig. 14.1, which is based on the UN projections of 1966 and in which the main regions of the world are arranged roughly in order of the expected pace of growth. The range of assessments indicated is from the high figures to the low figures in the UN Population Division's calculations on the subject. A fall in fertility is assumed on the highest alternative.

In a paper read to the Second World Population Conference, 1965, Boyarsky presented his own independent forecast of future world population, according to which it would be around 4,600 millions in the year 2000. The method used was equivalent in simplicity to the system adopted in the first UN assessment. The number of births per annum was assumed to be constant over a considerable past and future period. Thus the future population size would depend mainly on improving longevity. As a basis for this argument he cited Western European experience, in which rising populations have been combined with falling fertility to produce constant total annual numbers of births. This is of very doubtful validity for developing countries: wherever sound data are available for these countries it is evident that the numbers of births are rising *pari passu* with population. Although for many areas the long-term trend of the numbers of births is unrecorded it is logical to expect that as total population has increased so also have the annual numbers of births — otherwise a fall in fertility would have occurred, which hardly seems possible having regard to its high level today.

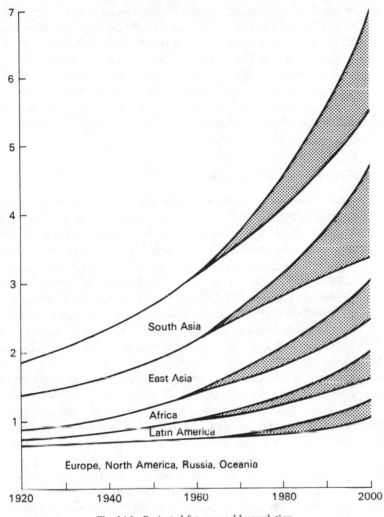

Fig. 14.1. Projected future world population.

14.3 World population growth beyond the year 2000

While it is both convenient and prudent to limit projections of population to the end of the present century, it is important to remember that on present prospects growth is likely to continue thereafter. Even a population for which the intrinsic rate of increase is zero may, as a consequence of its age-composition, get larger for several decades before stability is reached. In its most recent work the Population Division of the UN looked into the twenty-first century, during which it assumed that fertility would gradually

249

be reduced to net replacement level. That level would be reached in North America by 2005, in Europe by 2010, in East Asia by 2015 and so on, ending with Africa where it was assumed that it would not be achieved until 2075. The expectation of life at birth would ultimately reach 75 in a similar time-scale. On this approach, the world total population would settle down at some 12,000 millions by the year 2125. Of this, Europe, Russia, Oceania and North America would contribute together only about 11 per cent. Nearly one-half of this total relates to South Asia and second to this in size would be Africa.

14.4 Future demand for resources

If populations are going to grow in the manner indicated above, more resources are going to be needed. In order to be able to assess this increase in need it is desirable first to think about the requirements of the poor nations for their economic development. Most people accept as axiomatic that development is the first priority, though perhaps not all would agree with this. The peoples of lands suffering from lack of development seem, however, strongly to desire 'progress' even though it may bring disadvantages in its wake. Perhaps the overriding attraction is that it may give more control over the environment, and enables a more equitable distribution of wealth and benefits especially to the weak: children, women and the physically handi-capped.

Economic growth is the result of investment and the application of technical knowledge, and according to Rostow it is a process which has five stages. If the third stage of 'take-off'. is reached, it can then be expected to proceed under its own momentum. Whether or not this theory is tenable (and not all subscribe to it), poor countries, in the main, have failed to invest an adequate proportion of their national income in the past, and so have not achieved much advance. For investment to occur there has to be an excess of production over consumption. Economists sometimes work to an empirical rule that three units of capital investment will result in an addition of one unit to annual productive capacity. Where population is increasing at 2 per cent or more per annum, it follows that 6 per cent or more of the national output would need to be invested merely to maintain the income per head. This is a very difficult aim and the necessary saving seems to be beyond the capacity of so many of the subsistence economies.

Development may take place by either a predominantly industrial route or by a predominantly agricultural route. It may be that in many instances it is better that growth should occur first in the agricultural sector. In some countries, the emphasis has been placed on road-building, and on education, but the result does not appear to have been particularly beneficial: very probably these resources have not been properly used, at least initially.

250

Moreover, the trading pattern is unfavourable under present price structures, and the poorer countries' share of world markets is declining, so that attempts to export are not likely to be helpful. Under an agricultural development scheme, a better supply of food can be secured for the local population. The projects to be encouraged are those absorbing large amounts of labour in relation to a small amount of capital. A strong industrial sector would then be expected to emerge as a concomitant of the successful development of primary or resource industry exports. By trade the country can expand its resource base, but as the output of agricultural and other primary products grows, resources become available for industrialization catering for the home market. Metal and engineering trades, including an agricultural machinery industry, should develop, together with various consumers' goods industries.

The stages of development from the subsistence level could thus well be (a) greater consumption of home-produced food, (b) gradual diversion of a proportion of the labour force to non-agricultural work and (c) more trading with the rest of the world.

International aid is now substantial, and most of the poorer countries depend heavily on external resources to increase their income per head. Nevertheless, it can hardly give sufficiently massive help in such a development programme. It can, however, act as a catalyst when applied at crucial points, depending upon the needs of the recipient country at its current stage of development. It might for instance provide industrial capital that normal market incentives would not attract; or, in the early phase, it could take the form of food and consumption goods so as to release a proportion of the population for labour-intensive capital works designed to increase the productivity of agriculture. It might prove to be more useful, however, in the form of technical information or education – and indeed much assistance has been given in this manner.

Private foreign investment, acting in response to normal market incentives, can of course be attracted and have a beneficial effect. Extractive industries, such as oil, readily draw investment capital from overseas; but often the result is merely an industrial enclave, with little effect on the remainder of the country, and so a dual economy develops. Much of the progress in the poorer countries in the past has been of this kind, and capital works designed to diffuse development are vital to further growth.

The more capital a country acquires, the greater its absorptive capacity. A soundly-conceived development programme in the hands of a government providing sufficient incentive to save should produce good results and lead in time to the adoption of the production methods used in more advanced countries. In this way, eventually, saving capacity can be further expanded sufficiently to finance capital development projects without reliance on foreign aid.

251

14.5   Future resources

Two hundred years ago, 'resources' consisted wholly of land and its products and were measured in acres, pounds and bushels. Most of the real increase in product per head since then has been of non-agricultural origin, and is appropriately measured in terms of kilowatts and calories. Thus, resources have changed in character; ideas about them have also changed. Demand has been stimulated. Peoples' 'needs' have mostly increased; this is not always so: the precise attention given in some recent studies to the meaning and measurement of malnutrition and under-nutrition is significant. Also indicative are the references in the literature to the possibilities of algae and synthetic pills as potential foodstuffs.

It is to be expected that concepts of 'resources' will change still further in the future. Supplies of some materials will come to an end, and then use will be made of substitutes. Moreover, owing to changes in relative costs and prices, the manner of employment of resources may alter well before supplies are exhausted. Awareness will emerge for the first time of limitations in the supply of resources that have hitherto seemed illimitable, such as fresh water, open space and wild life. Our assessment of the relative importance of the various elements in our surroundings will alter correspondingly. This reappraisal will not be confined to 'natural' resources, because some of our needs are essentially man-made, such as political systems, education and culture. These are an important part, not only of man's adaptation of natural materials to his own requirements, but also of his adaptation of himself to the available supplies.

14.6   Agricultural resources

If the present standards of nutrition are to be maintained, then by and large it will be necessary to augment agricultural production in future at the rate of population growth indicated above, subject to the effects of any changes in age-distribution upon food requirements. If, however, calorie and protein deficiencies are to be eliminated, then the supply from the land must be raised even faster, as illustrated in table 14.2 for the developing areas.

It will be noted that roughly a trebling is necessary for these regions, and for the world as a whole, four alternative forecasts of demand on varying assumptions all lead to a total calorie consumption in the year 2000 in the region of 20×10^{12} per day, which is about three times as large as the 1960 figure.

An alternative form of assessment, over a different period, is given in table 14.3, in which the richer countries are included.

The views taken by agricultural experts as to the prospects of producing the food necessary to make an adequate rate of consumption possible vary ac-

Table 14.2. *Percentage increase of food supply 1965—2000 estimated to be necessary to treat all requirements of the developing countries*

Region	Total increase in 35 years (%)	Increase per annum (%)	Increase per head in 35 years (%)
Far East	244	3·6	72
Near East	181	3·0	17
Africa	220	3·4	28
Latin America	185	3·0	12

Table 14.3. *Percentage increase of food supply from 1958—80 estimated to be needed to meet requirements*

Region	Increase of food supply per head required to meet the minimum nutritional requirement	Projected population growth 1958—80	Total increase of food supply from 1958—80 required to meet the minimum requirements of the 1980 population	Rate of annual increase of food supply needed 1958—80	Recent annual rate of increase of food supply
Richer countries	—	28	28	1·2	3·6
Africa	28	36	75	2·6	1·3
Latin America	5	85	94	3·1	2·5
Near East	17	62	90	3·0	3·1
Far East (excluding mainland China)	41	55	118	3·6	3·0
World	14	48	69	2·4	2·9

cording to the method used and the outlook of the author. Malin, on the basis of chemical and biological assays, has argued that:

(1) water in the hydrosphere and atmosphere is in ample supply for a population many times greater than at present;

(2) nitrogen, vital for fertilizers, is freely available in the air, and chemists have devised successful methods of 'fixing', or combining this with other elements so as to bring the nitrogen into a form in which it can be absorbed by plants;

253

(3) although phosphorus and potassium are being used up, and stocks may run out within 1,000 years, it should be possible to recover some from the sea.

It may be added that the carbon cycle seems likely to ensure a sufficient supply of this other vital chemical element indefinitely.

Malin speaks of the possibility of setting up 'cycles' for elements such as phosphorus similar to the natural cycle by which water and water vapour interchange, or, alternatively, of the direct chemical production of food, which would eliminate the need for most of these elements. There is some doubt about the feasibility and economic value of these suggestions. But perhaps concentrated research efforts might be capable of solving such problems in the long run.

Zhavoronkov has drawn attention to the possibilities of:

(1) fuller use of the products of photosynthesis: forest vegetation alone produces over 10 tons of organic substance per head per annum;

(2) new methods of photosynthesis: from algae such as Chlorella it is theoretically possible to obtain a hundred tons of organic material per head annually;

(3) direct synthesis of carbohydrates from carbon dioxide, hydrogen and water.

From these rather airy prospects, it is a contrast to return to the problems of today. These can be typified by the information given for India by Sukhatme, where, he says, the chance of improvement in food production occasioned by extension of the land area is small. Lack of capital hampers more frequent cropping (which calls for irrigation). For the same reason, and also perhaps because of religious practices, it is difficult to secure better quality and higher yields (which demand fertilizers) and an expansion of fishing (which requires a greater provision of gear and more boats). Peasant conservatism is to blame for poor milk production, because of lack of knowledge and because holdings are too small. The most that can be hoped for, so Sukhatme believes, is support of the growing population at minimum subsistence level, and it is difficult to disagree with him.

When there are such divergencies, it is not easy to sum up. All that can be said is that the opportunities are there and it is up to mankind to take advantage of them as best it can.

14.7 Mineral and energy resources

Some forms of mineral resources are used as sources of energy while others form an essential part of the processes of manufacture; there is, however, a common factor in that the total supply is limited. Discussion of the prospects for the future normally takes one or other of two forms:

(1) extrapolations of growth in output, or in demand, in the light of recent experience, leading to short-term forecasts of total production; it is usually necessary to consider also the related question of cost, which is likely to determine the choice of metals or fuels where several are available; such methods have the usual limitations of forecasts based on only a partial understanding of the economic forces at work;

(2) comparisons of consumption with estimated reserves, leading to estimates of the number of years that will elapse before stocks are exhausted, or become uneconomic to use; the time scale involved in such comparisons tends to be much longer than for other economic forecasts; their value is rendered doubtful by the prospects of changing costs, as the cheapest resources tend to be used first.

Attitudes to the results of such exercises vary a good deal from person to person and from one time to another. In the 1950s pessimism predominated, but in the 1960s a more cheerful note was struck. More recently still, the word 'crisis' has been heard a good deal, in association with the decision of many oil-producing countries to charge much more than before for their resources. What can be said with confidence, however, is that recent advances in output have been well ahead of the growth in population. While prospects for the future are generally uncertain, at least the rate of progress in production has been well ahead of the growth of population, and it seems reasonable to assume that the pace can be maintained or even accelerated. Moreover, the rate of progress seems likely to be more rapid for the developing countries than for those that are already developed. True, known exploitable reserves of some metals, such as copper, lead and zinc, are likely to be exhausted before the end of the century (though according to Clark, the earth's crust *should* hold an ample reserve), but in any event it is expected that other materials, in more abundant supply, can be adapted for the same uses.

Production of atomic energy — as a source of industrial power — is expected to increase fifty-fold by the end of the century, at diminishing cost per unit. Even so, atomic energy will probably provide no more than one-fifth of all the supply of electric current needed in the year 2000.

For the longer future, man's security rests upon his ingenuity. All mineral resources available, as the word is understood today, are likely to be used up within a few hundred years and a reversion to an agrarian economy would be inescapable unless new discoveries opened up fresh prospects. Wind-power and water-power, sunlight and other non-mineral sources of energy may prove useful, but the present prospects seem to be that these sources cannot be fruitfully developed except in special and local situations. A much brighter prospect, potentially, is thermo-nuclear fusion, but after the high hopes of a few years ago this has become a long-term feasibility study only.

14.8 Other resources

Estimates of the future availability of resources, other than those of food, minerals and energy, are comparatively rare. The reason is probably that prediction is too difficult because of the imponderables involved.

Water is akin to food, in the sense that a certain minimum intake is required to support life. The world supply is at present more than ample, but its distribution and quality leave much to be desired. Good management is therefore needed in order to eliminate the possibility of future shortages. Some writers feel that it should be possible sufficiently to equalize the supply over the seasons of the year, and over the different areas of the world, and to arrange for chemical bacteriological purification to the extent necessary from time to time. This would, however, require considerable capital expenditure. Spengler is pessimistic as to the future, however.

In the long term, open space could become one of the scarcest of resources, but so far the sensation of acute need has been experienced only in a few places. At the present rate of expansion of man's numbers, it would take but a few hundred years to produce a world with standing room only. This state is unlikely ever to be reached, however; studies of insects and animals suggest that vitality falls away when there is overcrowding from which no escape is possible — in some cases as the result of instinctive mechanisms to regulate fertility and survival and in others as the result of psychological aspects affecting all behaviour. For the next few decades at least, space is a problem mainly of urban planning and of transport from crowded areas to open ones.

National Parks are an important aspect of the problem of recreational space. They are becoming more necessary as the wild life of the jungle and the prairie is reduced by the expansion of man's living and crop areas. Precise measurement of the diminution in the numbers of animals is hard to come by, but the fact of the decline is well attested from general observation. Perhaps 90 per cent of the larger African mammals have been lost. In Chile, millions of sea birds have died, at least in part because the fish they normally eat have been taken by man: the birds' skeletons record the cataclysm. Some of the smaller animals and insects are being eliminated by pesticides introduced with the aim of augmenting crop yields, and this has brought forth eloquent protests from Carson and others. In the USA, in order to visit the National Parks, it is already necessary to reserve accommodation at a considerable distance from them, and to reserve it many months beforehand; this is because of the pressure of demand.

The assessment of future housing supplies is not, perhaps, such an acute necessity because some form of dwelling sufficient to preserve life can usually be made available for everyone. The question for the future is therefore mainly one of the quality of the dwellings that people will occupy, and this raises issues of demand and supply, and competition with other scarce resources; the answer will vary geographically and in time. The nature of the demand for housing will clearly be a function of urbanization. Forecasts of the extent of any further move towards the cities are apt to be very imprecise. This is probably because the various contributory causes of the movement have not been precisely weighed and assessed.

If some form of housing, however poor, is likely to be available, much the same is true of education, of which a little can be obtained at the mother's knee or the father's side, even if schooling is not available. It is useful to have assessments of the capital requirements for housing and education at various levels of provision so that a system of development priorities can be drawn up and no doubt such estimates are prepared as part of the national plans of some countries. But in neither case is there any generally-agreed critical level dividing success from failure or any projection of the likely standards of the future. The rapid growth of populations puts an exceptional strain on education facilities, as the numbers of children are tending all the time to outpace the adults from among whom the teachers and school-builders must be found.

Among the other resources needed by mankind may be included clothing, health and security against the health hazards and other accidents of life. These add to the total problem but do not seem to change its fundamental nature.

The foregoing concerns only future resources in the aggregate. Much of the demand will undoubtedly come from the poorer countries, while much of the supply will come from the richer areas, where a rate of economic development of 5 per cent per annum on average was achieved during 1960–5. The more prosperous countries are growing from a mature foundation, and their development pattern appears to be a product of sophistication in which the degree of complexity of treatment of materials is growing faster than the quantity of materials consumed. Thus their industrial progress, though often seemingly wasteful, involves an unwitting economy of resources: structurally, they are favoured, while the poor countries are hampered.

In this situation, there will be an increasing moral obligation upon the favoured areas to be generous to the unfavoured ones, if population needs and resources are to be matched. Developed countries must try to advance as well as to provide a reasonable chance of progress to the underdeveloped.

14.9 General prospects for progress

A numerical assessment of the prospects for progress of the poorer countries is hardly feasible owing to inadequacy of data. Nevertheless, by collecting the work of numerous individual investigators and making assessments of the

257

absorptive capacities of such countries, Rosenstein-Rodan has estimated the growth rates that seem feasible. He paid regard to the volume of investment during the preceding five years, the average and marginal rates of saving, the scale of foreign aid and the administrative and developmental organization; on such bases, he projected rates of growth as being of the order of 2 per cent per head per annum – rather less than this in the immediate future but rather more in the medium term.

It is hardly possible to answer by a simple 'yes' or 'no' the question 'can resources be expanded fast enough to support growing world population?' Data on the recent growth of total output in developing countries suggest, first, that high rates of population increase have not prevented economic growth, and secondly that there has been a good deal of variation between countries. It does appear that high population growth in the developing areas prevents them from catching up to the standards of the economically more advanced countries and indeed the disparities in wealth between the two groups may well become sharper in future, in spite of the apparent current trend towards higher commodity prices, which would appear to favour the less-developed continents at the expense of the advanced countries.

14.10 Computerized models of world dynamics

Early in the 1970s Professors Forrester and Meadows of the Massachusetts Institute of Technology independently argued that, as world population grows and its economy develops, three kinds of restraint will be encountered: the limited land surface, the limited stocks of certain irreplaceable materials and the limited ability of the environment to absorb the polluting effects of economic activity. To illustrate their thesis they postulated a complex system of interrelationships, involving such elements as capital equipment, technical knowledge, output, births and deaths as well as land, materials and pollution. In the process they were able to use some established data but they also had to incorporate many untested assumptions. Having established the model, they 'set it in motion', in other words they made an economico-demographic projection of an elaborate kind on a large electronic computer; this showed that many dangers lay ahead if population continued to grow and resources were used up at increasing rates. Man's prosperity might be threatened and his life might be shortened unless some current habits were changed.

Subsequently, a number of rival model systems have been tested, each with postulates to the taste or belief of a particular economist, and many with analysis in greater detail with more parameters. It was soon shown that almost any outcomes could be found, depending on the postulates made. On the whole, those models which show the gloomiest prospects are those in which man's behaviour is assumed to be inflexible; those involving 'feedback' (a term deriving from the study of electric circuits and implying an automatic reaction of some sort — such as adaptation of behaviour in a stressful situation) are much less alarming. Studies are now proceeding to improve the quality of the assumptions with special reference to the feedbacks which in real life do tend to maintain stability in economic and political systems.

14.11 Past assessments of future world population

Before the publication of their most recent work, estimates had been made by the Population Division of the UN on four separate occasions. The first of these appeared in 1951. It was made on a relatively simple basis (extrapolation of curves representing crude birth and death rates for groups of regions) and suggested that the population of the world would lie within the range 3,000 to 3,600 millions in 1980.

A second attempt was made in 1954, in rather more detail as to area, and led to assessments for the year 1980 of 3,300–4,000 millions. The various regions of the world were considered independently and the results totalled. In a subsequent analysis the data for the regions were subdivided to give estimates for individual countries, and in some instances these estimates were clearly unrealistic in relation to more detailed work which had been done elsewhere for the countries in question.

The third assessment was published, in still more detail, in 1958. The method employed was one of population models (data for a more precise formulation being insufficient in many areas) and the range of figures given for the year 1980 was from 3,900 to 4,300 million persons.

The fourth UN assessment was published in 1967. The report does not disclose the exact methods used, but closer attention than before was given to the individual circumstances of sub-regions and individual countries, and as a result the expectation for the year 1980 has now risen to 4,100–4,600 million people.

Part of the increase from one projection to the next can be ascribed to the collection of better information. At least 100 millions is attributable to this source, and the most significant single event in this connexion is probably the Chinese Census of 1953, which showed that the population of China was much bigger than had been thought. As the years have passed doubts have crept in about the validity of this census, but the new enumerations which have been held in many countries have, in general, improved the quality of the available statistics.

Another reason for the increase in the estimates over the years is the use of more elaborate methods of estimation. It is not possible to ascertain at all precisely how much of the increase might be due to these newer methods, but perhaps 200 millions would stem from this source. Some might question

259

whether the application of more detailed analysis does really represent an improvement, but the general impression to be gained from reading the four reports is one of increasing confidence arising from developing (but simple) technique.

The rest of the increase in the estimate for the year 1980 is due to changing experience, which has led both to a rise in the starting population and to an increase in the rate of growth estimated for the future. By far the main element in this change in experience is the fall in the death rate. In the year 1937 the world death rate was assessed at 25 per thousand, and relatively little improvement on this level appears to have been assumed in the early projections. By 1960, however, the rate was down to 17 per thousand, and the latest of the four assessments sees this down to about 11 per thousand by the year 1980. One imagines that there is no room for further improvements from this source, and the main uncertainty is now fertility. So far, however, this element has not given rise to much doubt. In 1937 the world rate was assessed at 36 per thousand and in 1960 it was 37 per thousand. The latest UN assessment writes it down to about 30 per thousand by 1980.

14.12 Population projections for Britain

British population projections can be classed broadly into three groups. First, those made during the 1930s and early 1940s, when fertility was low and apparently still falling. Secondly, those made by the staff of the Royal Commission on Population, in the late 1940s, and after a careful re-assessment of fertility trends, made under the aegis of the Commission. Finally, the projection work carried out each year by the Government Actuary's Department, in conjunction with the Registrars General, over the period of the 1950s and 1960s. It is of interest to observe that the first group consists of the work of several demographers independently; the second represents the work of one team at one time, but using a large variety of bases; the third is wholly an official product but includes a series of single projections made at regular intervals over a period of nearly twenty years.

A detailed examination of the projections was undertaken in chapter 13 of the First Edition (1950) of *Demography*, and in view of the lapse of time there is now less need to refer to them, except in broad terms. Table 14.4 shows the range of the figures expected for Britain by the year 1970, by the authors of the various assessments, in comparison with the 'actual' total — a figure which can, at the time of writing, be estimated without risk of material error.

The actual population thus exceeds all the expectations by a comfortable, and sometimes very wide, margin. If a similar comparison is made in round millions for the principal age-groups, the following emerge:

Table 14.4 *Total population of Britain in 1970
as assessed in projections made over
the period 1935—44, compared with
the actual total*

(Millions)

Demographer	Date of projection	Total population
Charles		
No. 1	1935	42
No. 2	1935	37
No. 3	1935	48
Honey	1937	38
Glass		
No. 1	1940	43
No. 2	1940	47
No. 3	1940	41
Registrar General for England and Wales	1942	46
Notestein	1944	42
Actual		56

Ages 65 and over: *Actual* 7 millions. *Expected* 6—7 millions.
Ages 45—64: *Actual* 14 millions. *Expected* 13—14 millions.
Ages 15—44: *Actual* 22 millions. *Expected* 15—19 millions.
Ages 0—14: *Actual* 14 millions. *Expected* 4—9 millions.

The inaccuracy of the projections is slight at the oldest ages, and indeed from middle life onwards the agreement between actual and expected is very reasonable; hardly any one could have been seriously incommoded by the discrepancies. The tendency of the actual numbers to be a little higher than the projected is probably attributable in part to a decline in mortality and in part to net immigration. At ages 15—44 the deficiency in the projected numbers varies from about 15 to 30 per cent of the actual; this group consists as to roughly one-half of persons who were already alive in the late 1930s, and as to the other half of children born after the time of the projection. Much of the deficiency must therefore be attributable to lack of success in assessing births, although a part may be due to migration. At ages 0—14, however, all the children alive in 1970 must have been born after the moment of the projection, and some of them will actually be the offspring of people born after it. The errors in the projections, which range from 30 to 70 per cent of the actual numbers, must therefore consist largely of inaccuracies in fertility estimation; but, because those inaccuracies have been to some extent duplicated, the percentage errors in the expected fertility rates would be expected to be rather less than 30—70 per cent.

Without detailed calculations, which would hardly be worth while, the exact degree of error cannot be stated; but it may be surmised that the projected level of fertility over the period 1940—70 was understated by perhaps 25—50 per cent of the actual outcome, i.e. the projected level should, to have achieved accuracy, have been raised by between 33 and 100 per cent. The basis producing the highest numbers of children and young people in fact assumes a continuation of the women's fertility of 1931. As may be seen from table 16.5 the average birth rate in England and Wales over the period 1941—65 was 17 per thousand, which is 14 per cent higher than the figure of 15 per thousand for 1931. The corresponding figures for the gross reproduction rate are 0·9 in 1931 and 1·15 in 1941—65 — an excess of more than 25 per cent. Earlier marriage, and higher marriage rates, will also have contributed to the excess of the actual population over the expected.

14.13   The projections of the Royal Commission on Population

In the analyses of the Commission's projections which were made in chapter 11 of the Third Edition (1959) of *Demography*, it was shown that, over the period of thirty years 1947—77, variations in the marriage, mortality and migration bases selected by the staff of the Commission had a modest effect on the projected outcome in each of the major age-groups. The ranges of projected figures quoted for the main age-groups in 1977 were (population in millions):

0—14	$8\frac{3}{4}$—$9\frac{1}{4}$
15—64	30—32
65 and over	7—8

In contrast, the corresponding ranges of results in respect of variations in the fertility bases selected were (in millions):

0—14	$9\frac{1}{2}$—$11\frac{1}{2}$
15—64	32—33
65 and over	8

As would be expected, the width of the range is greatest at the youngest ages, and is unimportant at the oldest. According to the 1973 expectations, the British population in 1977 will be:

0—14	$12\frac{1}{2}$
15—64	$34\frac{1}{2}$
65 and over	8
Total	55

As with the earlier projections, therefore, considerable prognosticative success has been achieved at the oldest ages but there is likely to be a marked shortfall at the youngest ages. The expected numbers of children and young adults were too low. Although the figure of $12\frac{1}{2}$ millions now projected could conceivably prove to be too high, the actual outcome is still likely to be in excess of the number expected according to the maximum of the range of the projections. There will also be an excess of actual over expected numbers at the working ages, as all the persons who will be aged 15—64 in 1977 were already born by the time of the making of the 1973 projection used above. The excess of the actual population size over the projected size is the result of fertility in excess of expectation, aided by earlier marriage and perhaps also by immigration.

The range of Royal Commission projections for the total population of Britain in 1970 was 48—53 millions, with a preferred narrower range of 49—51 millions: compare 37—48 millions in table 14.4. Thus the Commission, as a result of its careful and original analyses of fertility over the period 1920—45, removed the fear of a declining population and raised the general level of the previous projections, but it did not open up the prospect of materially expanding numbers, as it is now seen it should have done.

14.14   British official projections

Apart from showing the prospects as seen in each successive year, the series of official projections is of interest because it indicates how far the recorded population changes have had an influence upon the outlook from time to time. The projections that started from the populations of the years 1953, 1958 and 1963 respectively will be used as illustrative examples.

The prospects, according to the 1953 projection, were for a total British population in 1970 of 52 millions, i.e. one slightly above the average level projected by the Royal Commission but still within the wider range of possibilities offered by the Commission. Much the same total — a little over 50 millions — was expected for 1993, and this is also in a similar position in relation to the Commission's work. Little had happened, indeed, between the publication of its Report in 1949 and the issue of the 1953 official projection to change the prospects.

In what follows, the prospects up to 1995 will be studied, as 1977 is now too near to allow room for the effects of major differences in expectations to show themselves clearly. Fig. 14.2 shows the course of the numbers of births in England and Wales over the period 1945—73 and the trend lines which the projections of 1953, 1958, 1963 and 1973 assumed for the future.

The official projection starting from 1953 was based on the assumption that births would stay at their current level, subject to a gentle fall reflecting a slight expected diminution in the number of married couples. When the upward movement in births began, no one could be sure whether or not it represented a minor fluctuation, and at the start at least the most reason-

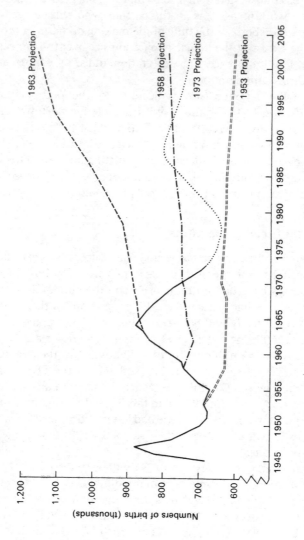

Fig. 14.2. Number of actual and projected births, England and Wales.

264

able assumption was that it did. Thus, the projection made from the year 1958, for instance, assumed that the numbers of births would, in general, remain at the level they had reached. With the passage of time, it became evident that the rise in births did in fact, represent a significant development, and hence in the 1963 projection it was assumed that the numbers of children born would continue to increase, though rather less rapidly than during 1955–63. A rise of one-half in these numbers was expected by the end of the century, although much of this was attributable to the growth in the number of parents, which was itself a consequence of the developments. The fall in births between 1965 and 1973 has altered the outlook once again, and subject to wave-like variations the numbers are now expected to remain fairly constant. The implications of the changes of outlook for the total population are indicated in the following statement. Even by 1963, the total had increased by 2 millions more than the 1953 expectation. By the 1970s there is a rise of 5 millions (10 per cent) and by the end of the century the difference is no less than 19 million persons, or 40 per cent. However, on the 1973 projections this is reduced.

Year from which projection was made	Projected total population of England and Wales				
	1963	1973	1983	1993	2003
1953	45	46	47	46	46
1958	46	48	50	51	53
1963	47*	51	55	59	65

* Actual.

Such a change has an enormous impact, for instance upon the need for building new towns, on the degree of crowding and on the need for teachers and schools. It also transforms the age-distribution, as the above figures show, with important consequences for the financing of national pension provision. It is especially noteworthy that the rise in the proportion of persons of over pension age is now expected to end and even to be reversed for a time, in some small degree.

Table 14.5 shows the projected age-distribution according to the projections of 1953, 1958, 1963 and 1973, illustrating the effects upon it of an increase in the assumed flow of births.

14.15 Analysis of changes in the outcome of projections made over the period 1953–73

In table 14.6 there appears an approximate analysis of the principal reasons for the changes in the projected numbers in 1993. This gives a good idea of the relative importance of the various elements involved.

265

Table 14.5 *Population age-distributions in the year 1993 according to the*
official projections of 1953, 1958, 1963 and 1973, England and Wales

Age-group	1953 projection	1958 projection	1963 projection	1973 projection
Under 15	196	221	251	220
15—29	200	212	224	212
30—44	202	200	188	207
45—59	189	171	162	168
60—74	151	136	123	133
75 and over	62	60	52	60
Total	1,000	1,000	1,000	1,000

Table 14.6 *Analysis of changes in projected numbers in 1993,*
England and Wales

(Numbers in millions)

	1953 and 1958 projections	1958 and 1963 projections	1963 and 1973 projections
Actual total population size in year of projection *minus* expected population size according to the earlier projection	$\frac{1}{2}$	1	−2
Increase in expected births from the date of the later projection			
(1) up to 1973	$1\frac{1}{2}$	$1\frac{1}{2}$	—
(2) during 1973—93	3	$5\frac{1}{2}$	−6
Residue, attributable to mortality, migration, etc.	—	—	—
Total difference in 1993	5	8	−8

14.16 Population projections for other countries and their outcome

The British experience in respect of success and failure in population projection is fairly typical of the degree of error in projections for other countries. Thus, in Finland, the total population size in 1960 was 4·4 millions, and this exceeded the numbers expected according to a projection made in 1947. The excess was about 0·2 millions and was attributable to fertility having proved to be higher than expected; it would have been greater if migration in excess of the projected amount had not reduced the numbers of adults below expectation.

A comparison by Myers of the actual population of the USA in 1950 with ranges of projections made in 1937 and in 1943 revealed that all the projections were in deficit in total numbers, the shortfall being from 3 to 12 per cent. The percentage deficits within certain age-groups were:

Age-group	Shortfall (%)
0–4	32–83
5–9	3–35
10–69	−7 to +12
70 and over	8–45

Here again, it is clear that it is the fertility bases that were the least successful, although the extent of error at the oldest ages is unusually high – so much so as to suggest great inaccuracy at censal enumeration in respect of the oldest people.

Of particular interest is the work performed by Notestein and his colleagues at Princeton University in respect of Europe, in which a standard pattern of methods was applied to a number of different countries. This work was published in 1944, but the statistical base-line for many countries was necessarily a good deal earlier – in fact the date of the latest pre-war census. Table 14.7 shows the actual total population in 1965 in comparison with the projected, for some of the countries in question.

In every one of these countries (except Greece), only a small part of the excess in the actual population was attributable to ages 65 and over. In every one, the numbers aged 0–14 in 1965 were well ahead of the expectation, and

Table 14.7. *Actual total population in 1965 in certain European countries in comparison with the 1944 projections*

(Millions)

Country	Actual	Expected	Excess (% of Expected)
Austria	7·3	6·4	14
Belgium	9·5	8·0	19
Denmark	4·8	4·0	20
Finland	4·6	4·0	15
France	48·9	38·1	28
Greece	8·6	8·6	—
Ireland	4·3	3·2	34
Italy	51·6	49·4	4
Netherlands	12·3	10·0	23
Norway	3·7	3·0	23
Portugal	9·2	9·0	2
Spain	31·6	28·0	13
Sweden	7·7	6·0	28
Switzerland	5·9	4·0	48

267

in most this difference at the youngest ages accounted for more than one-half of the total discrepancy for all ages together. As usual, therefore, fertility had been underestimated and this reflects a very natural failure — after the long falling trend in fertility rates — to recognize the temporary effects of the depression and the potential strength of a subsequent recovery from it.

It is readily possible to discern, in the smallness of the excess population in Italy, the effects of emigration and, in the high surplus in France and Switzerland, the result of an unexpected influx of population.

14.17   The implications of recent projections for Britain

Even though they may well fail to be borne out in the event, and may even, indeed, have been superseded by the moment when this account is read, the projections current at the time of writing (1975) have a special importance and can hardly be ignored. The assumptions upon which they are based are broadly as follows:

Mortality: declining for forty years at all ages, the extent of the fall varying from one quarter of the present level to about 10 per cent at younger and older ages.

Migration: a net outflow rising to 50,000 persons a year, representing a difference between intake and a larger gross outflow.

Fertility: a mean ultimate family size of 2·2 children per woman born in 1960 or later representing a level of fertility 5 per cent above the requirement for replacement. (This applies to England and Wales, with suitable regional variations for Scotland and Northern Ireland.)

These assumptions represent an appreciable change from those on which earlier projections were based; for instance, in 1968, lower mortality rates and higher fertility rates were adopted than in 1973, and the assumed balance of migration was inward, not outward.

If past experience is borne out, any differences in actual experience from the 'expectation' in respect of mortality and migration will be of relatively little significance, but departures from the fertility basis may well have a more profound outcome. Some regard was paid to birth expectations surveys in arriving at the fertility basis, although in the nature of things these could hardly do more than indicate the likely trend for the next two or three years ahead.

Table 14.8 indicates the percentage changes in numbers expected for future years, as compared with the 1973 population. The figures in the table bring out an expectation of a growth of 8 per cent in 40 years and a modest ageing of the population. They contrast with the expectations in earlier years, e.g. with those entertained in 1966, when a much more substantial total growth (35 per cent) was envisaged with a tilt in the age-distribution

Table 14.8. *Percentage changes expected in the British population in future years, as compared with 1973, according to the 1973 projections*

Age-group	1981	1991	2001	2011
Under 15	−11	− 4	− 1	− 4
15—44	+ 9	+14	+14	+14
45—64 (59)	− 6	− 7	+ 5	+15
65 (60) and over	+ 6	+ 6	+ 2	+ 8
Total	—	+ 4	+ 6	+ 8

towards youth. Among the economic consequences of the 1966 prospect would have been:

(1) a big rise in education costs and expenditure on child welfare;

(2) a small increase in national assistance;

(3) growth of intermediate size in the cost of the health services, housing and other expenditure;

(4) a modest rise in income from taxes,

but the current outlook is for a saving on the first item and probably for a greater increase in the other three than appeared likely seven years earlier. The disparity arises mainly from the fall in fertility which took place between 1966 and 1973 and the implications it has for the future.

14.18   The USA

In table 14.9 there appears a selection of the projected population sizes, according to calculations made at different times, in the years 1975, 2000 and 2025. The assessments were made by different authors.

Fertility after the Second World War was for many years higher than expected in 1946, and this development accounts for the sharp upward revision in expectations between 1946 and 1957. During the past 15 years, fertility has

Table 14.9. *Total population of the USA, according to various projections, in the years 1975, 2000 and 2025*

Date of projection	1975	2000	2025
1946	147—191	124—241	—
1957	215—238	263—343	291—441
1964	219—230	290—362	—
1972	213—216	251—301	265—392
1974	233	271	305

declined — at first slowly, and more recently very sharply — to about replacement level, and so the prospects for a long-continued rapid growth have receded. Even so, the working out of the effects of past trends are still expected to lead to an increase of about one-third in total population size within the next fifty years.

A recent projection for the USA began with a population of about 220 millions. This related to 1 January 1973 and included Puerto Rico and citizens of the USA resident abroad as well as the armed forces and merchant marine. The calculations were not subdivided by race, as a separation between Negroes, Japanese, and others did not seem likely, in the circumstances of the country, to have a significant effect. The purpose of the projection was to provide a foundation for assessments of the cost of social security in future years, but it is unlikely that this particular aim influenced the nature of the underlying assumptions made as to the course of fertility, mortality and migration (though it may well have helped to decide the date of the projection, the classes of people included and the lack of racial subdivision). Very probably, it is the assumptions made as to the levels and trends of demographic elements which are of major interest in this projection, rather than the results which flow from them — migration was taken as a constant inflow of 300,000 persons a year, which seems in line with recent experience.

Mortality rates, classified by sex and age, were projected separately for each classification, having regard to the movements of the figures in recent years and to the medical prospects — as well as they can be assessed. For this purpose calculations were made for each of ten groups of causes of death: as many groups as this being necessary in order that a clear distinction between different diseases (or modes of dying) with different trends could be made. The number of groups was, however, kept small so that the spurious influence of developments in medical science (and medical fashion) in diagnosis should be minimized. (If two similar kinds of heart disease are combined, little can be lost, but the addition of accidental drowning would not make sense; accidental drowning might, however, be grouped with accidents in the home without loss of prognostic efficiency).

The most interesting, and the most hazardous, part of the exercise lay in framing the assumptions for future fertility. The course of the experience in the USA over the period 1948—73 illustrates the problem:

Year	Fertility index
1948	3·11
1953	3·42
1958	3·70
1963	3·33
1968	2·48
1973	1·90 (provisional)

The index used is the 'total fertility rate', or sum for all ages of the woman's age-specific fertility rates and it shows a fall from well above replacement level to just below it by 1973. The history gives little clue to the prospects except to indicate the hazards.

The projected populations arrived at showed increases in total number, at a declining rate, leading to a grand total population of some 320 millions by the year 2050. The rise of nearly 50 per cent in 77 years, in spite of near-replacement-level fertility, shows the working out of the consequences of past trends. One corollary is an expected increase in the proportion of the aged (65 and over) from 10 to 16 per cent of the total population, or from 19 to 29 per cent of the active population (ages 20—64).

A recent projection for West Germany had the population of 1 January 1972 (62 millions) as a base. This was expected to decline slowly, to reach 57 millions by the end of the century. The fall arises from the youngest age groups and little change in the active or pensioner population is expected. 'According to all observations so far made, ... the declining birth rate is due to the changing attitudes of married couples regarding the desirable number of children ... the net reproduction rate which was about 1·2 in 1964 sank to about 0·81 by 1972 ... a continued, if somewhat weaker, birth rate decline was applied to the projection ... yielding a net reproduction rate of 0·73 for 1975 ... given this assumed fertility level, a woman could expect 1·5 births in her life-time'.

A projection made in Rumania, in contrast, assumed an increase in fertility, the current gross reproduction rate of about $1\frac{1}{4}$ being expected to rise to nearly $1\frac{1}{2}$ by the year 2000. This is the country in which a dramatic change in fertility was recently brought about by Government action. The outcome of this assumption is a growth in population from 20 millions to 28 millions by the end of the century, with little change in the distribution by age except for a rise in the proportion of pensioners — resulting no doubt from falls in fertility from a higher level in the early part of the century.

14.19 France

One of the most recent projections of the population of France was included in a book on the demography of that country published for World Population Year — 1974 — by the *Institut National d'Etudes Demographiques*. Mortality was assumed to continue to decline, at all ages, bringing the expectation of life at birth from 69 years for men and 75 years for women in 1970 to 73 and 78 years respectively by the end of the present century. Such a development, or indeed any other reasonable basis for projection, cannot have much effect on the results of the exercise. For migration, two convenient hypotheses were adopted, namely one of continued immigration of 135,000 people each year, and the other of no migration at all. The outcome of this difference is clearly one of about 3 (namely 25 × 0·135) million people after twenty-five years and this can hardly be significantly altered as a result of the operation of mortality or fertility in such a period.

As to fertility, the two similarly reasonable assumptions made were of constant rates at the current level and of rates about 15 per cent lower, which implies an approximation to replacement level. The disparity between these bases expresses itself as a difference in the number of annual births of some 150,000 on the average, in the decades to come, and so of about 4 million people in all by the end of the century. If these assumptions are well-pitched, the prospects for the French population, at present composed of about 52 million people, lie between a total size at the end of the twentieth century of 60 millions and one of 67 millions. The projection thus shows that without any births surplus to replacement needs, and without any migration, the population would in any event rise by about 8 millions, or 15 per cent; with these additions, on a realistic scale, its increase would be roughly doubled.

14.20   Other countries

Some contrasts in the outlooks for a variety of developed countries, as they appeared in 1963, are given in table 14.10. The table shows the percentage changes in the principal age-groups expected, according to these projections, between a recent date — usually 1963 — and 1980. It will be observed

Table 14.10. *Percentage changes in population size expected between 1963 (or thereabouts) and 1980 in broad age-groups*

(The figures show expected increases unless they are preceded by a minus sign.)

Country	Ages 0—14	Ages 15—44	Ages 45—64 (59 for women)	Ages 65(60) and over	All ages (see text)	
West Germany	− 7	8	− 6	21	6	
Austria	24	14	−15	8	8	
Denmark	19	13	− 2	30	14	
Spain	10	13	27	29	16	(13)
France	7	15	11	21	13	
Greece	− 2	9	26	47	14	(8)
Eire	44	46	− 7	18	31	(20)
Italy	15	5	20	33	14	
Norway	17	18	—	53	18	
Holland	40	23	14	36	27	
Portugal	23	26	27	48	29	(18)
United Kingdom	21	10	− 4	23	12	(13)
Sweden	23	3	− 5	36	11	(13)
Switzerland	11	21	15	22	10	(18)
USA	25	33	9	31	26	(30)

that a rise in total population is expected in all countries, but that there is a considerable diversity in the rate of growth, which varies from just under $\frac{1}{2}$ per cent per annum in West Germany and Austria to about $1\frac{1}{2}$ per cent per annum in Eire, Holland, Portugal and the USA.

When individual age-groups are considered, the most noticeable feature is the expected decline, or relatively low rate of increase, in many countries, in the numbers of people in middle life; as all those who will be in the age-range 45–64 (59 for women) in 1980 are already alive today, this is necessarily the result of unevenness in the age-distribution at the present time. Such persons were born in the period 1916–35 and their age range in 1942 was 7–26 years. This group therefore reflects the low birth rate during the First World War and afterwards, and perhaps also some direct losses in the Second World War. The persons aged 45–64 in 1963 were much less exposed to all these factors. This feature is not so evident in countries unaffected by the wars and in those where fertility has remained relatively high, for example, Spain and Portugal.

A rapid rate of total population growth is often associated with high fertility and with a big expected increase in the number of children – as it is in Eire, Holland and the USA; Austria is however an exception. But where a fertility decline has in the past proved less marked than in the generality of Western countries, a further decline may be occurring now, and this probably explains the relatively low rise for the numbers of children aged 0–14 in Greece, Portugal and Spain. A concomitant feature in these countries is a prospective big rise in the numbers of the aged. Substantial increases in this oldest group are also expected, however, in most other countries. The exceptions are Austria – because of special features associated with the political history of this country   and Eire, in which the balance of fertility, mortality and migration is keeping the population and its age-distribution relatively steady.

The figures shown are those arrived at before making any allowance for future migration. The alternative assessments of total population, shown in brackets at the extreme right, illustrate the revised expected percentage changes for all ages together when allowance is made for probable migratory flows, where they are likely to have a significant effect. It will be seen that losses in numbers are thought likely for Eire, Greece, Spain and Portugal, but gains in Switzerland, the USA, Sweden and the United Kingdom. These expectations are of course a reflection of recent trends and of the differentials in economic wealth which have given rise to the population movements.

The figures given earlier in this chapter for West Germany, France, Britain and the USA show how the prospect has changed in ten years. West Germany's population is now expected to fall, instead of rise, and the British and US populations to rise much more slowly than appeared likely ten years ago. The outlook for France has changed less. These developments in the prospects all reflect in the main the changes in fertility which have taken place during the past ten years.

SELECT BIBLIOGRAPHY

Brass, W. 'Perspectives in Population Prediction: Illustrated by the Statistics of England and Wales', *Journal of the Royal Statistical Society*, (1975).

Report of the Population Panel (Cmnd. 5258) (HMSO, London, 1973).

Recent Population Trends and Future Prospects. World Population Conference (United Nations, 1974).

Population Projections, No. 4, 1973—2013, prepared by the Government Actuary (HMSO, London, 1974).

Benjamin, B., Cox, P. R. and Peel, J. (editors). *Population and the New Biology* (Academic Press, London, 1974).

Hyrenius, H. *New Techniques for Studying Demographic—Economic—Social Interrelations* (Göteborg University, 1965).

Technical analysis

15   Life tables

15.1   Field of application

A few of the basic characteristics of life tables were mentioned in § 2.11. The purpose of the present chapter is to explain life table technique further, with some illustrations of its use in demography. The essential features of its field of application are:

(1) a group of people, all in some defined status or condition; and
(2) changes away from this status or condition which gradually deplete the group.

In the example given in § 2.11, item (1) represented people alive and item (2) represented deaths.

The technique is to show the numbers remaining in the defined status or condition at any stage, the numbers leaving it at that stage, and some related functions. It can be applied to animals, to plants, or even to inanimate objects — such as railway engines or houses — but, in demographic work, normally only people are concerned. The usual 'stages' in the life-table process are successive ages, expressed in years, but examples of other stages that may be encountered are the period of time elapsed since some event, and the number of children borne by a woman.

The nature of the departure from the status or condition may be single (such as death) or multiple (such as marriage and death for bachelors) and is irreversible — for the time being at least. For repeated events, other techniques are preferable.

If sufficient information is available, a life table may be formed very simply by setting forth the complete history of past events as they occurred, but the opportunities for doing so do not often arise. Moreover, the result would, in the main, be so much in the past as to be of little relevance at the time of its preparation. More commonly the technique is used to represent what such a history would be if certain conditions constantly prevailed, for example, to show the numbers living at any age on the basis of an indefinite continuation of a certain set of mortality rates. The result can be misleading if its limitations are not borne in mind. A specimen life table may be seen in table 15.1.

Table 15.1. *English Life Table No. 11, 1950—2, Males*

Age x	lx	dx	px	qx	ex	Age
0	100,000	3,266	0·96734	0·03266	66·42	0
1	96,734	233	0·99759	0·00241	67·66	1
2	96,501	136	0·99859	0·00141	66·82	2
3	96,365	98	0·99898	0·00102	65·91	3
4	96,267	81	0·99916	0·00084	64·98	4
5	96,186	78	0·99919	0·00081	64·04	5
6	96,108	72	0·99925	0·00075	63·09	6
7	96,036	61	0·99937	0·00063	62·13	7
8	95,975	56	0·99942	0·00058	61·17	8
9	95,919	53	0·99945	0·00055	60·21	9
10	95,866	50	0·99948	0·00052	59·24	10
11	95,816	50	0·99948	0·00052	58·27	11
12	95,766	50	0·99948	0·00052	57·30	12
13	95,716	54	0·99944	0·00056	56·33	13
14	95,662	61	0·99936	0·00064	55·36	14
15	95,601	70	0·99927	0·00073	54·40	15
16	95,531	78	0·99918	0·00082	53·44	16
17	95,453	87	0·99909	0·00091	52·48	17
18	95,366	101	0·99894	0·00106	51·53	18
19	95,265	114	0·99880	0·00120	50·58	19
20	95,151	123	0·99871	0·00129	49·64	20
21	95,028	128	0·99865	0·00135	48·71	21
22	94,900	129	0·99864	0·00136	47·77	22
23	94,771	130	0·99863	0·00137	46·84	23
24	94,641	132	0·99861	0·00139	45·90	24
25	94,509	133	0·99859	0·00141	44·96	25
26	94,376	135	0·99857	0·00143	44·03	26
27	94,241	138	0·99854	0·00146	43·09	27
28	94,103	140	0·99851	0·00149	42·15	28
29	93,963	143	0·99848	0·00152	41·21	29
30	93,820	147	0·99843	0·00157	40·27	30
31	93,673	152	0·99838	0·00162	39·34	31
32	93,521	158	0·99831	0·00169	38·40	32
33	93,363	165	0·99823	0·00177	37·46	33
34	93,198	173	0·99814	0·00186	36·53	34
35	93,025	183	0·99803	0·00197	35·60	35
36	92,842	195	0·99790	0·00210	34·67	36
37	92,647	209	0·99774	0·00226	33·74	37
38	92,438	226	0·99756	0·00244	32·81	38
39	92,212	244	0·99735	0·00265	31·89	39
40	91,968	267	0·99710	0·00290	30·98	40
41	91,701	292	0·99682	0·00318	30·06	41
42	91,409	322	0·99648	0·00352	29·16	42
43	91,087	356	0·99609	0·00391	28·26	43
44	90,731	395	0·99565	0·00435	27·37	44
45	90,336	439	0·99514	0·00486	26·49	45
46	89,897	488	0·99457	0·00543	25·61	46
47	89,409	543	0·99393	0·00607	24·75	47
48	88,866	604	0·99320	0·00680	23·90	48
49	88,262	671	0·99240	0·00760	23·06	49

Table 15.1 (continued)

50	87,591	745	0·99150	0·00850	22·23	50
51	86,846	824	0·99051	0·00949	21·42	51
52	86,022	911	0·98941	0·01059	20·62	52
53	85,111	1,004	0·98820	0·01180	19·83	53
54	84,107	1,103	0·98689	0·01311	19·06	54
55	83,004	1,208	0·98545	0·01455	18·31	55
56	81,796	1,318	0·98389	0·01611	17·57	56
57	80,478	1,432	0·98221	0·01779	16·85	57
58	79,046	1,551	0·98038	0·01962	16·15	58
59	77,495	1,672	0·97843	0·02157	15·46	59
60	75,823	1,796	0·97631	0·02369	14·79	60
61	74,027	1,921	0·97405	0·02595	14·14	61
62	72,106	2,047	0·97161	0·02839	13·50	62
63	70,059	2,173	0·96899	0·03101	12·88	63
64	67,886	2,297	0·96616	0·03384	12·28	64
65	65,589	2,420	0·96311	0·03689	11·69	65
66	63,169	2,539	0·95981	0·04019	11·12	66
67	60,630	2,653	0·95625	0·04375	10·57	67
68	57,977	2,762	0·95236	0·04764	10·03	68
69	55,215	2,865	0·94812	0·05188	9·50	69
70	52,350	2,958	0·94349	0·05651	9·00	70
71	49,392	3,041	0·93843	0·06157	8·49	71
72	46,351	3,112	0·93286	0·06714	8·02	72
73	43,239	3,167	0·92675	0·07325	7·56	73
74	40,072	3,205	0·92002	0·07998	7·12	74
75	36,867	3,221	0·91262	0·08738	6·70	75
76	33,646	3,214	0·90449	0·09551	6·29	76
77	30,432	3,178	0·89558	0·10442	5·90	77
78	27,254	3,111	0·88584	0·11416	5·54	78
79	24,143	3,013	0·87522	0·12478	5·19	79
80	21,130	2,880	0·86371	0·13629	4·86	80
81	18,250	2,714	0·85129	0·14871	4·54	81
82	15,536	2,517	0·83796	0·16204	4·25	82
83	13,019	2,294	0·82377	0·17623	3·97	83
84	10,725	2.051	0·80876	0·19124	3·72	84
85	8,674	1,795	0·79301	0·20699	3·48	85
86	6,879	1,537	0·77663	0·22337	3·26	86
87	5,342	1,284	0·75973	0·24027	3·07	87
88	4,058	1,045	0·74247	0·25753	2·88	88
89	3,013	829	0·72499	0·27501	2·71	89
90	2,184	639	0·70745	0·29255	2·56	90
91	1,545	479	0·69003	0·30997	2·42	91
92	1,066	349	0·67288	0·32712	2·30	92
93	717	246	0·65616	0·34384	2·19	93
94	471	170	0·63998	0·36002	2·08	94
95	301	113	0·62448	0·37552	1·99	95
96	188	73	0·60975	0·39025	1·91	96
97	115	47	0·59584	0·40416	1·84	97
98	68	28	0·58284	0·41716	1·78	98
99	40	17	0·57073	0·42927	1·72	99
100	23	10	0·55955	0·44045	1·67	100
101	13	6	0·54928	0·45072	1·62	101
102	7	3	0·53989	0·46011	1·58	102
103	4	2	0·53136	0·46864	1·53	103
104	2	1	0·52364	0·47636	1·50	104

15.2   The origins of life tables

Ulpian's 'life table', consisting of a series of values diminishing with increasing age, and having the appearance of expectations of life, survives from Roman times, but the way in which it was constructed, and even the manner of its use, are uncertain. Probably the ideas of life expectation and of a diminishing l_x column have been long appreciated. The following extracts from *The Vision of Mirza: An Oriental Allegory* by Joseph Addison (1672–1719) are of interest: '"I see a bridge", said I, "standing in the midst of the tide." "The bridge thou seest", said he, "is human life; consider it attentively." Upon a more leisurely survey of it, I found that it consisted of three-score and ten entire arches, with several broken arches, which, added to those that were entire, made up the number about a hundred ... "I see multitudes of people passing over it" ... I saw several of the passengers dropping through the bridge into the great tide that flowed underneath it; and, upon further examination, perceived that there were innumerable trap-doors that lay concealed in the bridge, which the passengers no sooner trod upon, but they fell through them into the tide, and immediately disappeared. These hidden pitfalls were set very thick at the entrance of the bridge ... They grew thinner towards the middle but multiplied and lay close together towards the end of the arches that were entire. There were indeed some persons, but their number was very small, that continued a kind of hobbling march on the broken arches, but quite tired and spent with so long a walk.'

No attempt to base a life table on statistics appears to have been made until the end of the seventeenth century AD (see chapter 20). Because the concept of exposure to risk had not yet been fully appreciated, the earliest efforts were faulty, but, by the end of the eighteenth century, valid life tables were being developed for the purposes of life assurance. Quite soon, it came to be realized that the chances of death were not the same for all groups and populations but that variations in mortality, such as those discussed in chapter 7, could occur. Study of these variations took place in due course. The application of the technique was not extended to marriage and fertility until the need arose with the advent of social insurance systems and pension schemes. Members of such systems and schemes may cease participation for a number of reasons, for example, change of occupation, or retirement, as well as death, and in order to estimate the future course of the finances it is valuable to know the relative numbers doing so at each age — a purpose for which the life-table technique is admirably suited. In demography, the technique is useful in the analysis of fertility by age, marriage duration and parity.

15.3   Some life-table functions

In life-table work the ages are usually shown in ascending order on the left-hand side of a table. The corresponding functions l_x, d_x and the like are set out in successive columns to the right. For purposes of general reference it is very convenient to discuss these functions in mathematical terms, and so to show their relationships for any age x. Here are definitions of the functions shown in table 15.1:

l_x the number living at age x exactly
d_x the number dying at age x last birthday
p_x the probability of survival from age x exactly to age $x + 1$ exactly
q_x the probability of death between age x and age $x + 1$
$\overset{o}{e}_x$ the complete expectation of life at age x.

If the l_x column is summed up for all ages $x + 1$ and over, and the result is divided by l_x, the outcome of this calculation is called the 'expectation of life' (usually denoted as e_x). Thus

$$e_x = \left(\sum_{t=1}^{\infty} l_{x+t} \right) \div l_x. \tag{15.1}$$

It represents the average numbers of complete years lived after attaining age x. It is often misunderstood, by people who believe that the expectation represents in some way the actual future lifetime of an individual person; whereas, of course, out of a group of persons aged x many will die before the age $x + e_x$ is reached, and many others will die after that age. Indeed all those who survive to age $x + e_x$ must die at age higher than the 'expectation'. Because of possible misunderstandings, use of the expression 'expectation of life', and of the function it represents, is better avoided wherever possible.

The 'complete' expectation of life represents the average number of years lived after attaining age x, including part years, and is related to the expectation of life by the formula

$$\overset{o}{e}_x = e_x + \tfrac{1}{2} \tag{15.2}$$

The probability of survival from age x exactly to age $x + t$ exactly is written as $_tp_x$. Here are some of the algebraic relationships which hold between life-table functions:

$$p_x = \frac{l_{x+1}}{l_x}, \tag{15.3}$$

$$_tp_x = \frac{l_{x+t}}{l_x}, \tag{15.4}$$

$$q_x = \frac{d_x}{l_x}, \tag{15.5}$$

$$p_x = 1 - q_x, \tag{15.6}$$

$$l_{x+1} = l_x \cdot p_x = l_x - d_x, \tag{15.7}$$

$$l_{x+t} = l_x \cdot {_tp_x} = l_x - \sum_{n=0}^{t-1} d_{x+n}. \tag{15.8}$$

279

These may be verified from table 15.1 and the student would do well to calculate a few values from the figures in it. He could check, for instance, that $_{20}p_{30} = 0.9336$ and find the chance of a man aged 75 dying before he is 95.

15.4 Multiple-decrement tables

It is not difficult to envisage situations in which a person's status may change in one of several ways. For instance, a bachelor may die, or he may marry. Either development will bring to an end his status of bachelorhood. A 'life table' for bachelors may thus be constructed with decremental rates of q_x representing the total chance at age x of leaving the status of bachelor. It is usually of more interest to analyse the decrements between the causes of exit, and so form a table in the following manner:

Age	Number of bachelors living ($^b l_x$, say)	Number of deaths ($^{bd}d_x$, say)	Number of marriages ($^{bm}d_x$, say)
.			
.			
.			
20	961	4	35
21	922	4	46
22	872		
.			
.			
.			

Such a table is usually termed a 'double-decrement' table. Other examples in demography are tables for (*a*) married women dying or being widowed, and (*b*) citizens dying or emigrating. If three or more decrements are involved, the table is known as a 'multiple-decrement' table and an example of this is a statement showing the numbers of occupied men (i.e., those at work) dying, emigrating or retiring.

The use of these tables adds little complication to the use of single-decrement tables, because if the various decrements are all added together a single-decrement table is arrived at, but care is required in their construction.

Table 15.2 gives a specimen portion of a multiple-decrement table, and some illustrative examples are given below it.

15.5 Marriage analyses

Marriage may be analysed in life-table form without allowance for the chance of death. An example of an analysis of this kind was given in table 10.5, which shows the numbers remaining unmarried out of 1,000 at age 16 according to the experience of generations of men and women. Such a table
280

Table 15.2. *A typical multiple-decrement table*

Age	Number at work	Deaths	Resignations	Retirements
16	1,000	4	108	—
17	888	5	85	1
18	797	5	70	1
19	721	6	57	1
20	657	5	42	1
21	609	5	33	2
22	569	5	28	2
23	534	4	21	2
24	507	4	17	3
25	483			

Chance of death in service while aged 22 = 5/569 = 0·0088.
Chance of work ending while aged 18 = (5 + 70 + 1) ÷ 797 = 0·095.
Chance of staying at work from age 18 to age 24 = 507 ÷ 797 = 0·636.

is sometimes referred to as a 'gross nuptiality' table — the word 'gross' referring to the absence of any allowance for mortality, as in the gross reproduction rate. Correspondingly, a 'net nuptiality' table is one based on the two decrements of marriage and mortality. Table 10.5 illustrates a tendency towards earlier marriage in more recent years, and any adjustments for losses attributable to mortality would be unlikely to affect the picture materially.

A gross nuptiality table could be constructed on the basis of the remarriage rates shown in table 5.6, which vary according to age and duration. The l_x column would then take a similar form; it would be defined in terms of $x + n$, if $n < 5$, and of only x where $n \geqq 5$. Such a form of presentation is sometimes called a 'select' table, by analogy with the experience of lives selected for insurance by health tests.

As the proportion ultimately marrying tends to be fairly constant, the principal function of nuptiality tables is to reveal changes in the distribution of marriages by age. Although such changes are of much interest, it should be borne in mind that some of them at least are temporary in character and may be of limited significance from a long-term point of view. A nuptiality table has a superficial appearance of permanence, but this may be deceptive.

Decremental tables may also be constructed, with or without allowance for mortality, widowhood and divorce, to show the numbers of married men or women at each age and the numbers of entrants (marriages and remarriages) to this class and perhaps exits (widowhoods and divorces) also. Furthermore, such tables can be subdivided to show distributions of married persons according to both age and duration of time since marriage; or married persons of either sex may be classified according to duration of marriage alone.

281

15.6   Use of life-table technique in fertility studies

As fertility is repetitive, and not a single final event, its connection with life-table techniques is not immediately apparent. A first birth can only happen once, however, and so it would be possible to construct a 'life table' for married women (or even all women) in which l_x represented those who had never borne a child and the decrements consisted of women having their first baby — and perhaps also of deaths, widowhoods and divorces. Such a table might well be prepared for successive marriage durations rather than successive ages.

Similarly, women who had borne one child only might be the subject of a table in which the decrements consisted of those bearing a second child. Another such table could relate to third births, and so on, and in this manner all fertility could eventually be incorporated. The axis of reference could be the number of years since the previous birth, or it could be the age or marriage duration; if either of the latter two were used, it would also be possible to construct a stratified fertility table in which the successive 'l_x' columns were formed from the previous 'd_x' columns. An example is given in table 15.3.

Without the use of age or duration as an axis of reference, 'parity' (the number of children a woman has borne) could be made the sole abscissa, and then a statement would be formed similar to that shown in table 15.4.

In table 15.3, mortality and other decrements are ignored, and so:

$$^1l_m = \sum_{n=0}^{m-1} (^0d_n - {}^1d_n) \tag{15.9}$$

(children born outside the marriage are ignored); similarly for ^2l_m and so on. Deaths of children are not taken into account. The table is over-simplified,

Table 15.3. *Specimen entries in a table showing the numbers of births according to parity and duration of marriage*

Duration of marriage in years (n)	Married women with no children (^0l_n)	First births (^0d_n)	Married women with one child (^1l_n)	Second births (^1d_n)	Married women with two children (^2l_n)	Third births (^2d_n)	
	(1)	(2)	(3)	(4)	(5)	(6)	...
0	1,000	48	0	0	0	0	...
1	952	101	48	11	0	0	...
2	851	147	138	95	11	7	...
3	704	133	190	123	99	56	...
4	571	119	200	111	166	69	...
.	.	.	.	.	.	.	
.	.	.	.	.	.	.	

Table 15.4. *A 'life table' by parity alone*

Parity n	Number of married women who have borne n children	Number of married women bearing their $(n + 1)$th child
0	1,000	84
1	916	189
2	727	463
3	264	199
4	65	51
.	.	.
.	.	.
.	.	.

because the possibility of multiple births, or of two maternities in one year, is overlooked.

In general, the use of such tables is not of much value unless they are constructed upon a generation basis and reflect an actual experience – in which event they represent little more than the historical statistical analysis discussed in chapter 6. The Registrar General of England and Wales publishes tables each year, showing, for each year of marriage and for each marriage duration, women classified according to the number of children they have had – a statement essentially in the form of a series of tables 15.3.

In table 6.6, fertility rates were shown classified by marriage duration. It would be possible to sum up the figures into a single-figure index by weighting by a standard distribution of women by duration of marriage, which might be arrived at by means of a life-table technique. To do so would, however, be of limited value because some information would be lost in the process.

15.7   Life tables in studies of migration and other topics

A method of using life-table techniques in migration studies is described in § 16.30 below, and in principle there is no reason why life tables should not be applied to the analysis of population movement of this kind. Life-table techniques may also be adopted in medical studies. In one American study, the l_x column was subdivided at each age into two groups: people who had lost all their teeth (or were 'edentulous') and those who had some natural teeth left. This is equivalent to a double-decrement table, the edentulous column representing the survivors of the combined forces of mortality and of loss of all natural teeth. By the age of 70, the US analysis showed, more than one-half of men and women were edentulous.

15.8   Construction of life tables for demographic purposes

A great deal has been written on the construction of life tables, and the algebra involved can be intricate. Much of the literature is concerned, however, with the treatment of forms of data that are unlikely to be available to demographers, in respect of national or regional populations, and is thus inessential to them. The following short account of the subject will be concerned with the basic principles and with the manner in which the demographer is likely to need to apply those principles. Methods based on incomplete data are considered in chapter 19.

If the full history of a group of persons in some status could be traced from their xth birthday to their $(x + 1)$th birthday, then rates of mortality, marriage, etc., could be accurately measured as the ratio of the number of moves out of the status occurring during this year of life to the numbers initially in the group at age x exactly (§ 2.9). A series of decremental rates so derived for all ages x could then be used to construct a life or multiple-decrement table. The main problem that could arise would be random fluctuations in the values of the rates at successive ages arising from the smallness of the numbers of persons observed. Reference to this problem is made in § 15.13 below.

In practice, however, it is not possible in population analysis to observe a group so closely, for the following reasons:

(1) at the moment when a census is held, only a tiny fraction of the population are celebrating their birthdays, and often the particular people constituting this fraction will not be known, because the exact date of birth is not required to be stated in the schedule;

(2) deaths, marriages and the like are usually recorded in calendar years, and not for the periods between the dates of censuses (which are rarely held on 31 December or 1 January);

(3) censuses are not held annually; decennial enumerations are more common;

(4) migrants arrive from overseas, and leave for other countries, and their experience can be observed only while they are present in the country;

(5) the records may be incomplete and inaccurate;

(6) data may well be available only for age-groups, or otherwise may not be subdivided as far as would be desirable.

15.9   The need for approximations

The problems that arise from item (1) in § 15.8 are not difficult to deal with. A rate of exit q_{x+t} may be calculated for any age $x + t$, where x is integral and t fractional, by the formula:

$$q_{x+t} = d_{x+t}/l_{x+t}, \tag{15.10}$$

where d_{x+t} represents the deaths between age $x + t$ and age $x + t + 1$. Summing for all convenient values of t between 0 and 1, it would be possible to regard

$$\sum_{t=0}^{1} d_{x+t} \Big/ \sum_{t=0}^{1} l_{x+t} \qquad (15.11)$$

as a weighted average of q_{x+t}. The denominator of this expression would be obtained from the census. Assuming for the moment that the numerator was available, q_{x+t} could be calculated, and it would then be necessary only to estimate the average value of t. This could often be assumed, on the basis of a uniform distribution, to be $\frac{1}{2}$, but allowance could if necessary be made for any factor, such as a fluctuation in the relevant number of births x years before, known to have caused this assumption to be inaccurate.

As item (2) indicates, the numerator, $\sum_{t=0}^{1} d_{x+t}$, is not available for the period between the censuses (which may not, indeed, be held on the same date in different years) but for some different 12-month period. Thus, exact tracing of the deaths relevant to the population enumerated is not possible; this is a more serious problem. Interpolation needs to be made with care, because, for example, of variations in weather and in economic conditions.

The lack of exact correspondence between the population and the deaths, and the adjustments and assumptions that therefore have to be made, are cardinal features of this type of mortality investigation, which is commonly known as the 'census method'.

The infrequency of censuses – item (3) above – accentuates the demographer's difficulties, because mortality, marriage and fertility rates are changing so rapidly in most countries today that a 10-year period of investigation is too long to render the data of much value. Thus it is normally necessary to base the examination of the experience upon one census and the registrations made in the census year and in the years preceding and succeeding it. The enumerated population is thus used as an approximation to the 'exposed to risk'.

This being so, no additional complications are caused by the migratory movements mentioned at item (4), except in countries where the migratory flows are relatively strong.

15.10 The census method in practice

If censuses are held at decennial intervals, as is normal, it is unlikely that complete life tables based on the experience of the whole population, or of broad segments of it, can be prepared any more frequently. In these circumstances it is important that the results should be reasonably representative. If, therefore, a severe influenza epidemic happened to be raging in the census year, it would not be of much value to have a life table on the deaths in that year alone. It would be preferable to include the preceding year and the succeeding year, or perhaps even the preceding and succeeding two years. The choice of the period must be governed by the particular circumstances; lengthening it would tend to increase the representativeness of the experience, but would perhaps also render the use of the census method less accurate, because the population used as the denominator would less truly represent the true exposed to risk. The following formula would be fairly normal:

$$\frac{\text{deaths in year } Y - 1, Y \text{ and } Y + 1}{3 \times (\text{population enumerated in year } Y)}. \tag{15.12}$$

As censuses are not normally held on 30 June, however, the enumerated population would probably need some adjustment to convert it to the size of the estimated population at the middle of the 3-year period, or on average over the whole of this period.

15.11 Continuous life-table functions

For many purposes it is useful to consider, not the number of people alive at exact age x but the number aged x last birthday. This is written as L_x, and from it is derived the 'central' death rate:

$$m_x = d_x/L_x. \tag{15.13}$$

As L_x is approximately equal to $l_x - \tfrac{1}{2}d_x$, (15.13) can be written as

$$m_x \doteq d_x/(l_x - \tfrac{1}{2}d_x), \tag{15.14}$$

and so $\dfrac{1}{m_x} \doteq \dfrac{1}{q_x} - \dfrac{1}{2}$. Hence:

$$m_x \doteq 2q_x/(2 - q_x) \tag{15.15}$$

or

$$q_x \doteq 2m_x/(2 + m_x). \tag{15.16}$$

These relationships do not hold if the distribution of deaths over the year of age is materially skew, as it is in the first year of life or at very advanced ages.

An exact expression for L_x involves the use of the integral calculus. Thus

$$L_x = \int_0^1 l_{x+t}\, dt. \tag{15.17}$$

If the central rate of mortality at age x applicable over a period of $1/n$th of a year is designated as $(1/n) \cdot m_x^{(n)}$, then

$$m_x^{(n)} = n \left[\frac{l_x - l_{x+1/n}}{l_x} \right] = -\frac{1}{l_x} \left[\frac{l_{x+1/n} - l_x}{1/n} \right]. \tag{15.18}$$

As n increases, and tends towards infinity, $m_x^{(n)}$ tends towards

$$-\frac{1}{l_x} \cdot \frac{dl_x}{dx}$$

to use the notation of the calculus. This limit is known as the force of mortality' and is usually written as μ_x. Thus.

$$\mu_x = -\frac{1}{l_x} \cdot \frac{dl_x}{dx}. \tag{15.19}$$

For the benefit of those unversed in the differential calculus, μ_x represents the rate of mortality at a point of time, rather than over a year, and is approximately equal to $m_{x-1/2}$. μ_x can be written as

$$\frac{-d(\log_e l_x)}{dx} \tag{15.20}$$

and it follows that $\log_e l_x = -\int_0^\infty \mu_{x+r} \, dr + C$, where C is a constant. Hence

$$\log_{et} p_x = -\int_0^t \mu_{x+r} \, dr. \tag{15.21}$$

From (15.19), l_x may also be written as $\int_0^\infty l_{x+t} \cdot \mu_{x+t} dt$ and it follows that

$$d_x = \int_0^1 l_{x+t} \cdot \mu_{x+t} dt \tag{15.22}$$

and (dividing by l_x) that

$$q_x = \int_0^1 {}_t p_x \cdot \mu_{x+t} dt. \tag{15.23}$$

The expression $\int_0^\infty l_{x+t} dt$ represents the total number of years of life lived after age x, and so the average number of years so lived, per person aged x, is

$$\frac{1}{l_x} \int_0^\infty l_{x+t} dt. \tag{15.24}$$

This is known as the 'complete' expectation of life, and is written as $\overset{\circ}{e}_x$. Thus also

$$\overset{\circ}{e}_x = \int_0^\infty {}_t p_x dt. \tag{15.25}$$

287

15.12 Influence of life tables on demographic studies of mortality

The existence of a life table provides a series of functions for study, for example, l_x, q_x and d_x, the mathematical relationship of which to x is a matter of interest. The search has been made for 'laws' of mortality which both represent tenable hypotheses and can be shown to reflect the data with sufficient accuracy. Even before data became available, Graunt based a table on the supposition that, between the ages of 6 and 56 at least, d_x was constant whatever the value of x. In searches of this kind it has so far proved necessary to omit the first few years of life, because of the quite different type of experience found there. Attempts to include these years render the analysis too complex.

The first famous 'law' is that of Benjamin Gompertz, who in 1825 propounded the hypothesis that μ_x increases in geometrical progression as x advances. Thus he developed the relationship

$$\mu_x = Bc^x \qquad (15.26)$$

where B and c are constants. This is a reasonable hypothesis because:

(1) it bears out the tendency of the chance of death to rise with increasing rapidity as the age increases; and

(2) it could be explicable in biological terms as the result of a steadily-declining resistance to dissolution.

Nevertheless, this law does not fit the data closely or provide theoretically for the accidents of life, such as collisions, falls, or infections. Makeham (in 1867) therefore added a constant A, giving

$$\mu_x = A + Bc^x. \qquad (15.27)$$

Fig. 15.1 shows the curve of μ_x for males in England and Wales in 1950–2; its shape is more complex than that of a Gompertz or Makeham curve.

In modern times, the focus of attention has shifted from μ_x or q_x to d_x, which, after the end of infancy, rises steadily to a peak and then falls ultimately to zero (see fig. 15.2). Attempts have been made to represent this by the combination of two bell-shaped curves, one for accidental death and one for the distribution of the population in regard to normal longevity.

15.13 Graduation

Incompleteness and inaccuracy in the data either must be corrected, using the methods described elsewhere in this book, or else must lead to rejection of any idea of preparing a life table. Of the various difficulties that are likely to arise, there remain only (*a*) grouping in the data, and (*b*) random

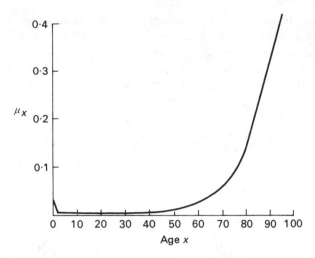

Fig. 15.1. μ_x according to English Life Table No. 11 (males).

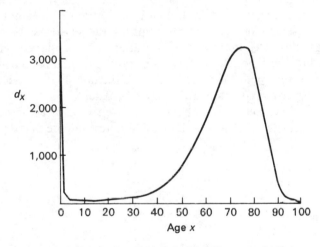

Fig. 15.2. d_x according to English Life Table No. 11 (males).

variations attributable to the smallness of numbers of decrements. The process of graduation may, if circumstances warrant it, be used in order to cope with these problems. Often, smoothness in the results will not be of great desirability. Occasionally, however, there may be some merit in graduation, on the basis that 'nature does not proceed in jumps' and that the data would have proceeded more smoothly if they had been more plentiful.

In Britain, the preparation of national life tables includes a process of graduation, in which considerable attention is paid to detail. This is done mainly for a very special purpose: the tables are used by insurance companies to calculate premiums for industrial life assurance, and it is important in practice that the premium scale should proceed smoothly from age to age. Demographers are unlikely normally to require such a careful application of graduation, and the processes employed will therefore not be developed in detail here, though a few explanatory notes are needed to give some idea of what is involved.

The principal methods of graduation are:

(1) graphical;
(2) curve-fitting;
(3) summation;
(4) reference.

Broadly speaking, the first of these involves plotting the observations on squared paper and drawing a freehand curve through the points, in the manner illustrated below. The second method involves choosing a suitable formula and finding the constants so as to minimize the differences between the curve and the data. The third consists of a process of averaging together adjacent observations. The fourth requires the existence of a suitably graduated life table, from which the ratios of the observed rates to the graduated rates can be calculated; these ratios are then smoothed by a simple process, and the application of the result to the rates in the graduated table should produce a graduation of the observed data.

Details of these methods may be obtained from standard actuarial works of reference. Only the first will be illustrated here. Suppose that the data are:

Age group	Marriage rate
15–19	0·10
20–24	0·28
25–29	0·22
30–34	0·11
35–39	0·05
40–44	0·02

Then the first step is to represent these figures on a chart, as illustrated in fig. 15.3. The second step is to draw a continuous curve, similar to the one shown in the figure, in such a way that the area under the curve is the same as the area of the corresponding 5-year block. Thus, at ages 15–19, the 'triangles' A and B are made of equal size; and at 20–24 D is made equal in area to C and E.

15.14   Special problems

In the preparation of national mortality tables, special problems arise in infancy, where an adjustment is often necessary to the census population

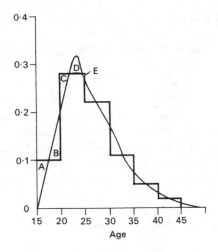

Fig. 15.3. Graphic graduation.

for understatement in the numbers of young children. Special formulae have been derived for correcting the exposed to risk, which frequently is based on the birth registrations. Thus, in England and Wales in 1931, use was made of the formula

$$q_0 = q_0^1 + q_0^2 + q_0^3 + q_0^4,$$ \hfill (15.28)

where

$$q_0^1 = \frac{\text{deaths in 1930, 1931 and 1932 at ages under 3 months}}{\tfrac{1}{2}B^4_{1929} + B_{1930} + B_{1931} + B_{1932} - \tfrac{1}{2}B^4_{1932}},$$

$$q_0^2 = \frac{\text{deaths in 1930, 1931 and 1932 at ages 3—6 months}}{\tfrac{1}{2}B^3_{1929} + B^4_{1929} + B_{1930} + B_{1931} + B^1_{1932} + B^2_{1932} + \tfrac{1}{2}B^3_{1932}},$$

and so on, where q_0^n represents the rate of mortality in the nth quarter of the first year of life; B_y represents the births in year y and B_y^m represents the births in the mth quarter of year y.

Special problems sometimes arise at the ages of childhood and again in extreme old age. These are connected with the difficulties of applying one formula of mortality at all ages above infancy.

Rates of mortality for particular occupations and statuses may be calculated, for example, for married women. These should not, in general, be formed into life tables, because people do not normally spend all their lives in one such status, and movement selection is exercised at entry and exit. Thus, conclusions drawn from an artificial life table, based upon some such occupation or status, may be wrong.

15.15 Abridged life tables

If it is essential to base a life table upon the experience of a year or years in which there was no census, it may be possible to construct one on the foundation of the registered deaths and an estimate of the population (prepared perhaps as indicated in § 9.2). In these circumstances, the data will be both less reliable and less detailed than if a census had been held. It may thus be suitable to draw up an 'abridged' table using approximate methods. Values will then be derived at only quinquennial or even decennial intervals. The requirement for this process is an approximate formula linking crude rates — for example, death rates — in age groups x to $x + n$ with the chances of 'survival' from x to $x + n$.

A number of formulae have been derived for this purpose. One such formula is that of Reed and Merrell, namely

$$\log(_tp_x) = -tM - at^3M^2,\qquad (15.29)$$

where a is a constant and M is the crude death rate for the age-range x to $x + t$. By the use of this formula, a set of l's may be derived for every t'th age.

Another simple and convenient method of constructing abridged life tables is King's method of calculating 'pivotal values'. Let it be supposed that the following data have been collected; the Δ and Δ^2 columns are obtained by simple differencing:

Age-groups	Population (P)	ΔP	$\Delta^2 P$	Deaths (D)	ΔD	$\Delta^2 D$
15–19	1,047			7		
20–24	1,031	−16	−22	8	+1	−1
25–29	993	−38	+ 3	8	0	+1
30–34	958	−35		9	+1	

The pivotal values at age $x + 2$ are taken, by 'King's formula':

Population $\qquad 0{\cdot}2\,P - 0{\cdot}008\,\Delta^2 P$ ⎫

Deaths $\qquad\quad 0{\cdot}2\,D - 0{\cdot}008\,\Delta^2 D$ ⎬. $\qquad$ (15.30)

The values in question are then as follows, and from them q_x may be derived by division:

Age	Population	Deaths	Rate
17	209·6	1·41	0·0067
22	206·2	1·59	0·0077

This approach gives quinary values of q_x and (by suitable modification) the values of the death rate at any other interval of years may be assessed.

Neither of the two methods immediately supplies values of both q_x and l_x, and if both are needed for the abridged life table a further step is necessary. This is to use a relationship such as

$$\log {}_5p_{x+5} = 5\log p_{x+2} + 7\Delta\log p_{x+2} +$$
$$+ 1{\cdot}6\Delta^2\log p_{x+2} - 0{\cdot}2\Delta^3\log p_{x+2}, \qquad (15.31)$$

where $p_{x+2} = 1 - q_{x+2}$ and is thus derived from the pivotal value of q.

A comparison of seven different methods of constructing abridged life tables has been given by Benjamin (see Bibliography below).

SELECT BIBLIOGRAPHY

Decennial Supplement, 1951: Part 1 — Life Tables (Registrar General for England and Wales, H.M. Stationery Office, London, 1957).

Spiegelman, M. *Introduction to Demography* (Harvard University Press, Cambridge, Massachusetts, 1958).

Benjamin, B. *Health and Vital Statistics* (Allen and Unwin, London, 1968).

16 Methods of summary and comparison

16.1 Introduction

Brief reference was made in §2.8 to standardization, and mention was also made of the possibility of comparing demographic ocurrence rates, such as fertility rates, very simply by setting them side by side, at individual ages or age-groups. Rates of mortality, marriage, fertility or migration may thus be aligned for comparison. Such tabulations can, however, become very tedious if a large number of groups is involved, for instance if there are many different occupations and several calendar years of experience. A process by which the amount of comparison can be greatly reduced is the construction of index figures. An index is a number expressive in some way of the properties of a group of numbers; a simple example is the unweighted mean. The efficiency of an index (that is, how completely it represents all the attributes of its constituents) will vary from case to case, but no single-figure index number can express *all* the qualities of the group it represents, and some information − often much − is lost by the amalgamation of the detailed figures. Consider the following simple example:

Age	Mortality rates A	Mortality rates B
20	0·0014	0·0019
21	0·0017	0·0021
22	0·0023	0·0024
23	0·0031	0·0028
24	0·0040	0·0033

Both sets of rates have the same unweighted mean (0.0025), but this fact alone does not tell us that the dispersion of the rates A is wider than that of the rates B or that B are the higher of the two at the younger ages and A are the higher at the older ages. The value of the index naturally depends on the relative importance of this suppressed information.

16.2 Use of life tables

Where life tables for two groups are available for approximately the same period of time, direct comparison can be made between the q_x at suitable

294

age-points, with the benefit of any graduation incorporated in the tables. One may also compare values of tp_x and even of l_x. If life tables for some previous year and mortality indexes for each group in subsequent years are available, it should be possible to combine the life-table figures with the index figure to provide up-to-date comparative measures. An index which is sometimes used in comparisons of mortality in the 'Equivalent Average Death Rate' or the unweighted average of the q's or m's. This depends on the life-table property:

$$_np_x = \exp\left(-\sum_{t=0}^{n-1} m_{x+t}\right) \qquad (16.1)$$

which is based on (15.21) above.

A further possible index of mortality is suggested by the use of the life table, namely the sum of the d's, over a given age range, divided by the sum of the l's or the L's. If the weights are the L's; the average death rate is then

$$\frac{\sum_{x=a}^{a+n} {}^tL_x \cdot {}^tm_x'}{\sum_{x=a}^{a+n} {}^tL_x}, \qquad (16.2)$$

where ${}^tm_x'$ is the graduated rate.

If $n = \infty$, the expression becomes $1/\overset{\circ}{e}_a$; if $a = 0$, this is sometimes called the 'Life Table Death Rate'. The advantage of this expression is that the weights naturally arise from the experience. The disadvantage is that they differ between every life table and every other life table and are never the same as any standard; thus the ratio of two average death rates may be written as

$$\frac{\Sigma^tL_x{}^tm_x'}{\Sigma^tL_x} \cdot \frac{\Sigma L_x}{\Sigma L_x \cdot m_x'}. \qquad (16.3)$$

Where rates are changing rapidly with increasing age, this type of index needs to be used with care, and may be of value only over short ranges of ages.

16.3 Comparisons based on the methods of descriptive statistics

The methods of descriptive statistics are infrequently used in comparing the features of life tables.

An index on a life table basis (see § 16.2) is related to the mean value t of the probability distribution ${}^tp_x \cdot \mu_{x+t}$ which represents the relative values of the ordinates of the 'death curve' of the life table. To give further information about the mortality level of the life table the obvious course is to employ the second moment of the distribution ${}^tp_x \cdot \mu_{x+t}$, or its standard

295

deviation. For further information still, the third and fourth moments or β_1 and β_2 might be used. As the curve of deaths has a second peak at age 0, descriptive statistics are of only limited value over the whole of life, but if infant ages and early childhood are omitted the difficulty caused by having ordinates of very high value at the extreme end of the distributions is eliminated.

The difficulty about these additional measures is that their meaning is not readily seen except by those trained in the methods of descriptive statistics, and it is probably for this reason that they have not come into common use. As a simpler device for supplementing the above mean as a comparative measure, it might be appropriate to compare one or two values of μ_x or q_x or to compare the modes of the distributions $^t p_x \cdot \mu_{x+t}$ and the heights of the ordinates at the modes. This is better than to use a single index for comparing two life tables.

16.4 The general form of demographic index

In the study of population, not only the methods of descriptive statistics, but also geometric means and more advanced mathematical formulae of this kind have so far found little application; in general the arithmetic average is used. Normally this is not the unweighted mean illustrated in § 16.1 but a 'weighted' average, which may be expressed in the form

$$R = \frac{\Sigma w_x \cdot \phi_x}{\Sigma w_x}, \tag{16.4}$$

where w_x is the 'weight' of the data at age (or duration) x, and ϕ_x is the demographic function towards which interest is being directed. The summation may be made over any chosen range for x.

Two or more weighting processes can be combined, for example, in assembling the data for the two sexes together; the grand average is then

$$\frac{\Sigma(w_x^m \cdot \phi_x^m + w_x^f \cdot \phi_x^f)}{\Sigma(w_x^m + w_x^f)}, \tag{16.5}$$

where the affixes m and f are used to denote males and females respectively.

Index figures are usually calculated as the ratio of two values of R, e.g.

$$I = \frac{R_1}{R_2}.$$

16.5 Crude rates

In this case the actual numbers at successive ages (or durations) x in the particular population are used as the weights and the weighted average is

$$R_t^A = \frac{\Sigma^t P_x \cdot {}^t\phi_x}{\Sigma^t P_x}, \qquad (16.6)$$

where A denotes the method, t refers to the particular experience, and P represents the population size. If two populations have identical occurrence rates but different age-distributions, their crude rates will not normally be the same; consequently comparison of the crude rates will probably be misleading. More generally, the difference between two crude rates may be analysed into the two parts, namely, those attributable respectively to (a) disparities in the population weights; and (b) differences in the experience in which interest resides. The first of these is a spurious effect; the extent to which an incorrect picture may be presented may be seen by considering two communities, one of settlers in a new territory, mostly of early adult age, and the other consisting mainly of retired persons living at a spa. If the crude mortality rate for the first group is lighter than the crude rate for the second group, the difference is clearly attributable mainly to the different age-constitutions of the groups and only partially to any differences in the level of mortality.

Two populations may have the same crude death rate and yet be experiencing very different intrinsic mortality. Similarly the crude birth rate is an unreliable indicator of intrinsic fertility. The 'net rate of natural increase', defined as the excess of the crude birth rate over the crude death rate, is doubly unreliable as an indicator of intrinsic growth because it is a difference item. In fact, because of a temporarily favourable age-distribution, a population may continue to increase in size for many years after its real reproductivity has become insufficient to support growth in the long run.

16.6   Use of a standard population as weights

If the numbers of people at successive ages (or durations) in a standard population are used as the weights, the weighted average rate becomes

$$R_t^B = \frac{\Sigma P_x \cdot {}^t\phi_x}{\Sigma P_x} \qquad (16.7)$$

(where P_x represents the standard population). The result is often known as the 'standardized rate' because it represents the rate that would have occurred if the value of ${}^t\phi_x$ had applied to the standard population.

In the example quoted in § 6.13, the use of the population in the year Y as the standard population would lead to a standardized fertility rate over the age-range 15-44 of

$$X \quad 3940 \div 51{,}100 = 0{\cdot}0771,$$
$$Y \quad 3789 \div 51{,}100 = 0{\cdot}0741.$$

Alternatively, the use of population X as the standard population would lead to standardized fertility rates of:

$$X \quad 3858 \div 52{,}600 = 0{\cdot}0733$$
$$Y \quad 3711 \div 52{,}600 = 0{\cdot}0706.$$

The values $0{\cdot}0741$ for population Y in the first example and $0{\cdot}0733$ for population X in the second example are of course 'crude'. The values of $0{\cdot}0771$ and $0{\cdot}0706$ represent the results of the use of formula 16.7. Comparison of the crude figures suggests a higher level of experience in Y than in X. Standardization on the basis of either X or Y reveals, however, that the rates in X are about 4 per cent higher than those in Y and, having regard to the detailed figures shown in §6.13, this is evidently more reasonable.

In mortality studies, the ratio of R_t^B to the crude rate in the standard population gives an index which is known as the 'Comparative Mortality Factor' (CMF), namely

$$I_t^B = \frac{\Sigma P_x \cdot {}^t m_x}{\Sigma P_x} \bigg/ \frac{\Sigma P_x \cdot m_x}{\Sigma P_x} \tag{16.8}$$

$$= \Sigma P_x \cdot {}^t m_x / \Sigma P_x \cdot m_x.$$

This index may be written in the alternative form

$$\Sigma (P_x \cdot m_x) \cdot \frac{{}^t m_x}{m_x} \bigg/ \Sigma (P_x \cdot m_x), \tag{16.9}$$

and in this form is seen to represent a weighted average of ${}^t m_x / m_x$ with $(P_x \cdot m_x)$ as the weights. The weights for the CMF are thus the actual deaths in the standard population. This method is sometimes called the 'direct' method of standarization.

16.7 Use of standard rates as a measure

If the experience rates of a standard population are applied to the successive values of ${}^t P_x$, a weighted average of these standard rates can be obtained, i.e.

$$R_t^C = \frac{\Sigma {}^t P_x \cdot \phi_x}{\Sigma {}^t P_x}. \tag{16.10}$$

The ratio of the crude rate R_t^A to this average provides a useful index of the experience, which may be written

$$I_t^C = \frac{\Sigma {}^t P_x \cdot {}^t \phi_x}{\Sigma {}^t P_x} \bigg/ \frac{\Sigma {}^t P_x \cdot \phi_x}{\Sigma {}^t P_x} = \frac{\Sigma {}^t P_x \cdot {}^t \phi_x}{\Sigma {}^t P_x \cdot \phi_x}. \tag{16.11}$$

The numerator of this index is the actual number of occurrences (for example, deaths or births) in population t, while the denominator is the number of occurrences that would have taken place in population t if the standard rates had applied. The denominator may be called the 'expected' occurrences, and the index thus measures the ratio of actual to expected occurrences.

If the fertility figures quoted in § 16.6 are rearranged, an example of this form of standardization is seen, as follows:

Population	Rates	Standardized rate
X	X	0·0733
X	Y	0·0706
Y	Y	0·0741
Y	X	0·0771

If the rates of population Y are employed in the standardizing process, the value of I_t^c arrived at for X/Y is 0·0733/0·0706, or 1·038. Similarly, if the rates of population X are used, the index figure for the ratio Y/X is 0·0741/0·0771. In this very simple example, the results coincide (in reverse order) with those given in § 16.6. In normal mortality analysis the methods of § 16.6 and § 16.7 will give different results.

In mortality studies, the expression 16.11 is known as the 'Standardized Mortality Ratio' (SMR). It can be written in the alternative form

$$\frac{\Sigma(^tP_x \cdot m_x) \cdot {^t m_x}/m_x}{\Sigma(^tP_x \cdot m_x)}. \tag{16.12}$$

In this form it is seen to represent a weighted average of $^t m_x/m_x$ with $(^tP_x \cdot m_x)$ as the weights, namely, the 'expected deaths'; compare the use of the actual deaths in the CMF. The method of the SMR is sometimes referred to as 'indirect' standardization, and in some senses it is the complement of the direct method.

16.8 Compromise bases

It is possible to form standardized rates by some combination of the direct and indirect methods. One such 'compromise' basis, which was adopted at one time by the Registrar General for England and Wales, is to use weights relating neither to the actual population nor to the standard population but to the arithmetic mean of the two, after each has been expressed as a proportion of the total for all ages together. Writing c for $\Sigma^tP_x/\Sigma P_x$,

$$\frac{1}{2}\left(\frac{P_x}{\Sigma P_x} + \frac{^tP_x}{\Sigma {^tP_x}}\right) = \frac{1}{2\Sigma {^tP_x}}\left\{c \cdot P_x + {^tP_x}\right\}.$$

299

This shows that the weights are proportionate to $(c \cdot P_x + {}^t P_x)$. The weighted average rate on this basis is

$$R_t^D = \frac{\Sigma (cP_x + {}^t P_x)^t \phi_x}{\Sigma (cP_x + {}^t P_x)} \tag{16.13}$$

and it leads to the index

$$I_t^D = \frac{\Sigma (cP_x + {}^t P_x)^t \phi_x}{\Sigma (cP_x + {}^t P_x) \phi_x}, \tag{16.14}$$

which has been called the 'Comparative Mortality Index'.

Another possible compromise basis is the geometric mean of the CMF and the SMR. This type of function is sometimes known as 'Fisher's Ideal Index'.

16.9 Comparison between the various indexes and their uses

If several experiences are being compared, it is only on the bases of §§ 16.2 and 16.6 that the weights remain the same from experience to experience. On the bases of §§ 16.7 and 16.8 they are the same for any one experience and for the standard experience but between any other experiences they are different. It is obvious that if the weights change from experience to experience the index will change even if the mortality, or fertility, rates at each age are the same for each experience. Such indexes therefore measure the changing effect of the system of weights as well as the changes in the occurrence rates.

This does not mean that the basis of § 16.7 is necessarily inferior to those of §§ 16.6 and 16.8. The use of the same set of weights throughout may be inappropriate if the age-distributions of the various experiences are materially different, because the weights may result in the mortality (or fertility) at some ages in some of the experiences being allowed to influence the index too much or too little, according to whether the numbers exposed to risk at those ages in those populations are deficient or excessive compared with the rest of the populations. For example, the standard population may be reasonably spread over the age-range, while one of the other populations may be concentrated at the younger ages and yet another may consist largely of people at the older ages.

The use of the same set of weights in a series of index numbers is evidently valuable. Yet it is inappropriate to use the same set of weights if the age-distributions differ substantially. This paradox is inherent in the nature of index numbers and cannot be completely resolved. There can thus be no such thing as a perfect mortality, marriage or fertility index.

If in any experience the numbers exposed to risk at certain ages are small, the random errors in the experience rate will be correspondingly large. The use of too large a standardizing population at these ages will magnify the errors in the index. This is another reason why the direct method may not be the most desirable. The difficulty may be avoided by grouping the ages, or using an indirect or compromise method.

A numerical example, from which students may calculate various indexes and verify their results, is given in § 16.20 below, and an illustrative series of crude and standardized death rates is shown in table 16.1.

The main features of table 16.1 are:

(1) the progressive fall in the rates for all ages together, in spite of wars and economic crises, to about half their original value;

(2) the increased rate of decline in the second half of the period;

(3) the increasing discrepancies between the crude and standardized death rates since the twentieth century began; these have been partly associated with changes in the shape of the population pyramid;

Table 16.1. *Death rates, England and Wales, 1856–1970*

Period	Crude death rates per thousand living		Standardized death rates per thousand living†		Comparative mortality indexes (1938 = 1)	
	Males	Females	Males	Females	Males	Females
1856–60	22·6	21·0	21·6	19·9	2·04	2·33
1861–5	23·7	21·5	22·6	20·3	2·13	2·38
1866–70	23·7	21·2	22·6	20·0	2·14	2·36
1871–5	23·3	20·7	22·4	19·5	2·13	2·32
1876–80	22·1	19·5	21·3	18·4	2·05	2·22
1881–5	20·5	18·3	20·1	17·5	1·94	2·11
1886–90	20·0	17·8	20·0	17·2	1·92	2·08
1891–5	19·8	17·7	20·0	17·2	1·91	2·08
1896–1900	18·8	16·6	19·1	16·2	1·82	1·95
1901–5	17·1	15·0	17·4	14·6	1·67	1·77
1906–10	15·6	13·8	15·8	13·2	1·52	1·62
1911–15*	15·4	13·3	15·1	12·4	1·46	1·53
1916–20*	16·5	12·8	15·1	11·9	1·44	1·46
1921–5	12·9	11·4	12·0	9·8	1·19	1·26
1926–30	12·9	11·4	11·5	9·2	1·14	1·19
1931–5	12·7	11·4	10·7	8·6	1·08	1·13
1936–40*	13·5	11·6	10·4	7·9	1·07	1·07
1941–5*	15·1	11·1	Not available		0·98	0·93
1946–50*	12·8	10·9	Not available		0·87	0·85
1951–5	12·5	10·9	Not available		0·85	0·79
1956–60	12·3	10·9	Not available		0·83‡	0·73‡
1961–5	12·5	11·2	5·0	3·0	0·83‡	0·73‡
1966–70	12·3	11·1	5·0	3·0	0·80‡	0·71‡

* Civilians only.
† Obtained by using the 1901 Census age-distribution in conjunction with the death rates at each age for the period in question. The figures for 1961–5 and 1966–70 are estimated approximately.
‡ Estimated on the basis of the SMR's provided by the Registrar General.

(4) the decline in the percentage ratio of female to male mortality; the margin between the male and female rates has remained fairly constant in its absolute size in spite of the general reduction in mortality;

(5) the increase in the crude civilian death rate in war-time, due principally to alterations in distribution caused by calling up young and healthy men to the Armed Forces, but also in part to air-raids and other war causes;

(6) the spectacular decline in the infant death rate since the turn of the century, after a long period in which little change occurred.

16.10   Indexes designed for specific purposes in mortality analysis

In demographic work, mortality analyses often consist of one or other of the following types, namely comparisons between:

(1) the mortality at different times of the population of a given country or large region;

(2) the mortality in the same period of time of various subdivisions of the population of a given country;

(3) the mortality at different times of particular subdivisions of a given country;

(4) the mortality in the same, or nearly the same, period of time of the populations of two or more different countries;

(5) the mortality from different causes in the population of the same country over the same period of time.

In the remainder of this chapter reference will be made first to the use of particular mortality indexes for such specific purposes. Then the quite different problems of indexes associated with fertility will be explored, with special reference to reproduction rates. Now that reproduction rates have largely ceased to be used in demographic analysis and presentation, these attempts are mainly of historical interest. Nevertheless, some insight into the complexities of demography may be gained from an acquaintance with such developments, and they also provide a fitting prelude to the consideration of population mathematics in chapter 18. Finally, indexes for use in the study of migration and the features of whole populations will be mentioned.

16.11   Comparisons between the mortality in successive periods of the population of a given country

The numbers of deaths, either for males and females separately or for the sexes together, may give almost as much information about a trend as a set of indexes can. This is because, in the absence of substantial migration, the total population and the age-distribution normally change only slowly. If the total population is known, or can be closely estimated for each year, the calculation of the crude death rates will remove the effect of the changing total population, and all that is then being ignored is a leisurely change in the age-distribution. Standardization on the basis of the age-distribution of the population at some point of time within the periods being compared will modify the crude rates slightly, but this adjustment may not be worth making unless the periods in question are long ones. These remarks apply particularly if they seem to be quite appropriate for comparisons between adjacent or nearly adjacent years. For years more widely separated, the effect of the changing weights in the basis of § 16.8 will be larger, though not so large as with that of § 16.7. The difference between the mortalities will usually be much greater, so that the effect of the changing weights will be relatively small.

None of the indexes described in this section, as used in practice, has taken account of the possible association of mortality with year of birth as well as with year of experience (see § 7.9). The same types of indexes could, however, be applied if desired to the mortality rates of generations.

16.12 Comparisons between the mortality of subdivisions of the population of a country

When comparing the mortality of subdivisions of a given population in the same period of time, account needs to be taken of the possibility that the numbers living and the deaths at some ages or in some age-groups may be small, so that some of the death rates may contain large random errors and be quite unreliable. Standardization on the bases of §§ 16.6 and 16.8 might well, therefore, magnify the random errors and result in the comparative measure being unnecessarily inaccurate. For this reason, the basis of § 16.7 (ratio of actual to expected deaths on the basis of the mortality of the whole population) is often used. Strictly, this means that comparisons should be made only between the mortality of each subdivision and of the whole population, and should not be made between the mortality of the subdivisions among themselves. If, however, the age-distributions of two subdivisions of the population are not markedly dissimilar the comparison can be made without serious reservation on this account. (If the age-distribution were markedly dissimilar, no single-figure indexes could be devised which were suitably comparable. Thus the basis in § 16.7 has the merit that it continually raises the question of the comparability of the age-distributions.)

Further considerations of comparisons of subdivisions will be given below in connection with occupational mortality; here the Registrar General for England and Wales has supplied occupational mortality indexes on the basis of both §§ 16.6 and 16.7. Only infrequently did substantially disparate figures result. This was in part because (*a*) the age-range was limited to

303

20–65, (b) the sexes were separately treated, (c) the age-distributions were not often markedly dissimilar to that of the whole population, and (d) the ratios $^t m_x / m_x$ in most cases did not vary greatly from age-group to age-group.

As an example of a comparison of mortality indexes for subdivisions of a population some figures (without adjustment for racial and sex differences) may be given for the American States, Maine and South Carolina, in 1930. Each of the following figures is the ratio of a rate for South Carolina to the corresponding rate for Maine:

Crude death rates	0·93
Standardized death rates	1·43
Standardized mortality ratio	1·55
Equivalent average death rates for ages 0–65	1·68
Life-table death rates	1·11

These figures show the wide variations between the various methods that can arise, and bring out sharply the unsatisfactory results that can be obtained from single-figure indexes.

Comparisons of the mortality of the same subdivision of a population at different times are not made very often. The point of interest in such comparisons is to see how the departure of the mortality of the subdivision from that of the whole population has changed over the period. For example, a particular occupation may have shown heavy mortality in the past. It may be desired to see how the relative mortality has responded to industrial reforms designed to protect the workers in that occupation. In such comparisons, care is always necessary in drawing inferences because other factors affecting mortality may also have changed within the period; indexes of the form I_t^c may be appropriate, and the ratio of actual to expected deaths based on whole population mortality in the second period may be compared with the corresponding ratio in the first period.

16.13   Indexes based on incomplete data

Indexes on the basis described in § 16.7 can be computed even if the only information available about the deaths in population t is the total number of deaths for the range of ages entering into the index, as the numerator of the index, $\Sigma^t P_x \cdot {}^t m_x$, is the total actual deaths. The distribution of population over the ages is, however, required to form the denominator, which is the total expected deaths. Although it would be an unusual situation in practice for $^t P_x$ to be known at each age and for the deaths to be known only in total, the work involved in computing this index for several populations relative to a single standard population is considerably less than for the basis described in §§ 16.6 and 16.8.

Another case of partial data is when the deaths in population t are known at each age, but the only information available about the population is the total $\Sigma^t P_x$. In this situation an index can be formed by dividing $^tP_x \cdot {^t}m_x$ by m_x, the rates in the standard population, summing and dividing the total by the total of population t, namely

$$\frac{\Sigma^t P_x \cdot ({^t}m_x/m_x)}{\Sigma^t P_x},$$ (16.15)

which is a weighted average of $^tm_x/m_x$ with ^tP_x as the weights, although the individual values of ^tP_x are unknown.

A situation that commonly arises in practice is where the population and deaths at each age are known for a given census year both for a country as a whole and for various localities or other subdivisions of the country. For subsequent years, only the total deaths and the total or estimated total population of each of the localities are known. It is desired to adjust the crude death rates for the localities in the post-census years to obtain suitable locality indexes for comparisons between localities. An 'Area Comparability Factor' (ACF) has been devised by the Registrar General for England and Wales.

16.14 Area comparability factor

For the purpose of demonstrating this factor the prefix s will be used for the whole population in the census year, and the prefixes $'$ and t will be used for an individual locality in the census year and in year t respectively.

The area comparability factor is then given by

$$\frac{\Sigma^s P_x \cdot {^s}m_x}{\Sigma^s P_x} \bigg/ \frac{\Sigma^1 P_x \cdot {^s}m_x}{\Sigma^1 P_x}$$ (16.16)

Multiplying the crude death rate in year t in the locality by this factor, an adjusted death rate is then obtained as follows:

$$\frac{\Sigma^s P_x \cdot {^s}m_x}{\Sigma^s P_x} \cdot \frac{\Sigma^1 P_x}{\Sigma^1 P_x \cdot {^s}m_x} \cdot \frac{\Sigma^t P_x \cdot {^t}m_x}{\Sigma^t P_x},$$ (16.17)

If it can be assumed that the local population has changed between the census year and year t by the same proportion at each age, i.e. that

$$^tP_x = {^1}P_x \cdot \frac{\Sigma^t P_x}{\Sigma^1 P_x},$$

then ^tP_x can be substituted for ^1P_x in the numerator and denominator of the second factor in the above adjusted rate which, since $\Sigma^t P_x$ cancels, then becomes

$$\frac{\Sigma^s P_x \cdot {^s}m_x}{\Sigma^s P_x} \cdot \frac{\Sigma^t P_x \cdot {^t}m_x}{\Sigma^t P_x \cdot {^s}m_x} = K \cdot I^c_t.$$ (16.18)

305

The first factor (K) is then dependent only on the population and deaths of the whole country in the census year and is therefore constant for all localities. The second factor, I_t^c, is simply the ratio of actual to expected deaths in year t in the locality, where the expected deaths are computed on the basis of the mortality of the whole country in the census year.

The use of such adjusted rates to compare the mortality of various localities in year t thus depends on the suitability of the assumption made above about the nature of the change in the locality populations between the census year and year t. The comparison is also subject to the disadvantages mentioned earlier about the use of indexes of the SMR type.

16.15 Time comparability factor

As the standard population used in England and Wales for mortality index purposes was for a long time the 1901 population, the Registrar General devised another adjusting factor, called the 'Time Comparability Factor' (TCF) to be applied to the adjusted local death rates (i.e. to the ACF multiplied by the crude local rate). The object of this further adjustment was to approximate to standardization on the basis of the 1901 Census. The TCF used was

$$\frac{\Sigma^r P_x \cdot {}^t m_x}{\Sigma^r P_x} \bigg/ \frac{\Sigma^t P_x \cdot {}^t m_x}{\Sigma^t P_x}, \tag{16.19}$$

where all the functions referred to England and Wales, r to 1901 and t to the current year in question. As 1931 was used as the standard year for the adjusted death rates, it would seem that the 1931 data might just as well have been used instead of the data for year t.

As the TCF depended on the values of ${}^t m_x$, a different factor was required for every subdivision, for instance, by cause.

These adjustments were discontinued during the Second World War for various reasons, including the large internal migrations of that time, and have not since been resumed.

16.16 Other methods for local comparisons

A somewhat different method has been used by the Division of Vital Statistics of the New York State Department of Health for intercensal locality comparisons. Again using the prefix s for the standard population in the census year and the prefix t for the locality in a subsequent year, the standardized death rate for the locality (on the basis of § 16.16) is given by

$$\frac{\Sigma^s P_x \cdot {}^t m_x}{\Sigma^s P_x}. \tag{16.20}$$

By multiplying and dividing this rate by the crude death rate in the locality it can be expressed in the form

$$\left(\frac{\Sigma^s P_x . {}^t m_x}{\Sigma^s P_x} . \frac{\Sigma^t P_x}{\Sigma^t P_x . {}^t m_x}\right) \frac{\Sigma^t P_x . {}^t m_x}{\Sigma^t P_x}. \tag{16.21}$$

Thus, if a suitable approximation can be made to the expression in brackets (F_t, say), a factor will be obtained for adjusting the crude rate to the standardized rate. What is done is to assume that F_t is independent of t during the intercensal years by substituting for this expression the corresponding expression for the census year, i.e., F_1, where

$$F_1 = \frac{\Sigma^s P_x . {}^1 m_x}{\Sigma^s P_x} . \frac{\Sigma^1 P_x}{\Sigma^1 P_x . {}^1 m_x}. \tag{16.22}$$

This factor can be calculated because all the items entering into it are available for the census year. The reasonableness of the assumption that $F_t = F_1$ can be seen by taking the ratio and re-arranging the terms as follows:

$$\frac{F_t}{F_1} = \frac{\Sigma^s P_x . {}^1 m_x . ({}^t m_x / {}^1 m_x)}{\Sigma^s P_x . {}^1 m_x} \frac{\Sigma^1 P_x . {}^1 m_x}{\Sigma^t P_x . {}^1 m_x . ({}^t m_x / {}^1 m_x)} . \frac{\Sigma^t P_x}{\Sigma^1 P_x}. \tag{16.23}$$

The first term is a weighted mean of ${}^t m_x / {}^1 m_x$. If we assume that ${}^t P_x = {}^1 P_x . (\Sigma^t P_x / \Sigma^1 P_x)$ as in the basis of the ACF, the second and third factors together yield the reciprocal of another weighted mean of ${}^t m_x / {}^1 m_x$. Thus we have for F_t / F_1 a weighted mean divided by a weighted mean. ${}^t m_x / {}^1 m_x$ is not likely to vary greatly from unity during the intercensal years; moreover, the relative values of weights ${}^s P_x . {}^1 m_x$ and ${}^t P_x . {}^1 m_x$ are unlikely to be markedly dissimilar. Thus F_t / F_1 may be expected, in general, to be close to unity.

If we substitute ${}^s m_x$ for ${}^1 m_x$ in F_1 we obtain the Registrar General's ACF, and there seems to be little effective difference between the American system and that of the Registrar General. The American system approximates to the CMF and the British system approximates to the SMR.

16.17 Methods of weighting designed to give more emphasis to the younger ages

Some demographers have argued that the weights underlying the bases of §§ 16.6 and 16.7 give too much emphasis to the older ages. True, those ages are where the deaths occur; but, it is held, old lives are less valuable than young ones; a young life saved is a life that will probably endure longer and can be lived more fully: an old life is not preserved for long in any event. Expression of this viewpoint is given by, for instance, using $P_x e_x$ instead of P_x as the weight in the method of § 16.6. (Compare § 7.20.) The method of the equivalent average death rate achieves the opposite result, because populations are normally more numerous at the younger ages than at the old, but the substitution of unity for $P_x m_x$ in formula (16.9), which has been suggested by Yerushalmy, gives more weight to the young. The formula based on the equivalent average death rate is

$$\Sigma^t m_x / \Sigma m_x. \tag{16.24}$$

Instead of unity, some other system of weights may be used. If P_x is employed, the result is known as the Relative Mortality Index.

The use of $1/x$ instead of unity (Kohn) gives a greater — and perhaps excessive — weight to youth, but this may be reduced, if desired, by the employment of such factors as the reciprocal of $\log x$ or of $\sqrt{x}$. Having regard to the limitations of indexes generally, these refinements are all of somewhat questionable worth.

16.18   The two-ages method

By Taylor's theorem

$$f(x) = f(\overline{x} + h) = f(\overline{x}) + hf'(\overline{x}) + \frac{h^2}{2!}f^2(\overline{x}) + \frac{h^3}{3!}f^3(\overline{x}) + \dots,$$

where $h = x - \overline{x}$ and $f^n(\overline{x})$ is the value of the nth derivative of $f(x)$ where x is put equal to $\overline{x}$. A mortality index is of the form

$$\frac{\Sigma w_x . f(x)}{\Sigma w_x}$$

where $f(x)$ is a ratio of the form ${}^t m_x / m_x$. If $f(x)$ is deemed to be differentiable, this can be written as

$$\frac{\Sigma w_x . f(\overline{x})}{\Sigma w_x} + \frac{\Sigma w_x . (x - \overline{x}) . f'(\overline{x})}{\Sigma w_x} + \frac{\Sigma w_x . (x - \overline{x})^2 . f^2(\overline{x})}{\Sigma w_x} + \dots$$

$$= f(\overline{x}) + \mu_1 . f'(\overline{x}) + \frac{\mu_2}{2!}f^2(\overline{x}) + \frac{\mu_3}{3!}f^3(\overline{x}) + \dots. \tag{16.25}$$

If $\overline{x}$ is the mean of the distribution w_x, μ_1 is zero and $\mu_2, \mu_3, \dots$ are the successive central moments of the distribution of weights w_x.

As the weighting system operates largely to eliminate the random errors, because their average value is zero or nearly so, it may not be unreasonable to regard $f(x)$ as a differentiable function. Further, since the mortality curve is normally not tortuous, derivatives above the second may well be of negligible proportions in expression (16.25), which thus reduces to

$$\frac{\Sigma w_x . f(x)}{\Sigma w_x} \doteqdot f(\overline{x}) + \frac{\mu_2}{2}f^2(\overline{x}). \tag{16.26}$$

Now, by Taylor's theorem,

$$f(\overline{x} + \sigma) = f(\overline{x}) + \sigma f'(\overline{x}) + \frac{\sigma^2}{2}f^2(\overline{x}) + \ldots$$

and

$$f(\overline{x} - \sigma) = f(\overline{x}) - \sigma f'(\overline{x}) + \frac{\sigma^2}{2}f^2(\overline{x}) - \ldots,$$

where

$$\sigma^2 = \mu_2.$$

Adding, and ignoring derivatives above the second,

$$f(\overline{x} + \sigma) + f(\overline{x} - \sigma) \doteq 2\left[f(\overline{x}) + \frac{\sigma^2}{2}f^2(\overline{x})\right]. \qquad (16.27)$$

Thus $[\Sigma w_x . f(x)]/\Sigma w_x$ is approximately equal to $\frac{1}{2}[f(\overline{x} + \sigma) + f(\overline{x} - \sigma)]$, where σ equals $\sqrt{\mu_2}$, the standard deviation of the distribution. This suggests than when using an index such as the CMF, where the same system of weights is applied to a number of experiences, much numerical work could be avoided by obtaining the mean and the standard deviation σ of the system of weights and working on the mean of the values of the function to be standardized at the two ages $\overline{x} \pm \sigma$. Or, more simply, two ages x_1 and x_2 could be chosen arbitrarily for use without even going to the extent of constructing a system of weights.

The difficulty with this approach is that the crude values of the mortality rate at individual ages are subject to random errors or errors arising from age misstatements. This can be avoided by grouping. Thus in dealing with mortality at working ages, say 20–65, the two quinary age-groups 28–32 and 53–57 could be used. The mid-points of these groups represent approximately $\overline{x} + \sigma$ for a uniform system of weights.

16.19 Standardization of mortality in occupational mortality investigations

In the British occupational mortality investigation of 1931 it was decided to make comparisons of the SMR and the CMF in order to choose whichever proved to be the more appropriate for use as an index. It was found that the two produced closely similar results in many cases. In the actual data for men aged 35–65 there was only one instance in which they differed by more than 5 units when expressed as percentages. For men aged 20–65 there were only four such instances, of which three were statistically significant, the difference exceeding twice the standard error of the SMR. For married women only one occupation showed a material difference between its SMR and CMF. This was a case where the CMF was clearly unsatisfactory. Consequently the need for two indexes was not apparent, only the SMR was retained.

309

In the case of single women, larger differences between the SMR and CMF than these were observed at ages 20—65, but not so much at ages 35—65. For this class the age-group 20—35 represented no less than 65 per cent of the standard population, but much of the occupation was temporary, because it was given up on marriage, and so did not have an appreciable effect on mortality. It was, therefore, decided to limit the SMR to ages 35—65 only, even though only one-third of the data were thus used.

In 1921 the mortality standard upon which the SMR was calculated was that of all occupied and retired civilian males aged 20—65. The restriction to civilians was necessary on that occasion in view of the number of men still in the Forces, but some criticism of the inclusion of the age-group 20—24 was made on several grounds. First, it was argued that a man's occupation was not sufficiently established at age 20; secondly, that the data at these ages were less trustworthy both because of paucity of numbers and also because of misstatements; thirdly and perhaps most important, it was said that variations in mortality of these ages were a measure of the degree of selection exercised at entry into the occupation rather than the occupational mortality itself.

As it may also have been the case that the data for ages 25—34 were affected by these considerations, it was decided to use both of the two age-ranges 20—65 and 35—65, for calculating the SMR's in the principal tables, although, in fact, few important variations between the two were revealed.

After age 65 many persons retire, and data showing present occupations are in consequence of little value. The attempt to correlate mortality in old age with the occupation formerly followed, though desirable, has unfortunately been too much the subject of misstatements to be of value. Many retired persons appear to have described themselves as 'unoccupied' at the census and to have given no indication of having followed an occupation at any time. As, however, relatively few men under age 65 are unoccupied, it was decided in 1931 not to omit them from the standard as in 1921, but to use the experience of all males for this purpose.

Some illustrative figures from the 1931 inquiry have already been given (§7.27).

The SMR for all men aged 20—64 was again used in the report of the Registrar General on occupational mortality in 1949—53.

16.20 Numerical illustration of mortality standardization

Table 16.2 summarizes the mortality indexes referred to in this chapter. In order to help students who would like to work through a simple numerical example, the figures on page 312 have been assembled to represent two hypothetical 'populations' over the limited age-range 70—74 and the

Table 16.2. *Summary of mortality indexes*
(For definitions of symbols used, see text)

Name	Formula	Formula reference number	Brief notes
Comparative Mortality Factor	$\dfrac{\Sigma P_x \cdot {}^l m_x}{\Sigma P_x \cdot m_x}$	(16.8)	The 'direct' method; equals the ratio of the standardized local death rate to the crude national death rate
Standardized Mortality Ratio	$\dfrac{\Sigma {}^t P_x \cdot {}^t m_x}{\Sigma {}^t P_x \cdot m_x}$	(16.11)	The 'indirect' method; equals the ratio of actual to expected deaths
Comparative Mortality Index	$\dfrac{\Sigma({}^e P_x + {}^t P_x) \cdot {}^l m_x}{\Sigma({}^e P_x + {}^t P_x) \cdot m_x}$	(16.14)	A compromise between above two approaches
—	$\dfrac{\Sigma {}^l m_x}{\Sigma m_x}$	(16.24)	Uses equal weights at all ages; is the ratio of the equivalent average death rates in local and national populations
—	$\dfrac{\Sigma {}^l L_x \cdot {}^l m_x'}{\Sigma {}^l L_x} \cdot \dfrac{\Sigma L_x}{\Sigma L_x \cdot m_x'}$	(16.3)	Is the ratio of the local and national lifetable death rates. Each uses a different system of weights
—	$\dfrac{\Sigma {}^t P_x \, ({}^l m_x / {}^t m_x)}{\Sigma {}^t P_x}$	(16.15)	For use when deaths at each age are known but only the total population
Area Comparability Factor	$\dfrac{\Sigma {}^s P_x \cdot {}^s m_x}{\Sigma {}^l P_x \cdot {}^s m_x} \cdot \dfrac{\Sigma {}^l P_x}{\Sigma {}^s P_x}$	(16.16)	Used to correct local crude death rates in years between censuses
Time Comparability Factor	$\dfrac{\Sigma {}^l P_x \cdot {}^l m_x}{\Sigma {}^t P_x \cdot {}^l m_x} \cdot \dfrac{\Sigma {}^t P_x}{\Sigma {}^l P_x}$	(16.19)	Used to approximate to standardization of local death rates on basis of a given census population
—	$\dfrac{\Sigma {}^s P_x \cdot {}^l m_x}{\Sigma {}^l P_x \cdot {}^l m_x} \cdot \dfrac{\Sigma {}^l P_x}{\Sigma {}^s P_x}$	(16.22)	Used in America instead of Area Comparability Factor

mortality experience of each. The results of the calculations of the various indexes are given below.

It will be noted that multiplication of the ratio of the crude death rates by the Area Comparability Factor produces the same ratio as that obtained by indirect standardization; multiplication by the Time Comparability Factor produces the same ratio as that obtained by direct standardization.

	Population I			Population II		
Age x	Numbers exposed to risk at age x	q_x	Deaths in a year at age x	Numbers exposed to risk at age x	q_x	Deaths in a year at age x
70	2,000	0·032	64	3,000	0·027	81
71	1,200	0·035	42	3,500	0·032	112
72	1,400	0·040	56	3,000	0·039	117
73	1,800	0·045	81	4,000	0·046	184
74	1,600	0·050	80	2,500	0·056	140
Total	8,000	—	323	16,000	—	634

The following statements shows alternative summary measures of mortality:

Name of index or method	Average mortality rate for population		Ratio of average mortality rate for Population II to that for Population I	Formula number for	
	I	II		Average mortality rate	Ratio
Crude death rate	0·04038	0·03962	0·981	16·6	—
Direct method (I as standard)	0·04038	0·03992	0·989	16·7	16·8
Indirect method (I as standard)	0·04022	0·03962	0·985	16·10	16·11
Comparative mortality index	0·04030	0·03978	0·987	16·13	16·14
Equivalent average death rate	0·04040	0·04000	0·990	—	16·3
Life-table death rate	0·04005	0·03946	0·985	—	—
Index based on incomplete data (I as standard)	—	—	0·971	—	16·15
Area comparability factor (I as standard)	—	—	1·004	—	16·16
Time comparability factor (I as standard)	—	—	1·008	—	16·19

16.21   Demographic comparisons: fertility

Unweighted averages may be used in fertility comparisons; for example, the function

$$\sum_{x=0}^{\infty} i_x$$

is sometimes used, where i_x is the fertility rate at age x. The rates used may relate either to men or to women. They may be restricted to births of the same sex as the parent, ^si_x (say). The function

$$\sum_{x=0}^{\infty} {}^si_x \qquad (16.28)$$

is known as the 'gross reproduction rate'.

If mortality is ignored, and migration gains and losses are disregarded, then it may be said that if a person experienced at each successive age x the fertility rates i_x, the total number of children he or she would have, of the same sex, would be given by expression (16.28). This expression then gives the number of children replacing him, or her, in the next generation.

Table 16.3 shows how the woman's gross reproduction rate would be calculated on the basis of the hypothetical data given in tables 6.3 and 6.4. Thus, ignoring fertility at ages 45 and over, total fertility equals 5 × 0·4353 = 2·176. This relates to children of both sexes; for comparison the crude fertility rate = (3,858/52,600) × 30 = 2·200. If the proportion of female births to all births were (say) 0·487, then the woman's gross reproduction rate would be 2·176 × 0·487, or 1·060. In these calculations the use of the factor 5 and, in the crude rate, of 30 is to correct for the width of the age-grouping and thus to ensure that the result is of the same order of size as would be obtained by the use of individual ages.

The gross reproduction rate is a function lying in the region of unity and may be regarded as a measure of the extent to which a sex is replacing itself, unity being the criterion for exact replacement. The value of the function as a measure of actual reproduction is, however, small, as there are serious objections to ignoring mortality and to combining fertility rates at different ages in the same calendar year. To this statement there are two qualifications. First, the use of a 'generation' approach is possible and would remove a major objection. Secondly, the unweighted addition of i_x is a justifiable procedure for obtaining an index of fertility, if not of reproduction.

Table 16.3. *Calculation of woman's gross reproduction rate for year X*

| Age-group | Number of women | Number of births | | | Fertility rate (4) ÷ (1) |
		Legitimate	Illegitimate	Total	
	(1)	(2)	(3)	(4)	(5)
15–19	9,000	100	40	140	0·0156
20–24	9,200	1,300	12	1,312	0·1426
25–29	8,900	1,065	2	1,067	0·1199
30–34	8,600	711	—	711	0·0827
35–39	8,400	468	—	468	0·0557
40–44	8,500	160	—	160	0·0188
Total	52,600	3,804	54	3,858	0·4353

16.22 Analysis of gross reproduction rates

Changes in gross reproduction rates can be analysed into their component parts. If the rates are considered only as indexes of fertility, such analyses can be valuable. The function ^si_x in expression (16.28) may be expressed as the sum of its legitimate and illegitimate components as follows:

$$^si_x = (mw)_x \cdot {}^mi_x + \left[1 - (mw)_x\right] \cdot {}^ui_x, \tag{16.29}$$

where $(mw)_x$ is the proportion married at age x among the sex under consideration and ^mi_x, ^ui_x are the fertility rates of married and unmarried women (or men) respectively.

If the experience of a second year is indicated by accented function throughout, then

$$^si'_x - {}^si_x = (mw)'_x {}^mi'_x + \left[1 - (mw)'_x\right] \cdot {}^ui'_x - (mw)_x \cdot {}^mi_x - \left[1 - (mw)_x\right] {}^ui_x,$$

or, by rearranging the right-hand side,

$$\begin{aligned}^si'_x - {}^si_x = (mw)_x \cdot ({}^mi'_x - {}^mi_x) &+ \left[1 - (mw)_x\right]({}^ui'_x - {}^ui_x) \\ &+ \left[(mw)'_x - (mw)_x\right]({}^mi'_x - {}^ui'_x).\end{aligned} \tag{16.30}$$

The first two expressions on the right-hand side represent the effects of the changes in legitimate and illegitimate fertility respectively; the third shows the effect of the change in proportions married.

The summation of expression (16.30) for all values of x thus provides an analysis of the difference between two gross reproduction rates into the amounts contributed by alterations in the three elements: legitimate fertility, illegitimate fertility and proportions married.

From the data given in tables 6.3 and 6.4, the gross reproduction rate in year Y was 1·059. Using the above method of analysis, the difference of 0·001 from the corresponding value in year X (1·060) is due to a growth in the proportion married, mainly at ages 20–24, in year Y, to the extent (as regards the reproduction rate) of 0·041; this was almost entirely offset by a fall of 0·038 caused by the lower legitimate fertility. The contribution of the slight change in illegitimate fertility was only 0·004. Thus

$$1\cdot059 \text{ (year } Y) = 1\cdot060 \text{ (year } X) - 0\cdot038 - 0\cdot004 + 0\cdot041.$$

In obtaining these results, X has been treated as the year with accented functions and Y as the year with unaccented functions.

The calculation of the difference due to legitimate fertility is shown in table 16.4. Hence the effect on the gross reproduction rate $= 5 \times 0\cdot0156 \times 0\cdot487$ (see § 16.21) $= 0\cdot038$.

Table 16.4. *Analysis of differences in legitimate fertility between years X and Y*

Age-group	Proportion of women married in year Y (from table 6.3)	Excess in legitimate fertility rate in year X (from table 6.4)	(1) × (2)
	(1)	(2)	(3)
15–19	0·118	0·010	0·0012
20–24	0·626	0·010	0·0063
25–29	0·809	0·010	0·0081
30–34	0·916	—	—
35–39	0·926	—	—
40–44	0·927	—	—
Total			0·0156

16.23   Net reproduction rates

It was shown in § 16.21 that an index of fertility could be formed by summing for all ages the fertility rates of persons of either sex, and that if the fertility under consideration was limited to issue of the same sex as the parent, then this index was called the gross reproduction rate. It was further explained that this rate had some significance in connexion with the measurement of the replacement of one generation of people by another, but that the omission of any adjustment for losses attributable to mortality was one of a number of factors that rendered the index rather artificial for this purpose. Using life-table factors, it is possible to make some allowance for such mortality losses. These factors are of the form l_x/l_0, or $_xp_0$, and if they are calculated on the basis of a life table constructed from the experience of the relevant sex in the same country in the same period as for the fertility rates, then the result is called the net reproduction rate, viz.

$$\sum_{x=0}^{\infty} {}^s_x p_0 \cdot {}^s i_x \qquad (16.31)$$

As an index of fertility, this function is perhaps less useful than the gross reproduction rate, because exactly equal and constant weights at all ages are easier to explain and use than the slightly unequal and variable weights $_xp_0$. As a measure of reproduction, however, the net rate is less unrealistic than the gross rate and therefore preferable to it. Nevertheless, the net reproduction rate based on the fertility experience of a given year is nowadays regarded as of little importance as a measure of reproduction. Formula (16.31) is valuable only if based on the experience of a generation. In practice, the net reproduction rate exhibits about as much variation from year to

315

year as does the crude birth rate, whereas the underlying idea of true reproductivity is of something more fundamental, constant and unaffected by short-term fluctuations.

The value of the net reproduction rate corresponding to the gross rate of 1·06 mentioned in § 16.21 might be of the order of 1·00, in an economically well-developed country. Mortality now has little effect on rates of reproduction in developed countries, as may be seen from table 16.5.

As will be seen from chapter 18, however, the net reproduction rate is a function of central importance in the mathematics of 'stable' populations,

Table 16.5. *Indexes of the trend of fertility in England and Wales since 1841*

Years	Average annual crude birth rate per thousand population	Average annual number of legitimate births per thousand married women aged 15—45	Approximate average women's reproduction rate	
			Gross	Net
1841—5	32·3†	*	2·25	1·30
1846—50	32·9†	*	2·25	1·30
1851—5	33·9†	281†	2·25	1·35
1856—60	34·3	281	2·25	1·35
1861—5	35·1	285	2·25	1·40
1866—70	35·3	289	2·30	1·40
1871—5	35·3	295	2·35	1·45
1876—80	35·3	206	2·35	1·45
1881—5	33·5	282	2·25	1·50
1886—90	31·3	267	2·10	1·45
1891—5	30·5	258	2·00	1·40
1896—1900	29·3	242	1·85	1·30
1901—5	28·2	230	1·70	1·25
1906—10	26·3	213	1·60	1·20
1911—15	23·6	191	1·45	1·15
1916—20	20·1	157	1·35	1·10
1921—5	19·9	157	1·30	1·10
1926—30	16·7	131	1·10	0·95
1931—5	15·.0	115	0·87	0·78
1936—40	14·7†	107‡	0·87‡	0·79‡
1941—5	15·9	105	0·96	0·88
1946—50	18·0	122	1·15	1·11
1951—5	15·3	105	1·05	1·02
1956—60	16·4	113	1·20	1·16
1961—5	18·1	126	1·40	1·36
1966—70	16·8	118	1·20	1·17

* Not available.
† May be understated owing to incompleteness of registration.
‡ The figures for 1939 and onwards are based on the number of births actually occurring in the year, whereas those for earlier periods relate to the numbers registered in the year; the effect of the change on the figures shown is unimportant.

because it can be developed by logical methods as representing the rate of growth over a generation if certain conditions rigidly apply.

Various other forms of reproduction rate may be encountered in demographic literature. They have usually been constructed in an attempt either to reconcile the differences between the rates for the two sexes or to eliminate the effect of variations in proportions married by the use of marriage standardization. The modifications so made have been ingenious, but none of them has mitigated the fundamental objection that reproduction rates based on the experience of calendar years do not measure true reproductivity.

Net reproduction rates can be analysed in a manner similar to that appropriate to gross reproduction rates (compare § 16.22). The following equation is self-evident:

$$ {}^{s}i'_x \cdot {}^{s}_{x}p'_0 - {}^{s}i_x \cdot {}^{s}_{x}p_0 = {}^{s}_{x}p_0({}^{s}i'_x - {}^{s}i_x) + {}^{s}i'_x({}^{s}_{x}p'_0 - {}^{s}_{x}p_0). \tag{16.32} $$

The first term on the right-hand side of (16.32) may be broken down into its three components, as in equation (16.30), while the second term represents the contribution of the changed mortality.

16.24 Marriage standardization in fertility analyses

In analyses of differential fertility, differential marriage experience may complicate the picture. Thus married women in each age-group may have differing numbers of children, not because (or not wholly because) of disparities in fertility but because — at least in part — of disparities in marriage duration. In one social class, married women aged 25–29 might have an average duration of (say) 7 years but in another they might have an average duration of 3 years — because later marriage was common in that other class. This would affect current fertility, and more especially the total number of children borne to date. Use has been made of 'marriage standardization' to bring out more clearly the contribution of fertility differences. In this process, for instance, the distribution of married women by age and duration in the country as a whole might be used as a basis (direct method) and to this would be applied the fertility rates, classified by age and duration, of each separate class. The results could then be summed up on one index figure or in separate indexes for each age-group.

If the experience of married and unmarried women together was being analysed, standardization could be effected by marital status. If that of men and women had been combined, standardization by sex might be used.

In the differential fertility analyses for England and Wales associated with the 1961 Census, a number of indexes of this kind were shown. For instance, the following figures relate to the ratio of the fertility of workers in the food, drink and tobacco industries to the fertility of all workers:

317

	Standardized for marriage duration	Unstandardized for marriage duration
Mean family size		
Standardized for age	1·02	0·97
Unstandardized for age	1·04	0·98
Proportion infertile		
Standardized for age	0·94	0·97
Unstandardized for age	0·90	0·94
Fertility rate		
Standardized for age	1·01	1·14
Unstandardized for age	1·03	1·17

16.25 Standardization of fertility for age or duration of marriage

A simple kind of age-standardization of fertility is involved in the calculation of Area Comparability Factors. These are arrived at by means of multiplications similar to those for mortality described in § 16.14 above. The proportion of the number of women aged 18–44 to the total population has been calculated for the whole country, and for each local area. The comparability factor is then the ratio of the national proportion to the local proportion. The crude birth rate for any area may be corrected by multiplication by the comparability factor, thus arriving at an adjusted rate.

In the example given in § 6.13, the difference between years X and Y may, of course, be due to a changed durational distribution of marriages or to others of the many types of variation which have been mentioned in the preceding paragraphs. In the long term it may be a quite unimportant variation, not deserving of close attention. The matter may be investigated by studying any other available fertility information, for example births analysed by duration of parity. Standardization in respect of either or both of these elements would then be a possibility.

Henry's method involves the use of the formula

$$(\text{number of } n\text{th births in year } Y) \left/ \sum_{t=1}^{\infty} x_t \cdot b_t^{n-1} \right. \qquad (16.33)$$

where b_t^{n-1} is the number of $(n-1)$th births t years before Y; x_t is a factor, derived from the experience of Czechoslovakia, relating to the frequency of birth of children in the family (see § 6.15 above).

16.26 Reproductivity

For many purposes it is desirable to know the underlying truth about population trends; one way in which an assessment may be made is to 'project' the population, that is, to estimate its future development on the basis of suitable assumptions as to the course of fertility and mortality. The uncertainties attaching to estimates of future fertility render this method somewhat speculative. A correct assessment of current reproductivity would often be more valuable. Indeed, it might almost be said that the chief practical aim in studying fertility is to determine the real tendencies in population size; these can have a tremendous impact on the social and economic life of a nation.

As has been indicated, however, reproduction is essentially a matter for study in terms of completed generations. All too frequently, accurate knowledge is available only in respect of events so long past as to be of little value as pointers to the present state of affairs. It is difficult to measure current reproductivity without the importation of some element of speculation as to the future. For this reason, demographers often prefer to study relatively stable elements in fertility, such as average family size, rather than its more variable components, so as to minimize uncertainties.

Nevertheless, attempts have been made, in the past, to improve the validity and usefulness of reproduction rates, and some examples of the kind of work that has been done are given in the following sections.

16.27 Sex differences in reproduction rates

In many European countries, conventional reproduction rates assessed in relation to the experience of men have exceeded the corresponding rates for women. Surpluses of up to 20 per cent have been recorded. One reason for this is that the length of a generation is greater for men than for women. Values of 33 years and 29 years respectively might be taken as typical. It is shown in chapter 18 that, in stable population mathematics, the net reproduction rate is approximately equal to $(1 + r)^G$, where r is the intrinsic annual rate of population growth and G is the average length of a generation. Thus it is not surprising that the male reproduction rate is greater than the female (where r is positive).

There are other reasons why the net reproduction rates for the sexes are not the same. Different mortality is one. Fertility within a given marriage is the same for men and women, except in regard to its incidence by age. It is, however, not marital fertility but all-men's and all-women's fertility that appears in expression (16.28). This may be regarded as being the product of the 'stock' element of proportion married and the 'flow' element of marital fertility. The proportion married is the chief cause of sex differences in reproduction rates; for whereas in a monogamous population the number of married men and women must be equal (except where one of the couple has migrated) the total numbers of men and women need not be so. The proportion of male to female births exceeds unity, but excess male mortality (especially in wartime) and emigration have frequently led to relatively

319

small male numbers at the reproductive ages, and hence to relatively high proportions married and high reproduction rates. (The reverse tends to be true in countries to which male emigrants are moving.)

16.28 Other attempts to measure reproductivity

In a paper published by the British Royal Commission on Population, Hajnal inquired whether by importing successive refinements into the net reproduction rate — for instance, by taking into account marriage duration or order of birth — demographers could ever reach a true measure of reproduction. The requirements of such a true measure were suggested as being (a) that it should summarize experience rates, the maintenance of which would not 'involve any changes which make it unlikely that these rates will continue in operation', and (b) that it should properly reflect fundamental characteristics of the population and not merely the temporary aspects of the situation in a given year. In our present state of knowledge, he argued, these requirements cannot be fulfilled. Instead of attempting to refine the net reproduction rate, therefore, he turned to a reconsideration of the underlying assumptions on which it is based. Hajnal used various combinations of these types of information to produce a number of different reproduction rates adjusted or developed in various ways. He obtained results varying from 0·81 to 1·00 and admitted that 'the variety of reproduction rates is only a reflection of the limits of knowledge about demographic prospects'.

The Royal Commission decided that an optimum measure of replacement would be obtained by the use of 'stock' data — average family sizes according to marriage duration — for fertility (see illustrative figures in table 16.6) and 'flow' data for marriage. This particular combination was considered suitable at that time, but would not automatically be suitable for use on all occasions.

Redington and Clarke, in their review of the work of the Commission, suggested that a table should be compiled showing the total number of live female births before age x to women born in a given year, according to age of women (and preferably subdivided to show the proportion of women who had had 0, 1, 2, 3 ... children — this is a 'cohort' study.

The following are a selection of estimated 'generation replacement rates' for England and Wales; the years shown are groups of calendar years of birth:

1848—53	1·358
1868—73	1·093
1888—93	0·806
1908—13	0·704
1928—33	0·963
1948—53	1·038

Table 16.6. *Estimated average number of births to cohorts of married women reaching similar durations of marriage at the end of (a) 1938 and (b) 1948, Britain*

(Women whose first marriages terminated before they reached age 45 are excluded)

	End of 1938		End of 1948		
Number of years since end of calendar year in which the group of couples were married (1)	Year of marriage (2)	Average number of births per married couple (3)	Year of marriage (4)	Average number of births per married couple (5)	Number of births to end of 1948 as a percentage of corresponding duration group in 1939 (6)
1	1937	0·40	1947	*	*
2	1936	0·64	1946	*	*
3	1935	0·84	1945	*	*
4	1934	1·02	1944	1·01	99
5	1933	1·16	1943	1·20	104
6	1932	1·31	1942	1·26	96
7	1931	1·43	1941	1·42	100
8	1930	1·56	1940	1·46	93
9	1929	1·61	1939	1·56	97
10	1928	1·71	1938	1·70	100
11	1927	1·80	1937	1·75	97
12	1926	1·89	1936	1·82	96
13	1925	1·99	1935	1·89	95
14	1924	2·09	1934	1·92	92
15	1923	2·15	1933	1·96	91
16	1922	2·23	1932	2·02	91
17	1921	2·34	1931	2·04	87
18	1920	2·47	1930	2·12	86
19	1919	2·60	1929	2·11	81
20	1918	2·51	1928	2·12	84
21	1917	2·50	1927	2·16	86

* Not available.

Of the increase from 1908–13 to 1948–53, about one-half is attributable to improved mortality, one-quarter to higher proportions marrying and one-quarter to increased family size.

16.29 Joint reproduction rate

A number of writers have suggested methods by which the fertility experience of the sexes could be combined in a single measure instead of remaining separate. Pollard, for instance, developed formulae in terms of the probability that a male aged x would have a female child and the probability that a female aged x would have a male child. Reproduction was considered over a period of two generations. He thus arrived at a 'joint

321

reproduction rate' which was equal to the product of the male and female reproduction rates.

As indexes of fertility, the joint reproduction rate and its square root are useful measures, more especially as it is reasonable to suppose that where the male and female functions differ a better result lies between them. The mathematical analysis involves some improbabilities, however, and many of the principal disadvantages of reproduction rates are not eliminated by this ingenious approach.

Another way of dealing with the problem of disagreements between the data for the sexes separately has been to study the discrepancies and the conditions under which they occur. Efforts have also been made to establish principles of 'dominance' by which the data for one sex could be shown to have more significance than the data for the other because the first was 'dominant'; for example, if marriages occurred more at the behest of the man than the woman, or if births happened more because of the wishes of the husband than of those of the wife, then the male sex would be dominant. These interesting speculations have not, however, solved any of the important problems of fertility measurement or indexing.

16.30   Use of life tables in studies of migration

Where statistics of migration are not available, or are suspected to be incomplete, life-table functions can be used in conjunction with the data obtained at two successive censuses in order to make an estimate of the net migratory movement. Suppose that at a census in 1953 the number of women enumerated at age 34 was A and that at a census in 1964 the number of women enumerated at age 45 was B. The expected number of women in 1964 at age 45 would, on the basis of mortality alone, be $Al_{45} \div l_{34}$ (provided that the life table employed was appropriate). Thus the difference

$$B - A \cdot l_{45}/l_{34} \tag{16.34}$$

is an estimate of the net migratory movement. It is of course important that errors due to misstatements of age should be eliminated, as far as possible, for example, by age-grouping.

16.31   Economic effects of a change in age-distribution

How much a member of a population can contribute towards the production of the goods and services necessary for the well-being of the community in which he lives depends upon his age; how much he needs to draw from the common pool for his subsistence is again associated with age, although in a smaller degree. Production and consumption also differ between the sexes. In order to illustrate the economic influence of an alteration in the structure of a population by sex and age, systems of proportional values have from time to time been devised. As with many economic measurements, precision is impracticable, but a broad idea of the relative importance of the various demographic groups may be obtained from the factors in the following statement; the figures, which were quoted by Abrams, show the effects of sex and age on production and consumption:

Age-group	Producer units		Consumer units	
	Males	Females	Males	Females
0–4	—	—	0·33	0·33
5–14	—	—	0·50	0·50
15–24	0·83	0·62	1·00	0·85
25–44	2·50	0·38	1·00	0·85
45–64	2·50	0·25	1·00	0·85
65 and over	0·83	0·12	0·60	0·60

From test calculations using units such as these, it seems probable that in the first half of the present century the demographic developments in some Western European countries gave rise to a favourable change economically owing to an increase in the proportion of producers and a decrease in the proportion of consumers. This was in part the effect of the upward move ment of the 'bulge' in the population pyramid which was also — for a time — a favourable feature from the point of view of reproduction.

A much simpler mode of presentation of the economic effects of a changing age-distribution is often employed. It consists of exhibiting the ratios of the numbers of persons aged (say) 65 and over to the total population size or, better, to the number of persons aged 15—64, at different times or in dif ferent countries. If children are included in the calculation, they are some times given a 'weight' of one third that of adults, though if the cost of their education were included a higher ratio might be justified.

SELECT BIBLIOGRAPHY

Benjamin, B. *Health and Vital Statistics* (Allen and Unwin, London 1968).

Hajnal, J. 'Births, Marriages and Reproductivity in England and Wales, 1938—47', in *Reports and Selected Papers of the Statistics Committee of the Royal Commission on Population* (London, 1950).

Yule, G. U. 'On some Points relating to Vital Statistics, more especially Statistics of Occupational Mortality', *Journal of the Royal Statistical Society*, **97** (1934), 1.

'Indexes of Mortality and Tests of their Statistical Significance', *Human Biology*, **38** (1966), 280.

Kitagawa, E. M. 'Standardized Comparisons in Population Research', *Demography*, **1**, (1964), 296.

17 Techniques of population projection

17.1 Calculations on an international scale

The most notable assessments involving several countries at one time are those made by the Population Division of the UN Organization on a world-wide basis. The methods adopted are necessarily those appropriate to countries with limited demographic data, for a more refined approach would be possible for only a relatively small part of the population of the globe. The first projections, made quite early in the history of the Organization, were on a relatively simple basis of extrapolation of curves representing crude birth rates and death rates for groups of regions. In a second approach, the same system was carried out in greater detail as to area, but in a third assessment the method employed was one of population models. Particulars of the method of calculation in the fourth and most elaborate exercise are not available, but still closer attention than before was devoted to the individual circumstances of sub-regions and countries. The results of these projections are discussed in chapter 14 above. Simplified methods of projection have also been devised by the UN Population Commission for the use of relatively unskilled staff in under-developed and partly-developed countries. The principal elements of the methods are (a) a standard series of model life tables by means of which future improvements in longevity could be estimated, and (b) a discussion of methods of appraisal and correction of incomplete and inaccurate birth and death registration data.

Series of population projections are sometimes made for several countries at the same time. In such exercises there is a tendency to try to find some feature common to all the countries concerned, such as a uniform curve of mortality improvement or a connexion between fertility trends in the various areas.

17.2 Essentials of the component method

Where mathematical curves for the total population are to be used, a straight-forward application of formulae such as those set out in § 9.8 above is all that is necessary. But calculations of future population by the component method may be made in a variety of ways. The minimum data requirements are (a) the age-distribution of the commencing population, (b) a set of

324

mortality factors (which can be most conveniently expressed for the purpose in the form of survival ratios) and (*c*) a set of fertility factors: the sets in (*b*) and (*c*) being associated with age. Given the initial population and the mortality factors, the projection can proceed very simply according to the pattern illustrated in fig. 17.1:

Age	Starting population (year 0)	Survival factor for one year	Population in year 1	Population in year 2	Population in year 3
23	$^0P_{23}$	p_{23}	—	—	—
24	$^0P_{24}$	p_{24}	$^0P_{23}\cdot p_{23} = {}^1P_{24}$	—	—
25	$^0P_{25}$	p_{25}	$^0P_{24}\cdot p_{24} = {}^1P_{25}$	$^1P_{24}\cdot p_{24} = {}^2P_{25}$	—
26	$^0P_{26}$	p_{26}	$^0P_{25}\cdot p_{25} = {}^1P_{26}$	$^1P_{25}\cdot p_{25} = {}^2P_{26}$	$^2P_{25}\cdot p_{25} = {}^3P_{26}$
27	—	—	$^0P_{26}\cdot p_{26} = {}^1P_{27}$	$^1P_{26}\cdot p_{26} = {}^2P_{27}$	$^2P_{26}\cdot p_{26} = {}^3P_{27}$
28	—	—	—	$^1P_{27}\cdot p_{27} = {}^2P_{28}$	$^2P_{27}\cdot p_{27} = {}^3P_{28}$
29	—	—	—	—	$^2P_{28}\cdot p_{28} = {}^3P_{29}$
—	—	—	—	—	—
—	—	—	—	—	—
—	—	—	—	—	—

Fig. 17.1. Pattern of population projection by the component method.

Assuming that the populations are tabulated at age x last birthday, the survival factors p_x represent (approximately) $1 - q_{x-\frac{1}{2}}$. The products are entered at one age lower at one step to the right, and thus the calculations proceed diagonally downwards. The survival factors need not remain constant, as in fig. 17.1, but can be changed as often as required as the years roll on.

In order to assess the number of infants aged under 1 year in year N, it would be suitable on this method to multiply the population in year $N - 1$ at each age by the appropriate fertility factor, and then to sum up the products for all ages. This process would give an estimate of the number of births in the period of 12 months between year $N - 1$ and year N. Multiplying this by an appropriate survival factor ($L_0 \div l_0$), the expected number of infants at age 0 last birthday in year N would then be obtained; this could be entered in the diagram, and then successively 'survived' down a diagonal.

As fertility in human populations begins effectively at age 15 (say), it is possible for the whole projection to proceed in the following stages:

(1) assess the population at ages N and over in the Nth year ahead for as many values of N as required;

(2) estimate the number of births in as many future years as required, but not exceeding 14 years at this stage, and the corresponding number of infants;

(3) enter the number of infants in future years, as estimated at (2), in the projection schedule and calculate their survivors for all future years, thus

arriving at the whole projected population for each of years 1—14 and the populations at age $N - 15$ and over in later years;

(4) assess the births in years 15 ... (maximum 29) as in (2), and their survivors as in (3);

and so in 15-year stages until all requirements are fulfilled.

17.3 Flow chart

A flow-chart, suitable for use in conjunction with the component method of population projection, is illustrated in fig. 17.2. It is envisaged that constant fertility and mortality rates, specific for age, would be used; that migrants would be 'fed in' at each age in each year; that the exercise would be carried forward for $5N$ years, and that the results would be printed out for every fifth year.

17.4 Projection matrices

In mathematics, a matrix is an algebraic array involving $n \, . \, m$ variables, which is normally written as:

$$
M = \begin{vmatrix}
a_1 & b_1 & c_1 & \ldots & n_1 \\
a_2 & b_2 & c_2 & \ldots & n_2 \\
\cdot & \cdot & \cdot & & \cdot \\
\cdot & \cdot & \cdot & & \cdot \\
a_m & b_m & c_m & \ldots & n_m
\end{vmatrix}
$$

A vector is defined as a matrix with one column only, namely

$$
V = \begin{vmatrix}
a \\
b \\
c \\
d \\
\cdot \\
\cdot \\
\cdot \\
m
\end{vmatrix}
$$

The mathematical theory of matrices and vectors incorporates rules for the addition and multiplication of matrices and vectors. It so happens that the rule for multiplying a vector and a matrix together provides an outcome which corresponds to the procedures described in § 17.2, where V represents the starting population, and M represents the fertility and mortality factors set out as described below. Thus the process of projection by the component method may be written as

$$
V \, . \, M. \tag{17.1}
$$

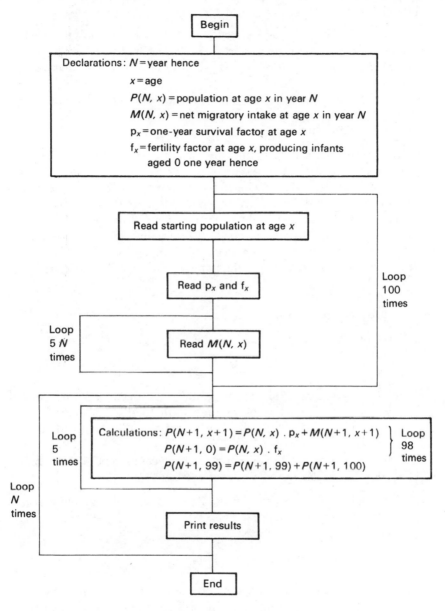

Fig. 17.2. Illustrative flow-chart for a population projection by the component method.

If V shows the initial members of people written down age by age or age-group by age-group from 0 to (say) 100, then M is a matrix consisting of:

(1) in the top row, the age-related fertility factors, running from left to right as the age increases (including zeros for ages 0–14);

(2) in the second line, the first-year survival factor p_0, and then a series of zeros;

(3) in the third line, first a zero, then the second-year survival factor, p_1, and then a series of zeros;

(4) in the fourth line, 0, 0, p_2, 0, 0 ... and so on.

In this way, the mathematical rules and theorems concerning matrices and vectors can be used to study the projection process and its outcome. Such methods are of particular value in relation to stable population mathematics. Thus, Keyfitz has used them, with the aid of an electronic computer, to make projections for a very long period ahead, and thus to measure the rate of growth in the ultimate state, and to verify its asymptotic tendency. (With or without mathematical treatment, electronic computers are very suitable for use in projection work, owing to the iterative nature of the processes.)

17.5   Projection formulae

In British official projections, the basic formula is given as follows:

$$ {}^nP_x = {}^{n-1}P_{x-1} (1 - {}^{n-1}q_{x-\frac{1}{2}}) \pm {}^nM_x \qquad (17.2) $$

where ${}^nP_x$ = number of persons at mid-year n aged x last birthday;
${}^nM_x$ = net number of migrants in the period mid-year $n - 1$ to mid-year n who were aged x last birthday at mid-year n;
${}^{n-1}q_{x-\frac{1}{2}}$ = probability of death within a year for a person aged $x - 1$ last birthday at mid-year $n - 1$.

The mortality of migrants between the date of migration and mid-year n is small and has been ignored.

At age 0, the formula used was:

$$ {}^nP_0 = {}^nB(1 - {}^{n-1}\tfrac{1}{2}q_0) \pm {}^nM_0 $$

where ${}^nB$ = number of live births in period mid-year $n - 1$ to mid-year n;
${}^nM_0$ = net number of migrants in same period who were under age 1 at mid-year n;
${}^{n-1}\tfrac{1}{2}q_0$ = probability that a baby born in the period mid-year $n - 1$ to mid-year n will die before the end of that period.

The work is carried out on a computer by a programme that provides figures for each sex, for single years of age and for each future year for the next forty years.

17.6 The use of marriage rates

The methods outlined in §§ 17.3 and 17.4 above are based on fertility rates specific for age but irrespective of sex or marital status. In practice, calculations are usually made separately for each sex, and future births are assessed on the basis of fertility data for women. The work can, however, be refined, where it seems appropriate to do so, by making specific allowance also for marital status. The relative merits of proportions married and marriage rates, and of aggregate and select fertility rates, as indicators have already been discussed.

Thus the number of births could be obtained as the sum of the following items:

(1) births on the assumption of no migration after the starting date of the projections:

    (*a*) births to women married once only;

    (*b*) births to remarried women;

    (*c*) illegitimate births; and

(2) effect of the assumed net inward migration.

To estimate the principal item, (1)(*a*), one might thus analyse the expected female population at annual intervals for the next fifteen years according to marital status. Then a series of expected mean ultimate family sizes, varying according to year of marriage, could be decided upon. From these, a set of fertility rates could be derived, classified by age at marriage, year of marriage and duration of marriage, and this set could be applied to the numbers of once-married women. Less elaborate methods would be needed for items other than (1) (*a*).

The example that will now be followed through in detail, in order to illustrate techniques of projection, involves the separation of marital statuses. Marriage and fertility rates have been analysed only by age; thus variations by marriage duration have not been directly taken into account. (Due consideration is assumed to have been given to the influence of duration in the choice of an aggregate basis, which should then produce results broadly similar to those obtained by the use of a more refined process.) The use of marriage rates and the segregation of spinsters, married women and widows is illustrated as an operation of some technical interest and not as the approach to be made in normal circumstances. It is important not to make calculations in greater detail than the conditions warrant and, having regard to the possible extent to which the actual marriage and fertility rates experienced in

329

future may differ from the assumptions made, the demographer may well decide in practice that the additional work involved in their use is not justified.

Fundamentally, as indicated in § 7.2, only two types of calculation schedule are needed: the first, an example of which is shown in table 17.1, is for estimating the future survivors of the population; the second is for working out the numbers of births in any period, of which table 17.5 gives an example. Within this general framework there can be many variations of detail, for instance according to the width of the age-groupings employed. Tables 17.1–17.5 show how the women's population could be projected for five years on given mortality, marriage and fertility bases; similar methods would apply in the case of men. Nothing important is omitted by not carrying this illustrative calculation further, as the general process for each succeeding quinquennium would be no different; only the factors and resulting assessments would be altered.

It is assumed for the purposes of this illustration that the projection will be made on a desk calculator, and not on an electronic computer. The survival and other factors which have been employed are arbitrary, and have not been derived directly from any factual experience; at the same time, they have been chosen so that the projected population at the end of the five years is of not unreasonable size and distribution.

17.7   Projection of total female population

The numbers shown in column (1) of table 17.1 were taken from a Census Volume. The first point to be considered is whether any adjustments are needed, and can conveniently be made, for misstatements and omissions in the data. In order to allow for any understatement in the numbers of young children, the estimated numbers of survivors of the preceding five years' births were used instead of the enumerated population at ages 0–4; this adjustment is similar to that made in recent English life tables for the purpose of obtaining mortality rates. Minor errors of age were largely eliminated by the use of quinary age-groupings. Apart from these 'corrections', the census data have been used without amendment.

A further series of possible adjustments to the data arise from special classes, such as persons in the armed forces overseas and in the merchant navy afloat at the time of the census and therefore not enumerated. For some purposes it might be necessary to include these; but as table 17.1 relates only to the female sex the figures in column (1) hardly require augmentation. Other examples of adjustments to the commencing population that might be required according to circumstances, are war casualties not provided for in the mortality basis, and special migratory movements.

The factors in column (2) relate to all-women's mortality. It may be noted in passing that it is not essential to use for this purpose functions derived from the latest published national life table. Survival ratios based on more recent experience can rapidly be evaluated by a variety of approximate methods. For example, it is possible to calculate the ratios of the crude mortality rates in any year to those of the years around the last census, in quinary age-groups, and to use them to adjust the mortality rates in the national life table relating to that census.

It is not essential to graduate the adjusting factors or the final rates, though in some circumstances to do so may be convenient and desirable. To smooth the set of mortality rates used is, however, of much less importance than to pay adequate attention to the appropriateness of the bases for marital status and fertility, and it would in fact be inconsistent to graduate unless the marriage and fertility rates used were similarly treated, a procedure which is unlikely to be necessary.

The formula for the factors in column (2) of the table is of the type:

$$\int_5^{10} l_{x+n}\,dn \bigg/ \int_0^5 l_{x+n}\,dn \qquad (17.3)$$

or for practical purposes (except at ages 0—4)

$$\sum_{n=5}^{9} l_{x+n+\frac{1}{2}} \bigg/ \sum_{n=0}^{4} l_{x+n+\frac{1}{2}}. \qquad (17.4)$$

These are approximations, as the actual age-distribution of the population within a group does not necessarily correspond to that of the life table. Other approximations may be appropriate according to the circumstances of the case; for example $_5p_{x+2}$ might be used. The age-group 0—4 requires special consideration owing to the heavy mortality in the first year of life.

The choice of quinary age-groupings was made with a view to reducing the amount of arithmetical calculation involved while maintaining a sufficient degree of accuracy. The interval between the years for which the projected population will be available must depend on the width of the age-groupings used, because persons in the age-group x to $x + n$ now will be aged $x + n$ to $x + 2n$ in precisely n years' time. Consideration must, therefore, be given to both these points together in practice. For approximate calculations, the population for a year lying between two years for which the numbers have been calculated by projection may be obtained by first difference interpolation, but this method would not be sufficiently accurate for detailed work.

In practice, table 17.1 would normally be completed by the addition of subtotals for certain wider age-groups of special interest, such as 0—14, 15—44, 45—64 and 65 and over. It must be borne in mind that the numbers in 1976 relate, not to the middle of the year, but to the census date.

Table 17.1. *Projection of female population*

(Numbers in thousands.)

Age-group	Population at 1971 Census	Survival factor for 5 years	Projected population in 1976 (1) × (2)
	(1)	(2)	(3)
0—4	1,486·2	0·9850	1,363·5*
5—9	1,644·8	0·9930	1,463·9
10—14	1,586·8	0·9924	1,633·3
15—19	1,725·0	0·9877	1,574·7
20—24	1,795·3	0·9861	1,703·8
25—29	1,728·1	0·9852	1,770·3
30—34	1,622·0	0·9814	1,702·5
35—39	1,520·0	0·9745	1,591·8
40—44	1,434·2	0·9624	1,481·2
45—49	1,367·4	0·9489	1,380·3
50—54	1,265·3	0·9273	1,297·5
55—59			1,173·3
—			
—			
—			
Total			

* From table 17.5.

17.8 Calculation of the numbers of marriages

The first three columns of table 17.2 are similar in character to those of table 17.1 but here it is necessary to make calculations only in respect of the fertile ages. So far as the period 1971—6 is concerned the main purpose of the table is to obtain the expected numbers of first marriages during the period, and their survivors as married women in 1976; but it is also necessary, in order to prepare for projections beyond 1976, to calculate the numbers of spinsters in 1976, and hence the second and third columns have to be inserted. The method of procedure in columns (1), (2) and (3) is the same as for table 17.1, and the formula for the survival factors is of the same type. In this case, however, the numbers living must be calculated from a double decrement table with contingencies of death and marriage. The mortality rates used should be those appropriate to spinsters.

If $(fm)_{x+n}$ be the number of spinsters' marriages at age $x + n$ last birthday in the double decrement table, then, in respect of spinsters aged x exactly, the number of marriages in the ensuing five years is proportionate to:

$$\sum_{n=0}^{4} (fm)_{x+n} = (f)_x \quad \text{(say),} \qquad (17.5)$$

Table 17.2. *Projection of spinster population and of first marriages*
(Numbers in thousands.)

Age-group	Spinster population at 1971 Census	Survival factor as spinsters for 5 years	Estimated spinster population in 1976	Factor to obtain number surviving as married women after 5 years	Estimated number of surviving married women in 1976 (1) × (4)
	(1)	(2)	(3)	(4)	(5)
10–14	1,586·8	0·9775	1,633·3*	0·0148	—
15–19	1,693·8	0·7142	1,551·1	0·2722	23·5
20–24	1,332·1	0·4618	1,209·7	0·5196	461·1
25–29	702·1	0·5406	615·2	0·4324	692·2
30–34	403·3	0·7756	379·6	0·1909	303·6
35–39	313·0	0·8621	312·8	0·1023	77·0
40–44	260·0	0·9122	269·8	0·0500	32·0
45–49	229·2	—	237·2	—	13·0

* From table 17.1.

and, for the age-group x to $x + 4$ last birthday in 1971, to

$$\int_0^5 (f)_{x+t}dt. \tag{17.6}$$

In practice this may be written approximately as:

$$\tfrac{1}{2}(fm)_x + 1\tfrac{1}{2}(fm)_{x+1} + 2\tfrac{1}{2}(fm)_{x+2} + 3\tfrac{1}{2}(fm)_{x+3} + 4\tfrac{1}{2}(fm)_{x+4} +$$
$$4\tfrac{1}{2}(fm)_{x+5} + 3\tfrac{1}{2}(fm)_{x+6} + 2\tfrac{1}{2}(fm)_{x+7} + 1\tfrac{1}{2}(fm)_{x+8} + \tfrac{1}{2}(fm)_{x+9}$$
$$= (FM)_x \text{ (say).} \tag{17.7}$$

The factor to obtain the number of first marriages between mid-1971 and mid-1976 among spinsters aged x to $x + 4$ in 1971 is, therefore,

$$\frac{(FM)_x}{\sum_{n=0}^{4} l_{x+n+\frac{1}{2}}}, \tag{17.8}$$

where l represents the numbers alive or unmarried.

17.9 Survival between marriage and end of quinquennium

If the married woman's survival factor as a married woman for r years from age y be written as $_r p'_y$, the number of married women aged precisely $x + 5$ in 1976 with a duration of marriage under five years, arising from spinsters

333

aged x exactly in 1971, may be obtained by the following development of formula (17.5):

$$\sum_{n=0}^{4} (fm)_{x+n \cdot \, 4\frac{1}{2}-n}p'_{x+n+\frac{1}{2}} = (m)_x \quad \text{(say)}, \tag{17.9}$$

so that formula (17.6) is adjusted to:

$$\int_0^5 (m)_{x+t}dt. \tag{17.10}$$

For practical use it is probably sufficient to assume that the marriages take place at age $x + 5$ on average (see formula (17.7)) and hence that the survival factor for the women after marriage is

$$\frac{\displaystyle\sum_{n=5}^{9} l'_{x+n+\frac{1}{2}}}{5l'_{x+5}}. \tag{17.11}$$

This factor, multiplied by expression (17.8) above, is that employed in column (4) of table 17.2.

If desired, of course, the calculation of spinsters' marriages may be made at individual ages for the important years 20–30, but this should not normally be necessary in projections of this type.

17.10 Projection of numbers of married women

In table 17.3 the population of married women in 1971 is projected for five years using factors similar in form to those in column (2), table 17.1, but allowing for the element of widowhood as well as for mortality. Married women's mortality rates may be calculated conveniently in the same manner as that described for spinsters in the first paragraph of § 17.8. Widowhood rates are not generally available and must be obtained by calculation on the basis of married men's mortality used in conjunction with the relative age-distribution of husbands and wives at the latest census enumeration.

In column (4) of table 17.3 the numbers of married women in 1976 arising from spinster marriages 1971–6 are brought forward from table 17.2. Similarly, in column (5), the numbers of married women arising from the remarriages of widows and divorced persons are brought in from table 17.4.

17.11 Calculation of the numbers of remarriages

The number of remarriages is relatively small, and does not contribute more than about 1 per cent to the population of married women in any age-group. This is fortunate, because it permits approximate estimates of re-marriages to be substituted for exact calculations, which would be troublesome

334

Table 17.3. *Projection of married women population*
(Numbers in thousands.)

Age-group	Population of married women at 1971 Census	Survival factor for 5 years married women	Survivors of (1) in 1976 (1) × (2)	Survivors of 1971–6 marriages		Estimated population of married women in 1976 (3) + (4) + (5)
				Of spinsters (table 17.2 col. (5))	Of widows (table 17.4 col. (4))	
	(1)	(2)	(3)	(4)	(5)	(6)
15–19	31·1	0·9748	—	23·5	—	23·5
20–24	461·0	0·9719	30·3	461·1	0·4	491·8
25–29	1,014·4	0·9663	448·0	692·2	4·1	1,144·3
30–34	1,188·9	0·9572	980·2	303·6	10·5	1,294·3
35–39	1,147·4	0·9399	1,138·0	77·0	14·2	1,229·2
40–44	1,074·7	0·9133	1,078·4	32·0	11·9	1,122·3
45–49	1,002·2	—	981·5	13·0	6·8	1,001·3

Table 17.4. *Calculation of number of remarriages of widows and divorced women*
(Numbers in thousands.)

Age-group	Population of widows and divorced women at 1971 Census	Mean of numbers in (1) at ages x to $x + 4$ and $x - 5$ to $x - 1$	Factor to obtain number surviving as married women after 5 years	Number of surviving married women in 1976 (2) × (3)	Population of widows and divorced women in 1976 (table 17.5 col. (6) *minus* table 17.2 col. (3)
	(1)	(2)	(3)	(4)	(5)
15–19	0·1	—	—	—	0·1
20–24	2·3	1·2	0·3095	0·4	2·3
25–29	11·6	6·9	0·5934	4·1	10·8
30–34	29·8	20·7	0·5050	10·5	28·6
35–39	59·6	44·7	0·3169	14·2	49·8
40–44	99·5	79·6	0·1499	11·9	89·1
45–49	136·6	117·8	0·0580	6·8	141·8

to make. Difficulties arise, first, because divorced women should strictly be dealt with separately from widows, as their remarriage experience is different; secondly, because the numbers of remarriages in the quinquennium depend to some extent on the numbers of widowhoods in that period, which in turn depend on the remarriages themselves; thirdly, because 'select' remarriage rates should be used, and this would require very detailed calculation; fourthly, some adjustment should strictly be made to allow for

335

misstatements in marital status at the census enumeration; and finally, the corresponding estimate of the numbers of widows in 1976, even if made in detail, would not necessarily harmonize exactly with the difference between the numbers of all females and of spinsters and married women, so that special adjusting factors would have to be introduced to remove any inconsistencies.

Short methods are justified on practical grounds for the calculation of the numbers of remarriages in table 17.4. Assuming for convenience that the numbers of widows are constant during the quinquennium, average numbers exposed to the risk of remarriage are calculated in column (2), and factors similar in form to those in column (4) of table 17.2 are applied in column (3) to obtain the number of remarriages in column (4).

The results having been transferred to table 17.3 in order to calculate the numbers of married women in 1976, the estimated numbers of widows in 1976 may then be obtained by deducting the numbers of spinsters from the numbers of non-married females (shown in table 17.5), obtained in turn by deducting the numbers of married women from those for all women. The results are shown in column (5). A recalculation of column (4) making use of the information now available as to the projected numbers of widows in 1976 would reduce the number of remarriages by about 2,500 at ages under 50, which is of little importance having regard to the size of the population of married women.

17.12 Calculation of the numbers of births

Table 17.5 shows how suitable fertility rates (obtained by dividing the births at each age of mother by the numbers of potential mothers) may be applied to the populations of married and unmarried women in 1971 and 1976 (see remarks in §6.11 as to the appropriateness of relating all legitimate births to married women and illegitimate births to unmarried women). Hence the expected total number of births in the quinquennium is derived. Births are subdivided between males and females by using factors based on average experience (which varies very little from year to year in this respect) and then projected into the corresponding numbers in the first age-group in 1976 by the use of the factor

$$\int_0^5 l_t\, dt / 5l_0. \tag{17.12}$$

In times of rapid or sudden changes in the numbers in the women's age-groups or in the number of births, for example, in a period of demobilization following a major war, a more refined method may be substituted for the simple interpolation used in table 17.5.

For the purpose of formula (17.12), $\int_n^{n+1} l_t\, dt$ may be assumed to be

Table 17.5. *Calculation of numbers of future births and their survivors*
(Numbers in thousands.)

Age of mother	Legitimate fertility rate (applicable to married women)	Illegitimate fertility rate (applicable to spinsters and widows)	Number of women in 1971		Number of women in 1976		Number of births in 1971		Number of births in 1976	
			Married women (table 17.3 col. (1))	Spinsters and widows (table 17.2 col. (1)) *plus* table 17.4 col. (1))	Married women (table 17.3 col. (6))	Spinsters and widows (table 17.1 col. (3) *minus* table 17.5 col. (5))	Legitimate (1) × (3)	Illegitimate (2) × (4)	Legitimate (1) × (5)	Illegitimate (2) × (6)
	(1)	(2)	(3)	(4)	(5)	(6)	(7)	(8)	(9)	(10)
15–19	0.2872	0.0021	31.1	1,693.9	23.5	1,551.2	8.9	3.6	6.7	3.3
20–24	0.2120	0.0064	461.0	1,334.4	491.8	1,212.0	97.7	8.5	104.3	7.8
25–29	0.1966	0.0093	1,014.4	713.7	1,144.3	626.0	199.4	6.6	225.0	5.8
30–34	0.1168	0.0069	1,188.9	433.1	1,294.3	408.2	138.9	3.0	151.2	2.8
35–39	0.0677	0.0042	1,147.4	372.6	1,229.2	362.6	77.7	1.6	83.2	1.5
40–44	0.0206	0.0016	1,074.7	359.5	1,122.3	358.9	22.1	0.6	23.1	0.6
45–49	0.0031	0.0003	1,002.2	365.2	1,001.3	379.0	3.1	0.1	3.1	0.1
Totals							547.8	24.0	596.6	21.9
							571.8		618.5	

Total numbers of births in quinquennium ($2\frac{1}{2} \times 571.8 + 2\frac{1}{2} \times 618.5$)

of which $\begin{cases} \text{Males} & (\times 0.515) \\ \text{Females} & (\times 0.485) \end{cases}$

Survivors aged 0–4 in 1976 $\begin{cases} \text{Males} & (\times 0.930) \\ \text{Females} & (\times 0.944) \end{cases}$

2,975.7
1,532.5
1,443.2
1,426.1
1,363.5

equal to $l_{n+\frac{1}{2}}$, except where $n = 0$. In the first year of life, as the numbers of deaths are very unevenly distributed, an assumed life table distribution can be obtained directly from the actual deaths by simple ratio from their cumulative sum, and $\int_0^1 l_t dt$ may be written as:

$$\tfrac{1}{365}(l_{\frac{1}{2}\,\text{day}} + l_{1\frac{1}{2}\,\text{days}} + \ldots + l_{6\frac{1}{2}\,\text{days}} + 7l_{1\frac{1}{2}\,\text{weeks}} + \ldots + 91l_{10\frac{1}{2}\,\text{months}})$$
$$(17.13)$$

(taking care to include 365 values of *l* within the parentheses).

17.13 Projection beyond the first five years

The calculations made for the first five years provide the pattern for projections further into the future, of which nothing need be said except that some economy in space and time may be achieved by continuing the calculations on the same schedules, for example, in an extension of table 17.1, instead of using fresh sheets. The line drawn under the age-group 0–4 in column (3) of table 17.1 subdivides the 1976 population according to the survivors of births after 1971 and of the existing population in 1971 respectively. As 1981, 1986 and later years are reached this line will proceed downwards in quinquennial steps, indicating the increasing dependence of the projected numbers upon future fertility. Further, from fifteen years hence, the numbers of women at the fertile ages will themselves depend, at least in part, on the estimated births after 1971, so that thereafter the births will depend on fertility twice over. Long-term projections increase in speculativeness, therefore, broadly in geometric progression.

17.14 Alternative ways of making component-method projections

The method described in the preceding eight sections is just one illustration of how a projection calculation might be made. Many adaptations and variations are possible according to circumstances. In order to emphasize that what has been shown is by no means the only possible approach, some widely differing examples will now be briefly described.

Greater application to certain details would be required if it were desired to estimate (say) the number of children aged 2 in three years' time, or the number of persons of pension age in the next financial year. In the first instance, a year-by-year projection using individual ages would be desirable, and allowance might well be made for the effect on fertility of existing family size and duration of time since the last birth. In the second instance, the effects on mortality of weather and the seasons would be likely to be among the most important factors.

Projections of population have been made for about 1,600 separate administrative areas in England and Wales, as an aid to housing development plans. Here, simplicity was the essential feature of a task that without great care could have become too vast to be satisfactorily completed. Furthermore, data for local areas are less plentiful than for the regions as a whole, and the relatively unknown factor of migration loomed large. Broad age-groups and standardized methods were therefore adopted together with economical methods of setting out the working sheets.

A somewhat similar problem faced Tabah when he projected a population of working age with an analysis into all possible combinations of:

(1) sex;
(2) rural and urban;
(3) active or retired;
(4) one social class or another.

Here again, clarity of exposition was important, and the author laid much emphasis on the representation of the data in matrix form, so as to ease the problem of writing a computer programme.

The British Royal Commission on Population, which adopted fertility rates analysed by duration of marriage (but not by age) for the purpose of its own projections, had first to calculate the total expected numbers of marriages each year, and then to evaluate joint survival factors, for the husband and wife together. The estimated numbers of births in each future year then consisted of a summation for all marriage durations of the product of (a) the number of marriages n years earlier, (b) the n-year joint survival factor and (c) the fertility factor for the nth year of marriage; an addition had then to be made for illegitimate children.

In any given set of circumstances it is the task of the demographer to choose the most appropriate methods of projection having regard to the general nature of the work, the time available and the degree of accuracy required. Where possible, the type and form of data employed should be those exhibiting the greatest stability in the past and providing the best prospects for continued stability in the future.

SELECT BIBLIOGRAPHY

'Projecting the Population of the United Kingdom', *Economic Trends* (H.M.S.O., 1965), 139, (iii).

Tabah, L. 'Représentations Matricielles de Perspectives de Population Active', *Population*, **23** (1968), 437.

18 Introduction to population mathematics

18.1 Introduction

Elementary examples of the application of mathematics to population problems have been given above, for example, rates, indexes and graduation. Some formulae have also been mentioned which relate total population at one time to total population at another time, or which perform the same function in relation to separate sexes or ages. In the present chapter, some more comprehensive analyses will be discussed.

The aim of this more comprehensive form of population mathematics is to express certain aspects of demographic change in a series of comprehensive formulae. These formulae do not relate exclusively to the population situations and problems of today, to human populations or even to animate objects. The first step is to postulate a series of fundamental assumptions. The next is to develop statements and equations which derive from the assumptions; the aim is to proceed from these towards a 'solution', from which some new information of value about populations may be derived. In order to achieve such a development, it is usually necessary to concentrate attention upon assumptions and relationships by means of which the analysis can be completed, and population mathematics often proceeds along the paths determined by such assumptions. In this way, close contact with realistic situations may to some extent be lost. Nevertheless, some interesting and important results have been obtained, and familiarity with these results is necessary to the demographer who is to be completely equipped for the study of population.

18.2 Deterministic and stochastic processes

Vital processes occur in a series of steps or stages which follow one another in sequence and depend largely upon one another. Thus marriage normally succeeds the attainment of puberty and usually precedes parenthood. Coitus precedes conception, which is followed by abortion or by parturition. Widowhood may be succeeded by remarriage. With each of these steps is associated a degree of variation; thus one person may attain puberty before another; one will marry and another will not; marriage may occur early or late and may not be followed by parenthood. Some analytical methods are limited to

340

discrete portions of this complex, for example, to the association between marriage and age, or between fertility and marriage duration, and the demographer's work proceeds in a 'deterministic' manner, that is, he deals mainly in averages and not with associated variations. Other mathematical systems do, however, pay attention to the connexions between these patterns of recurrence. They treat a population sub-group, not as a collection of people all having the same average characteristic, but as a frequency distribution to each member of which an event may happen which itself has a probability distribution. This approach thus envisages a series of 'stochastic' processes.

The difference between the deterministic and stochastic approach can be illustrated very broadly by an example. The number of births to a group of married women aged x might be expressed by the former as $P_x.f_x$, where P_x represents the population of married women at age x and f_x their average fertility rate; or it might be calculated as $\sum_m \sum_n P_{xmn}.f_{xmn}$, where m is the length of time married and n is the number of children already borne and the summation is made first for all possible m's and then for all possible n's. In either event a single answer would be arrived at. But by the method of stochastic processes a distribution would be found in either case; in the first instance the analysis might begin with a set of probabilities of a married woman aged x having 0, 1, 2, ... children, and in the second it might begin from the moment of marriage with probabilities of first birth and following this of subsequent births. The end product would be a frequency distribution of which not only the mean but also the variance and other measures of dispersion would be of interest.

18.3 Stable populations

The concept of a stable population is very important in demographic studies, and it is essentially a deterministic one. Most people when they speak of a 'stable' population think of it as one with a constant total number. This is not, however, the technically correct concept, which can be explained as follows.

If a population, the total size of which varies in the course of time, has a fixed age-distribution and a constant mortality rate at each age, it follows that the death rate is also constant. Moreover, by virtue of the fixed age-distribution, the birth rate must also be unvarying. Hence the rate of annual growth (or decline) is constant, too. The population thus develops in geometrical progression. It is then called a 'stable' population. In the special case where the birth and death rates are equal, the stable population becomes a stationary (or life table) population.

If ^tP_x denotes the number of persons aged x at time t, $_np_x$ is the chance of survival from age x to age $x+n$, and r represents the annual rate of growth, then:

$$^{t+n}P_{x+n} = {_n}p_x \cdot {^t}P_x,$$ (18.1)

and in particular

$$^t P_x = {_x}p_0 \cdot {^{t-x}}P_0.$$ (18.2)

The total population at time t may be written as $\sum\limits_{x=0}^{\infty} {^t}P_x$ and similarly the

total population at time $t-z$ may be written as $\sum\limits_{x=0}^{\infty} {^{t-z}}P_x$. These two are connected by the equation

$$\sum_{x=0}^{\infty} {^t}P_x = (1+r)^z \cdot \sum_{x=0}^{\infty} {^{t-z}}P_x.$$ (18.3)

Let f_x = the proportion of the total population which consists of people aged x; by definition, this is independent of t. Thus f_x is the result of dividing the left-hand side of expression (18.2) by the left-hand side of expression (18.3). It is then also the result of dividing the right-hand side of expression (18.2) by the right-hand side of expression (18.3).

Choose a particular value of x, say z; then

$$f_z = ({_z}p_0 \cdot {^{t-z}}P_0) \div \left((1+r)^z \cdot \sum_{x=0}^{\infty} {^{t-z}}P_x \right)$$

or

$$f_z = {_z}p_0 \cdot f_0 \cdot (1+r)^{-z}.$$ (18.4)

The value of f_z declines as that of z increases, not only because of mortality but also because of the rate of population growth. The higher the growth-rate, the younger the age-distribution and *vice versa*. By definition, the sum of the values of f for all ages is unity. So, if both sides of equation (18.4) are summed for all the values x that z can take, we obtain

$$\sum_{x=0}^{\infty} f_x = 1 = \sum_{x=0}^{\infty} {_x}p_0 \cdot f_0 \cdot (1+r)^{-x}.$$ (18.5)

Thus:

$$f_0 = \left[\sum_{x=0}^{\infty} {_x}p_0 \cdot (1+r)^{-x} \right]^{-1}.$$ (18.6)

18.4 Further notes on stable populations

In figs. 10.1 and 10.2, the actual population pyramids for England and Wales for the years 1901 and 1931 were shown. Superimposed on each one was a curve representing the stationary population that would be supported by a constant inflow of young children in the same numbers as the recorded births

342

of those two years. If instead the curves had represented the corresponding stable populations, on the same base but with an assumed growth rate relevant to the period, then the curves would have fitted the pyramids much more closely, as may be seen from fig. 18.1 which relates to the year 1901.

It is more convenient to express population mathematics in the form of continuous functions than in the form of step functions. In § 15.11, it was shown how the force of mortality μ_x was arrived at as a limit of $m_x^{(n)}$ as n tends towards infinity. By a similar process, we can arrive at a momently rate of population growth, ρ (say), which is related to r by the formula

$$\rho = \operatorname*{Lt}_{x \to \infty} \left(1 + \frac{r}{n}\right)^n = \log_e(1 + r). \tag{18.7}$$

(Actuarial readers will recognize the exact similarity to the compound interest formula $\delta = \log_e(1 + i)$.)

Equation (18.6) may then be written as

$$f_0 = \left[\int_0^\infty e^{-\rho x} \cdot {}_x p_0 \cdot dx\right]^{-1}. \tag{18.8}$$

Expressions (18.6) and (18.8) provide the means for determining the age-distribution, in any instance of a stable population – given the rate of growth and the mortality table (using also (18.4)) – or for determining the rate of growth, given the birth rate and the death rates by age.

It may readily be shown that stable populations arise from a number of hypotheses, for example from the assumption of a fixed age-distribution of deaths and a fixed set of mortality rates. Such populations are more interesting and useful than stationary populations, because they are less unrealistic and inflexible: the rate of growth may vary from one population to another. They also have useful implications for the study of population age-distributions. Nevertheless, the bases of constant mortality, fertility and age-distribution hardly reflect the facts of most populations today, as will be evident from

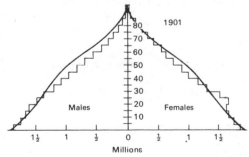

Fig. 18.1. Population pyramid illustrating the age and sex distribution of the population of England and Wales in the year 1901, together with curve for stable population based on the growth rate in that year.

343

the data quoted in other chapters in this book. It will be shown below how further realism can be introduced into population mathematics.

18.5   The rate of growth of stable populations

Equation (18.8) may be solved in a number of ways. No less than five are quoted by Keyfitz. For instance, a mathematical function may be fitted to $_xp_0$, and the integral may then be exactly evaluated. Again, an interative process, which may be programmed on an electronic computer, has been devised, in order to permit successive approximations. Furthermore, an approximate solution — with a satisfactory degree of accuracy — has been based on the mean and standard deviation of $_xp_0$. It is now appropriate to show a generalization of the formula which is of wide interest and to which the same (and other) methods of solution may be applied.

18.6   Populations tending towards the stable stage

It can be shown, as was first demonstrated by Lotka, that on certain assumptions populations will tend asymptotically towards a stable state. One example is a population with constant mortality and fertility rates at each age x, whatever the initial age-distribution. If the number of births between times t and $t + \delta t$ be written as $^tB\delta t$, then the number of persons aged x to $x + \delta x$ at time t may be written as

$$^{t-x}B \cdot _xp_0 \cdot \delta x \qquad (18.9)$$

and the births to which they give rise between times t and $t + \delta t$ will then be

$$^{t-x}B \cdot _xp_0 \cdot \phi_x \delta x \delta t, \qquad (18.10)$$

where ϕ_x is the rate of fertility at age x.

The total births between times t and $t + \delta t$ may thus be expressed as

$$\int_0^\infty {}^{t-x}B \cdot _xp_0 \cdot \phi_x \cdot \delta x \delta t, \qquad (18.11)$$

and, as this may be also written as $^tB\delta t$, it follows that

$$^tB = \int_0^\infty {}^{t-x}B \cdot _xp_0 \cdot \phi_x \delta x. \qquad (18.12)$$

If the average annual geometrical rate of growth over any period $t - x$ to t is ρ_t, then

$$I = \int_0^\infty e^{-\rho_t x} \, _xp_0 \cdot \phi_x \delta x. \qquad (18.13)$$

This equation (often called the 'intrinsic' equation) is similar in form to (18.8) and the statistically-trained reader will recognize that each is in the form of a moment-generating function. It may be solved in various ways. One solution is discussed in § 18.7 below; others are mentioned in §§ 18.8 and 18.9.

18.7 Approximate solution of the intrinsic equation

Given l_x and ϕ_x for all values of x, equation (18.13) determines the real value of ρ_t uniquely; for, since the value of the integral diminishes continuously from ∞ to 0 as ρ increases from $-\infty$ to ∞, it can be equal to 1 for only one real value of ρ.

If $_xp_0 \cdot \phi_x$ is written as r_x, if ρ_t is written as ρ and if $e^{-\rho x}$ is expanded in terms of x, equation (18.13) becomes:

$$\int_0^\omega r_x \left(1 - \rho x + \frac{\rho^2 x^2}{2!} - \frac{\rho^3 x^3}{3!} + \ldots \right) dx = 1. \qquad (18.14)$$

Writing the nth moment of r_x, namely $\int_0^w x^n r_x dx$, as v_n, equation (18.14) becomes:

$$v_0 - \rho v_1 + \tfrac{1}{2}\rho^2 v_2 - \ldots = 1. \qquad (18.15)$$

As ρ is fairly small, some approximate information about it may be obtained by ignoring ρ^2 and higher powers. Thus

$$v_0 - v_1 \rho \doteq 1,$$

therefore

$$v_0 \left(1 - \frac{v_1}{v_0}\rho \right) \doteq 1.$$

Taking logarithms,

$$\log_e v_0 + \log_e \left(1 - \frac{v_1}{v_0}\rho \right) \doteq 0.$$

Expanding the second term and again ignoring ρ^2 and higher powers

$$\log_e v_0 - \frac{v_1}{v_0}\rho \doteq 0.$$

Hence

$$v_0 \doteq e^{(v_1/v_0)\rho} \qquad (18.16)$$

Thus v_0 measures approximately the population increase in time v_1/v_0. v_1/v_0 is equal to

$$\frac{\int_0^w xr_x dx}{\int_0^w r_x dx} \tag{18.17}$$

and is thus equal to the average mother's age on bearing a female child.

Expression (18.17) is called the average length of a generation and may be written as, say G. Thus

$$v_0 \doteq e^{Gp},$$

or alternatively,

$$p \doteq \frac{1}{G} \log_e v_0. \tag{18.18}$$

But $v_0 = \int_0^v r_x dx$ and is thus equal to the net reproduction rate (when limited to parents and children of one sex). Its value is less than 1, unity or more than 1 according as p is negative, zero or positive. v_0 may be written as $(1 + r)^G$.

18.8 Other solutions of the intrinsic equation

It can be shown that, if k represents the ratio of the variance of the curve of fertility to the average length of a generation, then the error in equation (18.18) is of the order of $kp^2/2$. The range of the fertility curve is of the order of forty years and it is usually single-humped and thus virtually all the observations are contained within the range $+3\sigma$ to -3σ. Roughly therefore, $\sigma \doteq 40/6$. Hence $\sigma^2/G \doteq 45/30$, or $1\frac{1}{2}$, and thus k is of the order of unity. Since p is small, the error in equation (18.18) is thus small.

The general solution to equation (18.13) is complex and there are an infinite number of roots $u + iv$. It can be shown that $u < p_0$, and, provided that the death and birth rates are continuous functions of age, as t increases the roots converge towards the real exponential growth function. In other words, the tendency in the long run is towards a stable state. This has been demonstrated by calculation on an electronic computer, by a method of proceeding from one generation to another, which can be repeated many times very rapidly. Such a method (which is akin to population projection, as described in chapter 17) can be used as an effective way of measuring p for a given schedule of values of r_x.

The intrinsic rate of increase may also be calculated with the aid of an electronic computer by processes of successive approximation. Keyfitz has given a simple FORTRAN program which starts from the assumption that ρ has a given arbitrary value; tests its validity and finds a better value; tests the new value and finds a still better one; and so on.

18.9   Limits upon the value of stable population mathematics

The formulae and concepts which have been described in the last six sections are of value in the understanding of population processes. They provide the theoretical background to the net reproduction rate. They are sometimes of use in the consideration of populations for which few data are available, e.g. for the study of primitive tribes today or of the demography of past ages. The assumptions that mortality and fertility are constant in time, that these are related only to age, that marital status can be disregarded and that reproduction is a function of one sex alone, are not appropriate to the population of any developed country today; nor are they likely to be in accordance with the demographic situation of any other country for which extensive and accurate population data are available. Nevertheless, some of these features are sufficiently representative, for instance the shape of the age-distribution shown in fig. 18.1 above. The theory is historically important and has a particular fascination of its own. Moreover it may be possible to modify the theory for practical purposes, and some demographers are still finding new ways of making such modifications today, as will be seen in chapter 19.

18.10   Simple 'birth and death' processes

The approach to population development by means of stochastic processes may now be illustrated with some simple examples. The expression 'a birth and death process' relates to the study of variable populations subject to random increments and decrements. If, for instance, there is a constant incremental rate and no decrement, it can be shown that the population size at time t is a Poisson random variable with a mean proportionate to t. If it be supposed that a population ^tP is subject to fixed birth and death rates, b and d respectively, and that there is no migration, writing ^tQ_n for the probability that $^tP = n$ at time t, then for the reasons given below:

$$
\begin{aligned}
^{t+\delta t}Q_n = {} & {}^tQ_{n+1} \cdot (n+1)d \cdot \delta t \\
& + {}^tQ_{n-1} \cdot (n-1)b \cdot \delta t \\
& + {}^tQ_n \cdot \left[1 - n(b+d)\delta t \right],
\end{aligned}
\tag{18.19}
$$

where δt is a very small unit of time.

Of the three expressions on the right-hand side of (18.19), the first represents approximately the chance of a population at time t of size $n+1$ being

347

reduced by one death in time δt; the second similarly indicates the probability of an increase in numbers from $n - 1$ at time t to n at time $t + \delta t$ by reason of a birth; the third correspondingly shows the chance that no change in size occurs, because there are no deaths or births. Other possibilities, for example, two deaths, or a death and a birth, in time δt are omitted, as terms of $(\delta t)^2$ would be involved; as δt is so short these may be treated as *de minimis*.

The solution of equation (18.19) can be found with the aid of generating functions; particular interest attaches to ${}^tQ_0$; the probability of the extinction of the population at time t. This is equal to:

$$\left[\frac{de^{rt} - d}{be^{rt} - d} \right]^x \tag{18.20}$$

where $x = {}^0P$, namely the initial population, and $r = b - d$. If $r \leqq 0$, expression (18.20) tends to unity as t tends to infinity. Thus, a 'stable' population tends to zero in the end if $r < 0$, as is obvious; but less evident is the fact that the chance of extinction tends to unity also when $r = 0$. A 'stationary' population is thus bound to die out at some time or other, because of random movements. If r is positive, the probability of ultimate extinction is very small, unless the initial population z is itself very small, but it is still not zero; the value of this probability has been shown to be $(d/b)^x$.

From this form of analysis, it is possible to deduce the distribution of lengths of life and of the numbers of children per person in a stable population.

18.11 Some other stochastic models

General population models devised by Bartlett and Kendall have been described by J. H. Pollard, who has also produced his own stochastic version of a 'stable population' model. The mathematics involved are advanced in character; they become very complex and produce results which cannot be presented in a form suitable for the present work. A simpler form of analysis can be used to study the development of a population which is stratified with a series of groups, for example, geographic regions or socio-economic classes. It is supposed that the probabilities of transferring from the ith group at one time to the jth group at another time, p_{ij} say, are known. Then, if the state of the population at time t is characterized as

$${}^tP_1, {}^tP_2 \ldots {}^tP_n,$$

where $1 \ldots n$ are the groups in question, it follows that

$${}^{t+1}P_j = \sum_{i=1}^{n} p_{ij} \cdot {}^tP_i \tag{18.21}$$

Some broad conclusions about changes in population stratification have been drawn by treating the analysis in terms of a multinomial distribution, with i and j as axes. For instance, social mobility has been analysed into factors attributable to industrial changes (affecting the distribution of occupations) and factors attributable to competition for better jobs.

18.12 The use of electronic computers

The advent of electronic computers has made the investigation of stochastic variations much easier in two ways; first, an extensive volume of calculations can be readily undertaken, whereas formerly these would have been impracticable. Secondly, both measured data and mathematical expressions can alike be 'fed in' to a programme and manipulated; this is particularly useful where it would not be possible to handle the mathematical equations alone. A few examples will be quoted below; again, these take separate and distinct forms. At present the subject appears too new to be treated in a more general manner.

The aspects of demography that have so far benefited the most from investigations of stochastic processes are assessments of fecundity and of the effectiveness of birth control and analyses of fertility and family-building.

18.13 The study of reproductive processes

During married life before the menopause, a woman who is not permanently sterile is always in one or other of the three following states: (*a*) fecundable but not pregnant, (*b*) pregnant, and (*c*) temporarily sterile following a pregnancy. The time spent in each of these states may be treated as a random variable, in order to study such matters as the distribution of the intervals between pregnancies, the distribution of pregnancies per person in a given period of time, and the fertility rate. Such studies are important in the assessment of natural uncontrolled human fertility and of the efficiency of various contraceptive methods. The time spent in state (*b*) depends upon the outcome of that state — whether it is a live birth, a still-birth or an abortion. The time spent in state (*c*) will also depend upon that outcome. By general mathematical reasoning it can be shown that:

(1) the average time taken to complete one 'cycle', involving a pregnancy, post-partum sterility and the fecundable state until the next pregnancy begins, is the sum of the mean times in states (*a*), (*b*) and (*c*), allowing for the various chances of outcomes of (*b*); this is of course evident from general reasoning;

(2) the average time elapsing between one live birth and the next is the sum in (1) divided by the chance that (2) ends in a live birth;

(3) the fertility rate is the reciprocal of item (2);

(4) the variances of the items can be expressed mathematically in terms of the basic functions involved.

18.14 The effectiveness of birth control programmes

One use to which computers have been put is in predicting the types of person most likely to adopt family planning. A kind of factor analysis was employed. A social survey having provided data on (*a*) family-planning behaviour and (*b*) place of residence, age, occupation and other factors, the computer was programmed to ascertain by statistical methods which of these factors had the most powerful associations with the use of family planning.

Barrett and Brass constructed a Monte Carlo simulation model of fertility in which *inter alia* fecundability varied between women in proportion to the distribution of .

$$p^{a-1}(1 - p)^{b-1}, \tag{18.22}$$

where *a* and *b* are constants, in addition, allowance was made for (i) a decline in fecundability with advancing age, and (ii) a family-planning strategy in which couples prefer certain sizes of families and seek to lengthen the last planned birth interval. One of the outcomes of the model was a relationship between recorded family-size preferences and observed family-size distributions showing the extent to which couples are unable, because of the operation of chance in human biology, to achieve their preferences.

Besides their use in population projection by deterministic methods, computers have been employed on projections in which allowance is made for stochastic processes and for the influence of economic factors on marriage and birth rates. The device of 'simulation' was adopted — alternatively known as 'Monte Carlo methods'. The basis of operation is a set of random numbers. If it is desired to incorporate a probability that a certain event occurs, and that probability is to be one-fifth, this could be simulated by regarding the event as having happened wherever the digits of (say) either 2 or 7 were encountered in a process of scanning all the random numbers. If some number other than 2 or 7 were found, the event would be regarded as not having happened. In a large number of tests, the event should occur about one time in five on this basis; in the short run the actual outcome would be random. In such a simple example, no special advantage is conveyed by· simulation, but the speed of the computer is very useful in more complex instances. Thus, supposing that the probability of first conceiving between $t - 1$ and t months after marriage were to be expressed as

$$p_t = C - a\sqrt{t}, \tag{18.23}$$

where C and a are constants, and, having conceived, a woman had a chance of a live birth equal to d^{-ft}, then the distribution of the number of months elapsing between marriage and first conception leading to a live birth would be difficult to evaluate by mathematical methods and would be very laborious to calculate by using a desk calculating machine. An electronic computer could, however, rapidly calculate p_t for all practical values of t (say 1, 2 ... 120) and then by life-table methods assess the relative numbers first conceiving after t months. The corresponding number of first births could then be obtained by simulation for each value of t; and the distribution of t thereafter assembled.

18.15   Analysis of family-building

Hyrenius constructed a model based upon the following factors:

(1) initial age;
(2) fecundability;
(3) proportion sterile;
(4) chances of abortion and still-birth;
(5) probability of permanent post-partum sterility;
(6) duration of pregnancy;
(7) distribution of duration of temporary post-partum sterility; and
(8) age at menopause.

In this model, 20 was chosen as the initial age, and fecundability was assumed constant. The proportion sterile was assumed (in one version) to be a linear function of age. The chances of reproductive wastage were assumed constant, but those of permanent sterility arising after a conception were taken as a linear function of parity. Distributions based on practical experience were taken for items (6) and (7), the second of these varying according to the nature of the outcome of the pregnancy, and for item (8).

Using a flow-chart broadly akin to that shown in chapter 2, but more complex in detail, simulation methods were used to produce a series of age-specific fertility rates. As no control of fertility was assumed, other than that imposed by natural biological processes, the result was suitable for comparison with data collected in respect of communities where it is known that no man-made controls are imposed. The object of the exercise was to see whether the assumptions made in respect of fecundability and sterility were reasonable.

Potter and Sakoda, who carried out a similar type of exercise, included in addition the following two factors:

(1) desired family size and child-spacing; and
(2) contraceptive effectiveness.

The end-products of this model were a distribution of married women according to the number of children born, and distributions of the length of time elapsing between marriage and the *n*th birth. The object was to measure the effectiveness of control over family building in varying circumstances as to fecundability and pregnancy wastage.

In a further exercise, Hyrenius *et al.* introduced the following basic elements: woman's age at death; woman's age at marriage; woman's age at illegitimate birth; husband's age at death; husband's age at marriage; risk of divorce; number of children born; woman's age at confinement; woman's age at remarriage; husband's age at remarriage. Among the derived distributions were:

(1) a distribution of intervals of time between successive live births; and
(2) a distribution of marriages by the woman's age at marriage and the number of children born.

The object of the exercise was, *inter alia*, to measure the progress in Sweden of the demographic transition from high mortality and fertility — as in the eighteenth century, when demographic data were first collected there — to modern low mortality and fertility.

SELECT BIBLIOGRAPHY

Tabah, L. 'Relationships between Age-structure, Fertility, Mortality and Migration: Population Replacement and Renewal', *World Population Conference, 1965* (United Nations Organization, New York, 1967).

Keyfitz, N. 'The Intrinsic Rate of Natural Increase and the Dominant Root of the Projection Matrix', *Population Studies,* **18** (1965), 293.

Pollard, J. H. *Mathematical Models for the Growth of the Human Population* (Cambridge University Press, 1973).

Joshi, D. D. 'Stochastic Models Utilised in Demography', *World Population Conference, 1965* (United Nations Organization, 1967), **3**, 227.

Hyrenius, H. and Adolfsson, I. *A Fertility Simulation Model* (Almquist and Wiksell, Göteborg, 1964).

Sheps, M. C. and Perrin, E. B. 'The Distribution of Birth Intervals under a Class of Stochastic Fertility Models', *Population Studies,* **17** (1964), 321.

Ross, J. A. and Bang, S. 'The AID Computer Programme used to Predict Adoption of Family Planning in Koyang', *Population Studies,* **20** (1966), 66.

Barrett, J. C. and Brass, W. 'Systematic and Chance Components in Fertility Measurement', *Population Studies,* **28** (1974), 473.

19 The handling of suspect or scanty data

19.1 Introduction

Demographic data tend to be incomplete and inaccurate in some degree even at the best of times. Quite often the statistical material available for study is deficient, and attempts to remedy the trouble by means of new enquiries may be frustrated by the smallness of practical samples or the refusal of respondents to co-operate. For remote subjects, for developing countries or for the past the information may indeed by very patchy and very difficult to interpret. In spite of these handicaps, demographers persevere and often produce meaningful results. The first need is clearly to test the data for completeness and accuracy, and this is an important aspect of population analysis. A number of methods for doing so have been evolved, and the earlier part of the present chapter is concerned with these.

If completeness or inaccuracy has been established, unless the degree of shortfall or error is small the ideal procedure is to discontinue all demographic analysis and devote all available resources to the collection of more representative material. Often, however, this is impracticable; or it would take so long to achieve the necessary improvement in the available information that demographic studies urgently required — perhaps for policy formulation — ought to proceed by other means.

The second part of this chapter is devoted to these alternative means. Many demographers have described what they have done in particular circumstances, but it is clear that the best solution in any given instance depends very much on the nature of the subject under investigation and on the seriousness of the deficiency in the data. The method must, in other words, be well adapted to the local situation if it is to be of value. In these circumstances it is not easy to lay down rules as to what should be done in future eventualities. All that is possible is to enunciate a few general principles, give some relevant examples, and rely upon the ingenuity and common sense of the demographer to deal appropriately with each new problem as it arises. Broadly speaking, the devices to be used, as an alternative to correcting the data or instituting an improved system of records, fall into two classes: (a) the use of abstract models, and (b) the making of special *ad hoc* surveys: general reference has already been made in chapters 3 and 4 to sample investigations, but these have been discussed mainly in the context of a developed system

353

of demographic data. In this chapter, methods appropriate to less-developed areas will be touched upon.

The most comprehensive of the available models have been discussed in chapter 18, under the heading of population mathematics, but in the present chapter some less extensive examples adapted to more specific problems can appropriately be considered, for example, those relevant to particular aspects of population: mortality, age-distribution and the like. The advent of electronic computers has enabled much more extensive calculations to be made than were possible before within a reasonable allowance of time and expenditure. Models that have been developed, or proposed for construction, with the aid of computers have been touched on in chapter 18, and some further examples of these will now be given.

19.2   The detection of errors

The basis for all tests of inaccuracy in demographic data is comparison. The only variations arise from the nature of the objects with which comparison is made. First, the statistics may be studied to investigate internal consistency between one part and another of a single record system. Secondly, they may be contrasted with other information relating to the same population or area. Thirdly, the data may be examined in the light of reliable tabulations from comparable countries. Finally, comparison may be made with mathematical models, or with the results of special samples.

The first method should always be used if possible. Internal consistency can be a valuable feature even in data that are incomplete; thus if registrations of vital events disclose that no more than 50 per cent of occurrences are recorded, but that at all times the data represent just one-half of the true total, then the trend in time may well be correctly described – unless of course the nature of the 'selection' varies. The second method is also useful but may present problems if the other information is itself of uncertain accuracy: if there is a disagreement, it will not be easy to determine which set of data is at fault, or how any discrepancies should properly be shared between the two. The third method tends to suffer from international differences of definition and circumstance. The use of models presents problems not only of choosing the right type of model but also of the selection of an appropriate scale for its adaptation to the circumstances.

The studies that have been made indicate that a number of further aids may help the demographer to overcome these difficulties; these aids take one or other of three general forms, namely:

(1) *analysis*: subdivision of the data by factors such as age, duration, or geographical area, and examination of trends in time, may well reveal inconsistencies which should point to the source of error;

(2) *pattern likelihood*: an appreciation of actual demographic experience over a wide area gives a good idea of whether the picture apparently presented by a particular set of data does or does not conform to a reasonable pattern;

(3) *local knowledge*: it will obviously help if the demographer knows something of the people enumerated — their beliefs, prejudices, habits and customs — and of the conditions under which the data were assembled.

19.3 The detection of omissions

Completeness or incompleteness of coverage is unlikely to be revealed by 'internal' checks, which are more useful in relation to questions of accuracy; but the second, third and fourth general systems of analysis mentioned at the beginning of § 19.2 above may help in assessing degree of coverage. These may perhaps be termed 'external' checks. To them may be added, for current inquiries, the process of re-enumeration, in whole or in part, often with the aid of new field workers (see § 19.5 below).

19.4 Some useful forms of internal analysis

A simple example of such a check is a comparison of the numbers of persons enumerated at each successive age. Associated with such a comparison there must be a conceptual model of the picture that the trend of the numbers from age x to age y should present. Such a trend would perhaps be expected to take the form of a straight line. Unusual fluctuations in the numbers of births x to y years before (such as might have been caused by a war) or in mortality or migration could alter the picture, but some allowance for their effect might be made. There should be little confusion with typical misstatements of age, which take quite a different pattern, and usually stand out quite clearly.

Comparison of successive cohorts is useful because temporary secular fluctuations are largely eliminated in cohort analysis. To set results for one area alongside those for other areas (especially adjacent ones) can be very revealing if there is a difference between the areas in the degree of misstatement. Durational comparisons are important in detecting lapses of memory, which normally increase as the duration since the event lengthens.

Internal checks can be applied to individual returns as well as to tabulated statistics. In this way discrepancies can be discovered, for instance, as between date of marriage and number of children born to the marriage. In countries where fertility may be expected to have remained constant for some years, for instance in many developing countries, measures of current fertility may be compared with measures of total fertility (for example, family size) obtained from the same census: the cumulation of the 'flow' type data should tie in reasonably well with the 'stock' type information. Needless to say, the same kind of comparison may be made where the stock and flow information derive from independent sources.

19.5 External comparisons

Stock and flow comparisons from independent sources usually involve both census and registration material. Thus, data of birth and infant death occurrences shortly before a census may be compared with the numbers of characteristics of infants enumerated. Similarly, items registered in respect of deaths occurring shortly after a census may be compared with the census data for the same persons. The shortness of the time is important, so that migratory movement cannot interfere too much with the matching of the records.

Such work may be of one or other of two types: individual and group. The records may either be contrasted person by person or the totals may be set side by side in statistical aggregates. In the longer term, one census may be compared with another, for example, the numbers of persons aged x enumerated in year Y may be put alongside the numbers of persons aged $x + N$ enumerated at the census in year $Y + N$. If N is large, variations attributable to mortality and migration may complicate the interpretation of the results. The mortality aspect could be made much less troublesome if the numbers of deaths registered at the appropriate ages in the relevant years could be brought into the calculation.

Another way in which the accuracy and completeness of the data may be tested is by the making of a duplicate survey, for example, a repeat census or count. A proviso attaching to this process is that the repeat enumeration should be able to furnish reliable and truly independent evidence; it should perhaps be made by different enumerators from those who made the first count. Repeated surveys of this kind have been used widely, for example in India and the USA. Finally, from the national point of view, census data may be checked against information of a similar kind obtained for non-demographic purposes, for example, tax returns or social security data.

International comparisons, subject as they are to differences of definition, are of more limited value, but can occasionally be effective as a rough and ready test of reliability. This is so especially where data from a number of different countries can all be used in the verification process. Thus, a low fertility rate, in a poorly-developed country, by comparison with neighbouring and similar areas, unless explained by special climatic, health or social factors, would suggest under-registration of births. Exceptional apparent longevity would suggest under-registration of deaths, unless supported by medical or other independent valid evidence. An unusual age-distribution, unexplained by special past developments, might suggest material over-enumeration or under-enumeration or else a misunderstanding of the local method of assessing ages.

19.6 Examples of the testing of suspect data

Methods such as the foregoing were extensively used by Kuczynski in appraising the demographic statistics of the British Colonial Empire, and he was able to show that many of the data collected before independence were highly unreliable, owing to the nature of the techniques used in collecting them, which were primitive judged by the standards of today. It was easier to demolish the value of the records than to improve or correct them, as reliable independent standards were lacking.

Here are some more specific examples:

(1) In relation to modern Greek population data, Valaoras tested the seasonal distribution of birth registration against a reasoned expectation. He found that under-registration occurred in the months of November and (more especially) December; this was balanced by an over-registration in January, February and March.

(2) Valaoras also compared the total of registered births in the five years preceding a census, *less* the appropriate registered deaths, with the numbers enumerated; this analysis revealed that fewer births are registered than should be recorded, more especially for girls.

(3) The same demographer contrasted assessments of mortality early in life, based on the available records, between the sexes in Greece, and between Greece and other countries; and this work suggested an under-registration of infant deaths, markedly for boys and in the rural areas.

(4) Valaoras further measured the trend of mortality from year to year at the oldest ages. He thus found an overstatement of the age at death for old people. The data for this test are exhibited in table 19.1, and the essential points are:

(*a*) the reasonable progression of the numbers of deaths from year to year, allowing for the general ageing of the population and for normal annual fluctuations;

(*b*) the unreasonable jump in the population size in 1961, when there was a census, and the fact that the estimates for 1952—60 were based on the 1951 enumeration and registered deaths;

(*c*) the corresponding excessively rapid rise and then sudden fall in the death rate; as migration is negligible at the oldest ages, overstatement of the age at death — thus unduly reducing the estimate of population — seems to be by far the most reasonable possible explanation of the observations. This means that the number of deaths at ages 85 and over, and the mortality rate based upon them, are overstated generally.

This fourth example might be described as a test of consistency based on census and registration data taken together, or a test of the death records using the census as a guide. The second example also falls into the latter

357

Table 19.1. *Mortality in Greece, 1951—63, at ages 85 and over*

(Numbers in thousands.)

Year	Estimated population	Deaths	Death rate
1951	30·9	5·6	0·180
1952	31·2	5·6	0·181
1953	31·6	6·9	0·217
1954	31·5	7·4	0·235
1955	32·0	6·7	0·211
1956	32·5	8·1	0·248
1957	32·5	8·3	0·255
1958	32·4	8·1	0·250
1959	31·9	8·6	0·268
1960	31·4	8·8	0·281
1961	48·0	9·6	0·200
1962	47·4	9·9	0·209
1963	46·3	10·1	0·218

category, and is unusual because such calculations are more often used to show under-enumeration at the census. (Such under-enumeration indeed probably occurred, but in the circumstances cannot be tested by this procedure.) The third example essentially used international data as a standard. The first used a 'model', but probably this model was in fact largely based on experience in other countries.

(5) Another example of the use of a mathematical model in order to detect inaccuracy in data was the use of a Poisson distribution to test the grouping of dates of births of children reported by village headmen in Israel; it was found that, to save themselves work, the headmen were giving notional dates which were too closely grouped together, i.e. in effect they were treating all birth occurrences as happening on certain convenient days.

(6) In the USA, the National Health Survey asked people, at household interviews, whether they had been in hospital within the past 12 months. What they said was then compared with hospital records of admissions. It was found that memories are short. The rate of under-reporting in the interviews increased from 4 per cent when the admission was less than two months before the date of interview to as much as one-half when the interval was 10 or 11 months. The degree of error was similar in relation to hospital visits of members of the household other than the person interviewed.

(7) In Indian demographic work, extensive use has been made of 'interpenetrating networks' of samples. In these, the total number of units in a survey is subdivided into a number of parallel random groups. The mean and variance of the results are then calculated for each group. Using the technique

358

of 'analysis of variance' it is then possible to assign the total variance to the portions which are attributable to variance within samples, variance between samples, variance between enumerators and so on. By consulting statistical tables, it is then possible to assess whether bias has crept in, particularly between enumerators, some of whom may be tempted to short-cut their work and so in one way or another falsify the findings. (For instance they may not visit the most distant places in the survey but pretend that data collected nearer the base of operations were collected further afield). Analysis of this kind may eliminate the need for more costly re-surveys by independent enumerators.

19.7 The use of models in demography

It is not difficult to devise mathamatical expressions for use in the study of population. The choice is very wide, and a great number of techniques have been developed for a variety of purposes. The problem is, however, to find the models most likely to produce meaningful results, and to decide which of a number of possibilities is the most appropriate. The greater the absence of reliable data, the more severe the difficulty of selection. A number of principles may be enunciated as a guide; of these the most important are as follows:

(1) the model should be appropriate in theory; in other words, it should provide a reasonable interpretation not only over the range of ages, durations and areas in question but also over the maximum possible range of occurrences;

(2) the model should also be right in relation to the nature of the data or population under examination;

(3) the philosophical touchstone of 'Occam's razor' should be applied: unnecessary elaboration should be avoided, and a complex expression should not be used if a simpler one would be sufficient;

(4) the method by which the parameters are calculated should be such as to make the best possible use of the potentialities of the model in relation to the available information.

To illustrate these principles, reference may be made to the common practice of constructing a life table for countries where mortality data are absent or unreliable. This table may be based on a given formula for the relationship of the death rate with the age. Such a formula would be unsuitable if it were capable of producing a negative mortality rate at any age or one of infinite size at any age within the human span; ideally, it should conform with general biological knowledge of the ageing and death processes. Instead of a formula, the life table appropriate to another country might be used, in which

359

event the choice of this other country should be a reasonable one having regard to race, geography, economy and climate.

In economically-advanced countries, highly sophisticated statistical techniques have been developed in connexion with the interpretation of complex data on the basis of much accumulated knowledge. Newly-trained demographers in developing countries are often enthusiastic in their application of these techniques in circumstances where a simpler procedure might be just as appropriate and a good deal safer from the risk of technical error.

Fitting the model to the available data is a process for which mathematical techniques are available, and there are also devices for testing the goodness of fit. The assumptions upon which these mathematical techniques and devices are founded rarely, however, apply in demographic practice. Normally, the variations observed in population data greatly exceed 'random' fluctuations. It is difficult, therefore, to give good general guidance as to the mode of fitting models to the information. Perhaps the most important test is whether or not the result appears reasonable in relation to experience elsewhere. In such circumstances, it is far more important to comment cautiously on the results than to to fit a model in the neatest fashion.

The next few paragraphs give some more detailed examples of the use of models of various kinds in demography.

19.8 Substitute methods

A variety of special techniques has been assembled for dealing, *inter alia*, with people who may have no record of how old they are. Success in demographic analysis of this kind requires a knowledge of the people, ingenuity in devising ways of obtaining accurate information in the face of many difficulties, and a talent for the appraisal of the quality of any material that may have been collected. Fertility statistics have been obtained, for instance, from a sample of women by asking them either how many children they had had in the past year or the total number of children ever born to them. What are known as 'substitute' methods have been employed in assessing their age-distribution.

Substitute methods depend on comparison between one population and another. If the data for one country, town, social class or occupation are inadequate, a search is made for another country, town, social class or occupation with similar general characteristics, and for which more plentiful information can be obtained. Some idea of the scope for inaccuracy in the use of substitute methods may be formed by making several alternative substitutions and measuring the variability of the results.

One example of the use of substitute methods arises in the calculation of conventional paternal reproduction rates for places where the father's age is not ascertained when a birth is registered. In a few countries, the father's age is recorded whenever a birth occurs, and fertility rates at each man's age are therefore available. The shape of the curve of male fertility rates according to attained age in one or other of those few countries may be assumed to be applicable, and hence the required reproduction rates may be assessed.

The substitution need not be made from an actual population. In some circumstances a suitable theoretical model may be employed. A stable population is an example of such a model, and its influence on the measurement of reproduction has been indicated. A special case is a life table. If only the age-distribution of a population is known, the ratio (say k_y) of the number of male children aged y in it to the number of the total male population may, for instance, be compared with the corresponding life-table function:

$$\frac{\int_y^{y+1} {}^m l_x \, dx}{\int_0^\omega {}^m l_x \, dx} = k_y' \qquad (19.1)$$

The extent to which k_y exceeds or falls short of k_y' gives a rough indication of the relationship of the male reproduction rate $y + \frac{1}{2}$ years ago to unity. Needless to say, this method is open to great inaccuracy because of migration and other factors, but in some circumstances it would be better than no analysis at all.

A more highly-developed form of substitute method is based on large-scale international comparisons in which the data for a number of countries are brought into the analysis. If two measures of (say) fertility are available for several countries for a number of years, it may be possible to find either that these measures are closely correlated or that some fairly reliable relationship exists between them. Thus Bogue has found that the child–woman ratio is highly correlated with the general fertility rate. This fact can then be used for other countries, e.g. to deduce the general fertility rate, not otherwise available, from child–woman ratios which are known from census statistics.

19.9 The estimation of fertility rates from limited family data

Brass has shown how, among primitive peoples and in under-developed countries where fertility is not changing rapidly, fertility and reproduction rates may be assessed on the basis of data as to families. After discussing the difficulties of collecting any useful data at all from such peoples, Brass showed that the statistic likely to be of the least unreliability is the ratio of (*a*) the total number of children born to women of reproductive age to (*b*) the number of those women. He then showed that the following relationship holds

$$F = C \cdot A. \qquad (19.2)$$

In this expression, F is the sum of the age-specific fertility rates, such as is required in order to assess reproduction rates, C is the observed ratio $(a)/(b)$. Finally

$$A = \left[\frac{n-m}{n} + \frac{p}{2n} \left\{ m(n-m) - \sigma^2 \right\} \right]^{-1}. \qquad (19.3)$$

In this expression, n is the upper limit of age (say, 50), p the slope of the age-distribution curve, and m the mean and σ the standard deviation of this distribution.

Brass derived the values of p, m, and σ from a study of international data. Later, he modified the formula to incorporate the ratio of first births to all births. In this way he adjusted, in effect, for infertile women and so improved the accuracy of the method. His work is of interest because it involves international comparisons, substitute methods and the statistical study of variations, as well as a knowledge of the limitations of the actual data, in order to derive an improved result.

Studies in the USA suggest that women do not always report correctly the number of children they have borne, when they are approached in population surveys. The young may wish to conceal a birth, whereas the old may have forgotten about children who died young. Analysis of the data by age of respondent should provide a reasonable base for adjustment of such defects, if (as was the case in the USA) they are not too substantial.

19.10 Model life tables

A study of life tables prepared from the mortality experience of a number of populations of different types, at different points of time, revealed that they fell into one or other of a series of patterns. Generally speaking, the higher the mortality at one age x, the higher the mortality at another age y. In other words, the correlations between the death rates at different (and especially adjacent) ages were markedly positive. These correlations were measured as between successive age groups, and on the basis of the regression equations a set of model life tables was constructed: the curves of q_x and also those for l_x ran in broadly parallel lines. It was suggested that the most important single indicator, for any given population, was the infant mortality rate. This is also the demographic measure that it is easiest to assess, where data are generally unreliable, because infant welfare is one of the first health services to be provided. Thus, it was supposed, given a reasonably accurate measurement of the infant mortality rate, the appropriate model life table could be regarded as representing approximately the current mortality experience of the population in question.

This method has proved to be of some use in studies of primitive people and in historical demography, but is inaccurate — often very inaccurate — because the correlations between the mortality rates at different ages are a good way short of perfect. Instead, therefore, of the single parameter of the infant mortality rate, at least a second indicator might be a mortality rate at another age, or a geographical or climatic index or economic measure. A number of such indicators have been proposed for use.

In a set of model life tables published by Coale and Demeny in 1966, the expectation of life at birth was selected as the most appropriate parameter for the indication of mortality levels, as it depends on the mortality of the whole life span. Their work was founded on a collection, made by them from many sources, of life tables reflecting recorded experience in various countries. By grouping on a geographical basis they produced four basic age-patterns of mortality, and within each of these patterns selected 24 mortality levels (the range of expectations of life at birth was from 20 years to nearly 80 years). In this way they constructed a set of standard life tables. The demographer in possession of scanty information about death rates from some new country or region should be able to select, from among the 96 standard tables, one which seemed appropriate on the basis of his information, and this would then provide him with additional details which might be useful to him.

19.11 Graduation

Graduation represents a more flexible method of producing complete data than is provided by some forms of model, for example, those mentioned in § 19.8. Its use is not very common in demography, however, because the need for smooth series of rates and proportions is not great. Nevertheless, on occasions it may be helpful, for example, where only a small sample has been surveyed. A fairly simple curve of potential value in relation to mortality rates is Bc^x, the 'Gompertz' curve of geometric progression, representing a straightforward ageing process (see § 15.12). The 'Makeham' form $A + Bc^x$ may prove more flexible. Curves of greater complexity have been developed, but are hardly likely to be of use in relation to scanty statistics.

In relation to fertility, it is important that the curve used should rise from zero at about age 15 rapidly to a peak and thereafter decline, falling to zero at perhaps age 50 for women or age 100 for men. Polynomial curves have been used for this purpose by Brass.

There are a variety of methods of graduation, and a number of statistical tests are available for verifying the success of the process. As the subject is not of great importance in demography, no attempt will be made here to give a fuller account of the processes of graduation than has already been provided in § 15.13. Instead, the following brief notes are intended to draw

363

the reader's attention to matters which can be studied more deeply by using standard works of reference:

(1) statistically, variability tends to decrease as the number of observations increases;

(2) it is therefore the aim of graduation to show the nature of the results that would have been obtained from a sample, or population, larger than the one actually observed;

(3) tests of the validity of a graduation are concerned, *inter alia*, with assessments of whether the observed data could have occurred by chance on the basis of the underlying experience represented by the graduated data;

(4) graduation may be effected not only by the use of a mathematical trend curve but also by systems of weighted averages of the observations or by graphical means;

(5) the graphical method, which can be carried out freehand, may be helpful for many purposes; the smoothness of the result and the degree of adherence to the data, may be judged by eye; an example is shown in fig. 15.3.

19.12 Population surveys in less-developed areas: general principles

Experience has shown that registration is often too incomplete, in countries other than those with a developed, modern economy, for the data to be of much value demographically. Even censuses may be less than fully satis-factory. In these circumstances, smaller-scale surveys are essential for pro-gress in population studies; the basic requirements for success are:

(1) an understanding of local customs and habits of thought;
(2) the selection of suitable questions;
(3) the recruitment of good interviewers;
(4) independent verification of results.

With the aid of (2) and (3) it should be possible to overcome local pre-judices and to ascertain the facts with the minimum of error.

As with the use of models, it is not easy to generalize about surveys. One or two rules of wide application, mainly in relation to types of question, are as follows.

Specific inquiries about a single event are more likely to be answered correctly than those requiring an aggregate response covering more than one event.

Investigations into the current state of affairs usually produce more reliable results than those involving a memory of past occurrences. The longer ago an event happened, the less likely it is to be remembered accu-

364

rately, or indeed remembered at all. It is more fruitful to question people about past happenings, even with the inevitable loss of information due to lapses of memory, than it is to try to link the registration of enumeration of individual events and characteristics over a long interval of time.

A very close study of small communities, by frequent visits or continuous observation over a period of time, may be of more interest than a single survey of a more diffuse population. With some primitive people, an accurate account of age is not kept, but a good record of approximate age, in broad groups, can often be obtained in relation to religious and tribal ceremonies associated with events in life, for example, initiation rites at puberty.

Measurement in terms of 'life intervals', for example, childhood, re-productive period, and post-reproductive period, may be more suitable than measurement in terms of fixed time intervals.

19.13 Techniques of surveys in less-developed areas

The following special devices have been used in particular recent surveys in less-developed countries:

(1) classification of events according to the time elapsed; in this way a trend-line can be established showing the degree of failure of memory as a function of time; the earlier records can thus be corrected; the intensity of memory lapses, and the speed with which they increase with the duration of time since the event, vary according to the subject of inquiry and the society or social class of the person interviewed — even so there are now plenty of data available from a number of countries (for example, those mentioned in § 19.6 (6) above), and these data may be of assistance in the process of correction;

(2) sub-sampling, on a random basis, and allotting a separate sub-sample to each enumerator; enumerator-bias can thus be tested, and suitable corrections made after discussion with the enumerators; (this is a somewhat simpler version of the technique of interpenetrating samples mentioned at (7) in § 19.6 above);

(3) re-surveys of a proportion of a sample, using more detailed question-naires and more highly-skilled interviewers;

(4) point-sampling; this involves the placing of enumerators at pre-arranged geographical points and counting the persons found there; all the persons so enumerated are given an identifying card or button; shortly afterwards, the same enumerators repeat the process at a different set of geographical points; on this second occasion they note separately (a) the persons with a card or button and (b) those who have not such an identi-fication; the ratio of ((a) + (b)) to (a), when applied to the first count, leads to an estimate of the total population; this method, which has also been used in assessing animal and insect numbers, is valuable where the popula-

tion is very mobile within a limited area, for example, nomads in a bounded desert, or butterflies on a remote island.

Such devices have, in the main, been arranged to meet particular local situations; nevertheless, the methods could evidently be of value in a wider range of circumstances, and as such are worthy of mention here.

19.14 Quasi-stable populations and similar models

Few or no real populations have age-structures which are completely unchanging in time; but many have structures which are changing, or have changed, slightly, and if this can be recognized by an adaptation of the mathematics then the theoretical distribution so modified may have useful practical applications. The situation with which quasi-stable populations deal is that of the large number of populations today which are still in the stage of unvarying fertility but their mortality rates are falling steadily. Coale has therefore developed a type of model in which these features appear. In the Lotka analysis presented in the first part of chapter 18, the three basic features of stable populations (constant birth rate, constant death rate, constant age-distribution) were reduced to two (constant birth rate, constant death rate). Coale has further reduced them to one (constant birth rate). Mortality rates, instead of remaining the same, may in his analysis take any one of a number of forms at a given moment: forms derived from a set of model life tables. The population is accordingly in a position of tending ultimately to one or another of a set of stable situations. The advantage of this approach is that, where only very limited information is available about a population, for example, the age-distribution, it is possible to make approximate estimates of fertility and population growth. The method is essentially one of approximation, and errors can arise from the data available, from the assumption that age-distribution is little affected by the declining mortality, from the use of model life tables and so on.

The UN Organization has produced a series of tables from which one can be selected, as required, on the basis of such parameters, known to apply to the population of a particular developing country, as death rate; age-distribution of the population; age-distribution of deaths; or rate of natural increase. Another possible variation of the Lotka analysis is to make a special allowance for migration − thus rendering the population 'open' rather than 'closed'. If net migration rates are constant at each age, it can be shown that much of stable population theory can be applied, with a decrement of migration and mortality combined in place of mortality alone. It does not matter if net immigration is higher than mortality, except that special verification is then needed in order to establish that the rate of growth (or decline) converges towards a stable state.

SELECT BIBLIOGRAPHY

Brass, W. 'Methods of Obtaining Basic Demographic Measures where Data are Lacking or Defective', *World Population Conference, 1965* (United Nations Organization, New York, 1967), **1**, 88.

Carrier, N. H. and Farrag, A. M. 'The Reduction of Errors in Census Populations for Statistically Underdeveloped Countries', *Population Studies*, **12** (1959), 240.

Gabriel, K. R. and Ronen, I. 'Estimates of Mortality from Infant Mortality Rates', *Population Studies*, **12** (1958), 164.

Brass, W. 'The Derivation of Fertility and Reproduction Rates from Restricted Data on Reproductive Histories', *Population Studies*, **7** (1953), 137.

Methods of Estimating Basic Demographic Measures from Incomplete Data (United Nations Organization, Manuals on Methods of Estimating Population, New York, 1962) (ST/SOA/Series A/42).

Conclusion

20 History and Prospects of Demography

20.1 Introduction

No attempt will be made, in this concluding chapter, to give a succinct summary of the whole contents of this book. Each student should make his own condensed assessment from his notes, and should find this process helpful. A more fitting end for the text would seem to consist of a broad examination of the status of the subject today and its prospects for the future. Some introduction to the past history of population study is desirable as a prelude to this examination.

20.2 The beginnings

Theories of population preceded the scientific study of demographic statistics by many centuries. For instance, ancient Chinese philosophers, including Confucius, held that excessive growth in the numbers of people may depress the standard of living. Aristotle, too, argued that land and property could not be increased as rapidly as the number of inhabitants and that poverty was likely to be the outcome. Hebrew and Moslem authors placed emphasis, however, on the desirability of rapid multiplication and density of population. Similar ranges of views were expressed by European writers in the seventeenth and eighteenth centuries. These views were not derived from any inspection of the results of the early enumerations. The idea of using such statistics for any purpose other than the practical matter in hand does not appear to have occurred to the collectors. Indeed, the very concept of a 'population' does not appear to have been entertained until the beginning of the seventeenth century AD.

Not long after this, men appeared who were able to develop an interest in the numbers of their fellow creatures for the sake of these numbers alone, and for what they implied for the society of the day. Along with this interest went a will to investigate the reasons for the figures, and to inquire into the characteristics of population without preconceived notions. The pioneer in this field was the Englishman John Graunt (1620–74), who was the author of a book entitled *Natural and Political Observations ... upon the Bills of Mortality*. These Bills were weekly statements showing the numbers of deaths in certain places, and their causes, and were virtually the only demo-
368

graphic data available at that time. Nevertheless, Graunt used this material to good purpose, as may be seen from his dedicatory epistle addressed to Lord Roberts, of which the following are extracts: 'Now having ... engaged my thoughts upon the Bills of Mortality and so far succeeded therein, as to have reduced several great confused Volumes into a few perspicuous Tables and abridged such Observations as naturally flowed from them ... I have presumed to sacrifice these my small, but first published Labours upon your Lordship ... I conceive, That it doth not ill become a Peer of the Parliament ... to consider how few starve of the many that beg; That the irreligious Proposals of some, to multiply people by Polygamy, is withal irrational, and fruitless ... That the greatest Plagues of the City are equally, and quickly repaired from the Country. That the wasting of Males by Wars and Colonies do not prejudice the due proportion between them and Females ... That London, the Metropolis of England, is perhaps a Head too big for the Body, and possibly too strong: That this Head grows three times as fast as the Body unto which it belongs ... That the Trade, and very City of London, removes Westward: That the walled City is but a fifth of the whole Pyle ... All which being new, to the best of my knowledge ... I did make bold to trouble your Lordship with a perusal of it ...'

About one-half of Graunt's book was devoted to an analysis of the causes of death shown on the Bills (see § 3.5). The remainder dealt, in such manner as the author was able, with population, fertility, migration, housing, family data, differences between town and country, and numbers of men at the military ages; finally, the author made recommendations for the closer study of the distribution of the population by 'Sex, State, Age, Religion, Trade, Rank, or Degree, etc.'. The special virtue of his approach to these subjects was that he studied his data carefully and examined their sources critically. Where information was non-existent or scanty he sometimes took samples (however small and unrepresentative) for the purpose of estimation. He formed the first 'life table', and made some of the earliest assessments of the size and trend of the population of London. Graunt's work covers so wide an area of interest that it may be said that a large part of demography was born all at once. The developments that occurred subsequently were in the nature of consolidation.

20.3 Graunt's contemporaries and immediate successors

Although the collection of demographic data on a nation-wide scale did not begin, except in a few countries, until the nineteenth century, interest in population grew rapidly after Graunt's time, and during the next hundred and fifty years great controversies arose. Opinions were based on local data, on small samples or on general observation. Some of these controversies died away when censuses and registration began, but the importance of

369

others has not diminished today, in spite of the relative wealth of data that has been assembled. A famous contemporary of Graunt was William Petty (1623–87) who is remembered chiefly because of the fertility of his ideas. He developed a 'political arithmetick', involving the measurement of the influence of population in human affairs, and proposed the establishment of a Central Statistical Office, and went so far as to draw up a proposed census enumeration schedule for completion in respect of each parish. Petty's enthusiasm, sometimes rather hot-headed, was in contrast with the critical and scientific spirit of Graunt.

In the following generation, men eminent in other fields of science took an interest in population matters. For instance, Edmund Halley (1656–1742) – better known as an astronomer – was the first to attempt to construct a life table on the basis of recorded statistics. Some particulars of births and deaths had been compiled from the church records of a German town, Breslau, over the period 1687–91, and these were sent to Halley, who wrote down the number of deaths at successive ages and (with slight adjustments) summed these upwards to form an l_x column. Halley realized that this would be a correct procedure only in a population stationary in size, but he noted that the recorded numbers of births and deaths were in approximate balance, and that migration did not appear important, and concluded that his table would be representative. Only later was it realized that populations are so rarely stationary that this is an unsatisfactory mode of procedure.

Richard Price constructed a life table correctly from the population and deaths in Sweden, but his better-known work, the Northampton Table, published in 1783, was based on only the death returns in a Northampton parish, again in the belief that the population was stationary. This belief was based on the number of baptisms recorded, but in fact these omitted many of the births that had occurred, and so the table materially overstated the rates of mortality.

Johann Süssmilch, with Germanic thoroughness, assembled large masses of demographic data from parishes in Germany during the first half of the eighteenth century, and studied them in detail, investigating such matters as the relative numbers of the sexes, at birth and at the time of marriage; the tendency of populations to grow; the relative frequencies and causes of deaths at different ages; and conditions affecting fertility.

20.4 Malthus and his opponents

The purpose of Süssmilch, a Lutheran clergyman, was to expound the goodness of God on the basis of the population statistics. But the eighteenth century was, in general, the 'age of reason', and men in Europe began to develop the study of the social order and to consider whether and how the lot of the poor could be improved. Some of those who gave thought to these matters were optimistic as to the future and believed, as many still do today, that there was no limit to the potentialities for the betterment of man's economic and moral state. Godwin and Condorcet believed that scientific progress would lead to great abundance while man's reason would keep his numbers within bounds. Others were chiefly impressed by the difficulties in the way. The expression of the views of this second group was most strikingly made by Thomas Malthus (1766–1834). One of his main arguments was that the natural ability of humans to reproduce is such that man's numbers are capable of being doubled within a short period – perhaps in as little as twenty-five years – and that this is faster than the rate at which subsistence obtained from the land can be increased: thus population always tends to press on the available resources so hardly as to lead to misery and starvation. This kind of argument, in various modified forms, still has many proponents today. It is of interest to note that similar views were being propounded at the same period of time in the Far East, notably by the Chinese philosopher Hung Liang Chi.

At this time, comprehensive data were beginning to be collected. Early examples of the modern type of census are those conducted in Quebec in the year 1665 and in Iceland in 1703. The practice did not, however, become general until the early nineteenth century: periodical enumerations began in the USA in 1790 and in Britain and France in 1801.

Malthus's first essay (1799) was an example of general reasoning, unsupported by any statistical evidence, but shortly after its publication he undertook a tour of the Scandinavian countries, during which he carefully inquired into the condition of the people. Later editions of his book were fully illustrated with statistics in support of his arguments. Consistently, Malthus advocated 'moral restraint' (i.e. absence of sexual intercourse) in order that starvation, pestilence and vice could be avoided. ('Vice', it may be noted, in his view included contraceptive practices.)

Karl Marx disagreed profoundly with Malthus on the question of the living conditions of the poor, which Malthus appeared to suggest could not be improved. Marx argued that an improvement could be achieved by a fundamental change in the social structure from capitalism to communism, and today the name of Malthus is still reviled in communist countries. Engels, too, maintained that the productive power of mankind was unlimited, and he rejected the law of diminishing returns which is implicit in Malthus's theory.

20.5 The nineteenth century

Although many efforts to collect complete demographic data had been made in the eighteenth century, the results were only partially successful. Their assembly on a nation-wide scale was delayed in some countries by prejudice and in others by a lack of the will or the means for an undertaking of such magnitude. Eventually, however, the requisite data began to emerge in European countries and in the United States, and with them came the birth of demography as we know it today. Along with this development, the tools of measurement were also being sharpened. The Carlisle Life Table (1815) constructed by Joshua Milne represented a great advance in relevance, correctness and accuracy, and was the first of a long line of valid and useful mortality tables.

Thoroughness and capacity for the systematic analysis of a large column of information were desirable qualities in dealing with the new masses of figures relating to a complex of matters. Among those who possessed these and other qualities and successfully pioneered in this field in England was William Farr (1807–83) who held office under the Registrar General and was responsible for preparing census and registration reports during the early and middle parts of Queen Victoria's reign. It was he who drew the attention of the general public to the high mortality in certain districts and trades resulting from insanitary conditions and dangerous work, and paved the way for social legislation leading to the great reductions in mortality that were eventually effected. During roughly the same period there developed an association between actuaries and demography. In 1837, John Finlaison, later to be the first President of the Institute of Actuaries, gave advice on the inauguration of vital registration and accurately forecast the number of births, deaths and marriages that were to be recorded. This interest has continued to the present day.

Attempts began to be made to assemble information about the populations of colonial territories but at first these were of little value. The local conditions were not so favourable as in Europe and the administrators were not sufficiently skilled to be able to conduct effective censuses.

The end of the nineteenth century saw the awakening in many European countries of a public consciousness of the potentialities of modern means of birth control. As a result, increasing attention has had to be paid in more recent times to the statistical analysis of fertility as well as of mortality in the study of population.

20.6 The beginning of fertility studies

When the birth rate began to fall in many European countries, and in North America, the fact was noted by a number of contemporary writers, but there was little opportunity for demographers to analyse the change in any detail, because the necessary data were not available. In the second half of the nineteenth century, however, this branch of demography began to develop. Among the factors that stimulated the advance mention should be made of two events which attracted particular attention in France, namely:

(1) the total recorded number of deaths first exceeded the total recorded number of births in the year 1854; and

(2) France was heavily defeated by Prussia in the year 1870.

Such happenings suggested to many people that France was becoming too weak through lack of population growth. Moreover, it became apparent that the decline in fertility had started earlier, and gone further, in the upper classes of society than in the lower.

Events and tendencies such as these caused attention to be directed to fertility, after a period in which progress in reducing mortality had seemed all-important. Theories began to be formed about social behaviour, which could explain the observed facts. Dumont advanced the idea of 'social capillarity'; just as water rises higher in a narrow tube than in a broad one, he argued, small family size is associated with the desire to rise in the social scale. Following the discoveries of Mendel and Darwin, Galton created eugenics, the science of the breeding of man. Differential fertility began to be studied, and it began to be feared that the quality of population might be eroded as a result of the tendency of the upper classes to have fewer children than the generality of the population.

20.7   Population mathematics

Quantitative theories of population were first advanced by Euler and his work was carried on by Ludwig Moser. Such theories were concerned with the conditions holding sway in populations experiencing constant fertility and mortality, in which there was no migration; they dealt with such parameters as the sex ratio and the age-distribution. The work of Alfred Lotka developed from this foundation. Böckh had already calculated the first reproduction rate, as early as 1884, but the theoretical foundation provided by Lotka created renewed interest in reproduction rates, which were extensively used in consequence in the work of demographers in the 1930s. The economic and political disturbances of this decade, and of the 1940s, however, gave rise to conditions in which the use of reproduction rates could be misleading, and on further analysis it was realized that the mathematical approach, interesting and important as it was, suffered from severe practical limitations. Even so, some academic writers have continued to develop the study of population formulae for their intrinsic interest and elegance.

20.8   Population projection

A mathematical approach had also been used in connexion with theories of population growth; for example, Malthus had entertained the idea of a geometric growth in numbers (and also of an arithmetical progression for food production). The regular and comprehensive censuses which were started in the eighteenth and nineteenth centuries in some countries were necessary before guesses as to the future could be transformed into projections. In many of the countries concerned the population was growing rapidly. In the New World, especially in the USA, this expansion was of interest in relation to the development of the untapped resources that were waiting to be used. In Europe there did not seem to be room for expansion, and prophecies were made of starvation, pestilence, and vice as the result of overcrowding. In these circumstances, any attempt at a precise prediction of the future did not seem to be called for.

The first estimates of future populations appeared at the end of the eighteenth century, when census material began to be available. They were made by extrapolating from the enumerated total numbers without taking any special account of such factors as mortality, fertility, migration or age-distribution, the incidence of which was mainly unknown. Interest was aroused by the rapid rate of human increase at that time, and the assumption that this would continue unchecked gave rise to fears that numbers would outstrip the growth of productive power and lead to a state of starvation. These ideas gave way in time, however, to the realization that there must be some limit to the size of the population imposed by the environment and that the rate of growth would, therefore, diminish. Verhulst suggested that the increase would fall to zero in due course and that the numbers would thus reach a stationary level, after progressing along a curve which he described as a 'logistic' (see § 9.7).

When, towards the end of the nineteenth century, and early in the twentieth, a progressive reduction in the average size of the family began, in certain countries, mortality was also falling. The numbers of children then remained for many years sufficiently large to provide the prospect of an increasing population, although at a diminished rate of growth, but eventually it seemed to some people that not only were too few children being born for replacement purposes but the shortage was serious and permanent and might become even more grave. Some population projections were published showing the long-term results of such apparent tendencies and, mainly because of differences of opinion on the extent of the insufficiency of births, the appearance of several further sets of calculations was stimulated.

One of the earliest demographers to attempt a projection was Cannan, who used an algebraic formula to estimate the future total population, but also suggested making estimates by dealing separately with the different sex and age components of an initial population. The work of Bowley and Pearl in the 1920s has already been referred to in chapter 9. Similar work was being done in the USA by Whelpton. By the 1930s, the practice of making projections was becoming common, and the use of alternative bases began to be established. No less than sixteen alternative projections were made for the British Royal Commission on Population in the late 1940s.

20.9   The influence of electronic computers on demography

The development of new methods of computation during the past forty years has had an important influence on the study of population. The rapidity and ease with which computers can make iterative calculations has rendered the process of projection a simple one. The gain from this is not, however, great, as it remains very difficult to choose with much confidence the assumptions as to mortality, fertility and migration which are most likely to be representative. The computer has, however, made possible a type of exercise which would not previously have been practicable, namely the construction of models for forecasting purposes incorporating a more numerous and complex set of assumptions, concerning for instance the development of food resources, the production of energy, the distribution of wealth and the progress of medicine and of science generally. Even so, the first models of this kind that have been produced have been criticized on the ground of the many assumptions they incorporate which are based on hazardous guesses. It has been shown that a quite different picture of the future can be produced by variations based on equally plausible hypotheses (see § 14.10 above).

Data-processing on computers is now in many developed countries the method preferred to less sophisticated systems for the production of census and registration data, and gains can be made in this way in the speed of publication of the results and in the degree of complexity of the tabulations. Considerations of manpower and cost often limit, however, the extent of the gain.

20.10   Administration and training

One of the major developments in the administrative field has of course been the setting up of organizations for the study of population and for the collection of demographic data. The first national censuses and vital registration systems were often entrusted to the care of existing official institutions, but in due course it was usually found necessary to set up separate departments of State in order to manage this highly specialized work. In order to co-ordinate the activities of the authorities in various countries, in the interests of uniformity and comparability of data between one area and another, various international bodies have been called together at different times. Valuable demographic work was carried out between the World Wars under the auspices of the League of Nations, and soon after the inception of the UN Organization a permanent Population Commission was established.

From the outset, the Population Commission was confronted with the need to secure an improvement in population statistics in all parts of the world, especially in the under-developed countries; it soon tackled this problem vigorously, and already there are successful results to report. Plans have been made for the holding of censuses in an ever-increasing number of countries, and standard lists of questions have been issued as a guide. The success of this venture is evidenced by the fact that a recent census has been held in some 250 countries whose population accounts for a high proportion of the world total.

Such data are recorded in an invaluable *Demographic Year Book* issued each year by the UN Organization, and a *Multi-lingual Demographic Dictionary* has been prepared to help in standardizing usage. Another urgent task facing the UN Organization at the time of its foundation was the study of the population situations in the areas devastated by the Second World War and in under-developed regions in all parts of the world. Reports on these matters, and also on the demography of the UN Trust Territories such as Western Samoa, have been issued. Among the many subjects on which papers have been written under the aegis of the Commission are training and research, demographic legislation, and methods of estimating population.

Besides the official work of government departments, much demographic research is now carried out by universities and other interested bodies. The International Union for the Scientific Study of Population, an organization of which the leading demographers in many countries are members, has sponsored various congresses — the first in 1927; one on a world-wide scale was held in Rome in 1954 under the auspices of the UN Organization. This was known as the World Population Conference, 1954. The Conference consisted of no less than thirty-one meetings spread over eleven days; over four hundred papers were presented. A Second World Population Conference, on an even larger scale, was held in Belgrade in 1965. A Third took place in Bucharest in 1974, in which emphasis was placed more on the politics of population than on the techniques of its study.

Among the more important national organizations may be mentioned the Institut National d'Etudes Démographiques in Paris, the Population Council in the USA, and the Population Investigation Committee in London.

Much attention has been paid in recent years to the training of demographers, and centres for this purpose have been set up in Chembur (India), in Cairo and in Santiago (Chile). Dissemination of information among the rapidly-growing numbers of workers in the field of population studies has been achieved by means of text books and periodical journals. Important examples of journals are *Demography*, *Milbank Memorial Fund Quarterly* and *Population Index* (USA), *Population* (France) and *Population Studies* and the *Journal of Biosocial Science* (Britain). Similar periodicals of much value are published in many other countries, including for example Hungary, India, South Korea and Poland. Where a language difficulty arises, the gist of the main articles is usually given in a summary written in English.

376

20.11   Recent technical developments

On the technical front much interest has resided in recent years in the study of such subjects as historical demography — which offers excellent opportunities for research; the interrelations between population trends and economic, social, labour and education developments; and the ingenious use of mathematical analysis and statistical comparison to elucidate the main characteristics of the demographic situations of countries in which population data are either not available or not credible. Much greater efforts, however, in terms of manpower and expenditure, have been devoted to the development and assessment of family-planning programmes in many countries in accordance with national policies or the activities of voluntary organizations; the student of demography must certainly recognize today the force of such practical endeavours as an influence upon fertility and perhaps other trends.

20.12   Prospects for the future

It is much easier to envisage future developments as a continuation of past trends than to imagine startling innovations or unexpected changes that might occur. It is probably also sounder. Speaking of the concept of a 'new biology', in relation to recent scientific advances, the author said, 'The new biology ... represents, maybe, nothing more than the current segment of a steadily upward trend line in scientific advance.' If this is true of biology, it is surely true also for demography, which depends so much less on the laboratory and so much more on observations in the field. Indeed, a part of the prospects is defined by the very deficiencies which are readily observable today, both in the extent of knowledge and in the adequacy and accuracy of the statistical data available for study.

Among the subjects on which new research seems necessary are:

(1) dynamic models ... which incorporate changes both in the economy and in the size and structure of populations;

(2) careful re-study of the historical record of the developed countries;

(3) attempts to study the record of population growth and economic development in the backward areas of relatively developed countries;

as well as further investigations of fertility, mortality and migration, of population projections and of disability.

The background to these suggestions is the general consciousness of the wide, and perhaps growing, disparity in wealth between countries such as Britain and the USA on the one hand and (say) Brazil and Indonesia on the other. Such as disparity is not healthy, because it breeds international jealousies and rivalries, and it is desirable to formulate plans for reducing

377

the differences in living standards between one area and another. Without preliminary research, however, such plans might be fruitless — for instance, if economic aid to an under-developed country merely served to cause its population to grow all the faster and so kept down or even depressed the average level of prosperity.

Much more could be (and has been) written on these topics. They lie, however, on the borderline of the scope of this book and cannot be pursued further here, except to say that (*a*) the possibilities of historical research do not yet appear to have been exhausted; and (*b*) some writers believe that demographic data should not be considered by themselves in isolation but that populations should always be regarded as subject to economic influences.

To these topics, the following could be added:

(1) the study and interpretation of demographic data known or suspected to be incomplete or inaccurate;

(2) proposals for improving the quality of population statistics and for broadening their scope;

(3) comparative analyses of communities of various sizes and locations and of conurbations;

(4) the classification of population according to various qualitative characteristics;

(5) the identification of social and psychological factors affecting fertility; and

(6) studies of the possibilities and uses of governmental action to influence population trends.

Some reference to these and other topics will be made in the remaining paragraphs of this chapter.

20.13   Better data

It is evident from chapter 4 above that the population data available in many parts of the world are most inadequate for even the simplest needs of the demographer. When some of his more detailed requirements are considered, the record systems even of the economically advanced countries soon appear deficient. Thus the classification of live births by father's occupation — today available for countries comprising only 7 per cent of world population — is not available at all in North America and can be found for only about one-quarter of Europe's population; and even the numbers of deaths subdivided by cause, age and sex can be traced only incompletely in Europe and North America and for only about one-quarter of the world's population. The amount of statistical information required for a close study of (say) birth spacing is such that few if any countries can give it from their present resources.

378

Even so, consideration of the qualities needed by an ideal system of population records is useful as an aim for the future: perhaps one that could be achieved, in the light of progress in the past. The main characteristics required of an ideal system of demographic statistics are probably:

Comprehensiveness: all the information needed by demographers and administrators should be available;

Unity: independent statistical systems such as censuses, registrations and national insurance records should be welded together under a single administration;

Accuracy: misstatements by people when specifying their ages, occupations, and other characteristics should as far as possible be eliminated;

Full and permanent identification of each individual: this should reduce the number of separate registrations and inquiries and do away with many of the forms now needing to be filled in by the public;

Speed: results should be available soon after the holding of an inquiry, and fresh investigations should be held as often as required in view of the rate of change of the population in any particular respect.

The most obvious weaknesses in the existing arrangements in Britain and the other countries of the West are the insufficient co-ordination between different types of inquiry, the infrequency with which censuses are taken, and more particularly the long intervals between special investigations, such as that into fertility, and the delays in the publication of some of the data.

Co-ordination between the data obtained from censuses and registrations cannot be complete until individuals can be traced from one event to another; but often the existing civil records of births, deaths and marriages are defective in so far as they do not completely identify the individuals concerned; a name such as John Smith may be common to many persons. In order to eliminate this deficiency it would be desirable to give, on each occasion of registration, an adequate reference to the birth record. It would also be useful to keep an account of near relatives, for example, to require the wife's name to be inserted on the death certificate, and the parents' date and place of marriage to be shown on the birth certificate. Any such extensions as these, even though designed only for their administrative advantages, would also enable better population data to be published. The first action along these lines is already beginning. The possibility has been considered of linking up the data obtained at one census with those from the ensuing enumeration. In the Chalk River project in Canada, birth certificates are being matched with marriage registrations, thus establishing a system of records of family units.

Among the more evident of the improvements needed in Western countries are the development of continuous registration systems, an increased use of sampling and an extension of the scope of migration statistics. Linkage of data from different sources may be considered as a less radical

379

step, in the collection of comprehensive demographic data, than the maintenance of population registers which permanently comprise information of censal and vital registration type. 'Data banks', incorporating such demographic data integrated with a variety of social and economic characteristics, are more radical still — so much so as to arouse the hostility of those who feel that administrators are thereby given too much power over individuals — the danger being that the use of the data would not be confined to the anonymity of statistical analysis. Though some steps have been taken in a few countries towards the maintenance of such systems, in general the gap between available data and the maximum possible cross-classifications is so enormous that there is vast room for development (and for the institution of democratic safeguards) in the future.

20.14 Historical research

Brief reference was made in § 10.6 to studies which have been conducted among the parish registers which were maintained during the period before formal registration began on a national scale. The technique has usually consisted in assembling all the items of information about birth, death and marriage that concern the members of any given family. Where this can be done over a substantial period of years, for groups of families, it is possible to assess values for such measures as fertility rates at each age, average family sizes per married couple, legitimate and illegitimate fertility, birth spacing, child mortality, and widowhood and remarriage. Church registers of adequate completeness and accuracy are now being studied in a variety of places, and there is scope for additional work over a wide area — so wide, indeed, that ultimately all such work might be assembled into a sample truly representative of national or even international experience as a whole. New techniques of analysis developed from work on parish registers may indeed be capable of fruitful application to civil registration material, where access to this material is possible. Where they can be so applied, not only will a useful link be established between the history just before and just after the start of registration but also new light may be thrown on subsequent developments, especially in relation to the inception of a decline in fertility in Western countries.

20.15 New directions in fertility research

Inquiries into the social and psychological factors affecting fertility indicate that these factors vary considerably from one country to another, especially when there are different cultural backgrounds and different economic and historical circumstances. Much therefore remains to be investigated. Because of these and other factors, which affect the fertility of the social classes within a country in varying ways and may give rise to differential rates of reproduction for different groups, changes in the qualitative composition of populations may be expected in future. For instance, it has been found in many countries that children in large families tend to score fewer marks in 'intelligence tests' than do children in small families, and it has been argued from this — although accepted by few nowadays — that a deterioration in average intelligence may result. The measurement of changes from time to time in qualities such as health and ability is important for the understanding of any developments which may be taking place as a result of differential fertility, mortality or migration, and for the making of 'eugenic plans' to combat any unfavourable trends.

The direction of research in this area has recently veered away from large-scale investigations involving the multivariate analysis of many conflicting factors and their effects. It is believed that smaller samples, investigated in greater depth, should prove more useful. Such inquiries would involve not only information about family-building in the past but also statements of intention as to the future: only in this way can a full picture of the current situation be obtained and, as has been seen in chapters 11 and 14, the situation and outlook can change so rapidly these days that such a picture is badly needed. Perhaps the most important matters to be investigated are those concerned with family size, for couples capable of using effective planning. Recent experience suggests that changes in the birth rate tend to be of the same magnitude irrespective of socio-economic category, religion, age, duration of marriage and other variables that demographers traditionally study. The changes are secular in character and it remains to be discovered what events and prospects motivate people; this can be done only by close and continuous sample investigations of a new kind. The causes may be political, economic, fiscal, psychological or biological (in the sense of the availability of new techniques of contraception or abortion) and the methods of study may well need to be varied in order to find out the relative importance of each one. This should be an exciting new field for research.

Another very live area in current research is the construction of mathematical and practical numerical models, and their analysis with the aid of electronic computers, bearing upon various aspects of population. Foremost among these has recently been the study of the biology of reproduction, and — against this background — of the effectiveness of various contraceptive and other birth-control techniques. Only a few initial clues to this rapidly-developing sphere of work have been provided in chapter 19, but more can be deduced from the reading proposed at the end of that chapter.

381

20.16 Other technical studies

Analysis and projection of mortality trends would probably be made more effective if research were directed to the connexions between the development of new drugs, treatments and medical techniques and their use in practice, between their use in practice and the survival of the sufferers, and between the incidence of new cases of illness and the population mortality rates. Such studies might have helped to throw light on the developments noted in chapters 10 and 11 above, though it is probably too late now for useful retrospective research. In old age, death is often the result of the action of multiple causes, and this makes analysis very difficult, but if any light is to be thrown, by demographic means, on the prospects for the improvement of longevity it will probably be by research in this area. Otherwise, medical and biological research will be the chief contributors to progress.

In migration research, the scope for new studies is wide, and begins with the collection and analysis of more extensive data, where practicable. The relationship between population and environment can perhaps be analysed in new ways, leading to new knowledge about the possibilities for redistribution of the population and ultimately to new economic theories of migration. Immigrant groups can be studied in this connexion, and also to ascertain how their social and personal behaviour affects rational measures of fertility and mortality.

20.17 The political background

The manner in which populations will develop in the years ahead, and hence the results which demographers will measure, analyse and project in future, must depend on the climate of opinion in each country or area, and on changes in that climate. This may influence government action or be influenced by it. It may also be affected by the predictions of demographers themselves or by the electronic models of 'ecodoomsters'. Even in the seventeenth century the study of population was called 'political arithmetic'. It seems possible to discern, from chapter 13 above, a tendency towards an increase in government involvement in demographic affairs, and this tendency was recognized in the organization of the Third World Population Conference along political lines — in contrast to its two predecessors, in 1954 and 1965, which were largely technical in character.

SELECT BIBLIOGRAPHY

Lorimer, F. 'The Development of Demography', in *The Study of Population: an Inventory and Appraisal* (University Press, Chicago, 1959).
Hauser, P. M. and Duncan, O. D. *The Study of Population: an Inventory and Appraisal* (University Press, Chicago, 1959).
Current Research in Human Fertility (Milbank Memorial Fund, New York, 1955).

Index to Tables

Index

Index

graduation of, 288–90
model, 362–3
multiple decrement, 280
origins of, 370
uses of, 294–5
literacy, 227
live birth, definition of, 24
Lotka, Alfred, stable population theory of, 344, 373
lung cancer, analysis of mortality from, 119

Maine, mortality indexes for S. Carolina and, 304
Makeham curve, 288, 363
Malaya, death rates in, 116
Malthus, Thomas, population theory of, 179, 371
marital status
estimates of population according to, 155–6
in population projection, 332–6
marriage rates, in population projection, 164–5
marriages,
age at, 72–4, 77–8; and fertility, 72, 81–2
causes of termination of, 78–80
consensual, 78–9
definition of, 24
proportion of population in, 78
rates of, 15, 73–4
recording of, 24–5, 47
standardization in fertility, 317–18
see also individual countries
Martinique, birth and death rates in, 201
Marx, Karl, 241, 371
Massachusetts, death rates from tuberculosis in, 117
maternity, act of, 24
mathematics in demography
in population projection, 156–8
of stable populations, 341–7
of stochastic variations, 347–9
matrices, in population projection, 326
Mauritius
current population trends in, 203
mortality data for, 114
measles, mortality from, 129–30, 133
medical certificate of cause of death, form of, recommended by WHO, 124
menarche, 83
menopause, 84
Merchant Shipping Act (1906), and collection of migration records, 62, 64
Mexico
birth data for, 201
households in, 224

illiteracy in, 227
mortality data for, 114
migration
differentials in, 150
interrelations of, with fertility and mortality rates, 149–50
life tables in study of, 283, 322
measures of, 148–9
politics and, 143
in population projection, 167
records of, inadequacy of, 39
theories of, 141
to urban areas, 175
see also countries involved
Milbank Memorial Fund Quarterly, 376
Milne, J., 372
minerals, resources of, 254–5
models, mathematical, for use where data are incorrect or scanty, 359–60
mortality
differential, 136–7
foetal, 110–11
industrial revolution and, 174
infant, 110–11
theories of, 118–20
see also individual countries
mortality indexes, summary of, 311
mortality rates
infant, 110–11
marital status and, 120–1
by occupation, 137–40
in population projection, 163–4
by race (USA), 112
by region, 122–3
by social class, 134–6
motor accidents, mortality from, 133
Multi-lingual Demographic Dictionary, 3, 8
multiple births, 24
multiple decrement tables, 280
multiple influences, 132

National Registration (Britain, 1939–52), 65
natural increase of population, 198
neonatal period, mortality in, 26
net reproduction rate, 315–17
Netherlands, *see* Holland
New York Department of Health, calculation of standardized death rate for localities by, 306–7
New Zealand
births in, 12
censuses in, 32
vital statistics in, 71
Nigeria, population of, 155, 212
nitrogen, supply of, 253
North America
energy consumption in, 219